Engraved by Emily Sartain, Phila.

Very truly Yours &c
W. A. Sparks

THE MEMORIES

OF

FIFTY YEARS:

CONTAINING

BRIEF BIOGRAPHICAL NOTICES OF DISTINGUISHED AMERICANS, AND ANECDOTES OF REMARKABLE MEN;

INTERSPERSED WITH SCENES AND INCIDENTS OCCURRING DURING A LONG LIFE OF OBSERVATION CHIEFLY SPENT IN THE SOUTHWEST.

BY

W. H. SPARKS.

Third Edition.

PHILADELPHIA:
CLAXTON, REMSEN & HAFFELFINGER,
MACON, GA.: J. W. BURKE & CO.
1872.

STEREOTYPED BY J. FAGAN & SON. PRINTED BY MOORE BROS.

TO

MY BROTHER AND NEPHEW,

THE HONORABLE OVID GARTEN SPARKS,

AND

COLONEL THOMAS HARDEMAN,

OF MACON, GEORGIA.

This Volume is Dedicated

BY THEIR AGED AND AFFECTIONATE RELATIVE, TRUSTING THEY WILL ESTEEM IT, WHEN HE SHALL HAVE PASSED TO ETERNITY, AS SOME EVIDENCE OF THE AFFECTION BORNE THEM BY

THE AUTHOR.

PREFACE.

IN the same week, and within three days of the same date, I received from three Judges of the Supreme Court, of three States, the request that I would record my remembrances of the men and things I had known for fifty years. The gentlemen making this request were Joseph Henry Lumpkin, of Georgia; William L. Sharkey, of Mississippi, and James G. Taliaferro, of Louisiana.

From Judge Sharkey the request was verbal; from the other two it came in long and, to me, cherished letters. All three have been my intimate friends — Lumpkin from boyhood; the others for nearly fifty years. Judge Lumpkin has finished his work in time, and gone to his reward. Judges Sharkey and Taliaferro yet live, both now over seventy years of age. The former has retired from the busy cares of office, honored, trusted, and beloved; the latter still occupies a seat upon the Bench of the Supreme Court of Louisiana.

These men have all sustained unreproached reputations, and retained through their long lives the full confidence of the people of their respective States. I did not feel at liberty to resist their appeal: I had resided in all three of the States; had known long and intimately their people; had been extensively acquainted with very many of the most prominent men of the nation — and in the following pages is my compliance.

I have trusted only to my memory, and to a journal kept for many years, when a younger man than I am to-day — hastening to the completion of my seventieth year. Doubtless, I have made many mistakes of minor importance; but few, I trust, as to matters of fact. Of one thing I am sure: nothing has been wilfully written which can wound the feelings of any.

Many things herein contained may not be of general interest; but none which will not find interested readers; for while some of the individuals mentioned may not be known to common fame, the incidents in connection with them deserve to be remembered by thousands who knew them.

These Memories are put down without system, or order, as they have presented themselves, and have been related in a manner which I have attempted to make entertaining and instructive, without being prolix or tedious. They will be chiefly interesting to the people of the South; though much may, and, I hope, will be read by those of the North. Some of my happiest days have been passed in the North: at Cambridge some of my sons have been educated, and some of my dearest friends have been Northern men. Despite the strife which has gone far toward making us in heart a divided people, I have a grateful memory of many whose homes and graves were and are in New England.

Would that this strife had never been! But it has come, and I cannot forego a parent's natural feelings when mourning the loss of sons slain in the conflict, or the bitterness arising therefrom toward those who slew them. Yet, as I forgive, I hope to be forgiven.

There are but few now left who began the journey of life with me. Those of this number who still sojourn in our native land will find much in these pages familiar to their remembrance, and some things, the reading of which may revive incidents and persons long forgotten. In the West, in Louisiana, Mississippi, Alabama, and Texas, there are many — the descendants of those who participated in events transpiring fifty years ago — who have listened at the parental hearth to their recital. To these I send this volume greeting; and if they find something herein to amuse and call up remembrances of the past, I shall feel gratified.

To the many friends I have in the Southwest, and especially in Louisiana and Mississippi, where I have sojourned well-nigh fifty years, and many of whom have so often urged upon me the writing of these Memories, I commit the book, and ask of them, and of all into whose hands it may fall, a lenient criticism, a kindly recollection, and a generous thought of our past intercourse. It is an inexorable fate that separates us, and I feel it is forever. This sad thought is alleviated, however, by the consciousness that the few remaining sands of life are falling at the home of my birth; and that when the end comes, as very soon it must, I shall be placed to sleep amid my kindred in the land of my nativity.

THE AUTHOR.

CONTENTS.

CHAPTER VI.

POPULAR CHARACTERISTICS.

CHAPTER VII.

WITS AND FIRE-EATERS.

CHAPTER VIII.

FIFTY YEARS AGO.

CHAPTER IX.

PEDAGOGUES AND DEMAGOGUES.

CHAPTER X.

INDIAN TREATIES AND DIFFICULTIES.

CHAPTER XI.

POLITICAL CHANGES.

CHAPTER XII.

GOSSIP.

CHAPTER XIII.

INFLUENCE OF CHILDHOOD.

CHAPTER XIV.

A REVOLUTIONARY VETERAN.

CHAPTER XV.

CHANGE OF GOVERNMENT.

CHAPTER XVI.

PARTY PRINCIPLES.

CHAPTER XVII.

CONGRESS IN ITS BRIGHTEST DAYS.

CHAPTER XVIII.

FRENCH AND SPANISH TERRITORY.

CHAPTER XIX.

THE NATCHEZ TRADITIONS.

CHAPTER XX.

EXPLORATION OF THE MISSISSIPPI VALLEY.

CHAPTER XXI.

TWO STRANGE BEINGS.

CHAPTER XXII.

THE ROMANCE CONTINUED.

CHAPTER XXIII.

WHEN SUCCESSFUL, RIGHT; WHEN NOT, WRONG.

CHAPTER XXIV.

THE SILVER-TONGUED ORATOR.

CHAPTER XXV.

A FINANCIAL CRASH.

CHAPTER XXVI.

ACADIAN FRENCH SETTLERS.

CHAPTER XXVII.

ABOLITION OF LICENSED GAMBLING.

CHAPTER XXVIII.

THREE GREAT JUDGES.

CHAPTER XXIX.

AMERICANIZING LOUISIANA.

CHAPTER XXX.

DIVISION OF NEW ORLEANS INTO MUNICIPALITIES.

CHAPTER XXXI.

BLOWING UP THE LIONESS.

CHAPTER XXXII.

GRADUAL EXTINCTION OF THE RED MAN.

CHAPTER XXXIII.

FUN, FACT, AND FANCY.

THE MEMORIES

OF

FIFTY YEARS.

CHAPTER I.

REVOLUTIONARY TRADITIONS.

MIDDLE GEORGIA — COLONEL DAVID LOVE — HIS WIDOW — GOVERNOR DUNMORE — COLONEL TARLETON — BILL CUNNINGHAM — COLONEL FANNON — MY GRANDMOTHER'S BIBLE — SOLOMON'S MAXIM APPLIED — ROBERTUS LOVE — THE INDIAN WARRIOR — DRAGON CANOE — A BUXOM LASS — GENERAL GATES — MARION — MASON L. WEEMS — WASHINGTON — "BILLY CRAFFORD."

MY earliest memories are connected with the first settlement of Middle Georgia, where I was born. My grandparents on the mother's side, were natives of North Carolina; and, I believe, of Anson county. My grandfather, Colonel David Love, was an active partisan officer in the service of the Continental Congress. He died before I was born; but my grandmother lived until I was seventeen years of age. As her oldest grandchild, I spent much of my time, in early boyhood, at her home near the head of Shoulderbone Creek in the county of Green. She was a little, fussy, Irish woman, a Presbyterian in religion, and a very strict observer of all the duties imposed upon her sect, especially in keeping holy the Sabbath day. All her children were grown up, married, and, in the language of the time, "gone away." She was in truth a lone woman, busying herself in household and farming affairs. With a few negroes, and a miserably poor piece of land, she struggled in her widowhood with fortune, and contrived, with North Carolina frugality and industry, not only to make a decent living, but to lay up something for a rainy day, as she phrases it. In her visits to her fields and garden, I ran by her side and listened to stories of Tory atrocities and Whig suffering in North Carolina during the Revolution. The infamous Governor Dunmore, the cruel Colonel Tarleton, and the murderous and thieving Bill Cunningham and Colonel Fannin, both Tories, and the latter natives to the soil, were presented graphically to me in their most hateful forms. In truth, before I had attained my seventh year, I was familiar with the history of the partisan warfare waged between Whig and Tory in North and South Carolina, from 1776 to 1782, from this good but garrulous old lady. I am not so certain she was good: she had a temper of her own, and a will and a way of her own; and was good-natured only when permitted this way without opposition, or cross. Perhaps I retain a more vivid memory of these peculiar traits than of any others characterizing her. She permitted no contradiction, and exacted implicit obedience, and this was well understood by everything about her. She was strict and exacting, and had learned from Solomon that to "spare the rod was to spoil the child." She read the Bible only; and it was the only book in the house. This Bible is still in existence; it was brought by my grandfather from Europe, and is now covered with the skin of a fish which he harpooned on his return voyage, appropriating the skin to this purpose in 1750. She had use for no other book, not even for an almanac, for at any moment she could tell the day of the month, the phase of the moon and the day General Washington captured Cornwallis; as also the day on which Washington died. Her reverence for the memory of my grandfather was idolatry. His cane hung with his hat just where he had habitually placed them during his latter days. His saddle and great sea-chest were preserved with equal care, and remained undisturbed from 1798 to 1817, precisely as he left them. I ventured to remove the cane upon one occasion; and, with a little negro or two, was merrily riding it around in the great lumber-room of the house, where scarcely any one ever went, when she came in and caught me. The pear-tree sprouts were immediately put into requisition, and the whole party most mercilessly thrashed. From that day forward the old buckhorn-headed cane was an awful reminder of my sufferings. She was careful not to injure the clothing of her victims, and made her appeals to the unshielded cuticle, and with a heavy hand for a small woman.

It was an ill-fashioned but powerfully-built house, and remains a monument to this day of sound timber and faithful work, braving time and the storm for eighty-two years. It was the first framed house built in the county, and I am sure, upon the poorest spot of land within fifty miles of where it stands. Here was born my uncle, Robertus Love, who was the first white child born in the State west of the Ogeechee River.

Colonel Love, my grandfather, was eccentric in many of his opinions, and was a Puritan in religious faith. Oliver Cromwell was his model of a statesman, and Praise-God Barebones his type of a Christian. While he was a boy his father married a second time, and, as is very frequently the case, there was no harmony between the step-mother and step-son. Their jarrings soon ripened into open war. To avoid expulsion from the paternal roof he "bundled and went." Nor did he rest until, in the heart of the Cherokee nation of Indians, he found a home with Dragon Canoe, then the principal warrior of the nation, who resided in a valley amid the mountains, and which is now Habersham County. With this chief, who at the time was young, he remained some four years, pursuing the chase for pleasure and profit. Thus accumulating a large quantity of peltries, he carried them on pack-horses to Charleston, and thence went with them to Europe. After disposing of his furs, which proved profitable, he wandered on foot about Europe for some eighteen months, and then, returning to London, he embarked for America.

During all this time he had not heard from his family. Arriving at Charleston he made his way back to the neighborhood of his birth. He was ferried across the Pedee river by a buxom lass, who captured his heart. Finding his father dead, he gathered up the little patrimony left him in his father's will, should he ever return to claim it: he then returned to the neighborhood of his sweetheart of the ferry; and, being a fine-looking man of six feet three inches, with great blue eyes, round and liquid; and, Othello-like, telling well the story of his adventures, he very soon beguiled the maiden's heart, and they were made one. About this time came off the battles of Concord and Lexington, inaugurating the Revolution. It was not, however, until after the declaration of independence, that he threw aside the plough and shouldered the musket for American independence.

That portion of North Carolina in which he resided had been mainly peopled by emigrants from Scotland. The war progressing into the South, found nearly all of these faithful in their allegiance to Britain. The population of English descent, in the main, espoused the cause of the colonies. With his neighbors Love was a favorite; he was very fleet in a foot-race, had remarkable strength; but, above all, was sagacious and strong of will. Such qualities, always appreciated by a rude people, at that particular juncture brought their possessor prominently forward, and he was chosen captain of a company composed almost to a man of his personal friends and acquaintances. Uniting himself with the regiment of Colonel Lynch, just then organized, and which was ordered to join the North Carolina line, they marched at once to join General Gates, then commanding in the South. Under the command of this unfortunate general he remained until after the battle of Camden. Here Gates experienced a most disastrous defeat, and the whole country was surrendered to the British forces.

South Carolina and North Carolina, especially their southern portions, were entirely overrun by the enemy, who armed the Tories and turned them loose to ravage the country. Gates's army was disorganized, and most of those who composed it from the Carolinas returned to their homes. Between these and the Scotch Tories, as the Loyalists were termed, there was a continual partisan strife, each party resorting to the most cruel murders, burning and destroying the homes and the property of each other. Partisan bands were organized by each, and under desperate leaders did desperate deeds. It was then and there that Marion and Fanning became conspicuous, and were respectively the terror of Whigs and Tories.

There were numerous others of like character, though less efficient and less conspicuous. The exploits of such bands are deemed beneath the dignity of history, and now only live in the memories of those who received them traditionally from the actors, their associates or descendants. Those acts constitute mainly the tragic horrors of war, and evidence the merciless inhumanity of enraged men, unrestrained by civil or moral law. Injuries he deems wanton prompt the passions of his nature to revenge, and he hastens to retaliate upon his enemy, with increased horrors, their savage brutalities.

As the leader of a small band of neighbors who had united for protection and revenge, Colonel Love became conspicuous for his courage and cruelty. It was impossible for these, his associates, as for their Tory neighbors and enemies, to remain at their homes, or even to visit them, except at night, and then most stealthily. The country abounds with swamps more or less dense and irreclaimable, which must always remain a hiding-place for the unfortunate or desperate. In these the little bands by day were concealed, issuing forth at night to seek for food or spoils. Their families were often made the victims of revenge; and instances were numerous where feeble women and little children were slain in cold blood by neighbors long and familiarly known to each other, in retaliation of like atrocities perpetrated by their husbands, sons, or brothers.

It was a favorite pastime with my grandmother, when the morning's work was done, to uncover her flax-wheel, seat herself, and call me to sit by her, and, after my childish manner, read to her from the "Life of General Francis Marion," by Mason L. Weems, the graphic account of the general's exploits, by the venerable parson. There was not a story in the book that she did not know, almost as a party concerned, and she would ply her work of flax-spinning while she gave me close and intense attention. At times, when the historian was at fault in his facts—and, to say the truth, that was more frequently the case than comports with veracious history — she would cease the impelling motion of her foot upon the pedal of her little wheel, drop her thread, and, gently arresting the fly of her spool, she would lift her iron-framed spectacles, and with great gravity say: "Read that again. Ah! it is not as it happened, your grandfather was in that fight, and I will tell you how it was." This was so frequently the case, that now, when more than sixty years have flown, I am at a loss to know, if the knowledge of most of these facts which tenaciously clings to my memory, was originally derived from Weems's book, or my grandmother's narrations. In these forays and conflicts, whenever my grandfather was a party, her information was derived from him and his associates, and of course was deemed by her authentic; and whenever these differed from the historian s narrative, his, of consequence, was untrue. Finally, Weems, upon one of his book-selling excursions, which simply meant disposing of his own writings, came through her neighborhood, and with the gravity of age, left verbally his own biography with Mrs. McJoy, a neighbor; this made him, as he phrased it, General Washington's preacher. He was never after assailed as a lying author: but whenever his narrative was opposed to her memory, she had the excuse for him, that his informant had deceived him.

To have seen General Washington, even without having held the holy office of his preacher, sanctified in her estimation any and every one. She had seen him, and it was the especial glory of her life. Yes, she had seen him, and remembered minutely his eyes, his hair, his mouth and his hands—and even his black horse with a star in his face, and his one white foot and long, sweeping tail. So often did I listen to the story, that in after boyhood I came to believe I had seen him also, though his death occurred twenty days before I was born. My dear, good mother has often told me that but for an attack of ague, which kept the venerable lady from our home for a month or more, I should have been honored with bearing the old hero's name through life. So intent was she in this particular, that she never liked my being named after Billy Crafford (for so she pronounced his name) for whom the partiality of my father caused him to name me. Few remain to remember the horrors of this partisan warfare. The very traditions are being obliterated by those of the recent civil war, so rife with scenes and deeds sufficiently horrible for the appetite of the curious in crime and cruelty.

CHAPTER II.

PIONEER LIFE.

Settlement of Middle Georgia — Prowling Indians — Scouts and their Dogs — Classes of Settlers — Prominence of Virginians — Causes of Distinction — Clearing — Log-Rolling — Frolics — Teachers Cummings and Duffy — The Schoolmaster's Nose — Flogging — Emigration to Alabama.

THE early settlement of Middle Georgia was principally by emigrants from Virginia and North Carolina. These were a rough, poor, but honest people, with little or no fortunes, and who were quite as limited in education as in fortune. Their necessities made them industrious and frugal. Lands were procured at the expense of surveying; the soil was virgin and productive; rude cabins, built of poles, constituted not only their dwellings but every necessary outbuilding. Those who first ventured beyond the Ogeechee generally selected some spot where a good spring of water was found, not overlooked by an elevation so close as to afford an opportunity to the Indians, then very troublesome, to fire into the little stockade forts erected around these springs for their security against the secret attacks of the prowling and merciless Creeks and Cherokees.

Usually several families united in building and living in these forts. As soon as this protection was completed, the work of clearing away the surrounding forest was commenced, that the land should afford a field for cultivation. While thus employed, sentinels were stationed at such points in the neighborhood as afforded the best opportunity for descrying the approach of Indians, and the watch was most careful. When those employed in hunting (for every community had its hunters) discovered, or thought they had discovered signs of the presence of the savages, scouts were immediately sent out to discover if they were lurking anywhere in the neighborhood. This was the most arduous and perilous duty of the pioneers, and not unfrequently the scout, or spy as he was usually termed, went to return no more. When seed-time came, corn, a small patch of cotton and another of flax were planted, and cultivation continued under the same surveillance.

The dog, always the companion of man, was carefully trained to search for the prowling Indians; and by daylight every morning the clearing, as the open lands were universally termed, was passed around by a cautious scout, always preceded by his dogs, who seemed as conscious of their duty and as faithful in its discharge as was their master. If he reported no Indians, the work of cultivation commenced, and the sentinels repaired to their posts. These were usually changed whenever the slightest sign of Indians anywhere in the country could be found, lest their posts might have been found and marked, and ambushed at night. Yet, despite this prudent caution, many a sentinel perished at his post. The unerring arrow gave no alarm, and the sentinel slain, opened an approach for the savages; and not unfrequently parties at labor were thus surprised and shot in full view of those in the fort.

Occasionally an emigrant brought with him a slave or two: these were rich, and invariably were the leading men in the communities. Those from Virginia were more frequently possessed of this species of property than those from the Carolinas, and, coming from an older country, had generally enjoyed better opportunities and were more cultivated. A common necessity harmonized all, and the state of society was a pure democracy. These communities were usually from twenty to fifty miles apart, and about them a nucleus was formed, inviting those who sought the new country for a home to locate in the immediate vicinity. Security and the enjoyment of social intercourse were more frequently the incentives for these selections than the fertility of the soil or other advantages. One peculiarity was observable, which their descendants, in their emigration to the West, continue to this day to practise: they usually came due west from their former homes, and were sure to select, as nearly as possible, a new one in the same parallel, and with surroundings as nearly like those they had left as possible. With the North Carolinian, good spring-water, and pine-knots for his fire, were the *sine qua non.* These secured, he went to work with the assiduity and perseverance of a beaver to build his house and open his fields. The Virginians, less particular, but more ambitious, sought the best lands for grain and tobacco; consequently they were more diffused, and their improvements, from their superior wealth, were more imposing.

Wealth in all communities is comparative, and he who has only a few thousand dollars, where no one else has so much, is the rich man, and ever assumes the rich man's prerogatives and bearing. All experience has proved that as a man estimates himself, so in time will the community esteem him; and he who assumes to lead or dictate will soon be permitted to do so, and will become the first in prominence and influence in his neighborhood, county, or State. Greatness commences humbly and progresses by assumption. The humble ruler of a neighborhood, like a pebble thrown into a pond, will continue to increase the circle of his influence until it reaches the limits of his county. The fathers speak of him, the children hear of him, his name is a household word; if he but assumes enough, in time he becomes the great man of the county; and if with impudence he unites a modicum of talent, well larded with a cunning deceit, it will not be long before he is Governor or member of Congress. It is not surprising, then, that in nearly every one of these communities the great man was a Virginian. It has been assumed by the Virginians that they have descended from a superior race, and this may be true as regards many families whose ancestors were of Norman descent; but it is not true of the mass of her population; and for one descendant from the nobility and gentry of the mother country, there are thousands of pure Anglo-Saxon blood. It was certainly true, from the character and abilities of her public men, in her colonial condition and in the earlier days of the republic, she had a right to assume a superiority; but this, I fancy, was more the result of her peculiar institutions than of any superiority of race or greater purity of blood. I am far, however, from underrating the influence of blood. That there are species of the same race superior in mental as well as in physical formation is certainly true. The peculiar organization of the brain, its fineness of texture in some, distinguish them as mentally superior to others, as the greater development of bone and muscle marks the superiority of physical power. Very frequently this difference is seen in brothers, and sometimes in families of the same parents—the males in some usurping all the mental acumen, and in others the females. Why this is so, I cannot stop to speculate.

Virginia, in her many divisions of territory, was granted to the younger sons of the nobility and gentry of England. They came with the peculiar habits of their class, and located upon these grants, bringing with them as colonists their dependants in England, and retaining here all the peculiarities of caste. The former were the governing class at home, and asserted the privilege here; the latter were content that it should be so. In the formation of the first constitution for Virginia, the great feature of a landed aristocracy was fully recognized in the organic law. The suffragist was the landed proprietor, and in every county where his possessions were this right attached. They recognized landed property as the basis of government, and demanded the right for it of choosing the lawmakers and the executors of the law. All power, and very nearly all of the wealth of the State, was in the hands of the landlords, and these selected from their own class or caste the men who were to conduct the government. To this class, too, were confined most of the education and learning in the new State; and in choosing for the Legislature or for Congress, State pride and the love of power prompted the selection of their brightest and best men.

Oratory was esteemed the first attribute of superior minds, and was assiduously cultivated. There were few newspapers, and the press had not attained the controlling power over the public mind as now. Political information was disseminated chiefly by public speaking, and every one aspiring to lead in the land was expected to be a fine speaker. This method, and the manner of voting, forced an open avowal of political opinion. Each candidate, upon the day of election, took his seat upon the bench of the judge in the county court-house, and the suffragist appeared at the bar, demanding to exercise his privilege in the choice of his representative. This was done by declaring the names of those he voted for. These peculiar institutions cultivated open and manly bearing, pride, and independence. There was little opportunity for the arts of the demagogue; and the elevation of sentiment in the suffragist made him despise the man, however superior his talents, who would attempt them. The voter's pride was to sustain the power of his State in the national councils, to have a great man for his Governor; they were the representatives of his class, and he felt his own importance in the greatness of his representative. It is not to be wondered at, under these circumstances, that Virginia held for many years the control of the Government, furnishing Presidents of transcendent abilities to the nation, and filling her councils with men whose talents and eloquence and proud and independent bearing won for them, not only the respect of the nation's representatives, but the power to control the nation's destinies, and to be looked upon as belonging to a superior race.

There were wanting, however, two great elements in the nation's institutions, to sustain in its pride and efficiency this peculiar advantage, to wit, the entailment of estates, and the right of primogeniture. Those landed estates soon began to be subdivided, and in proportion as they dwindled into insignificance, so began to perish the prestige of their proprietors. The institution of African slavery served for a long time to aid in continuing the aristocratic features of Virginia society, though it conferred no legal privileges. As these, and the lands, found their way into many hands, the democratic element began to aspire and to be felt. The struggle was long and severe, but finally, in 1829 or 1830, the democratic element triumphed, and a new constitution was formed, extending universal suffrage to white men. This degraded the constituent and representative alike, and all of Virginia's power was soon lost in the councils of the nation. But the pride of her people did not perish with her aristocracy; this continued, and permeated her entire people. They preserved it at home, and carried it wherever they went. Those whose consideration at home was at zero, became of the first families abroad, until Virginia pride became a by-word of scorn in the western and more southern States. Yet despite all this, there is greatness in the Virginians: there is superiority in her people, — a loftiness of soul, a generosity of hospitality, a dignified patience under suffering, which command the respect and admiration of every appreciative mind.

Very soon after the Revolution, the tide of emigration began to flow toward Tennessee, Kentucky, and Georgia. Those from Virginia who sought new homes went principally to Kentucky, as much because it was a part of the Old Dominion, as on account of climate and soil. Those from North Carolina and South Carolina preferred Tennessee, and what was then known as Upper Georgia, but now as Middle Georgia; yet there was a sprinkling here and there throughout Georgia from Virginia. Many of these became leading men in the State, and their descendants still boast of their origin, and in plenary pride point to such men as William H. Crawford and Peter Early as shining evidences of the superiority of Virginia's blood.

Most of these emigrants, however, were poor; but where all were poor, this was no degradation. The concomitants of poverty in densely populated communities — where great wealth confers social distinction and frowns from its association the poor, making poverty humility, however elevated its virtues — were unknown in these new countries. The nobler virtues, combined with energy and intellect, alone conferred distinction; and I doubt if the world ever furnished a more honest, virtuous, energetic, or democratic association of men and women than was, at the period of which I write, to be found constituting the population of these new States. From whatever cause arising, there certainly was, in the days of my early memory, more scrupulous truth, open frankness, and pure, blunt honesty pervading the whole land than seem to characterize its present population. It was said by Nathaniel Macon, of North Carolina, that bad roads and fist-fights made the best militia on earth; and these may have been, in some degree, the means of moulding into fearless honesty the character of these people. They encountered all the hardships of opening and subduing the country, creating highways, bridges, churches, and towns with their public buildings. These they met cheerfully, and working with a will, triumphed. After months of labor, a few acres were cleared and the trees cut into convenient lengths for handling, and then the neighbors were invited to assist in what was called a log-rolling. This aid was cheerfully given, and an offer to pay for it would have been an insult. It was returned in kind, however, when a neighbor's necessities required. These log-rollings were generally accompanied with a quilting, which brought together the youth of the neighborhood; and the winding up of the day's work was a frolic, as the dance and other amusements of the time were termed. Upon occasions like this, feats of strength and activity universally constituted a part of the programme. The youth who could pull down his man at the end of the hand-stick, throw him in a wrestle, or outstrip him in a foot-race, was honored as the best man in the settlement, and was always greeted with a cheer from the older men, a slap on the shoulder by the old ladies, and the shy but approving smiles of the girls,—had his choice of partners in the dance, and in triumph rode home on horseback with his belle, the horse's consciousness of bearing away the championship manifesting itself in an erect head and stately step.

The apparel of male and female was of home-spun, woven by the mothers and sisters, and was fashioned, I was about to say, by the same fair hands; but these were almost universally embrowned with exposure and hardened by toil. Education was exceedingly limited: the settlements were sparse, and school-houses were at long intervals, and in these the mere rudiments of an English education were taught—spelling, reading, and writing, with the four elementary rules of arithmetic; and it was a great advance to grapple with the grammar of the language. As population and prosperity increased, their almost illiterate teachers gave place to a better class; and many of my Georgia readers will remember as among these the old Irish preachers, Cummings, and that remarkable brute, Daniel Duffee. He was an Irishman of the Pat Freney stripe, and I fancy there are many, with gray heads and wrinkled fronts, who can look upon the cicatrices resulting from his merciless blows, and remember that Milesian malignity of face, with its toad-like nose, with the same vividness with which it presents itself to me to-day. Yes, I remember it, and have cause. When scarcely ten years of age, in his little log school-house, the aforesaid resemblance forced itself upon me with such *vim* that involuntarily I laughed. For this outbreak against the tyrant's rules I was called to his frowning presence.

"What are you laughing at, you whelp?" was the rude inquiry.

Tremblingly I replied: "You will whip me if I tell you."

"And you little devil, I will whip you if you don't," was his rejoinder, as he reached for his well-trimmed hickory, one of many conspicuously displayed upon his table. With truthful sincerity I answered:

"Father Duffy, I was laughing to think how much your nose is like a frog."

It was just after play-time, and I was compelled to stand by him and at intervals of ten minutes receive a dozen lashes, laid on with brawny Irish strength, until discharged with the school at night. To-day I bear the marks of that whipping upon my shoulders and in my heart. But Duffy was not alone in the strictness and severity of his rules and his punishments. Children were taught to believe that there could be no discipline in a school of boys and girls without the savage brutality of the lash, and the teacher who met his pupils with a caressing smile was considered unworthy his vocation. Learning must be thrashed into the tender mind; nothing was such a stimulus to the young memory as the lash and the vulgar, abusive reproof of the gentle and meritorious teacher.

There was great eccentricity of character in all the conduct and language of Duffy. He had his own method of prayer, and his own peculiar style of preaching, frequently calling out the names of persons in his audience whom it was his privilege to consider the chiefest of sinners, and to implore mercy for them in language offensive almost to decency. Sometimes, in the presence of persons inimical to each other, he would ask the Lord to convert the sinners and make the fools friends, first telling the Lord who they were by name, to the no small amusement of his most Christian audience; many of whom would in deep devotion respond with a sonorous "Amen."

From such a population sprang the present inhabitants of Georgia; and by such men were they taught, in their budding boyhood, the rudiments of an English education;—such, I mean, of the inhabitants who still live and remember Duffy, Cummings, and McLean. They are few, but the children of the departed remember traditionally these and their like, in the schoolmasters of Georgia from 1790 to 1815.

At the close of the war of 1812–15, a new impetus was given to everything throughout the South, and especially to education. The ambition for wealth seized upon her people, the high price of cotton favored its accumulation, and with it came new and more extravagant wants, new and more luxurious habits. The plain homespun jean coat gave way to the broad-cloth one; and the neat, Turkey-red striped Sunday frock of the belle yielded to the gaudy red calico one, and there was a sniff of aristocratic contempt in the upturned nose towards those who, from choice or necessity, continued in the old habits.

Material wealth augmented rapidly, and with it came all of its assumptions. The rich lands of Alabama were open to settlement.

The formidable Indian had been humbled, and many of the wealthiest cultivators of the soil were commencing to emigrate to a newer and more fertile country, where smiling Fortune beckoned them.

The first to lead off in this exodus was the Bibb family, long distinguished for wealth and influence in the State. The Watkinses, the Sheroos, and Dearings followed: some to north, some to south Alabama. W. W. Bibb was appointed, by Mr. Madison, Territorial Governor of Alabama, and was followed to the new El Dorado by his brothers, Thomas, John Dandridge, and Benajah, all men of substance and character.

For a time this rage for a new country seemed to threaten Georgia and South Carolina with the loss of their best population. This probably would have been the result of the new acquisition, but, in its midst, the territory between the Ocmulgee and Chattahoochee was ceded by the Indians, and afforded a new field for settlement, which effectually arrested this emigration at its flood. The new territory added to the dominion of Georgia was acquired mainly through the energy and pertinacity of George M. Troup, at the time Governor of Georgia.

I have much to record of my memories concerning this new acquisition, but must reserve them for a new chapter.

CHAPTER III.

THE GEORGIA COMPANY.

Yazoo Purchase — Governor Mathews — James Jackson — Burning of the Yazoo Act — Development of Free Government — Constitutional Convention — Slavery: Its Introduction and Effects.

THE grant by the British Government of the territory of Georgia to General Oglethorpe and company, comprised what now constitutes the entire States of Georgia, Alabama, and Mississippi, except that portion of Alabama and Mississippi lying below the thirty-first degree of north latitude, which portions of those States were originally part of West Florida.

The French settlements extended up the Mississippi, embracing both sides of that river above the mouth of Red River, which discharges into the former in the thirty-first degree of north latitude. The river from the mouth of the Bayou Manshac, which left the river fourteen miles below Baton Rouge, on the east side, up to the thirty-first degree of north latitude, was the boundary line between West Florida and Louisiana. Above this point the French claimed jurisdiction on both sides; but Georgia disputed this jurisdiction over the east bank, and claimed to own from the thirty-first to the thirty-sixth degree of latitude. There were many settlements made by Americans upon this territory at a very early day,—one at Natchez, one at Fort Adams, and several on the Tombigbee, the St. Stephens, at McIntosh's Bluff, and on Bassett's Creek. These settlements formed the nucleus of an American population in the States of Mississippi and Alabama. The lands bordering upon these rivers and their tributaries were known to be exceedingly fertile, and proffered inducements to settlers unequalled in all the South. Speculation was very soon directed to these regions. A company was formed of citizens of Georgia and Virginia for the purchase of an immense tract of territory, including most of what is now Mississippi and Alabama. This company was known as the Georgia Company, and the territory as the Yazoo Purchase. It was a joint-stock company, and managed by trustees or directors. The object was speculation. It was intended to purchase from Georgia this domain, then to survey it and subdivide it into tracts to suit purchasers. Parties were delegated to make this purchase: this could only be done by the Legislature and by special act passed for that purpose. The proposition was made, and met with formidable opposition. The scheme was a gigantic one and promised great results, and the parties concerned were bold and unscrupulous. They very soon ascertained that means other than honorable to either party must be resorted to to secure success. The members to be operated upon were selected, and the company's agents began the work. Enough was made, by donations of stock and the direct payment of money by those interested in the scheme, to effect the passage of the Act and secure the contract of purchase and sale. The opposition denied the power of the Legislature to sell; asserting that the territory was sacred to the people of the State, and that those, in selecting their representatives, had never contemplated delegating any such powers as would enable them to dispose by sale of any part of the public domain; that it was the province of the Legislature, under the Constitution, to pass laws for the general good alone, and not to barter or sell any portion of the territory of the State to be separated from the domain and authority of the State. They insisted that the matter should be referred to the people, who at the next election of members to the Legislature should declare their will and intention as to this sale.

On the other side they were met with the argument, that the Legislature was sovereign and the supreme power of the State, and might rightfully do anything, not forbidden in the Constitution, pertaining to sovereignty, which they in their wisdom might deem essential to the general welfare; that the territory included in the grant to Oglethorpe and company was entirely too extended, and that by a sale a new State or States would be formed, which would increase the political power of the South — especially in the United States Senate, where she greatly needed representation to counterbalance the influence of the small States of the North in that body. These arguments were specious, but it was well understood they were only meant to justify a vote for the measure which corruption had secured.

The Act was passed by a bare majority of both branches of the Legislature, and the sale consummated. Before the passage of this measure, the will of the people had been sufficiently expressed in the indignant outburst of public feeling, as to leave no doubt upon the minds of the corrupt representatives that they had not only forfeited the public confidence, but had actually imperilled their personal safety. Upon the return to their homes, after the adjournment, they were not only met with universal scorn, but with inappeasable rage. Some of the most guilty were slain; some had their houses burned over their heads, and others fled the State; one was pursued and killed in Virginia, and all not only entailed upon themselves infamy, but also upon their innocent posterity; and to-day, to be known as the descendant of a Yazoo man is a badge of disgrace. The deed, however, was done: how to undo it became an agitating question. The Legislature next ensuing was elected pledged to repeal the odious Act; and upon its convening, all made haste to manifest an ardent zeal in this work.

At the time of the passage of this Act, the Legislature sat in Augusta, and the Governor who by the Act was empowered to make the sale was George Mathews. Mathews was an Irishman by birth, and was very illiterate, but a man of strong passions and indomitable will. During the war of the Revolution he had, as a partisan officer, gained some distinction, and in the upper counties exercised considerable influence. Many anecdotes are related of his intrepidity and daring, and quite as many of his extraordinary orthography. At the battle of Eutaw Springs, in South Carolina, he was severely wounded, at the moment when the Continental forces were retiring to a better position. A British soldier, noticing some vestiges of a uniform upon him, lifted his musket to stab him with the bayonet; his commander caught the weapon, and angrily demanded, "Would you murder a wounded officer? Forward, sir!" Mathews, turning upon his back, asked, "To whom do I owe my life?" "If you consider it an obligation, sir, to me," answered the lieutenant. Mathews saw the uniform was British, and furiously replied, "Well, sir, I want you to know that I scorn a life saved by a d——d Briton." The writer had the anecdote from a distinguished citizen of Georgia, who was himself lying near by, severely wounded, and who in one of his sons has given to Georgia a Governor.

General Wade Hampton, George Walker, William Longstreet, Zachariah Cox, and Matthew McAllister were the parties most active in procuring the passage of the Yazoo Act. That bribery was extensively practised, there is no doubt, and the suspicion that it even extended to the Executive gained credence as a fact, and was the cause of preventing his name ever being given to a county in the State: and it is a significant fact of this suspicion, and also of the great unpopularity of the Act, that to this day every effort to that end has failed. No act of Governor Mathews ever justified any such suspicion. As Governor of the State, and believing the sovereign power of the State was in the Legislature, and consequently the power to dispose of the public domain, he only approved the Act as the State's Executive, and fulfilled the duties assigned to him by the law. But suspicion fastened upon him, and its effects remain to this day.

The pertinacious discussions between the parties purchasing and those opposed to the State's selling and her authority to sell, created immense excitement, and pervaded the entire State. The decision of the Supreme Court of the United States was invoked in the case of Fletcher *versus* Peck, which settled the question of the power of the State to sell the public domain, and the validity of the sale made by the State to the Georgia Company. In the meantime the Legislature of Georgia had repealed the law authorizing the Governor to sell. This decision of the Supreme Court brought about an amicable adjustment of the difficulties between the Company and the State, with the Government of the United States as a third party.

The excitement was not so much on account of the sale, though this was bitter, as of the corruption which procured it. The test of public confidence and social respect was opposition to the Yazoo fraud. Every candidate at the ensuing election for members of the Legislature was compelled to declare his position on the subject of repealing this Act, and, almost to a man, every one who believed in the power of the State to sell, and that rights had vested in the purchasers and their assigns, was defeated.

James Jackson, a young, ardent, and talented man, who had in very early life, by his abilities and high character, so won the public confidence that he had been elected Governor of the State, when he was ineligible because of his youth, was at this time a member of Congress. He made a tour through the State, preaching a crusade against the corrupt Legislature, and denouncing those who had produced and profited by this corruption, inflaming the public mind almost to frenzy. He resided in Savannah, and was at the head of the Republican or Jeffersonian party, which was just then being organized in opposition to the administration of John Adams, the successor of Washington. His parents had emigrated from England, and fixed their home in Savannah, where young Jackson was born, and where, from the noble qualities of his nature, he had become immensely popular.

Talent and virtuous merit at that period was the passport to public confidence. Had it continued to be, we should never have known the present deplorable condition of the country, with the Government sinking into ruin ere it has reached the ten o'clock of national life.

His Shibboleth was, that the disgrace of the State must be wiped out by the repeal of the Yazoo Act; and *repeal* rang from every mouth, from Savannah to the mountains. Jackson resigned his seat in Congress, and was elected a member of the Legislature. Immediately upon the assembling of this body, a bill was introduced repealing the odious Act, and ordering the records containing it to be burned. This was carried out to the letter. Jackson, heading the Legislature and the indignant public, proceeded in procession to the public square in Louisville, Jefferson County, where the law and the fagots were piled; when, addressing the assembled multitude, he denounced the men who had voted for the law as bribed villains—those who had bribed them, and the Governor who had signed it; and declared that fire from heaven only could sanctify the indignation of God and man in consuming the condemned record of accursed crime. Then, with a Promethean or convex glass condensing the sun's rays, he kindled the flame which consumed the records containing the hated Yazoo Act.

Jackson was a man of ordinary height, slender, very erect in his carriage, with red hair and intensely blue eyes. His manners were courteous, affable, and remarkable for a natural dignity which added greatly to his influence with the people. He was the model from which was grown that chivalry and nobility of soul and high bearing so characteristic of the people of Southern Georgia. In truth, the essence of his character seemed subtilly to pervade the entire circle in which he moved, inspiring a purity of character, a loftiness of honor, which rebuked with its presence alone everything that was low, little, or dishonest. Subsequently he was elected Governor of the State, bringing all the qualities of his nature into the administration of the office; he gave it a dignity and respectability never subsequently degraded, until an unworthy son of South Carolina, the pus and corruption of unscrupulous party, was foisted into the position. Strength of will, a ripe judgment, and purity of intention, were the great characteristics distinguishing him in public life, and these have endeared his name to the people of Georgia, where now remain many of his descendants, some of whom have filled high positions in the State and United States, and not one has ever soiled the honor or tarnished the name with an act unworthy a gentleman.

The Revolutionary struggle called out all the nobler qualities nature has bestowed on man, in those who conceived the desire and executed the determination to be free. The heroic was most prominent: woman seemed to forget her feebleness and timidity, and boldly to dare, and with increased fortitude to bear every danger, every misfortune, with a heroism scarcely compatible with the delicacy of her nature. To this, or some other inexplicable cause, nature seemed to resort in preparation for coming events. In every State there came up men, born during the war or immediately thereafter, of giant minds—men seemingly destined to form and give direction to a new Government suited to the genius of the people and to the physical peculiarities of the country where it was to control the destinies of hundreds of millions of human beings yet unborn, and where the soil was virgin and unturned, which nature had prepared for their coming. This required a new order of men. These millions were to be free in the fullest sense of the word; they were only to be controlled by laws; and the making of these laws was to be their own work, and nature was responding to the exigencies of man.

The early probation of independent government taught the necessity of national concentration as to the great features of government, at the same time demonstrating the importance of keeping the minor powers of government confined to the authority of the States. In the assembling of a convention for this purpose, which grew out of the free action of the people of each State, uninfluenced by law or precedent, we see congregated a body of men combining more talent, more wisdom, and more individuality of character than perhaps was ever aggregated in any other public body ever assembled. From this convention of sages emanated the Constitution of the United States; and most of those constituting this body reassembled in the first Congress, which sat as the supreme power in the United States. It was these men and their coadjutors who inaugurated and gave direction to the new Government. Under its operations, the human mind and human soul seemed to expand and to compass a grasp it had scarcely known before. There were universal content and universal harmony. The laws were everywhere respected, and everywhere enforced. The freedom of thought, and the liberty of action unrestrained, stimulated an ambition in every man to discharge his duties faithfully to the Government, and honestly in all social relations. There was universal security to person and property, because every law-breaker was deemed a public enemy, and not only received the law's condemnation, but the public scorn. Under such a Government the rapid accumulation of wealth and population was a natural consequence. The history of the world furnishes no example comparable with the progress of the United States to national greatness. The civilized world appeared to feel the influence of her example and to start anew in the rivalry of greatness. Her soil's surplus products created the means of a widely extended commerce, and Americans can proudly refer to the eighty years of her existence as a period showing greater progress in wealth, refinement, the arts and sciences, and human liberty, than was ever experienced in any two centuries of time within the historical period of man's existence. My theme expands, and I am departing from the purposes of this work; yet I cannot forbear the expression of opinion as to the causes of this result. I know I shall incur the deepest censure from the professors of a mawkish philanthropy, and a hypocritical religion which is cursing with its cant the very sources of this unparalleled progress, this unexampled prosperity.

Slavery was introduced into the Colonies by English merchants about two centuries since: this was to supply a necessity — labor — for the purpose of developing the resources of this immense and fertile country. The African was designed by the Creator to subserve this purpose. His centre of creation was within the tropics, and his physical organization fitted him, and him alone, for field labor in the tropical and semi-tropical regions of the earth. He endures the sun's heat without pain or exhaustion in this labor, and yet he has not nor can he acquire the capacity to direct profitably this labor. It was then the design of the Creator that this labor should be controlled and directed by a superior intelligence. In the absence of mental capacity, we find him possessed of equal physical powers with any other race, with an amiability of temper which submits without resistance to this control. We find him, too, without moral, social, or political aspirations, contented and happy in the condition of servility to this superior intelligence, and rising in the scale of humanity to a condition which under any other circumstances his race had never attained. I may be answered that this labor can be had from the black as a freeman as well as in the condition of a slave. To this I will simply say, experience has proved this to be an error. Such is the indolence and unambitious character of the negro that he will not labor, unless compelled by the apprehension of immediate punishment, to anything approaching his capacity for labor. His wants are few, they are easily supplied, and when they are, there is no temptation which will induce him to work. He cares nothing for social position, and will steal to supply his necessities, and feel no abasement in the legal punishment which follows his conviction; nor is his social status among his race damaged thereby. As a slave to the white man, he becomes and has proved an eminently useful being to his kind—in every other condition, equally conspicuous as a useless one. The fertility of the soil and the productions of the tropical regions of the earth demonstrate to the thinking mind that these were to be cultivated and made to produce for the uses and prosperity of the human family. The great staples of human necessity and human luxury are produced here in the greatest abundance, and the great majority of these nowhere else. The white man, from his physical organization, cannot perform in these regions the labor necessary to their production. His centre of creation is in the temperate zones, and only there can he profitably labor in the earth's cultivation. But his mental endowments enable him to appropriate all which nature has supplied for the necessities of life and the progress of his race. He sees and comprehends in nature the designs of her Creator: these designs he develops, and the consequence is a constant and enlightened progress of his race, and the subjection of the physical world to this end.

He finds the soil, the climate, the production, and the labor united, and he applies his intelligence to develop the design of this combination; and the consequence has been the wonderful progress of the last two centuries. I hold it as a great truth that nature points to her uses and ends; that to observe these and follow them is to promote the greatest happiness to the human family; and that wherever these aims are diverted or misdirected, retrogression and human misery are the consequence. In all matters, experience is a better test than speculation; and to surrender a great practical utility to a mere theory is great folly. But it has been done, and we abide the consequences.

In all nations, a spurious, pretentious religion has been the *avant-coureur* of their destruction. In their inception and early progress this curse exercises but slight influence, and their growth is consequently healthy and vigorous. All nations have concealed this cancerous ulcer, sooner or later to develop for their destruction. These wear out with those they destroy, and a new or reformed religion is almost always accompanied with new and vigorous developments in a new and progressive Government. The shackles which have paralyzed the mind, forbidding its development, are broken; the unnatural superstition ceases to circumscribe and influence its operations; and thus emancipated, it recovers its elasticity and springs forward toward the perfection of the Creator. Rescued from these baleful influences, the new organization is vigorous and rapid in its growth, yielding the beneficent blessings natural to the healthful and unabused energies of the mind. But with maturity and age the webs of superstition begin to fasten on the mind; priests become prominent, and as is their wont, the moment they shackle the mind, they reach out for power, and the chained disciple of their superstition willingly yields, under the vain delusion that he shares and participates in this power as a holy office for the propagation of his creed—and retrogression commences.

The effects of African slavery in the United States, upon the condition of both races, was eminently beneficial to both. In no condition, and under no other circumstances, had the African made such advances toward civilization: indeed, I doubt if he has not attained in this particular to the highest point susceptible to his nature. He has increased more rapidly, and his aspirations have become more elevated, and his happiness more augmented. With his labor directed by the intelligence of the white race, the prosperity of the world has increased in a ratio superior to any antecedent period. The production of those staples which form the principal bases of commerce has increased in a quadruple ratio. Cotton alone increased so rapidly as to render its price so far below every other article which can be fashioned into cloth, that the clothing and sheeting of the civilized world was principally fabricated from it. The rapidity of its increased production was only equalled by the increase of wealth and comfort throughout the world. It regulates the exchanges almost universally. It gave, in its growth, transportation, and manufacture, employment to millions, feeding and clothing half of Europe—increasing beyond example commercial tonnage, and stimulating the invention of labor-saving machinery—giving a healthy impulse to labor and enterprise in every avocation, and intertwining itself with every interest, throughout the broad expanse of civilization over the earth. To cotton, more than to any other one thing, is due the railroad, steamboat, and steamship, the increase of commerce, the rapid accumulation of fortunes, and consequently the diffusion of intelligence, learning, and civilization.

Sugar, too, from the same cause, ceased to be a luxury, and became a necessity in the economy of living: coffee, too, became a stimulating beverage at every meal, instead of a luxury only to be indulged on rare occasions. How much the increased production of these three articles added to the commerce and wealth of the world during the last two centuries, and especially the last, is beyond computation. How much of human comfort and human happiness is now dependent upon their continued production, and in such abundance as to make them accessible to the means of all, may well employ the earnest attention of those who feel for the interest and happiness of their kind most. If these results have followed the institution of African slavery, can it be inhuman and sinful? Is it not rather an evidence that the Creator so designed?

But this is not all this institution has effected. Besides its pecuniary results, it has inspired in the superior race a nobility of feeling, resulting from a habit of command and a sense of independence, which is peculiar to privileged orders of men in civilized society. This feeling is manifested in high bearing and sensitive honor, a refinement of sentiment and chivalrous emprise unknown to communities without caste. This is to be seen in the absence of everything little or mean. A noble hospitality, a scorn of bargaining, and a lofty yet eminently deferential deportment toward females: in this mould it has cast Southern society, and these traits made the Southern gentleman remarkable, wherever his presence was found.

These were the men who led in the formation of the Government of the United States, and who gave tone and character to her legislative assembly, so long as they held control of the Government. A peer among these was James Jackson, and many of his confederates, of whom I shall have occasion to speak in the progress of this work.

CHAPTER IV.

POLITICAL DISPUTATIONS.

BALDWIN — A YANKEE'S POLITICAL STABILITY — THE YAZOO QUESTION — PARTY FEUDS AND FIGHTS — DEAF AND DUMB MINISTERS — CLAY — JACKSON — BUCHANAN — CALHOUN — COTTON AND FREE-TRADE — THE CLAY AND RANDOLPH DUEL.

AMONG the early immigrants into Georgia were Abraham Baldwin and William H. Crawford. Baldwin was from Connecticut, Crawford from Virginia. Baldwin was a man of liberal education, and was destined for the ministry; indeed, he had taken orders, and was an officiating clergyman for some time in his native state. His family was English, and has given many distinguished men to the nation. After he arrived in Georgia, where he came to engage in his vocation, he very soon ascertained his profession was not one which in a new country promised much profit or distinction; and possessing in an eminent degree that Yankee "*cuteness*" which is quick to discover what is to the interest of its possessor, he abandoned the pulpit for the forum, and after a brief probation in a law office at nights and a school-house by day, he opened an office, and commenced the practice of law in Augusta. He had been educated a Federalist in politics, and had not concealed his sentiments in his new home.

Mr. Jefferson and his political principles were extremely popular in Georgia, and though there were some distinguished Federalists in Augusta who were leaders in her society, their number in the State was too insignificant to hold out any prospect of preferment to a young, talented, and ambitious aspirant for political distinction. Baldwin was not slow to discover this, and, with the facile nature of his race, abandoned his political creed, as he had his professional pursuits. He saw Crawford was rising into public notice, and he knew his ability, and with characteristic impudence he thrust himself forward, and very soon was made a member of Congress. Here he was true to his last love, and became a leading member of the Republican party. By his conduct in this matter he made himself odious to his New England friends, who were unsparing of their abuse because of his treachery.

For this he cared very little; but bore well in mind that "the blood of the martyrs was the seed of the church," and that the hate of the Federalists was the passport to Republican favor. His zeal was that of the new convert, and it won for him the confidence of his party, and rapid preferment in the line of distinction. He was a man of decided abilities, and seemed destined to high distinction; but dying early, a member of the United States Senate, his hopes and aspirations here terminated. The State has honored and perpetuated his name by giving it to the county wherein is situated her seat of government.

Crawford, like Baldwin, taught, and studied law at the same time. He was usher in a school taught by his life-long friend, Judge Yates. When admitted to practise law, he located in the little village of Lexington, in the County of Oglethorpe, and very soon was not only the leading lawyer, but the leading man of all the up-country of Georgia.

Eminence is always envied: this was conspicuously the fortune of Crawford. The population of the State was increasing rapidly, and young aspirants for fame and fortune were crowding to where these were promised most speedily.

The Yazoo question had created deep animosities. General Elijah Clarke, and his son John, subsequently governor of the State, were charged with complicity in this great fraud. The father had distinguished himself in repelling the Indians in their various forays upon the frontiers, and was a representative man. With strong will and distinguished courage, he, without much talent, was conspicuous among a people who were, like himself, rude, unlettered, but daring, and abounding in strong common-sense.

There was a young man at the same time, a devoted friend of young Clarke, and follower of his father: he was an emigrant from one of the Middle States. Violent in his character, and incautious in the use of language, he very soon became offensive to his opponents, and sought every opportunity to increase the bad feeling with which he was regarded. Siding with the Yazoo Company, he soon made himself odious to their enemies. The parties of Republicans and Federalists were bitter toward each other, and feuds were leading to fights, and some of these of most deadly character. The conflicts with the Indians had kept alive the warlike spirit which the partisan warfare of the Revolution had cultivated at the South, and no virtue was so especially regarded by these people as that of personal courage. The consequence was that no man, whatever his deportment or qualifications, could long fill the public eye without distinguishing himself for the possession of personal bravery.

The Clarkes were the undisputed leaders of public opinion in the upcountry, until Crawford came, and, by his great abilities and remarkable frankness of manner, won away to his support, and to the support of his opinions, a large majority of the people. This was not to be borne; and young Van Allen was willingly thrust forward to test the courage of Crawford. Duelling was the honorable method of settling all difficulties between gentlemen, and Crawford was to be forced into a duel. If he refused to fight, he was ruined. This, however, he did not do; and Van Allen was slain in the affair.

This but whetted the rage of the Clarkes, and John Clarke was not long in finding an excuse to call to the field his hated foe. In this duel Crawford was shot through the left wrist, which partially disabled that arm for life. But this did not heal the animosity; its rancor became contagious, and involved the people of the State almost to a man; nor did it end until both Clarke and Crawford were in the grave.

The history and consequences of this feud, and the two factions which grew out of it, would be the history of Georgia for more than forty years. Each had an army of followers; and all the talent of the State was divided between and leading these factions. There were many young men of decided talent rising into distinction in the professions, who were of necessity absorbed by these factions, and whose whole subsequent career was tainted with the ignoble prejudices arising out of this association. Among the most prominent and talented of these was John Forsyth, Peter Early, George M. Troup, the man *sans peur, sans reproche,* Thomas W. Cobb, Stephen Upson, Duncan G. Campbell, the brother-in-law of Clarke, and personally and politically his friend, and who, from the purity of his character and elevated bearing, was respected, trusted, and beloved by all who knew him; Freeman Walker, John M. Dooly, Augustus Clayton, Stephen W. Harris, and Eli S. Sherter, perhaps mentally equal to any son of Georgia.

With the exception of Upson and Troup, these were all natives of the State. Upson was from Connecticut, and was the son of a button-maker at Watertown, in that State. He was a thorough Yankee in all the qualities of perseverance, making and saving money. He was a pure man, stern and talented; and as a lawyer, was scarcely equalled in the State. He and Cobb were students, and *protégés* of Crawford, and both signalized their whole lives by a devotion, amounting almost to fanaticism, to Mr. Crawford and his fortunes.

George Michael Troup was born at McIntosh's Bluff, on the Tombigbee River, in the State of Alabama. His father was an Englishman, who, during the Revolution, removed to the place since called McIntosh's Bluff. Mr. Crawford soon became prominent as a politician, and adopting the party and principles of Jefferson, was transferred in early life to the councils of the nation. In the United States Senate he was the compeer of Felix Grundy, John C. Calhoun, Harrison Gray Otis, Rufus King, Daniel D. Tompkins, William B. Giles, Henry Clay, and many others of less distinction; and was the especial friend of those remarkable men, Nathaniel Macon and John Randolph.

At this period, there was an array of talent in Congress never equalled before or since. The aggressions of English cruisers upon our commerce, and the impressing of our seamen into the English service, had aroused the whole nation, and especially the South; and the fiery talent of this section was called by the people, breathing war, into the national councils.

Crawford was in the Senate from Georgia, and was a war-man. John Forsyth, John C. Calhoun, David R. Williams, George M. Troup, John Randolph, Philip Doddridge, James Barbour, Henry Clay, and William Lomax from South Carolina, were all comparatively young men.

Lowndes, Calhoun, Clay, and Troup were little more than thirty years of age, and yet they became prominent leaders of their party, exercising a controlling influence over the public mind, and shaping the policy of the Government. Crawford was the Mentor of this ardent band of lofty spirits — stimulating and checking, as occasion might require, the energies and actions of his young compeers. So conspicuous was he for talent, wisdom, and statesmanship, that he was proposed by the Republican party as a proper person to succeed Mr. Madison; and nothing prevented his receiving the nomination

4*

of that party but his refusal to oppose Mr. Monroe. His magnanimity was his misfortune. Had he been nominated, he would have been elected without opposition. The golden opportunity returned no more. He had succeeded Chancellor Livingston as minister to France, and of these two, Napoleon said "the United States had sent him two plenipotentiaries—the first was deaf, the latter dumb." Livingston was quite deaf, and Crawford could not speak French. At the court of Versailles, he served faithfully and efficiently the interests of his country, and returned with increased popularity. He filled, under Mr. Monroe, the office of Secretary of War for a short time, and then was transferred to the Secretaryship of the Treasury.

In the Cabinet of Mr. Monroe there were three aspirants for the Presidency: Adams, Crawford, and Calhoun. Between Crawford and Calhoun a feud arose, which was mainly the cause of Mr. Calhoun's name being withdrawn as a candidate, and the substitution of that of General Jackson. Crawford was one of the three highest returned to the House, and from whom a choice was to be made.

Some twelve months anterior to the election he was stricken with paralysis; and both body and mind so much affected that his friends felt that it would be improper to elect him. Nevertheless he continued a candidate until Mr. Adams was chosen.

Mr. Clay had been voted for as a fourth candidate, but not receiving electoral votes enough, failed to be returned to the House. Being at the time a member of the House of Representatives, it was supposed he held the control of the Western vote; and consequently the power to elect whom he pleased. Mr. Clay was a great admirer of Mr. Crawford, though their intimacy had been somewhat interrupted by a personal difficulty between Mr. Randolph and Mr. Clay. Mr. Randolph being an especial friend and constant visitor at Mr. Crawford's, it would have been unpleasant to both parties to meet at his house.

Only a few years anterior to Mr. Clay's death, and when he was visiting New Orleans, the writer had frequent interviews with him, and learned that he preferred Mr. Crawford to either Adams or Jackson; and was only prevented voting for him by the prostration and hopeless condition of his health.

The political friends of Mr. Clay from the West knew of this preference, and would have acted with him, only upon condition that Mr. Crawford should make him a member of his Cabinet.

This was communicated to Mr. Clay, who assigned his reasons for declining to vote for Mr. Crawford, and avowed his intention of giving his vote for Mr. Adams. Upon this announcement, it was urged upon Mr. Clay that Mr. Adams was uncommitted upon the policy which he had inaugurated as the American System; that he stood pledged to the country for its success; and that, without some pledge from Mr. Adams upon this point, he would be hazarding too much to give him his support — for this would certainly make him President. Mr. Clay's reply was:

"I shall, as a matter of necessity, give my vote for Mr. Adams: Mr. Crawford's health puts him out of the question, and we are compelled to choose between Adams and Jackson. My opinion with regard to General Jackson is before the nation, it remains unaltered. I can never give a vote for any man for so responsible a position whose only claim is military fame. Jackson's violent temper and unscrupulous character, independent of his want of experience in statesmanship, would prevent my voting for him. I shall exact no pledge from Mr. Adams, but shall vote for him, and hold myself at liberty to support or oppose his administration, as it shall meet my approval or disapproval."

Mr. Adams was elected; and the friends of Mr. Clay insisted that he should accept the position of Secretary of State in the new Cabinet, which was tendered him by Mr. Adams. Mr. Clay thought it indelicate to do so. Whether true or not, the nation awarded to him the making of Mr. Adams President.

General Jackson had received a larger vote in the electoral colleges than Adams, and his friends urged this as a reason that he was more acceptable to the nation, and the voting for Adams on the part of Clay and his friends was a palpable disregard of the popular will; and that Clay had violated all his antecedents, and had thus deserted the principles of the Republican party.

The friends of Mr. Crawford were silent until the organization of the new Cabinet. There had been a breach of amicable relations between Crawford and Jackson for some years, and of consequence between their party friends; and it was supposed from this cause that Mr. Crawford would unite in the support of the Administration; and when it was known that Clay had accepted the premiership, this was deemed certain, from the friendship long existing between Clay and himself. The terrible paralysis which had prostrated Mr. Craw ford extended to his mind, and he had ceased to hold the influence with his friends as controller, and had become the instrument in their hands.

General Jackson received a hint that it would be well to have healed the breach between himself and Crawford. This it was supposed came from Forsyth, and it is further believed this was prompted by Van Buren. It may or may not have been so: Mr. Jackson's acuteness rarely required hints from any one to stimulate or prompt to action its suggestions. All Washington City was astounded, one Sunday morning, at seeing the carriage of Jackson pull up at the residence of Mr. Crawford; for their quarrel was known to every one, and it was heralded through the newspapers that a reconciliation had taken place between these great men. The interview was a protracted one: what occurred can only be known by subsequent developments in the political world.

Van Buren had supported Crawford to the last extremity, and was greatly respected by him. His intense acuteness scented the prey afar off. Mr. Calhoun had been elected by the electoral colleges Vice-President, and this position, it was thought, notwithstanding his devotion to Jackson, would identify him with the Administration. He was young, talented, extremely popular, ambitious, and aspiring, and it was the opinion of all that he would urge his claims to the succession.

The indignation which burst from the Southern and Middle States, and from many of the Western, at Mr. Clay's course, and the great unpopularity of the name of Adams, was an assurance that without great changes in public opinion Mr. Adams' administration would be confined to one term. Mr. Crawford was out of the question for all time, and it was apparent the contest was to be between Calhoun, Clay, and Jackson.

They had all belonged to the Jeffersonian school of politics—had grown upon the nation's confidence rapidly through their support of and conducting the war to its glorious termination. But this party was now completely disrupted; and from its elements new parties were to be formed. It only survived the dissolution of the Federal party a short time, and, for the want of opposition from without, discord and dissolution had followed. The political world was completely chaotic—new interests had arisen. The war had forced New England to manufacturing; it had established the policy of home production, and home protection; the agricultural interest of the West was connected with the manufacturing interest of the North, and was to be her consumer; but the planting interest of the South was deemed antagonistic to them. Her great staple, forming almost the sole basis of the foreign commerce of the country, demanded, if not free trade, an exceedingly liberal policy toward those abroad who were her purchasers.

The war had given a new impetus to trade, new channels had been opened, the manufacture of cotton in England had become a source of wealth to the nation, and was rapidly increasing. America was her source of supply, and was the great consumer of her fabrics, and this fact was stimulating the growth of cotton into an activity which indicated its becoming the leading interest of the South, if not of the nation. The course of trade made it the great competitor of home manufactures: this would seem unnatural, but it was true — the one demanding protection, the other free trade. The source of supply of the raw material to both was the same, and America the great consumer for both. Protection secured the home market to the home manufacturer, compelling the consumer to pay more, and sell for less, by excluding the foreign manufacturer from the market, or imposing such burdens, by way of duties, as to compel him to sell at higher prices than would be a just profit on his labor and skill under the operation of free trade, and which should exempt from his competition the home manufacturer in the American market.

All these facts were within the purview of the sagacious politicians of the day; and were evidently the elements of new parties. Mr. Clay had already given shape to his future policy, and had identified the new Administration with it. It was certain the South with great unanimity would be in opposition, and the sagacity of Van Buren discovered the necessity of uniting the friends of Jackson and Crawford. Should he, after feeling the political pulse of his own people, conclude to unite with the opposition, such a union would destroy Mr. Clay in the South, but might greatly strengthen Mr. Calhoun; his destruction, however, must be left to the future. He was not long in determining. The reconciliation of Crawford and Jackson made the union of their friends no very difficult matter. Mr. Randolph, Mr. Macon, Mr. Forsyth, and Mr. Cobb had expressed themselves greatly gratified at this restoration of amity; and at an informal meeting of their friends, Randolph said, in allusion to this adjustment:

"I have no longer a fear that the seat first graced by Virginia's chosen sons will ever be disgraced by a renegade child of hers."

Soon after the inauguration of Mr. Adams, and the adjournment of Congress, the nation was startled with the charge of corruption in the election of Mr. Adams. At first this was vague rumor. Mr. Clay was charged by the press throughout the country with bargaining with the friends of Adams, to cast his vote, and carry his influence to his support, upon the condition of his (Clay's) appointment to the premiership in the Administration, should Adams be elected.

There was no responsible name for this charge; but at the ensuing session of Congress, a member from Pennsylvania, George Creemer, uttered from his seat the charge in direct terms. This seemed to give assurance of the truth of this damaging accusation. There was no public denial from Mr. Clay. The press in his support had from the first treated the story as too ridiculous to be noticed other than by a flat denial; but the circumstances were sufficiently plausible to predicate such a slander, and the effect upon Mr. Clay was beginning to be felt seriously by his friends. In the mean time, rumors reached the popular ear that the proofs of its veracity were in the hands of General Jackson, whose popularity was running through the country with the warmth and rapidity of a fire upon the prairies.

There was now a responsible sponsor, and Mr. Clay at once addressed a note to Creemer, demanding his authority for the charge. This was answered, and General Jackson's was the name given as his authority. Mr. Clay sent his friend, General Leslie Combs, with a note to Jackson, with a copy of Creemer's communication. Combs was a weak, vain man, and so full of the importance of his mission that he made no secret of his object in visiting Jackson at the Hermitage; and it was soon running through the country in the party press, each retailing the story as he had heard it, or as his imagination and party bias desired it. It was soon current that Mr. Clay had challenged General Jackson, and a duel was soon to occur between these distinguished men. General Jackson, however, gave as his author, James Buchanan, of Pennsylvania. In turn, Mr. Buchanan was called upon by Clay, but he denied ever having made any such communication to General Jackson; at the same time, making certain statements under the seal of secrecy to Mr. Letcher,

Clay's friend. What these revelations were will never be known: death has set his seal on all who knew them; and no revelation disclosed them in time. Long after this interview between Letcher and Buchanan, the former called on the latter, and asked to be relieved from this imputation, and for permission to give to the public these statements; but Mr. Buchanan peremptorily refused. Mr. Letcher insisted that they were important to the reputation of more than Mr. Clay: still Buchanan refused; and to this day the question of veracity remains unsettled between Jackson and Buchanan. The public have, however, long since declared that General Jackson was too brave a man to lie.

Toward the close of Mr. Clay's life, one Carter Beverly, of Virginia, wrote Mr. Clay some account of the part he himself had taken in the concoction of this slander, craving his forgiveness. This letter was received by Mr. Clay while a visitor at the home of the writer, and read to him: it dissipated all doubts upon the mind of Mr. Clay, if any remained, of the fact of the whole story being the concoction of Buchanan. Creemer was a colleague of Buchanan, and was a credulous Pennsylvanian, of Dutch descent; honest enough, but without brains, and only too willing to be the instrument of his colleague in any dirty work which would subserve his purposes.

Beverly was one of those silly but presumptuous personages who thrust themselves upon the society of men occupying high positions, and feel their importance only in that reflected by this association; and ever too fond of being made the medium of slanderous reports, reflecting upon those whose self-respect and superior dignity has frowned them from their presence. Creemer died without divulging anything; probably under the influence of Buchanan, and it is not improbable he was in ignorance of the origin of the slander. Beverly knew of its utter falsity, and was as guilty as the originator, and his conscience smote him too sorely to permit him to go to the grave without atonement, and consequently he made a clean breast of it to Mr. Clay.

Mr. Clay and Mr. Buchanan entered public life about the same time, when they were both young and full of zeal. They belonged to the same political party, and became warmly attached. They were, however, men of very different temperaments. The professions of Mr. Clay were always sincere, his love of truth was a most prominent feature in his nature, and his attachments were never dissimulations: to no other person of his early political friends was he more sincerely attached than to Buchanan — he was his confidential friend; he was never on any subject reserved to him; and so deep was this feeling with him that he had called a son after his friend — the late James Buchanan Clay. When he learned that all his confidences had been misplaced, and that the man whom he so loved had sought to rob him of his good name, he was wounded to the heart. He struggled to believe Buchanan was wronged by General Jackson; but one fact after another was developed — he could not doubt — all pointing the same way; and finally came this letter of Beverly's, when he was old, and when his heart was crushed by the loss of his son Henry at Buena Vista, of which event he had only heard the day before: he doubted no more. I shall ever remember the expression of that noble countenance as, turning to me, he said: "Read that!" Rising from his seat, he went to the garden, where, under a large live-oak, I found him an hour after, deeply depressed. It was sorrow, not anger, that weighed upon him. In reply to a remark from me, he said:

"How few men have I found true under all trials! Who has a friend on whom he can rely, and who will not, to gratify his own ambition, sacrifice him? I was deeply attached to Buchanan; I thought him my friend, and trusted him as such — through long years our intimacy continued. You see how unwisely this attachment was indulged; I have misplaced my confidence; I am willing to disbelieve this statement of Beverly; he is known to you; I believe he is a miserable creature, but his testimony is but a link in the chain of evidences I have of Buchanan's being the author of this infamous story. It was artfully concocted and maliciously circulated. He was too shrewd to commit himself, and employed this creature to go to Jackson, who lent a willing ear to it; and he communicated it to Creemer. Yet it was settled upon him by Jackson. Beverly told Jackson he was sent by Buchanan, and now the world has the story denied by Buchanan, and I have it confessed by Beverly. All the mischief it could do, it has done; and this death-bed repentance and confession must command my forgiveness of poor old Beverly.

"I was not unaware of the hazards of accepting office under Mr. Adams, and yielded my judgment to gratify my friends. I was deeply solicitous of rendering the country independent: our population was increasing; I was sure large immigration would add to the natural increase; and I felt it was the true policy of the Government to commence the manufacture of all articles necessary to its population, and especially the articles of prime necessity, iron and clothing. We had the minerals, the coal, and the cotton; and the sad experience of the recent war warned us to prepare against the same consequences should we unfortunately be again in a similar condition. I was satisfied that this policy would meet powerful opposition by those who supposed their interests affected by protection; and I knew, to build up the manufactures at home, they must be protected against foreign competition — at least for a time. Once capital was abundant and largely invested in manufacturing, with an abundance of educated skill, this protection could be withdrawn; as home protection would not prevent home competition, and high prices would stimulate this competition to the point of producing more than was necessary for home consumption; which would force the manufacturer to find a market abroad for his surplus; this would bring him into competition with the European manufacturer, and he would be compelled to be content with the prices he could obtain under this competition; this would necessarily, by degrees, reduce prices at home, and finally obviate the necessity of protection. Already this has come to pass. The good of the country I thought demanded this; and for this I exerted all my powers and all my influence; never for a moment doubting but that in time and from results the whole people would approve the policy. Nor did I ever anticipate any political result to my own interest. I have never thought of self, in any great measure of policy I may have advocated. I have looked to final results in benefits to the country alone, with a hope that my name should not be a disgrace to my children, who should witness the working and the effect of measures connected with my public life. With an honest purpose, I feared no consequences; and desiring, above temporary popularity, the good of the country, I assumed all the hazards and consequences which my enemies could torture out of the act of accepting office under Mr. Adams. I have never regretted it, and have lived to see the slanderers of my fame rebuked by the whole country.

"This terrible Mexican war now raging, I fear, is to result in consequences disastrous to our Government. That we shall drive Mexico to the wall there cannot be a doubt. We will avail ourselves of the conqueror's right in demanding indemnity for the expenses of the war. She has nothing to pay with, but territory. We shall dispossess her of at least a third, perhaps the half of her domain; this will open the question of slavery again, and how it is to be settled God only knows. For myself, I see no peaceful solution of the question. The North and the South are equally fanatical upon the subject, and the difficulties of adjustment augmenting every day. You will agree with me that the institution violates the sentiment of the civilized world. It is unnatural, and must yield to the united hostility of the world. But what is to be done with the negro? You cannot make a citizen of him, and clothe him with political power. This would lead rapidly to a war of races; and of consequence to the extinction of the negro. He will not labor without compulsion; and very soon the country would be filled with brigands; the penitentiaries would not hold the convicts; and the public security would ultimately demand that they should be sent from the country.

"To remove such a number, even to the West Indies, would involve an expense beyond the resources of the Government; to force them into Mexico would make her a more dangerous and disagreeable neighbor than she is; besides, this would only be postponing the evil, for I apprehend we shall want to annex all of Mexico before many years. As I remarked, I can see no peaceful solution of this great social evil; but fear it is fraught with fatal consequences to our Government."

John Randolph, soon after the election of Mr. Adams, was sent to the United States Senate by Virginia. His enmity to Mr. Clay had received a new whetting through the events of the year or two just past; and the natural acerbity of his nature was soured into bitter malignity. He believed every word of the story of Creemer, and harped upon it with the pertinacity of the Venetian upon the daughter of Shylock. He was scarcely ever upon the floor that some offensive allusion was not made to this subject. It was immaterial to him what the subject-matter was under discussion: he found a means to have a throw at the Administration, and of consequence, at Clay; and bargain and corruption slid from his tongue with the concentration of venom of the rattlesnake. The very thought of Clay seemed to inspire his genius for vituperation; his eye would gleam, his meagre and attenuated form would writhe and contort as if under the enchantment of a demon; his long, bony fingers would be extended, as if pointing at an imaginary Clay, air-drawn as the dagger of Macbeth, as he would writhe the muscles of his beardless, sallow, and wrinkled face, pouring out the gall of his soul upon his hated enemy. It was in one of these hallucinations that he uttered the following morsel of bitterness, in allusion to the story of bargain and corruption: "This, until now, unheard-of combination of the black-leg with the Puritan; this union of Luck George with Blifell," (an allusion from Fielding's novel of "Tom Jones.") Language could not have been made more offensive. But the fruitful imagination of Randolph was not exhausted, and he proceeded with denunciation which spared not the venerable mother of Mr. Clay, then living — denouncing her for bringing into the world "this being, so brilliant, yet so corrupt, which, like a rotten mackerel by moonlight, shined and stunk."

This drew from Mr. Clay a challenge, and a meeting was the consequence. There was no injury sustained by either party in this conflict, the full particulars of which may be found in Benton's "Thirty Years in the Senate;" and I have Mr. Clay's authority for saying that this account is strictly correct.

In General Jackson's letter to Carter Beverly, he states that Buchanan came to him and stated that the friends of Mr Adams had made overtures to Mr. Clay, to the effect that, if Mr. Clay would with his friends support Mr. Adams, and he should be elected, then he would appoint Clay to the position of Secretary of State; and that Buchanan recommended Jackson to intrigue against this intrigue.

Buchanan denied the statement *in toto*. Beverly wrote a letter, in 1841, admitting the falsehood of a former letter of his; and again, another to Mr. Clay, in 1844 or 1845, asking Clay's forgiveness for the part he had acted in the matter.

CHAPTER V.

GEORGIA'S NOBLE SONS.

A MINISTER OF A DAY — PURITY OF ADMINISTRATION — THEN AND NOW — WIDOW TIMBERLAKE — VAN BUREN'S LETTER — AMBRISTER AND ARBUTHNOT — OLD HICKORY SETTLES A DIFFICULTY — A CAUSE OF THE LATE WAR — HONORED DEAD.

IMMEDIATELY upon the inauguration of Mr. Adams, Mr. Crawford left Washington, and returned home. His residence was near Lexington, Georgia, upon a small farm. It was an unostentatious home, but comfortable, and without pretensions superior to those of his more humble neighbors. Mr. Crawford had held many positions in the service of the country, and had honestly and ably discharged the duties of these for the public good. As a senator in Congress, he won the confidence of the nation by the display of great abilities; and gave universal satisfaction of the pure patriotism of his heart, in all he said, or did. He was distinguished, as minister to France, for his open candor and simplicity of manners — so much so, as to cause Napoleon to remark of him "that no Government but a republic could create or foster so much truth and honest simplicity of character as he found in Mr. Crawford."

For years, he had served the nation as financial minister, and at a time when the method of keeping, transferring, and disbursing the moneys of Government afforded infinite opportunities for peculation — when vast amounts of money arising from the sale of the public domain in the West and the South was under his control, and when he had the selection of the depositories of this, and when these deposits were of great value to the local or State banks, so that they would have paid handsomely for them; yet this noble being came out of the furnace without the smell of fire upon his garments.

There was but one man who ever imputed dishonesty to him, or selfish motives in any act. When the claims of Mr. Adams and Mr. Crawford for the Presidency were being discussed, and party asperity sought to slay its victims, Ninian Edwards, a senator of Congress from Illinois, charged Mr. Crawford with impropriety of conduct in depositing, for selfish and dishonest purposes, the public moneys arising from the sale of lands in Illinois, in banks notoriously insolvent. Edwards had been appointed minister to Mexico, had left the Senate, and had gone to his home, preparatory to his leaving for Mexico; and from his home made this attack upon Mr. Crawford. The son-in-law of Edwards, a man named Cook, was the representative in Congress from Illinois, and, if I remember correctly, was the only representative who at the time reiterated these charges from his seat. Mr. Crawford immediately demanded an investigation of his conduct. This was had, and the result was a triumphant acquittal from all blame; and so damaging was this investigation to Edwards that the President recalled the commission of Edwards as minister to Mexico, and appointed Joel R. Poinsett, of South Carolina, in his stead. Edwards was at New Orleans when the letter of recall from the President reached him, that far on his way to Mexico: he returned in disgrace, and soon faded from public notice forever. At the time, it was asserted he was the brother-in-law of Mr. Adams, and knowing that some of the banks in which Crawford had deposited the public treasure had failed, he imagined complicity of a dishonest character, on the part of Crawford, with the officers of the banks, and expected to injure him and subserve the interest of Adams. In what contrast does this transaction place the purity of the Government, as then administered, with its conduct of to-day, and how peerless were those who were trusted then with public confidence and high places, in comparison with the public men who fill their places now!

Georgia has given to the nation two Secretaries of the Treasury — William H. Crawford and Howell Cobb; they were citizens of adjoining counties. Cobb was born within a few miles of Crawford's grave. They were both administering the office at a time in the history of the nation when she was surrounded with perils. The one, when she was just coming out of a war with the most powerful nation on earth; the other, when she was just going into a war, civil and gigantic. Both were afforded every opportunity for dishonest peculation, and both came out, despite the allurements of temptation, with clean hands and untainted reputation. They were reared and lived in the atmosphere of honesty; they sought the inspiration from the hills and vales, blue skies, and clear pure waters of Middle Georgia. The surroundings of nature were pure; the honest farmers and mechanics, her professional men and merchants, were and are pure. It was the home of Upson, Gilmer, Thomas W. Cobb, Peter Early, Eli S. Sherter, Stephen Willis Harris, William Causby Dawson, Joseph Henry Lumpkin; and now is the home of A. H. Stephens, Ben. Hill, Robert Toombs, Bishop Pierce, and his great and glorious father, and in their integrity and lofty manhood they imitate the mighty dead who sleep around them.

Glorious old State! though long trodden with the tyrant's foot, there is a resurrectionary spirit moving thy people, which will lift thee again to the high pinnacle from which thou wast thrust, purified and reinvigorated for a career of brighter glory than thou hast yet known—when the men who plague you now shall be driven from your State, and the sons of your soil, in the vigor of their souls, undefiled and untrammelled, shall wield your destinies.

Like a Roman of latter days, Mr. Crawford retired from the service of his country poorer than when he entered it. There was sweet seclusion in his retreat, and honest hearts in his humble neighbors to receive him with "Come home, thou good and faithful servant; we receive thee, as we gave thee, in thy greatness and thy goodness, undefiled." He had only partially recovered from his paralysis, though his general health was much improved; rest and retirement, and release from public duties and cares, served to reinvigorate him greatly. His estate was small, his family large, and his friends, to aid him, secured his election to the bench of the Superior Court, the duties of which he continued to discharge until his death. He survived to see General Jackson elected President, to whom he gave a cordial support. Mr. Calhoun had been nominated and elected Vice-President with General Jackson, both with overwhelming majorities. Crawford had carried all his strength to the support of the ticket, and the friends of Crawford and Calhoun were found acting in concert, notwithstanding the hostility yet unappeased between their chiefs. It was the union of necessity, not of sympathy or affection. At this juncture, there was perhaps as cordial a hatred between the people of South Carolina and those of Georgia, as ever existed betwen the Greek and the Turk.

Mr. Calhoun, it seemed now to be settled, was to be the successor of General Jackson. The new parties were organized, and that headed by General Jackson assumed the name of Democrat, and now held undisputed control of more than two-thirds of the States.

Mr. Calhoun had broken away from the usage of former Vice-Presidents, which was to retire, and permit a president of the Senate *pro tem.* to be chosen to preside over the deliberations of that body. He determined to fulfil the duties assigned by the Constitution, and in person to preside. His transcendent abilities and great strength of character by this course was constantly kept before the nation. His manners and presence gave increased dignity and importance to the office, daily increasing his popularity with the Senate and the nation. His position was an enviable one, and was such as seemed to promise the power to grasp, at the proper time, the goal of his ambition, the Presidency of the republic.

From the commencement of General Jackson's Administration there was a powerful opposition organized. It consisted of the very best talent in the Senate and House. The Cabinet was a weak one. Mr. Van Buren was premier, or Secretary of State, with John H. Eaton, a very ordinary man, Secretary of War; Branch, Secretary of the Navy, and Ingham, Secretary of the Treasury; with John M. Berrien, Attorney-General. Eaton was from Tennessee, and was an especial favorite of General Jackson. He had been in the Senate from Tennessee, and had formed at Washington the acquaintance of a celebrated widow of a purser in the navy, Mrs. Timberlake. This woman had by no means an enviable reputation, and had been supposed the mistress of Eaton, prior to their marriage. She had found her way to the heart of Jackson, who assumed to be her especial champion. The ladies of the Cabinet ministers refused to recognize her or to interchange social civilities with her. This enraged the President, and it was made a *sine qua non*, receive Mrs. Eaton, or quit the Cabinet. Van Buren was a widower, and did not come under the order. He saw the storm coming, and, to avoid consequences of any sort, after consultation with Jackson, resigned. His letter of resignation is a literary as well as a political curiosity. General Jackson, it is said, handed it to Forsyth, with the remark "that he could not make head or tail of it; and, by the eternal, Mr. Forsyth, I do not believe Van Buren can himself." This was the forerunner of a general dismissal of the entire Cabinet, save Eaton, who resigned. This rupture startled the whole nation, but nothing Jackson could do, seemed capable of affecting his growing popularity. A new Cabinet was organized, and soon after Mr. Van Buren was sent minister to England, and Eaton minister to Spain.

The opposition were in a majority in the Senate, led on by Clay and Webster. These were confronted by Forsyth, Benton, and Wright: the wrestle was that of giants. The world, perhaps, never furnished a more adroit debater than John Forsyth. He was the Ajax Telemon of his party, and was rapidly rivalling the first in the estimation of that party. He hated Calhoun, and at times was at no pains to conceal it in debate. In the warmth of debate, upon one occasion, he alluded in severe terms, to the manner in which Mr. Crawford had been treated, during his incumbency as Secretary of the Treasury, by a certain party press in the interest of Mr. Calhoun. This touched the Vice-President on the raw: thus stung, he turned and demanded if the senator alluded to him. Forsyth's manner was truly grand, as it was intensely fierce: turning from the Senate to the Vice-President, he demanded with the imperiousness of an emperor: "By what right does the Chair ask that question of me?" and paused as if for a reply, with his intensely gleaming eye steadily fixed upon that of Calhoun. The power was with the speaker, and the Chair was awed into silence. Slowly turning to the Senate, every member of which manifested deep feeling, he continued, as his person seemed to swell into gigantic proportions, and his eye to sweep the entire chamber, "Let the galled jade wince, our withers are unwrung," and went on with the debate.

The cause of the animosity of Jackson toward Crawford was a report which had reached Jackson, that Crawford, as a member of Mr. Monroe's Cabinet, had insisted in Cabinet meeting upon the arrest of Jackson for a violation of national law, in entering without orders, as the commanding general of the army of the United States, the territory of a friendly power, and seizing its principal city by military force. General Jackson had entered Florida, then a dependency of Spain, with which power we were in amity, and seized Pensacola.

A band of desperate men had made a lodgment in Florida, headed by two Scotchmen, Ambrister and Arbuthnot. These men had acquired great influence with the Indians, and were stimulating them to constant depredations upon the frontier people of Georgia. When pursued, they sought safety in the territorial limits of Florida. Remonstrances with the Government of Spain had produced no effect. It could not, or would not expel them, or attempt any control of the Indians; and it became necessary to put a stop to their aggressions. Jackson commanded, and was the very man for such a work. He placed before the President the difficulties, but said he could and would break up this nest of freebooters, if he had authority from the President to enter the territory, and, if necessary, take possession of it. It would be an act of war to authorize this course, he knew; but he was prepared for the responsibility (he generally was.) "I do not ask for formal orders: simply say to me, 'Do it.' Tell Johnny Ray to say so to me, and it shall be done." Johnny Ray was a member of Congress at that time from East Tennessee, and devoted to Jackson. This was done, and the work was accomplished. The two leaders were captured and summarily executed, claiming to be British subjects.

Mr. Monroe in some things was a weak man; he was surrounded by a Cabinet greatly superior to himself; he had not counselled with them, and he feared the responsibility he had assumed would not be sanctioned or approved by his constitutional advisers, and he timidly shrank from communicating these secret instructions to them. The matter was brought before the Cabinet, by a remonstrance from the Spanish Government, in the person of her representative at Washington. In the discussion which arose, a motion was submitted to arrest and court-martial Jackson. Calhoun was indignant that as Secretary of War he had not been consulted. General Jackson was sent for, and very soon the matter was quieted, and Spain satisfied.

It was in this discussion, or Cabinet meeting, that Mr. Crawford was represented to General Jackson as moving his arrest. Mr. Adams defended Jackson most strenuously, and it is not improbable that the President may have informed him, *sub rosa,* of what had been communicated to Jackson. The intimacy between Mr. Monroe and Mr. Adams was close, and it was thought he preferred him, and gave him more unreservedly his confidence than any of his ministers.

I believe it was in the early part of the year 1829, or 1830, (I have, where I write, no means of reference, and will not pretend to great accuracy in dates,) when Mr. Crawford received a visit from Mr. Van Buren, and his friend, Mr. Cambreling, at his home in Oglethorpe. What transpired during that visit, I do not pretend to know; but soon after, Mr. Forsyth received a letter from Mr. James Hamilton, of New York, making certain inquiries with regard to this move in Mr. Monroe's Cabinet. Mr. Forsyth appealed to Mr. Crawford, who responded, and in detail revealed the proceedings in council upon this matter, charging, without equivocation, Mr. Calhoun as being the secretary who had moved the arrest and trial of Jackson.

At the time of this development, General Jackson was absent from Washington, on a visit to his home in Tennessee, and Mr. Calhoun was in South Carolina. A correspondence ensued between the President and Vice-President of the most acrimonious character. Mr. Calhoun denied *in toto* the charge. Mr. Crawford appealed to the members of the Cabinet, Adams and Crowninshield, who sustained the truth of Mr. Crawford's statements, and Mr. Calhoun clearly implicated himself, by accusing Crawford of a breach of honor in disclosing cabinet secrets. It is not my purpose to enter into the minutiæ of this affair, further than to show the part taken in it by Mr. Crawford. Mr. Van Buren did not appear in this imbroglio; he doubtless had his agency, as his interest, in bringing this matter to General Jackson's knowledge. Mr. Calhoun was identified with the popularity of Jackson and his party, and was now, by common consent of that party, the prominent man for the presidential succession. Mr. Van Buren had been the Secretary of State of General Jackson, had studied him well, and knew him well. He knew also the temper of the Democratic party: through his agency the political morality of New York politicians had permeated the Democracy from one end of the country to the other: the doctrine subsequently enunciated by Mr. Marcy, that "to the victors belonged the spoils," was in full operation throughout the nation as the Democratic practice. This was the cement which closely held the politician to party fealty. Jackson rewarded his friends, and punished his enemies; Jackson was an omnipotent power; Jackson was the Democratic party. To secure his friendship was necessary to success; to incur his enmity, certain destruction. Van Buren was as artful as ambitious: he had indoctrinated Jackson with his own policy, by inducing him to believe it was his own; and the frankness of Jackson's nature prevented his believing anything was not what it professed to be. It was the ambition of Van Buren to be President, and his sagacity taught him the surest means to effect this end was to secure effectually and beyond peradventure the friendship and support of Jackson. Mr. Calhoun was between him and the aim of his ambition: to thrust him from Jackson's confidence was to effect all he desired. This was done; the breach was irreparable. Van Buren was sent, in the interim of the session of Congress, minister plenipotentiary to the Court of St. James.

Mr. Clay had come back into the Senate, and was heading and leading an opposition, then in the majority in the Senate; and the nomination of Van Buren was rejected. Jackson, assured that Calhoun had deceived him, was bitter in his denunciations of him, and Calhoun was sympathizing with this opposition. Jackson denounced Calhoun as his informant of Crawford being the Cabinet minister who had in Cabinet council moved his arrest. Calhoun gave the lie direct to the assertion; and that Jackson was capable of lying, referred as evidence to his statements relative to the charge of bargain and intrigue against Mr. Clay. But enough had been done to crush out the popularity and the hopes of Calhoun, beyond the limits of South Carolina. There never has been so sudden and so terrible a fall from such a height of any man in this nation — not excepting that of Aaron Burr. John C. Calhoun, in talent, learning, and statesmanship, was greatly superior to Jackson, and unsurpassed by any man of the age. But the breath of Jackson was the blight which withered his laurels, and crushed his prospects, and destroyed his usefulness forever, in a night.

What consequences have grown out of this quarrel, I leave for the pen of the historian. Yet I cannot forbear the speculation that the late and most disastrous war was one, and of consequence the ruin and desolation of the South, and the threatened destruction of the Government at this time. The agitation which led to these terrible consequences, commenced with Mr. Calhoun immediately subsequent to these events. Does any man suppose, if Mr. Calhoun had succeeded to the Presidency, that he would have commenced or continued this agitation? For one, I do not. The measure of his ambition would have been full: his fame would have been a chapter in the history of his country — his talents employed in the administration of the Government, the honor and boast of her people, and her preservation and prosperity the enduring monument of his fame and glory. But, wronged as he believed, disappointed as he knew, he put forth all his strength, and, Samson-like, pulled down the pillars of her support; and, disunited, crushed, and miserable, she is a melancholy spectacle to the patriot, and in her desolation a monument of disappointed ambition.

That Mr. Calhoun anticipated any such results, I do not believe.

To suppose he desired them, and to the end of his life labored to produce them, would be to suppose him little less than a fiend. Blinded by his prejudices and the hatred natural toward those who had accomplished his political ruin, he could not calmly and dispassionately weigh the influence of his acts upon the future of his country.

Mr. Crawford was now rapidly declining, his nervous system was completely undermined, and he felt the approach of death calmly and without fear. Still, he continued to give his attention to business, and was sufficiently strong to go abroad to calls of duty. In one of these journeys he stopped to spend the night in the house of a friend, and was found dead in his bed in the morning, after a quiet and social evening with his friend and family.

William Holt Crawford was a native of Virginia: his family were Scotch, and came early to the United States, and have been remarkable for their talents and energy. Since the Revolution, there has scarcely been a time that some one of the family has not been prominently before the public as a representative man. Mr. Crawford was an eminent type of his race, sternly honest, of ardent temperament, full of dignity, generous, frank, and brave. Plain and simple in his habits, disdaining everything like ostentation, or foolish display—strictly moral, firm in his friendship, and unrelenting in his hatred, his sagacity and sincerity forbade the forming of the one or the other without abundant cause. He was never known to desert a friend or shrink from a foe. In form and person he was very imposing; six feet two inches in height; his head was large, forehead high and broad; his eyes were blue and brilliant, and, when excited, very piercing. His complexion was fair, and, in early life, ruddy; he was, when young, exceedingly temperate in his habits, but as he advanced in years he indulged too freely in the luxuries of the table, and his physicians attributed mainly to this cause his attack of paralysis, which ultimately destroyed him. His mind had been very much excited during the Presidential canvass; the attacks of his enemies were fierce and merciless, and very irritating to him; and this doubtless had much to do with it. He lies buried in the garden of his home, without a stone to mark the spot. It is a reproach to the people of Georgia that her most eminent son should be neglected to sleep in an undistinguished grave. But this neglect does not extend alone to Mr. Crawford. I believe, of all her distinguished men, James A. Meriwether is the only one whose grave has been honored with a monumental stone by the State. Crawford, Cobb, Dooly, Jackson, Troup, Forsyth, Campbell, Lumpkin, Dawson, Walker, Colquitt, Berrien, Daugherty, and many others who have done the State some service and much honor, are distinguished in their graves only by the green sod which covers them.

CHAPTER VI.

POPULAR CHARACTERISTICS.

A Frugal People — Laws and Religion — Father Pierce — Thomas W. Cobb — Requisites of a Political Candidate — A Farmer-Lawyer — Southern Humorists.

THE plain republican habits which characterized the people of Upper Georgia, in her early settlement and growth, together with the fact of the very moderate means of her people, exercised a powerful influence in the formation of the character of her people. She had no large commercial city, and her commerce was confined to the simple disposal of the surplus products of her soil and the supply of the few wants of the people. It was a cardinal virtue to provide every thing possible of the absolute necessaries of life at home. The provision crop was of first necessity, and secured the first attention of the farmer; the market crop was ever secondary, and was only looked to, to supply those necessaries which could not be grown upon the plantation. These were salt, iron, and steel, first; and then, if there remained unexhausted some of the proceeds of the crop, a small (always a small) supply of sugar and coffee; and for rare occasions, a little tea.

The population, with the exception of mechanics, and these were a very small proportion, and the few professional men and country merchants, was entirely agricultural. This rural pursuit confined at home and closely to business every one; and popular meetings were confined to religious gatherings on Sunday in each neighborhood, and the meeting of a few who could spare the time at court, in the village county-seat, twice a year. There were no places of public resort for dissipation or amusement; a stern morality was demanded by public opinion of the older members of society. Example and the switch enforced it with the children. Perhaps in no country or community was the maxim of good old Solomon more universally practised upon, "Spare the rod and spoil the child," than in Middle Georgia, fifty years ago. Filial obedience and deference to age was the first lesson. "Honor thy father and mother, that thy days may be long in the land," was familiar to the ears of every child before they could lisp their a, b, c; and upon the first demonstration of a refractory disobedience, a severe punishment taught them that the law was absolute and inexorable. To lie, or touch what was not his own, was beyond the pale of pardon, or mercy, and a solitary aberration was a stain for life.

The mothers, clad in homespun, were chaste in thought and action; unlettered and ignorant, but pure as ether. Their literature confined to the Bible, its maxims directed their conduct, and were the daily lesson of their children. The hard-shell Baptist was the dominant religion; with here and there a Presbyterian community, generally characterized by superior education and intelligence, with a preacher of so much learning as to be an oracle throughout the land.

The Methodists were just then beginning to grow into importance, and their circuit-riders, now fashionably known as itinerants, were passing and preaching, and establishing societies to mark their success, through all the rude settlements of the State. These were the pioneers of that truly democratic sect, as of the stern morality and upright bearing which had so powerful an influence over the then rising population.

It is more than sixty years since I first listened to a Methodist sermon. It was preached by a young, spare man, with sallow complexion, and black eyes and hair. I remember the gleam of his eye, and the deep, startling tones of his voice — his earnest and fervent manner; and only yesterday, in the Baronne Street (New Orleans) Methodist Church, I listened to an old man, upward of eighty years of age, preaching the ordination sermon of four new bishops of the Methodist Church. It was he to whom I had first listened: the eye was still brilliant, the face still sallow, but wrinkled now, and the voice and manner still fervent and earnest; and the great mind, though not the same, still powerful. It was that venerable, good man, Lovie Pierce, the father of the great and eloquent bishop. What has he not seen? what changes, what trials, what triumphs! Generations before his eyes have passed into eternity; the little handful of Methodist communicants grown into a mighty and intelligent body; thousands of ministers are heralding her tenets all over the Protestant world — mighty in learning, mighty in eloquence — yet none surpass the eloquence, the power, and the purity of Lovie Pierce.

When I first heard him, Bishop Asbury, William Russell, and he were nursing the seed sown by John Wesley and George Whitefield, a little while before, upon the soil of Georgia. All but Pierce have long been gathered to their fathers, and have rest from their labors. He still remains, bearing his cross in triumph, and still preaching the Redeemer to the grandchildren of those who first welcomed him and united with him in the good work of his mission. How much his labors have done to form and give tone to the character of the people of the State of Georgia, none may say; but under his eye and aid has arisen a system of female education, which has and is working wonders throughout the State. He has seen the ignorant and untaught mothers rear up virtuous, educated, and accomplished daughters; and, in turn, these rearing daughters and sons, an ornament and an honor to parents and country. Above all, he has seen and sees a standard of intelligence, high-breeding, and piety pervading the entire State. The log-cabin gives way to the comfortable mansion, the broad fields usurping the forest's claim, and the beautiful church-building pointing its taper spire up to heaven, where stood the rude log-house, and where first he preached. He has lived on and watched this growing moral and physical beauty, whose germs he planted, and whose fruits he is now enjoying in the eighty-fourth year of his age, still zealous, still ardent and eloquent, and a power in the land. Should these lines ever meet his eye, he will know that the child whose head he stroked as he sat upon his knee — the youth whom he warned and counselled, loves him yet, now that he is wrinkled, old, and gray.

From parents such as I have described, and under the teaching of such men, grew up the remarkable men who have shed such lustre upon the State of Georgia.

The great distinguishing feature of these men was that of the masses of her people — stern honesty. Many families have been and continue to be remarkable for their superior talents and high character; preserving in a high degree the prestige of names made famous by illustrious ancestry. The Crawfords, the Cobbs, and the Lamars are perhaps the most remarkable.

Thomas W. Cobb, so long distinguished in the councils of the nation, and as an able and honest jurist in Georgia, was the son of John Cobb, and grandson of Thomas Cobb, of the County of Columbia, in the State of Georgia. His grandfather emigrated from Virginia at an early day, when Georgia was comparatively a wilderness, and selecting this point, located with a large family, which through his remarkable energy he reared and respectably educated. This was an achievement, as the facilities for education were so few and difficult as to make it next to impossible to educate even tolerably the youth of that day. This remarkable man lived to see his grandson, Thomas W. Cobb, among the most distinguished men of the State. He died at the great age of one hundred and fifteen years, at the home of his selection, in Columbia County, the patriarch pioneer of the country, surrounded by every comfort, and a family honoring his name and perpetuating his virtues; and after he had seen the rude forest give way to the cultivated field, and the almost as rude population to the cultivated and intellectual people distinguishing that county.

Thomas W. Cobb, in his education, suffered the penalties imposed in this particular by a new country; his opportunities, however, were improved to their greatest possible extent, and he continued to improve in learning to the day of his death. In boyhood he ploughed by day, and studied his spelling-book and arithmetic by night — lighting his vision to the pursuit of knowledge by a pine-knot fire. This ambition of learning, with close application, soon distinguished him above the youth of the neighborhood, and lifted his aspirations to an equal distinction among the first men of the land. He made known his wishes to his father, and was laughed at; but he was his grandfather's namesake and pet, and he encouraged his ambition. The consequence was that young Cobb was sent to the office of William H. Crawford at Lexington, to read law. He applied himself diligently, and won the respect and confidence of Mr. Crawford, which he retained to the day of his death. When admitted to the bar, he located with his fellow-student in Lexington; thus taking the place of Mr. Crawford, who was now in political life. He rose rapidly in his profession, and while yet a young man was sent to Congress as one of the representatives of the State.

At this time the representation in Congress was chosen by general ticket. The consequence was the selection of men of superior talent and character: none could aspire to the high position whose names had not become familiar for services to the State, or for the display of talent and character at the bar, or other conspicuous positions, their virtues and attainments distinguishing them above their fellow-men of the country. Throughout the State, to such men there was great deference, and the instances were rare where it was not deserved. The discipline and trickery of party was unknown, nor was it possible that these could exist among a people who, universally, honestly desired and labored to be represented by their best men. To attain to the high position of senator or representative in Congress was so distinguishing a mark of merit, that it operated powerfully upon the ambitious young men of the State, all of whom struggled to attain it by laboring to deserve it.

The standard of talent established by Crawford, Jackson, and Baldwin was so high, that to have public opinion institute a comparison between these and an aspirant was a sure passport to public favor; and this comparison was in no instance so likely to be made as between him and the pupils of his teaching. This fact in relation to Jackson and Crawford is remembered well by the writer.

In the low country of Georgia, the fiat of James Jackson fixed the political fate of every young aspirant. In the up-country, Crawford was as potent. In Crawford's office the student was required to apply himself diligently, and give promise of abilities, or he could not remain. The writer remembers to have heard the question asked of Mr. Crawford, in his later days, why a family in his own county, distinguished for wealth, had uniformly opposed him politically. In the frankness of his nature he said: "Aleck came, when a young man, to read law in my office, and though he was diligent enough, he was without the brain necessary to acquire a proper knowledge of the law. I liked his father, and in reply to an inquiry of his relative, as to Aleck's capacity, I told him 'his son would doubtless succeed as a farmer, for he was industrious; but he had not sense enough to make a lawyer.' He thanked me; and Aleck left the office, and, profiting by my advice, went to the plough, and has made a fortune, and a very respectable position for himself; but from that day forward, not a member of the family has ever been my friend. I think I did my duty, and have got along without their friendship."

Jackson had his *protégés*, and they were always marked for talent. In early life he discerned the germ of great abilities in two youths of Savannah — George M. Troup and Thomas U. D. Charlton. Through his influence, these young men, almost as soon as eligible, were sent to the Legislature of the State, and both immediately took high positions. Talent was not the only requisite to win and retain the favor of Jackson: the man must be honest, and that honesty of such a character as placed him above suspicion.

Under the operation of the Confiscation Act, many who had favored the mother country in the Revolutionary struggle had fled with their property to Florida. Conspicuous among these was one Campbell Wiley, a man of fortune. This man applied to the Legislature to be specially exempted from the penalties of this act, and to be permitted to return to the State. A heated debate ensued, when the bill was being considered, in which Charlton was silent, and in which Troup made a violent speech in opposition to its passage, ending with the sentence, "If ever I find it in my heart to forgive an old Tory his sins, I trust my God will never forgive me mine." This speech gave him an immediate popularity over the entire State. Charlton in secret favored the bill; but knowing its unpopularity with his constituents, he contrived to be called to the chair, and was forced to vote on a material motion which was favorable to the bill. The wealth of Wiley, and Charlton's equivocation, attached suspicion to his motives, and brought down upon him the wrath of Jackson, blighting all his future aspirations. As a member of the bar he attained eminence, and all his future life was such as to leave no doubt of his purity, and the cruel wrong those suspicions, sustained by the frown of Jackson, had done him.

Thomas W. Cobb was eminently social in his nature, and frank to a fault; his opinions were never concealed of men or measures; and these were, though apparently hasty, the honest convictions of his judgment, notwithstanding their apparent impulsive and hasty character. Like his tutor, Mr. Crawford, he cared little for ceremony or show; and in every thing he was the kernel without the shell: his character was marked before his company in five minutes' conversation, whether he had ever met or heard of them before; and in all things else he was equally without deceit. This openness to some seemed rude; and his enemies were of this class. He expressed as freely his opinion to the person as to the public; but this was always accompanied with a manner which disrobed it of offence. But human nature will not in every individual excuse the words because of the manner; and sometimes this peculiarity made him sharp enemies. It will be supposed such traits would have rendered him unpopular. At this day, when social intercourse is less familiar, they certainly would have done so; but they seemed a means of great popularity to Cobb, especially with those who were most intimate with him, as all who met him were, after an hour's acquaintance. His public life was as his private, open and sincere; he never had a sinister motive, and this relieved him from duplicity of conduct. His talents were of a high order: in debate, he was argumentative and explicit; never pretending to any of the arts of the orator; but logically pursued his subject to a conclusion; never verbose, but always perspicuous. As a lawyer, he was well read; and the analytical character of his mind appeared to have been formed upon the model of Judge Blackstone. Before the juries of the country he was all-powerful. These, in the main, were composed of men of very limited information — and especially of legal lore. But they were generally men of strong practical sense, with an honest purpose of doing justice between man and man. Cobb with these was always sincere; never attempting a deception, never seeking to sway their judgments and secure a verdict by appealing to their passions or their prejudices, or by deceiving them as to what the law was. Toward a witness or a party of whose honesty he entertained doubts, he was sarcastically severe; nor was he choice in the use of terms. As a statesman, he was wise and able — and in politics, as in everything else, honest and patriotic. In early life he was sent to the House of Representatives, in the Congress of the United States, and soon distinguished himself as a devoted Republican in politics, and a warm supporter of the Administration of Mr. Monroe. Here he was reunited socially with Mr. Crawford and family, and so close was this intimacy that he was on all political measures supposed to speak the sentiments of Mr. Crawford. Associated with Forsyth, Tatnall, Gilmer, and Cuthbert, all men of superior abilities, all belonging to the same political party, and all warm supporters of Mr. Crawford, he led this galaxy of talent — a constellation in the political firmament unsurpassed by the representation of any other State. Nor must I forget, in this connection, Joel Crawford and William Terrell, men of sterling worth and a high order of talent. Mr. Cobb was a man of active business habits, and was very independent in his circumstances: methodical and correct, he never left for to-morrow the work of to-day.

He was transferred from the House to the Senate, and left it with a reputation for integrity and talent—the one as brilliant as the other unstained—which falls to the lot of few who are so long in public life as he was. Unlike most politicians whose career has been through exciting political struggles, the blight of slander was never breathed upon his name, and it descended to his children, as he received it from his ancestry, without spot or blemish.

Toward the close of his life, he was elected by the Legislature of the State to the Bench of the Superior Court, then the highest judicial tribunal of the State. This was the last public station he filled. Here he sustained his high character as a lawyer and honest man; carrying to the tomb the same characteristics of simplicity and sincerity, of affability and social familiarity, which had ever distinguished him in every position, public or private. He assumed none of that mock dignity or ascetic reserve in his intercourse with the Bar and the people, so characteristic of little minds in elevated positions: conscious of rectitude in all things, he never feared this familiarity would give cause for the charge of improper bias in his decisions from the bench or his influence with the jury.

Mr. Cobb died at the age of fifty, in the prime of his manhood and usefulness. In person, he was a model for a sculptor—six feet in height, straight, and admirably proportioned. His head and face were Grecian; his forehead ample; his nose beautifully chiselled; gray eyes, with sparkling, playful expression, round, and very beautiful; his head round, large, and admirably set on; the expression of his features, variant as April weather, but always intellectual, they invited approach, and the fascination of his conversation chained to his presence all who approached him. In fine, he was a type in manner and character of the people among whom he was born and reared; and I scarcely know if this is the greater compliment to him or them.

With few exceptions, this peculiar population of Middle Georgia has furnished all of her distinguished sons, and to the traits which make them remarkable is she to-day mainly indebted for her exalted prominence among her sister States of the South. The peculiar training of her sons, the practical education and social equality which pervades, and ever has, her society, acquaints every one with the wants of every other; at the same time it affords the facility for union in any public enterprise which promises the public good. All alike are infused with the same State pride, and the equality of fortunes prevents the obtrusion of arrogant wealth, demanding control, from purely selfish motives, in any public measure.

This community of interests superinduces unity of feeling, and unity of action; and the same homogeneous education secures a healthy public opinion, which, at last, is the great controlling law of human action. Thus the soil is one, the cultivation is one, the growth is one, and the fruit is the same. Nowhere in the South have these been so prominent as in Middle Georgia, and no other portion of the South is so distinguished for progress, talent, and high moral cultivation. There is, perhaps, wanting that polish of manners, that ease and grace of movement, and that quiet delicacy of suppressed emotion, so peculiar to her citizens of the seaboard, which the world calls refinement; which seems taught to conceal the natural under the artistic, and which so frequently refines away the nobler and more generous emotions of the heart. I doubt, however, if the habit of open and unrestrained expression of the feelings of our nature is not a more enduring basis of strong character and vigorous thought and action, than the cold polish of refined society. Whatever is most natural is most enduring. The person unrestrained by dress grows into noble and beautiful proportions; the muscles uncramped, develop not only into beauty, but strength and healthfulness. So with the mind untrammelled by forms and ceremonies; and so with the soul unfettered by the superstition of vague and ridiculous dogmas. The freedom of action and familiarity of language, where there are few social restraints to prevent universal intercourse, familiarizes every class of the community with the peculiarities of each, and forms an outlet for the wit and humor of the whole. This was the stimulant to mirth and hilarity, for which no people are so much distinguished as the Georgians of the middle country. At the especial period of which I now write, her humorists were innumerable. Dooly, Clayton, Prince, Longstreet, Bacon (the Ned Brace of Longstreet's Georgia Scenes), and many others of lesser note, will long be remembered in the traditions of the people. These were all men of eminence, and in their time filled the first offices of the State. The quiet, quaint humor of Prince is to be seen in his Militia Muster, in the Georgia Scenes; and there too the inimitable burlesque of Bacon, in Ned Brace.

CHAPTER VII.

WITS AND FIRE-EATERS.

JUDGE DOOLY — LAWYERS AND BLACKSMITHS — JOHN FORSYTH — HOW JURIES WERE DRAWN — GUM-TREE *vs.* WOODEN-LEG — PREACHER-POLITICIANS — COLONEL CUMMING — GEORGE MCDUFFIE.

JOHN M. DOOLY was a native of Lincoln County, Georgia, where he continued to reside until his death, and where he now lies in an undistinguished grave. He was the son of a distinguished Revolutionary soldier, whose name, in consideration of his services in that struggle, has been given to a county in the State. In early life he united himself to the Federal party, and from honest convictions continued a Federalist in principle through life. But for his political principles, his name in the nation to-day would have been a household word, familiar as the proudest upon her scroll of fame. In very early life he gave evidence of extraordinary powers of mind. With a limited education, he commenced the study of the law when quite young. But despite this serious defect, which was coupled with poverty and many other disadvantages incident to a new country impoverished by war, and wanting in almost everything to aid the enterprise of talent in a learned profession, soon after his admission to the Bar he attracted the attention of the community, and especially the older members of the Bar, as a man of extraordinary capacity, and already trained in the law. So tenacious was his memory of all that he read or heard, that he not only retained the law, but the author and page where it was to be found. His mind was eminently logical and delighted in analytical investigation. In truth, the law suited the idiosyncrasy of his mind, and it was most fortunate for his future life, that he adopted it as a lifetime pursuit. Nature, it seems, gives to every mind a peculiar proclivity, as to every individual a peculiar mind: to pursue this proclivity is a pleasure; it makes work a delight, and this secures success. Hence it is fortunate to learn this peculiarity, and to cultivate it from the beginning. When the mind is strong and vigorous, this peculiar proclivity is generally well-marked to the inquiring observer in very early life.

It is related of Benjamin West, the great painter, that at five years of age he was continually soiling the floor of his good and sensible mother with charcoal sketches of the faces of the different members of the family; and of Napoleon, that in early childhood his favorite amusement was to build forts and array his playmates into column, and charge these, and assault and enter them. Stevenson, the great engineer, spent all his idle time, when a boy, in attempts at constructing machinery and bridges.

In these great minds this natural trait was so strongly marked, and so controlling in its influence, as to defy and overleap every obstacle, and develop its wonderful energy and capacity in the most stupendous manner. In such as these, this manifestation is early and palpable. Yet the same peculiarity exists wherever there is mind sufficient to connect cause and effect; but it is proportionate with the strength of the mind, and in ordinary or feeble minds it is less conspicuous, and requires close observation to discern it in early life.

The folly and ambition of parents and adverse circumstances too often disappoint the intentions of nature, and compel their offspring, or the victims of circumstance, to follow a pursuit for which they have a natural aversion, and absolutely no capacity: hence we see thousands struggling painfully through life in a hated avocation, and witness many a miserable lawyer whom nature designed to be a happy blacksmith. His toil of life is always up hill, without the possibility of ever attaining the summit. Sometimes the rebellion of nature is successful, and the misdirected will shake off the erroneously imposed vocation, and dash away in the pursuit for which the mind is capacitated; and immediate success attests the good sense and propriety of the act.

Fortunately, John M. Dooly selected, under the guidance of natural inclination, the profession of law. His eminence was early in life, and the public eye was directed to him as one worthy any public trust. He was frequently chosen a member of the Legislature from his native county, and was distinguished for extraordinary ability in the capacity of a legislator. His conspicuous position and commanding talents pointed him out as one to take a foremost rank with the first of the nation; and his friends urged his name as a fit representative in Congress for the State. At this time the acrimony of party was intense; the Republican, or Jeffersonian party, was largely in the ascendant in the State, and would accept no compromise. It was willing to receive new converts and prefer them according to merit, but would accord no favor to an unrepentant enemy. At this time there were many young, talented men rising to distinction in the State, who were Federalists. With some of them ambition was superior to principle; they recanted their principles, and, in the ranks of their former opponents, reaped a harvest of political distinction. Prominent among these was John Forsyth. He had delivered a Fourth of July oration at Augusta, distinguished for great ability and high Federal doctrines. Abraham Baldwin, who, with the astuteness of the Yankee — which he was — had renounced Federalism, and was now a prominent leader of the Republican party, spoke of this effort of Forsyth as transcendently great, and always, when doing so, would add: "What a pity such abilities should be lost to the country through the influence of mistaken political principle!" Whether this had any effect upon the views of Forsyth or not, certain it is that very soon after he repudiated Federalism, and published a formal renunciation of the party and its principles. From that time forward his march was onward, and now his name and fame are embalmed as national wealth.

Dooly was less facile: his convictions were honest and strong, and he clung to them. He won the confidence not only of his party, but of the people, for high integrity; but this was all. Out of his county he was intrusted with no political position, and those who most prized his talents and integrity could never be persuaded to aid in giving these to the country. He was more than once beaten for the Senate of the United States; and once by Forsyth, who was not announced as a candidate, and who was at the time minister plenipotentiary of the nation at the Spanish Court. His great legal abilities were, however, complimented by the Republican Legislature, by placing him upon the bench of the highest judicial tribunal of the State, where his usefulness was transcendent, and where most of his life was spent.

As a wit, Dooly never had an equal in the State, and there might now be written a volume of his social and judicial wit. Its compass was illimitable — from the most refined and delicately pungent to the coarsest and most vulgarly broad; but always pointed and telling. Nature had given him a peculiarity of look and voice which gave edge to his wit and point to his humor.

The judicial system of Georgia at this time was peculiar. The State was subdivided into districts, or circuits, as they were denominated; and one judge appointed to preside over each. These were elected by the Legislature, on joint ballot, for a term of three years; and until faction claimed the spoils of victory, the judge who had proven himself capable and honest was rarely removed, so long as he chose to remain. Dooly was one of these. Party never touched him, and both factions concurred in retaining him, because it was the universal wish of the people of his circuit. The law of the country was the common law of England and the statutes of the State. In the expounding of these, the judges frequently differed, and the consequence was that each circuit had, in many particulars, its own peculiar law, antagonistic to that which was received as law in the adjoining circuit. The uniformity of law, so essential to the quiet and harmony of a people, and so necessary in defining the title and securing the tenure of property, by this system was so greatly disturbed, that it led to the informal assembling of the judges at irregular periods, and upon their own responsibility, to reconcile these discrepancies. This in some degree obviated the necessity of a supreme court for the correction of errors; but was very unsatisfactory to the Bar, who were almost universal in their desire for the establishment of a tribunal for this purpose. But there was another feature peculiar to the judicial system of the State, to which her people were greatly attached: that of special juries. They feared the creation of a supreme court would abolish this, and for many years resisted it. This system of special juries, in the organization of her judiciary, was intended to obviate the necessity of a court of chancery. The conception was a new one, and in Georgia, with her peculiar population, its effects were admirable. It was an honest, common-sense adjudication of equity cases, and rendered cheap and speedy justice to litigants. It was unknown in the judiciary system of any other State, and I will be excused by the reader, who may not be a Georgian, for a brief description of it here.

By direction of the law of 1798, the justices of the Inferior Court took the tax list, which contained the name of every white man of twenty-one years and upwards in the county, and, from this list, selected a certain number of names, and placed them in a box marked "The grand-jury box." The remaining names were placed in another box marked "The petit-jury box." Those selected as grand jurors were chosen because of their superior intelligence, wealth, and purity of character. These selections were made at certain stated periods; and the jurors thus chosen from the mass never served on the petit jury, nor were they liable even as talesmen to serve on that jury. The same act made it the duty of the presiding judge of each circuit to draw, at the termination of each term of his court, and in open court, a certain number of names from each box, which were entered as drawn upon the minutes of the court, to serve as grand and petit jurors at the ensuing term of the court. The special juries, for the trial of cases in equity, and appeals from the verdicts of petit juries, were formed from the grand juries, and after the manner following: A list was furnished by the clerk of the court to the appellant and respondent. From this list each had the right to strike a name alternately — the appellant having the first stroke — until there remained twelve names only. These constituted a special jury, and the oath prescribed by law for these jurors was as follows: "You shall well and truly try the issue between the parties, and a true verdict give, according to law and equity, and the opinion you entertain of the testimony." Under the pleadings, the entire history of the case went before this jury, and their verdict was final. It was this method of trial which prevented so long that great desideratum in all judicial systems — a court for the correction of errors and final adjudication of cases.

Dishonest litigants feared this special jury. Their characters, as that of their witnesses, passed in review before this jury, whose oaths allowed a latitude, enabling them frequently to render a verdict, ostensibly at variance with the testimony, but almost always in aid of the ends of equitable justice.

The system was eminently promotive of honesty and good morals, as well as the ends of justice; for men's rights before it were not unfrequently determined by the reputation they bore in the community in which they lived. This fact stimulated uprightness of conduct, and often deterred the wrong-doer. It has passed away; but I doubt if what has replaced it has benefited the interests or morals of the people of the State.

Like Mr. Crawford, Judge Dooly relied more upon the practical good sense of the people as jurors, for justice between man and man, than upon the technicalities of the law; and especially upon that of special juries. Dooly had great contempt for petit juries, and evinced it upon one occasion by declaring in open court that he thought, if there was anything not known to the prescience of the Almighty, it was what the verdict of a petit jury would be, when they left the box for the jury-room. Dooly was an opponent of Crawford through life—a friend and intimate of John Clark, Crawford's greatest enemy. But his character was devoid of that bitterness and persistent hatred characteristic of these two. Crawford and Judge Tate were intimate friends, and between these and Clark there was continual strife. Tate and Clark were brothers-in-law; but this only served to whet and give edge to their animosity. Dooly, in some manner, became entangled with Tate in this feud; and an amusing story is told of the final settlement of the difficulty between these men.

Tate, it seems, challenged Dooly to mortal combat. Mr. Crawford was Tate's friend. Dooly, contrary to all expectation, accepted, and named General Clark as his friend, and appointed a day of meeting. Tate had lost a leg, and, as was usual in that day, had substituted a wooden one. On the appointed day, Tate, with his friend, repaired to the place of meeting, where Dooly had preceded them, and was alone, sitting upon a stump. Crawford approached him, and asked for his friend, General Clark.

"He is in the woods, sir."

"And will soon be present, I presume?" asked Crawford.

"Yes; as soon as he can find a gum."

"May I inquire, Colonel Dooly, what use you have for a gum in the matter we have met to settle?"

"I want it to put my leg in, sir. Do you suppose I can afford to risk my leg of flesh and bone against Tate's wooden one? If I hit his leg, why, he will have another to-morrow, and be pegging about as well as usual. If he hits mine, I may lose my life by it; but almost certainly my leg, and be compelled, like Tate, to stump it the balance of my life. I cannot risk this; and must have a gum to put my leg in: then I am as much wood as he is, and on equal terms with him."

"I understand you, Colonel Dooly; you do not intend to fight."

"Well, really, Mr. Crawford, I thought everybody knew that."

"Very well, sir," said Crawford; "but remember, colonel, your name, in no enviable light, shall fill a column of a newspaper."

"Mr. Crawford, I assure you," replied Colonel Dooly, "I would rather fill every newspaper in Georgia than one coffin."

It is scarcely necessary to say, that Tate and Crawford left the field discomfited, and here the matter ended.

Dooly never pretended to belligerency. When Judge Gresham threatened to chastise him, he coolly replied he could do it; but that it would be no credit to him, for anybody could do it. And when he introduced his friend to another as the inferior judge of the Inferior Court of the inferior County of Lincoln, and was knocked down for the insult, he intreated the bystanders not to suffer him to be injured. When released from the grasp of his antagonist, he rubbed his head, and facetiously said: "This is the forty-second fight I have had, and if I ever got the best of one, I do not now recollect it."

Judge Dooly was much beloved by the younger members of the Bar, to whom he was ever kind and indulgent, associating with them upon his circuit, and joining in all their amusements. His wit spared no one, and yet no one was offended at it. His humor was the life of the company wherever he was, and he was never so burdened with official dignity as to restrain it on the bench. Unbiassed by party considerations or personal prejudices, and only influenced by a sense of duty and wish to do right, it was impossible he could be otherwise than popular. This popularity, however, was personal, not political, and could never secure to him any political distinction. He was ambitious of a seat in the United States Senate, a distinction to which he more than once aspired; but here the grinning ghost of Federalism always met him, frightening from his support even the nearest of his social friends. Mr. Crawford's wishes controlled the State, through the instrumentality of those he had distinguished with his countenance. None doubted the patriotism or capacity of Dooly for the position; but he was a Federalist, and the friend of many of the prime movers of the Yazoo fraud; and these were unpardonable sins with Crawford and his friends. No one ever charged upon

Dooly the sin of a participation in this speculation, or the frauds through which it became a fixed fact, as a law of the State, by legislative act. But it was, for a very long time, fatal to the political aspirations of every one known to be personally friendly to any man in any way concerned in the matter. They were pariahs in the land, without friends or caste.

Of all the men prominent in his day, George M. Troup was the most uncompromising in his hostility to those engaged in this speculation. It certainly was the work of a few persons only, and did not embrace one out of fifty of the Georgia Company. All, or nearly all of these, honestly embarked in the speculation, not doubting but that the State had the power to sell, and knowing her pecuniary condition required that she should have money. Had they known that it required bribery to pass the measure, they would have scorned to become parties to such corruption; nevertheless they were inculpated, and had to share the infamy of the guilty few who thus accomplished the purchase, as they shared the profits arising therefrom. But it did not stop with the participants. Their personal friends suffered, and no one individual so fatally as Dooly. He asserted the power of the Legislature to sell — he was sustained by the decision of the Supreme Court — he was not a stockholder — he afforded no aid with his personal influence; yet the public clamor made him a Yazoo-man, and Troup was foremost in his denunciation of him. On this account it was that, upon a memorable occasion, Dooly declared that Troup's mouth was formed by nature to pronounce the word Yazoo. It had been proposed to Dooly, at the time Forsyth abandoned the Federal party, to follow his example; but he refused to part with his first love, and clung to her, and shared, without a murmur, her fortunes and her fate, which condemned him to a comparative obscurity for all the future.

It was long years after, and when Mr. Forsyth was in the zenith of his popularity, that the friends of Dooly proposed his name for the Senate of the United States. His was the only name announced as a candidate to the Legislature, but, on counting the ballots, it was found Forsyth had been elected. Dooly was present, and remarked to a friend that he was the only man he ever knew to be beaten who ran without opposition. He saw the aspiring companions of his youth favorites of the people, and thrust forward into public places, winning fame, and rising from one position to another of higher distinction. He witnessed the advance of men whom he had known as children in his manhood, preferred over him; and, in the consciousness of his own superiority to most or all of these, rather despised than regretted the prejudices of the public — influenced by men designing and selfish — which consigned him to obscurity because of an honest difference of opinion upon a point of policy which ninety out of every hundred knew nothing about. While the companions of his early youth were filling missions abroad, executive offices at home, and Cabinet appointments, he was wearing out his life in a position where, whatever his abilities, there was little fame to be won. Still he would make no compromise of principle. In faith he was sincere, and too honest to pretend a faith he had not, though honors and proud distinction waited to reward the deceit. As true to his friends as his principles, he would not desert either, and surrender his virtue to the seductions of office and honors. Toward the close of his life, his friends got into office and power. His friend, John Clarke, was elected Governor, upon the demise of Governor Rabun; but his day had passed, and other and younger men thrust him aside. Parties were growing more and more corrupt, and to subserve the uses of corruption, more tractable and pliant tools were required than could be made of Dooly.

The election of Clarke was a triumph over the friends of Crawford, who was then a member of Mr. Monroe's Cabinet, and had long been absent from the State. It revived anew the flame of discord, which had smouldered under the ashes of time. The embers lived, and the division into parties of the people of the United States, consequent upon the disruption of the Federal and Republican parties, and the candidacy of Mr. Crawford for the Presidency, caused a division of the old Republican party in Georgia. Clarke immediately headed the opposition to Crawford, and his election was hailed as an evidence of Mr. Crawford's unpopularity at home. This election startled the old friends of this distinguished son of Georgia, and revived the old feeling. Clarke was a man of strong will, without much mind, brave, and vindictive, and nursed the most intense hatred of Crawford constantly in his heart. The long absence of Crawford from the State, and the secluded retirement of Clarke, had caused to cool in the public mind much of the former bitterness of the two factions in the State, but now it was rekindled. There were very many young men, who had been too young to take any part in these factions, but who were now the active and ambitious element in the State. Many persons, too, had immigrated into the new-settled parts of the State, who were strangers to the feuds which had once divided her people, and which now began to do so anew. Each party sought to win and secure this element. Every newspaper in the State, every judge upon the bench, every member of Congress was in the interest of Crawford; and yet there was a majority of the people of the State attached to the Clarke faction. He and his friends had long been proscribed, and they pleaded persecution. The natural sympathies of the heart were touched by these appeals, and it was feared the State would be lost to Crawford in the coming Presidential election. Every effort was now to be made to defeat this faction against him, headed by Clarke. The election of Governor at this time was by the Legislature; and it was not anticipated that there would be any difficulty in the re-election of Rabun, and, consequently, there had been no agitation of the question before the people at the recent election of members of the Legislature. Scarcely a tithe of the people had even heard of the candidacy of Clarke when his election was announced; and, at the time, so little interest was felt on the subject, that very few objected to his election. Clarke was a man of violent passions, and had been, to some extent, irregular and dissipated in his habits. When excited by any means, he was fierce; but when with drink, he was boisterous, abusive, and destructive. Many stories were related of terrible acts of his commission — riding into houses, smashing furniture, glass, and crockery — of persecutions of his family and weak persons he disliked. This had aroused in the pious and orderly members of society strong opposition to him, and at this time all his sins and irregularities were widely and loudly heralded to the public. The preachers, with few exceptions, denounced him, and those who did not were very soon with him denounced. Very soon after his inauguration, the celebrated Jesse Mercer — the great gun of the Baptist denomination in Georgia — was invited to preach the funeral sermon of Governor Rabun. Mercer was an especial friend of Mr. Crawford, and a more especial enemy of Clarke. In many respects he was a remarkable man — a zealous and intolerant sectarian, and quite as uncompromising and bitter in his political feelings. His zeal knew no bounds in propagating his religious faith, and it was quite as ardent in persecuting his political opponents. It was doubtful which he most hated — the Devil or John Clarke. Rabun had been his neighbor, his friend, and, above all, a member and elder in his church. It was quite fitting under the circumstances that he should be selected to officiate in the funeral services in honor of the late Governor. From respect, Clarke and the Legislature were present. The moment Mercer's eye, from the pulpit, descried Clarke, he threw open his Bible violently, and for many minutes was busy searching from page to page some desired text. At last he smiled. And such a smile! It was malignant as that of a catamount. Turning down the leaf — as was the custom of his church — he rose and gave out to be sung, line by line, his hymn. This concluded, he made a short and hurried prayer — contrary to his custom — and, rising from his prayerful position, opened his Bible, and fixing his eye upon Clarke, he directed his audience to his text, and read:

"When the wicked rule, the land mourns."

The expression of his countenance, the twinkling of his eye, all pointed so clearly to Clarke as to direct the attention of every one present to the Governor. This was followed by a sermon half made up of the irregularities of Clarke's life. This was the tocsin to the church, and it came down in force with the opposition to the Governor elect. It was, too, the slogan of the Crawford party to rally for a new conflict.

Mr. Crawford's conduct as a representative of the State in Congress, and the representative of her people in his foreign mission, had been eminently satisfactory; and his present elevated position as Secretary of the Treasury of the United States was exceedingly gratifying to their pride. When it was determined by his friends to present his name to the nation as a candidate for the Presidency, it was supposed his support would be unanimous in Georgia. Time had given opportunity for the prejudices and hatreds of youth to wear out with the passions of youth. Those, however, who knew John Clarke, were not deceived when he successfully rallied a party in opposition. So little interest had been felt in the personal difficulty formerly existing between Clarke and Crawford, that even those who remembered it attached to it no importance, and they did not suppose Clarke's election was to be the commencement of an organized opposition to Crawford's election, and of the bitterness which was to follow.

There was scarcely the show of opposition to the election of

Clarke. Those who remembered the old feud, and how completely it had pressed down all the ambitious hopes and aspirations of Clarke, were willing to forget the past, and, though warm friends of Mr. Crawford, to vote for Clarke, and honor him with the first office in the State. Some felt his treatment had been too harsh, and that for his father's Yazoo antecedents he had been made to pay quite too severe a penalty, and were desirous to manifest their feelings in their votes. Besides, his family connections were most respectable. Griffin Campbell and Dr. Bird were his brothers-in-law, and were men of high character and great influence. The friends of these gentlemen united in his support. And there was still another, whose influence, to the writer's knowledge, carried four young, talented members of the House to the support of her father — Ann Clarke, the only daughter of John Clarke, who had no superior among her sex in talent, beauty, and accomplishments, in the State. During the incumbency of her father she did the honors of the executive mansion with a dignity, grace, and affability which won all hearts, and added greatly to the popularity of the Governor. She married Colonel John W. Campbell, and all her after-life has justified the promise of her girlhood. Left a widow with many children, she has reared and educated them to be an honor to their mother, and, as she was, an ornament to society. She is now an aged woman, and resides in Texas, honored and beloved by all who know her.

The election of Clarke was illy received by the old and tried friends of Crawford throughout the State. They knew him. His stern, inflexible character and indomitable will were sure to rally about him a party; and his personal bravery and devotion to his friends would greatly aid in keeping and inspiring these. His position now was one of strength, with the capacity to increase it, and the material was abundant; yet there were formidable difficulties in his way. All, or very nearly all of the leading families of the State — the Lamars, Cobbs, McIntoshes, Waynes, Telfairs, Cummings, Tatnals, Dawsons, Abercrombies, Holts, Blackshears, and many others — were Republicans, and active in the support of Crawford for the Presidency. These apparently insurmountable difficulties were to be overcome in the organization of new parties. The complete breaking up of the Republican party of the nation was favorable; and there was another element which the sagacity of Campbell soon discovered and laid hold upon. There were many ambitious and disappointed men and families in the State beside Clarke and his family.

The overwhelming popularity of Crawford as the head of the Republican party in the State had enabled his friends to monopolize all the offices, and give direction to every political movement and fix the destiny of every political aspirant. Under this *régime* many had been summarily set aside, and were soured. The talents of Troup, Forsyth, Cobb, Berrien, Tatnal, and some others, pointed them out as men to be honored, because they honored the State. They seemed to hold a possessory right to the distinguished positions, and to dictate who should be elected to the minor ones. Young ambition submitted, but was restless and impatient to break away from this dominion. Party stringency had enforced it, but this was loosened, and all that was now wanting was a head to rally them into a new and formidable party. Every old Federalist in the State who had clung to his principles attached himself to Clarke. There were many strong families, wielding a potent influence in their neighborhoods, attached to Federal principles. The Watkins, Hills, Walkers, Glasscocks, and Adamses all soon sided with the new party. A press in its support was greatly needed, and was soon established, and given in charge of Cosein E. Bartlett, than whom no man was better calculated for such a service as was demanded of him.

There were not at this time a dozen newspapers in the State. With all of them had Bartlett to do battle for the cause in which he had enlisted, and right valiantly did he do it. He was a fluent and most caustic writer, and was always ready, not only to write, but to fight for his party, and would with his blood sustain anything he might say or write. Like most party editors, he only saw the interest of his party in what he would write, and would write anything he supposed would further the ends of his party. Almost immediately after the election of Clarke, the opposition presented the name of George M. Troup, who had been voted for as an opposing candidate at the time of Clarke's election. It was but a little while before the State trembled with the agitation which seemed to disturb every breast. None could be neutral. All were compelled to take sides or be crushed between the contending parties or factions; for this division of the people was only factious. There was no great principle upon which they divided; it was men only. Clarke and his friends favored the pretensions of Mr. Calhoun to the Presidency solely because he was the enemy of Crawford, and they were subsequently transferred to the support of Jackson as readily as cattle in the market.

For two years was this agitation increasing in intensity, and so bitter had it made animosities arising out of it, that reason seemed to reel, and justice to forget her duty. Men were chosen indiscriminately to office because of party proclivities. Intelligence and moral worth were entirely disregarded — families divided — husbands and wives quarrelled — father and sons were estranged, and brothers were at deadly strife. There was no argument in the matter; for there was nothing upon which to predicate an argument. To introduce the subject was to promote a quarrel. Churches were distracted and at discord, and the pulpit, for the first time in Georgia, desecrated by political philippics. Pierce then, as now, was the leading minister of the Methodist Church in the State, and abstained in the pulpit, but made no secret of his preferences upon the street. Duffie travelled everywhere. He had by unkindness driven from him his wife with her infant child, and, in her helpless and desperate condition, she had taken refuge with the Shaking Quakers in the West, and remained with them until her death. His son came to him after maturity, and was established by him on a plantation with a number of slaves; but, having inherited all the brutal ferocity of his father, it was not long before he murdered one or two of them. Incarcerated in the county jail, his father invoked party aid to release him, openly declaring it was due to him for party services in opposing that son of the Devil — John Clarke. Whether his party or his money did the work I know not; but the miserable wretch escaped from jail, and was never brought to trial.

Peter Gautier was another prominent preacher-politician, and exercised his talents in the service of Clarke. He was by birth an American, but his parents were French. He was a bad man, but of eminent abilities, and exercised great influence in the western portion of the State. After Pierce, he was the superior of all of his denomination as a pulpit orator; and in will and energy unequalled by any other. Bold, unscrupulous, and passionate, he, regardless of his profession, mingled freely, at county musters and political barbecues, with the lowest and vilest of the community, using every art his genius suggested to inflame the mad passions of men already excited to frenzy. In after life the viciousness and unscrupulousness of his nature overmastered his hypocrisy and burst out in acts of dishonesty and profanity, which disgraced and drove him from the State. He sought security from public scorn in the wilds of Florida; but all restraint had given way, and very soon the innate perfidy of his nature manifested itself in all his conduct, and he was obliged to retire from Florida. At that time Texas was the outlet for all such characters, and thither went Gautier, where he died.

Every means which talent and ingenuity could devise was put into requisition by both parties to secure their ascendency. The men of abilities greatly preponderated in the Troup faction; and the pens of Cobb, Cumming, Wild, Grantland, Gilmer, and Foster were active in promoting the election of Troup, and thereby regaining the lost power of the old Crawford or Republican party. Many young men of talent had espoused the Clarke faction, and, under the guidance of Dooly, Campbell, and Clarke, were doing yeomen's work for the cause. Among these was Charles J. McDonald, whose fine character and family influence rendered him conspicuously popular. This popularity he retained to the end of his life. It elevated him to the Gubernatorial chair, after serving in the United States Congress and for years upon the bench of the Superior Court. His talents were not of the first order, but his honesty, sincerity, and goodness made him beloved.

Bartlett was struggling with all his energies to write up the administration and to defend the Governor against the fierce and reiterated attacks of the opposition. About this period there appeared some articles in a paper in Augusta, Georgia, reflecting upon Mr. Crawford, in reply to several papers signed "C.," which were written by Richard H. Wild, then a member of Congress from Georgia. These articles were attributed to Colonel William Cumming, of Augusta, and "C.," in reply, attacked him severely. He was not a man to be badgered by an anonymous writer in a newspaper. He demanded immediately of the editor the name of his correspondent, and that of George McDuffie, of South Carolina, was given. A challenge ensued — a meeting followed, in which McDuffie was seriously wounded, and which ultimately caused his death. This affair increased the hatred between the Georgians and Carolinians, as it did not cease with a single meeting. Cumming renewed his challenge in consequence of a statement made by McDuffie in a paper to the public, narrating offensively — as Cumming felt — the particulars of the affair. A second meeting was the consequence, at which a difficulty arose between the seconds, and it was adjourned to another day and another place. At this third meeting, in an exchange of shots, McDuffie's arm was broken, and this terminated the difficulty; but it did not appease the animosity of the friends of the parties.

These combatants were both men of remarkable abilities. Colonel William Cumming was a native of Augusta, Georgia. Born to the inheritance of fortune, he received a liberal education and selected the law as a profession. He read with the celebrated Judges Reeve and Gould, at Litchfield, Connecticut. At the period of his study this was the only law-school in the United States. Many anecdotes of his peculiarities during his residence at the school were related by his preceptors to the young gentlemen from Georgia who followed him in the office in after years. A moot court was a part of the system of instruction, in which questions of law, propounded by one of the professors, were argued by students appointed for the purpose. On one occasion, Cumming was replying to the argument of a competitor, and was so caustic as to be offensive. This was resented by insulting words. Turning to the gentleman, and without speaking, Cumming knocked him down. Immediately, and without the slightest appearance of excitement, addressing the presiding professor, he remarked: "Having thus summarily disposed of the gentleman, I will proceed to treat his argument in like manner."

Upon his return to Georgia, the war with England having broken out, he procured the commission of a captain and entered the army. He was transferred to the northern frontier — then the seat of active operations — and soon distinguished himself amid that immortal band, all of whom now sleep with their fathers — Miller, Brook, Jessup, McCrea, Appling, Gaines, and Twiggs. Cumming, Appling, and Twiggs were Georgians. At the battle of Lundy's Lane he was severely wounded and borne from the field. He was placed in an adjoining room to General Preston, who was also suffering from a wound. Cumming was a favorite of Preston's, and both were full of prejudice toward the men of the North. Late at night, Preston was aroused by a boisterous laugh in Cumming's apartment. Such a laugh was so unusual with him that the general supposed he had become delirious from pain. He was unable to go to him, but called and inquired the cause of his mirth.

"I can't sleep," was the reply, "and I was thinking over the incidents of the day, and just remembered that there had not in the conflict been an officer wounded whose home was north of Mason and Dixon's line. Those fellows know well how to take care of their bacon."

He was soon promoted to a colonelcy, and was fast rising to the next grade when the war terminated. In the reduction of the army he was retained — a compliment to his merits as a man and an officer. He was satisfied with this, and, in declining to remain in the army, wrote to the Secretary of War:

"There are many whose services have been greater, and whose merits are superior to mine, who have no other means of a livelihood. I am independent, and desire some other may be retained in my stead."

He was unambitious of political distinction, though intensely solicitous to promote that of his friends. His high qualities of soul and mind endeared him to the people of the State, who desired and sought every occasion which they deemed worthy of him, to tender him the first positions within their gift; but upon every one of these he remained firm to his purpose, refusing always the proffered preferment. Upon one occasion, when written to by a majority of the members of the Legislature, entreating him to permit them to send him to the Senate of the United States, he declined, adding: "I am a plain, military man. Should my country, in that capacity, require my services, I shall be ready to render them; but in no other." He continued to reside in Augusta in extreme seclusion. Upon the breaking out of the war with Mexico he was tendered, by Mr. Polk, the command of the army, but declined on account of his age and declining health, deeming himself physically incapable of encountering the fatigue the position would involve.

The habits of Colonel Cumming were peculiar. His intercourse with his fellow-men was confined to a very few tried friends. He never married, and was rarely known to hold any familiar intercourse with females. So secluded did he live, that for many years he was a stranger to almost every one in his native city. He was strictly truthful, punctual to his engagements in business matters, and honest in all things. In person, he was very commanding. In his walk the whole man was seen—erect, dignified, and impetuous. Energy and command flashed from his great, gray eyes. His large head and square chin, with lips compressed, indicated the talent and firmness which were the great characteristics of his nature. Impatient of folly, he cultivated no intercourse with silly persons, nor brooked for a moment the forward impertinence of little pretenders. To those whose qualities of mind and whose habits were congenial to his own, and whom he permitted familiarly to approach him, he was exceedingly affable, and with such he frequently jested, and hilariously enjoyed the piquant story in mirthful humor; but this was for the few. He was a proud man, and was at no pains to conceal his contempt for pert folly or intrusive ignorance, wherever and in whomsoever he met it.

In early life he was the close intimate of Richard Henry Wild, and was a great admirer of his genius, and especially his great and interesting conversational powers. Unexceptionable in his morals, he was severe upon those whose lives were deformed by the petty vices which society condemns yet practises in so many instances and universally tolerates.

It is greatly to be regretted that the talents and learning of such a man should not be given to mankind. Every one capable of appreciating these great attributes in man, and who knew Colonel Cumming, will, with the writer, regret that he persistently refused every persuasion of his friends to allow them to place him in such a position before the country as would bring his great qualities prominently forward in the service, and for the benefit of his fellow-men. His proud nature scorned the petty arts of the politician; and he doubtless felt place could only be had or retained by the use of these arts; he was of too high principle to descend to them, and held in great contempt those whose confidence and favor could only be had by chicanery. He was not a people's man, and had in his nature very little in common with the masses; and, like Coriolanus, scorned and shunned the great unwashed. He lived out his threescore years and ten, hiding the jewel God had given him, and appropriating it only to the use of his own happiness in the solitude he loved.

George McDuffie was a very different man. Born of humble parentage in one of the eastern counties of Georgia, he enjoyed but few advantages. His early education was limited: a fortuitous circumstance brought him to the knowledge of Mr. Calhoun, who saw at once in the boy the promise of the man. Proposing to educate him and fit him for a destiny which he believed an eminent one, he invited him to his home, and furnished him with the means of accomplishing this end. His ambition had often whispered to his young mind a proud future, and he commenced the acquisition of the education which was, as he felt, essential as a means of its attainment. In this he made rapid progress, and at the age of twenty-five graduated at the university of South Carolina. It was not long after graduating before he was admitted to the Bar, and commenced the practice of law in company with Eldridge Simpkins, at Edgefield Court House, who was, if I mistake not, at the time, a member of Congress.

The rise of McDuffie at the Bar was rapid; he had not practised three years before his position was by the side of the first minds of the State, and his name in the mouth of every one—the coming man of the South. It was probably owing to the defence made by him of William Taylor for the killing of Dr. Cheesboro, that he became famous as it were in a day. This case excited the people of the whole State of South Carolina. The parties were, so far as position was concerned, the first in the State. William Taylor was the brother of John Taylor, who at the time of the killing was Governor of the State. John Taylor, his grandfather, was a distinguished officer in the army of the Revolution: the family was wealthy, and extensively connected with the first families of the State. Cheesboro was a young physician of great promise and extensive practice. Jealousy was the cause of the killing, and was evidently groundless. The deed was done in the house of Taylor, in the city of Columbia, and was premeditated murder. Mrs. Taylor was a lovely woman and highly connected. In her manners she was affable and cordial; she was a great favorite in society, and her universal popularity attracted to her the host of friends who so much admired her. Dr. Cheesboro was one of these, and the green-eyed monster made him, in the convictions of Taylor, the especial favorite of his wife. McDuffie was employed in his defence, and he made a most triumphant success against evidence, law, and justice. His speech to the jury was most effective. The trial had called to Columbia many persons connected with the family; and all were interested to save from an ignominious death their relative. This, it was thought, could only be done by the sacrifice of the wife's reputation. This would not only ruin forever this estimable lady, but reflect a stain upon her extensive and respectable connections. She was appealed to, to save her husband's life with the sacrifice of her fame. In the consciousness of innocence, she refused with Spartan firmness to slander her reputation by staining her conscience with a lie. Her friends stood by her; and when hope had withered into despair, and the possibility gone forever of saving him by this means, the eloquence of McDuffie and the influence of family were invoked, and successfully.

In the examination of the witnesses he showed great tact, and successfully kept from the jury facts which would have left them no excuse for a verdict of acquittal. But it was in his address that his great powers made themselves manifest. The opening was impassioned and powerful. Scarcely had he spoken ten minutes before the Bench, the Bar, the jury, and the audience were in tears, and, during the entire speech, so entirely did he control the feelings of every one who heard him, that the sobs from every part of the court-room were audible above the sounds of his voice. When he had concluded, the jury went weeping from the box to the room of their deliberations, and soon returned a verdict of acquittal.

This effort established the fame of McDuffie as an orator and man of great mental powers. Fortunately at that time it was the pride of South Carolina to call to her service the best talent in all the public offices, State and national, and with one acclaim the people demanded his services in Congress. Mr. Simpkins, the incumbent from the Edgefield district, declined a re-election, that his legal partner, Mr. McDuffie, might succeed him, and he was chosen by acclamation. He came in at a time when talent abounded in Congress, and when the country was deeply agitated with the approaching election for President. Almost immediately upon his entering Congress an altercation occurred upon the floor of the House between him and Mr. Randolph, which resulted in the discomfiture of Mr. Randolph, causing him to leave the House in a rage, with the determination to challenge McDuffie. This, however, when he cooled, he declined to do. This rencontre of wit and bitter words gave rise to an amusing incident during its progress.

Jack Baker, the wag and wit of Virginia, was an auditor in the gallery of the House. Randolph, as usual, was the assailant, and was very severe. McDuffie replied, and was equally caustic, and this to the astonishment of every one; for all supposed the young member was annihilated — as so many before had been by Randolph — and would not reply. His antagonist was completely taken aback, and evidently felt, with Sir Andrew Ague-cheek: "Had I known he was so cunning of fence, I had seen him damned ere I had fought him." But he was in for it, and must reply. His rejoinder was angry, and wanting in his usual biting sarcasm. McDuffie rose to reply, and, pausing, seemed to hesitate, when Baker from the gallery audibly exclaimed: "Lay on, McDuff, and damned be he who first cries hold, enough!" The silence which pervaded the chamber was broken by a general laugh, greatly disconcerting Randolph, but seeming to inspire McDuffie, who went on in a strain of vituperation witheringly pungent, in the midst of which Mr. Randolph left his seat and the House. Here was a triumph few had enjoyed. Not even Bayard, in his famous attack upon Randolph, when the latter first came into Congress, had won so much. Every one seemed delighted. The newspapers heralded it to the country, and McDuffie had a national reputation. Everything seemed propitious for his fame, and every friend of Mr. Calhoun felt that he had a champion in his *protégé*, who, in good service, would return him fourfold for his noble generosity to the boy.

The contest with Cumming whetted more sharply the edge of the animosity between Georgia and South Carolina. The two were considered the champions of their respective States, as also the chosen knights of their respective friends — Crawford and Calhoun. The States and the friends of the parties in this quarrel very soon arrayed themselves in antagonism, which was made personal on many occasions, and between many parties. The young were especially prominent in their demonstrations of hostile feeling, not excepting the belles of the respective States. Between them, I believe, it never went beyond words; but they were frequent in conflict, and sometimes very bitter and very witty ones escaped from lovely lips, attesting that the face of beauty was underlaid with passion's deformity. With the young gallants it went to blows, and, on a few occasions, to more deadly strife; and always marred the harmony of the association where there were young representatives of both States. On one occasion of social meeting at a public dinner-party in Georgia, a young South Carolinian gave as a sentiment: "George McDuffie — the pride of South Carolina." This was immediately responded to by Mirabeau B. Lamar, the late President of Texas, who was then young, and a great pet of his friends, with another: "Colonel William Cumming —

"The man who England's arms defied,
A bar to base designers;
Who checked alike old Britain's pride
And noisy South Carolina's."

The wit of the impromptu was so fine and the company so appreciative, that, as if by common consent, all enjoyed it, and good feeling was not disturbed.

McDuffie was not above the middle size. His features were large and striking, especially his eyes, forehead, and nose. The latter was prominent and aquiline. His eyes were very brilliant, blue, and deeply set under a massive brow — his mouth large, with finely chiselled lips, which, in meeting, always wore the appearance of being compressed. In manners he was retiring without being awkward. His temperament was nervous and ardent, and his feelings strong. His manner when speaking was nervous and impassioned, and at times fiercely vehement, and again persuasive and tenderly pathetic, and in every mood he was deeply eloquent.

In the after period of life these antagonists were, through the instrumentality of a noble-hearted Hibernian, reconciled, and sincerely so — both regretting the past, and willing to bury its memory in social intimacy. McDuffie married Miss Singleton, of South Carolina, one of the loveliest and most accomplished ladies of the State.

Owing to the wound received in the duel with Cumming, his nervous system suffered, and finally his brain. The ball remained imbedded in the spine, and pressed upon the spinal chord. An attempt to remove it, the surgeons determined, would be more hazardous to life than to permit it to remain. There was no remedy. From its effects his mind began to decay, and finally perished, leaving him, long before his death, a melancholy imbecile. In all the relations of life this great man was faithful to his duties — a devoted husband, a sincere friend, a kind neighbor, and a considerate and indulgent master to his slaves. He was one of those rare creations for which there is no accounting. None of his family evinced more than very ordinary minds; nor can there be traced in his ancestry one after whom his nature and abilities were marked. His morals were as pure and elevated as his intellect was grand and comprehensive, and his soul was as lofty and chivalrous as the Chevalier Bayard's. His fame is too broad to be claimed alone by South Carolina. Georgia is proud of giving him birth, and the nation cherishes his glory.

CHAPTER VIII.

FIFTY YEARS AGO.

Governor Mathews — Indians — Topography of Middle Georgia — A New Country and its Settlers — Beaux and Belles — Early Training — Jesuit Teachers — A Mother's Influence — The Jews — Homely Sports — The Cotton Gin — Camp-Meetings.

IMMEDIATELY subsequent to the Revolution, all the country northwest of the Ogeechee River, in the middle portion of the State of Georgia, was divided into two counties, Franklin and Wilkes. It was a wilderness, and contiguous to both the Creek and Cherokee Indian nations. No country in the world was more beautiful in its topography, and few more fertile in soil. Governor Mathews had purchased a home in this region; and being at this time the principal man in the up-country, attracted to his neighborhood the emigrants who began to come into the country.

Mathew's Revolutionary services in the command of a regiment in the Virginia line were eminent; and his character for intrepidity naturally made him a leader among such men as were likely to seek and make homes in a new country.

Surrounded not only with all the difficulties presented to him by the unsubdued wilderness, but the perils of savage warfare, he unflinchingly went forward in his enterprise, daring and conquering every obstacle nature and the savages interposed. He was an uneducated man; but of strong mind, ardent temperament, and most determined will. Many anecdotes are related of his intrepidity, self-respect, and unbending will. He was a native of Augusta County, Virginia, and emigrated to Georgia about the same time that Elijah Clarke came from North Carolina and settled in that portion of the new territory now known as Clarke County.

These two remarkable men formed a nucleus for those of their respective States who came at subsequent periods to make a home in Georgia. They were models to the youth of their respective neighborhoods, and gave tone to the character of the population for many years after they were in their graves. About the same time, the Earlys came from Virginia, and the Abercrombies from North Carolina, and located respectively in the new counties of Greene and Hancock. They were all men of strong character, and all exercised great influence with those who accompanied or came to them at a subsequent period.

Among the very first to locate in Greene County was Colonel David Love, from North Carolina, and soon after came the Nesbits, Jacksons, and Hortons; all of whom settled upon the head-waters of the Ogeechee and upon Shoulderbone Creek.

The country was very attractive, the soil very generous, the water good, and the health remarkable. The general topography of Middle Georgia (as that portion of Georgia is now termed) is unsurpassed by any other portion of the State for beauty — hill and dale, the one not rising many feet above the other, generally with beautiful slopes, and scarcely at any place with so much abruptness as to forbid cultivation. Upon these lovely acclivities were built the cabins of the emigrants, at the base of which, and near the house, was always to be found a fountain of pure, sweet water, gushing and purling away over sand and pebbles, meandering through a valley which it fertilized, and which abounds in shrubs flowering in beauty, and sheltered by forests of oak, hickory, pine, and gum.

Those who first came were frequently compelled to unite in a settlement at some selected point, and, for defence against the inroads of the savages, were obliged to build stockade forts, with block-houses.

Nature seems to have prepared, during the Revolution, men for subduing the wilderness and its savage inhabitants. They cheerfully encountered all the difficulties and hazards thus presented, and constantly pursued their object to its consummation. They came from every section of the older communities, and all seemed animated with the same spirit. They were orderly, but rude; and though beyond the pale of the law, they were a law unto themselves; and these laws were strictly enforced by a public opinion which gave them being and efficiency. With remarkably simple habits and very limited opportunities, their wants were few; and these were supplied by their own industry and frugality upon the farm. Their currency was silver coin, Spanish milled, and extremely limited in quantity. The little trade carried on was principally by barter, and social intercourse was confined almost exclusively to the Sabbath. The roads were rough and uneven, consisting almost entirely of a way sufficiently wide for an ox-cart to pass, cut through the forest, where the stumps and stones remained; and in soft or muddy places, the bodies of small trees or split rails were placed side by side, so as to form a sort of bridge or causeway, so rough as to test and not unfrequently to destroy the wheels of the rude vehicles of the country. These obtained and to this day receive the sobriquet of Georgia railroads or corduroy turnpikes.

Very few of these immigrants were independent of labor; and most of them devoted six days of the week to the cultivation of a small farm and its improvement. Children learned early to assist in this labor, and those who were sent to school, almost universally employed the Saturday of each week in farm-work.

Man's social nature induces aggregation into communities, which stimulates an ambition to excel in every undertaking. From this emulation grows excellence and progress in every laudable enterprise. These small communities, as they grew from accessions coming into the country, began to build rude places for public worship, which were primitive log-cabins, and served as well the purposes of a school-house. Here the adult population assembled on the Sabbath, and the children during the week. This intercourse, together with the dependence of every one at times for neighborly assistance, was greatly promotive of harmony and mutual confidence. Close and familiar acquaintance revealed to all the peculiar character of every one — the virtuous and the vicious, the energetic or the indolent, the noble and the ignoble — and all very soon came to be appreciated according to their merit.

Rude sports constituted the amusements of the young — wrestling, leaping, and hunting; and he who was most expert at these was the neighborhood's pride: he rode from church with the prettiest girl, and was sure to be welcomed by her parents when he came; and to be selected by such an one was to become the neighborhood's belle.

At log-rollings, quiltings, and Saturday-night frolics, he was the first and the most admired.

The girls, too, were not without distinction — she who could spin the greatest number of cuts of cotton, or weave the greatest number of yards of cloth, was most distinguished, and most admired; but especially was she distinguished who could spin and weave the neatest fabric for her own wear, of white cloth with a turkey-red stripe — cut, and make it fit the labor-rounded person and limbs — or make, for father's or brother's wear, the finest or prettiest piece of jean — cook the nicest dinners for her beau, or dance the longest without fatigue.

The sexes universally associated at the same school, (a system unfortunately grown out of use,) and grew up together with a perfect knowledge of the disposition, temperament, and general character of each other. And, as assuredly as the boy is father to the man, the girl is mother to the woman; and these peculiarities were attractive or repulsive as they differed in individuals, and were always an influence in the selection of husbands and wives. The prejudices of childhood endure through life, particularly those toward persons. They are universally predicated upon some trait of manner or character, and these, as in the boy perceived, are ever prominent in the man. So, too, with the girl, and they only grow with the woman. This is a paramount reason why parties about contracting marriage-alliances should be well aware of whom they are about to select. The consequence of this intercommunication of the sexes from childhood, in the primitive days of Georgia's first settlement, was seen in the harmony of families. In the age which followed, a separation or divorce was as rare as an earthquake; and when occurring, agitated the whole community. For then a marriage was deemed a life-union, for good or for evil, and was not lightly or inconsiderately entered into.

The separation of the sexes in early youth, and especially at school, destroys or prevents in an eminent degree the restraining influences upon the actions of each other, and that tender desire for the society of each other, which grows from childhood's associations. Brought together at school in early life, when the mind and soul are receiving the impressions which endure through life, they naturally form intimacies, and almost always special partialities and preferences. Each has his or her favorite, these partialities are usually reciprocal, and their consequence is a desire on the part of each to see the other excel. To accomplish this, children, as well as grown people, will make a greater effort than they will simply to succeed or to gratify a personal ambition to that effect. Thus they sympathize with and stimulate each other. Every Georgia boy of fifty years ago, with gray-head and tottering step now, remembers his sweetheart, for whom he carried his hat full of peaches to school, and for whom he made the grape-vine swing, and how at noon he swung her there.

'T is bonny May; and I to-day
Am wrinkled seventy-four,
Still I enjoy, as when a boy,
Much that has gone before.

Is it the leaves and trees, or sheaves
Of yellow, ripened grain,
Which wake to me, in memory,
My boyhood's days again?

These seem to say 't is bonny May,
As when they sweetly grew,
And gave their yield, in wood and field,
To me, when life was new.

But nought beside—ah, woe betide!—
Which grew with me is here—
The home, the hall, the mill, the all
Which young life holds so dear.

The school-house, spring, and little thing,
With eyes so bright and blue,
Who'd steal away with me and play
When school's dull hours were through,

Are memories now; and yet, oh! how
It seems but yesterday
Since I was there, with that sweet dear,
In the wild wood at play.

The hill was steep where we would leap;
The grape-vine swing hung high,
And I would throw the swing up so
That, startled, she would cry.

But though she cried, she still relied
  (And seemed to have no fear)
On me to hold the swing, and told
  Me "not to frighten her."

But I was wild, and she no child,
  And not afraid, I deemed;
So tossed as high the swing as I
  Could — when she fell and screamed.

She was not harmed; but I, alarmed,
  Ran quickly to assist,
And lifted her, all pale with fear,
  Within my arms, and kissed

Her pallid cheek, ere she could speak:
  But I had seen, you know,
(Ah! what of this? that sight and kiss
  Was fifty years ago,)

That little boot and pretty foot,
  So neatly formed and small —
The swelling calf, and stifled laugh —
  How I remember all!

That lovely one has long since gone,
  Is dust, and only dust, now;
Yet I recall that swing and fall,
  As though it had been just now.

Take these lines, reader, if you please, as an evidence of how the memories growing out of the associations of boyhood's school-days endure through life. This association of the sexes operates as a restraint upon both, salutary to good conduct and good morals. Such restraints are far more effective than the staid lessons of some old, wrinkled duenna of a school-mistress, whose failure to find a sweetheart in girlhood, or a husband in youthful womanhood, has soured her toward every man, and filled her with hatred for the happiness she witnesses in wedded life, and which is ever present all around her. Her warnings are in violation of nature. She has forgotten she was ever young or inspired with the feelings and hopes of youth. Men are monsters, and marriage a hell upon earth. Girls will not believe this, and will get married. How much better, then, that they should cultivate, in association, the generous and natural feelings of the heart, and during the period allotted by nature for the growth of the feelings natural to the human bosom, as well as to the growth of the person and mind, than to be told what they should be by one disappointed of all the fruits of them, and hating the world because she is! It is the mother who should form the sentiments and direct the conduct of daughters, and in their teachings should never forget that nature is teaching also. Let their lessons always teach the proper indulgences of nature, as well as the proper and prudent restraints to the natural feelings of the human heart, and so deport themselves toward their daughters from infancy as to win their confidence and affection. The daughters, when properly trained, will always come with their little complaints in childhood, and seek consolation, leaning upon the parent's knee, and, with solicitude, look up into the parental face for sympathy and advice. Home-teaching and home-training makes the proper woman. When this is properly attended to, there needs no boarding-school or female-college finish, which too frequently uproots every virtuous principle implanted by the careful and affectionate teaching of pious, gentle, and intelligent mothers. But few mothers, who are themselves properly trained, forget nature in the training and education of their daughters; and a truly natural woman is a blessing to society and a crown of glory to her husband. I mean by a natural training a knowledge of herself, as well as a knowledge of the offices of life and the domestic duties of home. Every woman in her girlhood should learn from her mother the mission and destinies of woman, as well as what is due to society, to their families, to themselves, and to God. The woman who enters life with a knowledge of what life is, and what is due to her and from her in all the relations of life, has a thousand chances for happiness through life unknown to the belle of the boarding-school, who, away from home influences, is artificially educated to be in all things prominent before the world, and entirely useless in the discharge of domestic duties. She may figure as the lady-president or vice-president of charitable associa tions, or the lady-president of some prominent or useless society; but never as a dutiful, devoted wife, or affectionate, instructive mother to her children. Her household is managed by servants, and about her home nothing evinces the neat, provident, and attentive housewife.

The whole system of education, as practised by the Protestants of the United States, is wrong; religious prejudice prevents their learning from the Catholics, and particularly from the Jesuit Catholics, who are far in advance of their Protestant brethren. They learn from the child as they teach the child. In the first place, none are permitted to teach who are not by nature, as well as by education, qualified to teach; nature must give the gentleness, the kindness, and the patience, with the capacity to impart instruction. They learn, first, the child's nature, the peculiarities of temper, and fashion these to obedience and affection; they first teach the heart to love—not fear; they warn against the evils of life—teach the good, and the child's duties to its parents, to its brothers and sisters, to its teachers, to its playmates, and to its God. When the heart is mellowed and yields obedience in the faithful discharge of these duties, and the brain sufficiently matured to comprehend the necessity of them, then attention is directed to the mind; its capacities are learned and known, and it is treated as this knowledge teaches is proper: it is, as the farmer knows, the soil of his cultivation, and is prepared by careful tillage before the seed is sown. The vision of the child's mind is by degrees expanded; the horizon of its knowledge is enlarged, and still the heart's culture goes on in kindness and affection. The pupil has learned to love the teacher, and receives with alacrity his teaching; he goes to him, without fear, for information on every point of duty in morals, as on every difficult point of literary learning. He knows he will be received kindly, and dealt with gently. Should he err, he is never rebuked in public, nor harshly in private; the teacher is aggrieved, and in private he kindly complains to the offender, whose love for his preceptor makes him to feel, and repent, and to err no more. All this is only known to the two; his school-fellows never know, and have no opportunity for triumph or raillery. Thus taught from the cradle, principles become habits; and on these, at maturity, he is launched upon the world, with every safeguard for his future life. So with the girl. With the experience of forty-five years, the writer has never known a vicious, bad woman, wife, or mother trained in a Jesuit convent, or reared by an educated Catholic mother.

The daughters of the pioneers of Georgia's early settlements received a home education; at least, in the duties of domestic life. In the discharge of these duties, they gained robust constitutions and vigorous health; they increased the butcher's bill at the expense of the doctor's; and such women were the mothers of the men who have made a history for their country, for themselves and their mothers. I may be prolix and prosaic, but I love to remember the mothers of fifty years ago—she who gave birth to Lucius Q. C. and Mirabeau B. Lamar, to William C. Dawson, Bishop George Pierce, Alexander Stuart, Joseph Lumpkin, and glorious Bob Toombs. I knew them all, and, with affectionate delight, remember their virtues, and recall the social hours we have enjoyed together, when they were matrons, and I the companion of their sons. And now, when all are gone, and time is crowding me to the grave, the nobleness of their characters, the simplicity of their bearing in the discharge of their household duties, and the ingenuousness of their manners in social intercourse, is a cherished, venerated memory. None of these women were ever in a boarding-school, never received a lesson in the art of entering a drawing-room or captivating a beau. They were sensible, modest, and moral women, and their virtues live after them in the exalted character of their illustrious sons. Their literary education in early life was, of necessity, neglected, because of the want of opportunities; but in the virtues and duties of life, they were thoroughly educated; and none of these, or any of their like, was ever Mrs. President or Secretary of any pretentious or useless society or association.

The little education or literature they acquired was in the old log school-house, where boys and girls commingled as pupils under the teaching of some honest pedagogue, who aspired to teach only reading, writing, and arithmetic, in a simple way. It must not be supposed, from the foregoing remarks, that I object to female education; on the contrary, I would have every woman an educated woman. But I would have this education an useful and proper education; one not wholly ornamental and of no practical use, but one obtained at home, and under the parental care and influence—such an one as made Mrs. Ripley, of Concord, Massachusetts, the wonder and admiration of every sensible man. She who studied La Place's *Mécanique Céleste* when she was making biscuit for her breakfast, and who solved a problem in the higher mathematics when darning her stockings; an education where the useful may be taught and learned to grace the ornamental—where the harp and piano shall share with the needle and the cooking-stove, and the pirouettes of the dancing-master shall be only a step from the laundry and the kitchen.

The duties of wives and mothers are to home, husband, and children; and this includes all of woman's duty to the country, and in the intelligent and faithful discharge of which the great ends of life are subserved. Good neighborhood, good government, and happy communities secure the implanting and cultivation of good principles, and the proper teaching of proper duties. The wise direction of literary education to sons and to daughters, all comes within the range of home, and home duties especially incumbent upon mothers. The domestic duties and domestic labors should be a prime consideration in the education of daughters. The association of the mother and child from birth, until every principle which is to guide and govern it through life is implanted, makes it the duty of the mother to know the right, and to teach it, too. Example and precept should combine; and this necessity compels a constant watch, not only over the child's, but over the mother's language and conduct. All these duties imply a close devotion to home: for here is the germ which is to grow into good or into evil, as it is nursed and cultivated, or wickedly neglected. Begin at the beginning, if you would accomplish well your work; and to do this, application and assiduity are indispensable; and these are duties only to be discharged at home. They admit of a relaxation of time sufficient for every social duty exacted by society, if that society is such as it should be; and if not, it should neither occupy time nor attention.

In this is comprised all woman's duties, and they are paramount; for upon their successful application depend the well-being of society and the proper and healthful administration of wise and salutary laws. The world is indebted to woman for all that is good and great. Let every woman emulate Cornelia, the Roman mother, and, when a giddy, foolish neighbor runs to her to exhibit newly purchased jewels, be found, like the Roman matron, at her tambour-work; and like her, too, when her boys from school shall run to embrace her, say to the thoughtless one, "These are my jewels!" and Rome will not alone boast of her Gracchi and their incomparable mother.

The duties of home cultivate reflection and stimulate to virtue. For this reason, women are more pious than men; and for this reason, too, they are more eminent in purity. Contact with the domestic circle does not contaminate or corrupt, as the baser contact with the world is sure to do.

The home circle is select and chaste — the promiscuous intermingling with the world meretricious and contaminating. The mother not trained to the appreciation and discharge of the domestic duties, was never the mother of a great representative mind; because she is incapable of imparting those stern principles of exalted morality and fixity of purpose essential in forming the character of such men. The mother of Cincinnatus was a farmer's wife; of Leonidas, a shepherdess; and the mothers of Washington, Webster, Clay, Calhoun, William H. Crawford, and Andrew Jackson were all the wives of farmers — rural and simple in their pursuits, distinguished for energy and purity; constant in their principles, and devoted to husband, home, and children. They never dreamed it was woman's vocation or duty to go out into the world and mingle in its strifes and contentions — but at home, to view them, reflect upon their consequences to society, and upon the future of their sons and daughters, and warn them what to emulate and what to shun. They, as did their husbands, felt the necessity of preserving that delicacy of thought and action which is woman's ornament, and which is more efficient in rebuking licentiousness and profligacy in the young and the old than all the teaching of the schools without such example. Such were the mothers of the great and the good of our land, and such the mothers of those men now prominent and distinguished in the advocacy and support of the great principles of natural rights and humanity.

It is a mooted question whether the purposes of human life demand a high, classical education among the masses; or whether the general happiness is promoted by such education. In the study of the human mind in connection with human wants, we are continually met with difficulties arising from the want of education; and quite as frequently with those resulting from education. So much so, that we hear from every wise man the declaration that as many minds are ruined by over-education as from the want of education.

Man's curse is to labor. This labor must of necessity be divided to subserve the wants of society — and common sense would teach that each should be educated as best to enable him to perform that labor which may fall to his lot in life. But who shall determine this lot? Every day's experience teaches the observant and thinking man that no one individual is uselessly born. To deny this proposition would be to call in question the wisdom and goodness of the Creator. Every one possesses proclivities for some one avocation, and should be educated for its pursuit. This is manifested in very early life; in some much more palpably than in others. This is always the case when the aptitude is decisive. In such cases this idiosyncrasy will triumph over every adverse circumstance, educational or otherwise; but in the less palpable, it will not; and the design of nature may, and indeed constantly is, disappointed, and improper education and improper pursuits given. In these pursuits or callings, the person thus improperly placed there never succeeds as he would had his bent or mental inclination been observed, and his education directed to it, and he given to its pursuit. Such persons labor through life painfully; they have no taste or inclination for the profession, business, or trade in which they are engaged; its pursuit is an irksome, thankless labor; while he who has fallen into nature's design, and is working where his inclinations lead, labors happily, because he labors naturally. These inclinations the parent or guardian should observe; and when manifested, should direct the education for the calling nature has designed. Idiosyncrasies are transmissible or inherited. In old and populous communities, where every pursuit or profession is full, the father generally teaches his own to his son or sons. Where this has extended through three or four generations, the proclivity is generally strongly marked, and in very early childhood made manifest. Thus, in the third or fourth generation, where all have been blacksmiths, the child will be born with the muscles of the right arm more developed than those of the left, and the first plaything he demands is a hammer. So, where a family have been traders, will the offspring naturally discover an aptness for bargaining and commerce. This is illustrated in the instincts of the Jews, a people of extraordinary brain and wonderful tenacity of purpose. Five thousand years since, a small fragment of the Semitic race, residing in Mesopotamia between the waters of the Euphrates and the Tigris, consisting of two families, came into the land of Canaan, in Asia Minor; from them have descended the people known as Jews. The country over which they spread, and which is known as Judea, is not more than four hundred miles long by two hundred and fifty in breadth, situated between two populous and powerful empires, the Assyrian and Egyptian, who, waging war too frequently, made the land of Judea their battle-field, and its people the objects of persecution and oppression. The earnings of their labor were deemed legitimate prey by both, and taken wherever found: they were led into captivity by the Assyrians and by the Egyptians, enslaved, and denied the legal right to possess the soil—which, to the everlasting disgrace of Christian Europe, was a restriction upon this wonderful people until within the present century. A blind bigotry would have blotted them from the face of the earth, but for that energy, talent, and enterprise possessed by them in a superior degree to any people upon the globe. Inspired by a sublime belief that they were the chosen people of God, no tyranny nor oppression could subdue their energies. They prayed and labored, went forward with untiring determination, upheld by their faith, and always, under the direst distress, found comfort from this belief and the fruits of incessant labor. The soil of their loved Canaan was barren, and yielded grudgingly to the most persistent labor. This drove them to trade, and an extended intercourse with the world. Without a national government of sufficient power to protect them when robbed by the people or the governments surrounding their own, they were compelled, for self-protection, to resort to every means of concealing the earnings of their enterprise and superior knowledge and skill from Christian and pagan alike. They gave value to the diamond, that in a small stone, easy of concealment, immense wealth might be hidden. They invented the bill of exchange, by which they could at pleasure transfer from one country to another their wealth, and avoid the danger of spoliation from the hand of power and intolerance. Without political or civil rights in any but their own country, they were compelled to the especial pursuit of commerce for centuries, and we now see that seven-tenths of all Jews born, as naturally turn to trade and commerce as the infant to the breast. It has become an instinct.

To these persecutions the world is probably indebted for the developments of commerce—the bringing into communication the nations of the earth for the exchange of commodities necessary to the use and comfort of each other, not of the growth or production of each, enlarging the knowledge of all thus communicating, and teaching that civilization which is the enlightenment and the blessing of man—ameliorating the savage natures of all, and teaching that all are of God, and equally the creatures of His love and protection; and leading also to that development of mind in the Israelite which makes him conspicuous to-day above any other race in the great attributes of mind — directing the policy of European governments — first at the Bar, first in science, first in commerce, first in wealth — preserving the great traits of nationality without a nation, and giving tone, talent, wealth, and power to all.

A few men only are born to think. Their minds expand with education, and their usefulness is commensurate with it. This few early evince a proclivity so strong for certain avocations as to enable those who have the direction of their future to educate them for this pursuit. This proclivity frequently is so overpowering as to prompt the possessor, when the early education has been neglected, to educate himself for this especial idiosyncrasy. This was the case with Newton — with Stevenson, the inventor of the locomotive-engine, who, at twenty years of age, was ignorant even of his letters. Arkwright was a barber, and almost entirely illiterate when he invented the spinning-jenny. Train, the inventor of the railroad, was, at the time of its invention, a coal-heaver, and entirely illiterate.

These cases are rare, however. The great mass of mankind are born to manual labor, and only with capacities suited for it. To attempt to cultivate such minds for eminent purposes would be folly. Even supposing they could be educated — which is scarcely supposable, for it would seem a contravention of Heaven's fiat — they could no more apply this learning, which would simply be by rote, than they could go to the moon. Such men are not unfrequently met with, and are designated, by common consent, learned fools. Nature points out the education they should receive. In like manner with those of higher and nobler attributes, educate them for their pursuits in life. It requires not the same education to hold a plough, or drive an ox, that it does to direct the course of a ship through a trackless sea, or to calculate an eclipse; and what is essential to the one is useless to the other. — But I am wandering away from the purpose of this work. Turning back upon the memories of fifty years ago, and calling up the lives and the histories of men, and women too, I have known, I was led into these reflections, and ere I was aware they had stolen from my pen.

The rude condition of a country is always imparted to the character of its people, and out of this peculiarity spring the rough sports and love of coarse jokes and coarse humor. No people ever more fully verified this truth than the Georgians, and to-day, even among her best educated, the love of fun is a prevailing trait. Her traditions are full of the practical jokes and the practical jokers of fifty years ago. The names of Dooly, Clayton, Prince, Bacon, and Longstreet will be remembered in the traditions of fun as long as the descendants of their compatriots continue to inhabit the land. The cock-fight, the quarter-race, and the gander-pulling are traditions now, and so is the fun they gave rise to; and I had almost said, so is the honesty of those who were participants in these rude sports. Were they not more innocent outlets to the excessive energies of a mercurial and fun-loving people than the faro-table and shooting-gallery of to-day? Every people must have their amusements and sports, and these, unrestrained, will partake of the character of the people and the state of society. Sometimes the narrow prejudices of bigoted folly will inveigh against these, and insist upon their restraint by law; and these laws, in many of the States, remain upon the statute-book a rebuking evidence of the shameless folly of fanatical ignorance. Of these, the most conspicuous are the blue-laws of Connecticut, and the more absurd and criminal laws of Massachusetts against amusements not only necessary, but healthful and innocent. Even in the present advanced state of knowledge and civilization, do we occasionally hear ranted from the pulpit denunciations of dancing, as a sinful and God-offending amusement. Such men should not be permitted to teach or preach — it is to attenuate folly and fanaticism, to circumscribe the happiness of youth, and belie the Bible.

The emigrants to Kentucky, Tennessee, and Georgia were all persons of like character, combining a mixture of English, Irish, and Scotch blood. They were enterprising, daring, and remarkable for great good sense. Rude from the want of education and association with a more polished people, they were nevertheless high-principled and full of that chivalrous spirit which prompts a natural courtesy, courts danger, and scorns the little and mean — open-handed in their generosity, and eminently candid and honest in all their intercourse and dealings with their fellow-men. These elements, collected from various sections, combined to form new communities in the wild and untamed regions. In their conflicts with the savages were shown a daring fearlessness and a high order of military talent in very many of the prominent leaders of the different settlements.

They had no chronicler to note and record their exploits, and they exist now only in the traditions of the country.

The names of Shelby and Kenton, of Kentucky; of Davidson and Jackson, of Tennessee; of Clarke, Mathews, and Adams, of Georgia; Dale, of Alabama, and Claiborne, of Mississippi, live in the memory of the people of their States, together with those of Tipton, Sevier, Logan, and Boone, and will be in the future history of these States, with their deeds recorded as those whose enterprise, energy, and fearlessness won from the wilderness and the savage their fertile and delightful lands, to be a home and a country for their posterity.

The children of such spirits intermarrying, could but produce men of talent and enterprise, and women of beauty, intelligence, and virtue. In the veins of these ran only streams of blue blood—such as filled the veins of the leaders of the Crusades—such as warmed the hearts of the O'Neals and O'Connors, of Wallace and Bruce, and animated the bosoms of the old feudal barons of England, who extorted the great charter of human liberty from King John. There was no mixture of the pale Saxon to taint or dilute the noble current of the Anglo-Norman blood which flowed through and fired the hearts of these descendants of the nobility and gentry of Britain. They were the cavaliers in chivalry and daring, and despised, as their descendants despised, the Roundheads and their descendants, with their cold, dissembling natures, hypocritical in religion as faithless in friendship, without one generous emotion or ennobling sentiment.

It is not remarkable that conflict should ensue between races so dissimilar in a struggle to control the Government: true to the instincts of race, each contended for that which best suited their genius and wants; and not at all remarkable that all the generous gallantry in such a conflict should be found with the Celt, and all the cruel rapacity and meanness with the Saxon. Their triumph, through the force of numbers, was incomplete, until their enemies were tortured by every cruelty of oppression, and the fabric of the Government dashed to atoms. This triumph can only be temporary. The innate love of free institutions, universal in the heart of the Celtic Southerner, will *yet* unite all the races to retrieve the lost. This done, victory is certain.

The descendants of these pioneers have gone out to people the extended domain reaching around the Gulf, and are growing into strength, without abatement of the spirit of their ancestors. Very soon time and their energies will repair the disasters of the recent conflict; and reinvigorated, the shackles of the Puritan shall restrain no longer, when a fierce democracy shall restore the Constitution, and with it the liberty bequeathed by their ancestors.

With this race, fanaticism in religion has never known a place. Rational and natural, they have ever worshipped with the heart and the attributes of their faith. Truth, sincerity, love, and mercy have ever marked their characters. Too honest to be superstitious, and too sincere to be hypocrites, the concentrated love of freedom unites the race, and the hatred of tyranny will stimulate the blood which shall retrieve it from the dominion of the baser blood now triumphant and rioting in the ruin they have wrought.

In the beginning of the settlements, and as soon as fears of the inroads from the savages had subsided, attention was given to the selection of separate and extended homes over the country, to the opening of farms, and their cultivation. The first consideration was food and raiment. All of this was to be the production of the farm and home industry: grain enough was to be grown to serve the wants of the family for bread, and to feed the stock; for this was to furnish the meat, milk, and butter. Cotton enough to serve the wants of families, together with the wool from the flock, and some flax, were of prime consideration. All of this was prepared and manufactured into fabrics for clothing and bedding at home. The seed from the cotton was picked by hand; for, as yet, Whitney had not given them the cotton-gin. This work was imposed most generally upon the children of families, white and black, as a task at night, and which had to be completed before going to bed; an ounce was the usual task, which was weighed and spread before the fire; for it was most easily separated from the seed when warm and dry. Usually some petty rewards stimulated the work. In every family it was observed and commented upon, that these rewards excited the diligence of the white children, but were without a corresponding effect upon the black; and any one who has ever controlled the negro knows that his labor is only in proportion to the coercion used to enforce it. His capacity, physically, is equal to the white; but this cannot be bought, or he persuaded to exert it of himself, and is given only through punishment, or the fear of it.

The removal of restraint is to him a license to laziness; and the hope of reward, or the cravings of nature, will only induce him to labor sufficiently to supply these for immediate and limited relief.

Stock of every kind except horses was left to find a support in the forest, and at that time, when their range was unlimited, they found it in abundance. Increasing wants stimulated the cultivation of a market crop to supply them, and indigo and tobacco were first resorted to. Tobacco was the principal staple, and the method of its transportation was extraordinary. As at the present day in Kentucky, it was pressed into very large hogsheads. Upon these were pinned large wooden felloes, forming the circle of a wheel around the hogshead at either end, and in the centre of each head a large pin was inserted. Upon these pins were attached shafts or thills, as to a cart, and to these teams, and thus the hogshead was rolled along rough roads and through streams for sometimes ninety miles to Augusta, for a market. When sold, the shafts were reserved, and upon these was then erected a sort of box, into which the few articles purchased were placed, and dragged home. These articles almost universally consisted of some iron and steel, and a little coffee and sugar, and sometimes a quarter of a pound of tea — universally termed store-tea, to distinguish it from that made from the root of the sassafras and the leaf of the cassia or tepaun-bush.

Cotton was, to some little extent, cultivated near the seaboard in Georgia and South Carolina, and cleaned of the seeds by a machine similar to that used at the present day for preparing the sea-island cotton for market. This was a tedious and troublesome method, and was incapable of doing the work to any very great extent. Indigo, of a superior quality to the American, was being produced in British India and Central America, and the competition was reducing the price to the cost of production. The same difficulty attended the growing of tobacco. Virginia and Maryland, with their abundance of labor, were competing, and cheapening the article to a price which made its production unprofitable. At this juncture, Whitney invented the cotton-gin, and the growth of cotton as a marketable crop commenced upon a more extended scale. In a few years it became general — each farmer growing more or less, according to his means. Some one man, most able to do so, erected a gin-house, first in a county, then in each neighborhood. These either purchased in the seed the cotton of their neighbors, or ginned it and packed it for a certain amount of toll taken from the cotton. This packing was done in round bales, and by a single man, with a heavy iron bar, and was a most laborious and tedious method; and the packages were in the most inconvenient form for handling and transportation.

Up to this time the slave-trade had been looked upon most unfavorably by the people of the South. Among the first sermons I remember to have heard, was one depicting the horrors of this trade. I was by my grandmother's side at Bethany, in Greene county, and, though a child, I remember, as if of yesterday, the description of the manner of capturing the African in his native wilds — how the mother and father were murdered, and the boys and the girls borne away, and how England was abused for the cruel inhumanity of the act. Although unused to the melting mood, the old lady wiped from her eyes a tear, whether in sorrow or sympathy for outraged humanity, or in compliment to the pathos and power of her favorite preacher, I was too young to know or have an opinion. I remember well, however, that she cried, for she pinched me most unmercifully for laughing at her, and at home spanked me for crying. Dear old grandmother! but yesterday I was at your grave, where you have slept fifty-two years, and if I laughed above thy mould at the memory of the many bouts we had more than sixty years ago, and, from the blue bending above, thy spirit looked down in wrath upon the unnatural outrage, be appeased ere I come; for I should fear to meet thee, even in heaven, if out of humor! The roses bloomed above you — sweet emblems of thy purity and rest — and there, close by you, were the pear-trees, planted by your hands, around the roots of which you gathered the rods of my reformation; for I was a truant child. You meant it all for my good, no doubt; but to me it was passing through purgatory then, to merit a future good in time. Ah! how well I remember it — all of it. *Requiescat in pace.* I had almost irreverently said, "Rest, cat, in peace."

It was at this period that the competition for accumulating money may be said to have commenced in Middle Georgia. Labor became in great demand, and the people began to look leniently upon the slave-trade. The marching of Africans, directly imported, through the country for sale, is a memory of sixty-five years ago. The demand had greatly increased, and, with this, the price. The trade was to cease in 1808, and the number brought over was daily augmenting, to hasten to make from the traffic as much money as possible before this time should arrive. The demand, however, was greater than could be supplied. From house to house they were carried for sale. They were always young men and women, or girls and boys, and their clothing was of the simplest kind. That of the men and boys consisted of drawers, only reaching midway the thigh, from the waist. The upper portions of the person and the lower extremities were entirely nude. The females wore a chemise reaching a few inches below the knee, leaving bare the limbs. This was adopted for the purpose of exposing the person, as much as decency would permit, for examination, so as to enable the purchaser to determine their individual capacity for labor. This examination was close and universal, beginning with an inspection of the teeth, which in these young savages were always perfect, save in those where they had been filed to a point in front. This was not uncommon with the males. It was then extended to the limbs, and ultimately to the entire person. They were devoid of shame, and yielded to this inspection without the slightest manifestation of offended modesty. At first they were indifferent to cooked food, and would chase and catch and eat the grasshoppers and lizards with the avidity of wild turkeys, and seemed, as those fowls, to relish these as their natural food.

From such is descended the race which our Christian white brothers of the North have, in their devotion to their duty to God and their hatred to us, made masters of our destiny. Our faith in the justice and goodness of the same Divine Being bids us believe this unnatural and destructive domination will not be permitted to endure for any lengthy period. Could the curtain which veiled out the future sixty years ago, have been lifted, and the vision of those then subduing the land been permitted to pierce and know the present of their posterity, they would then have achieved a separation from our puritanical oppressors, and built for themselves and their own race, even if in blood, a separate government, and have made it as nature intended it should be to this favored land — a wise and powerful one.

Sooner or later these intentions of Divine wisdom are consummated. The fallible nature of man, through ignorance or the foolish indulgence of bad passions in the many, enable the few to delude and control the many, and to postpone for a time the inevitable; but as assuredly as time endures, nature's laws work out natural ends. Generations may pass away, perhaps perish from violence, and others succeed with equally unnatural institutions, making miserable the race, until it, like the precedent, passes from the earth. Yet these great laws work on, and in the end triumph in perfecting the Divine will.

To the wise and observant this design of the Creator is ever apparent; to the foolish and wicked, never.

John Wesley had visited Savannah,.and travelled through the different settlements then in embryo, teaching the tenets and introducing the simple worship of the church of his founding, after a method established by himself, and which gave name and form to the sect, now, and almost from its incipiency known as Methodist. This organization and the tenets of its faith were admirably suited to a rude people, and none perhaps could have been more efficient in forming and improving such morals. Unpretending, simple in form, devoid of show or ceremony, it appealed directly to the purer emotions of our nature, and through the natural devotion of the heart lifted the mind to the contemplation and inspired the soul with the love of God. Its doctrines, based upon the purest morality, easily comprehensible, and promising salvation to all who would believe, inspiring an enthusiasm for a pure life, were natural, and naturally soon became wide-spread, and as the writer believes, has done more in breaking away the shackles of ignorance and debasing superstition from the mind, than any other system of worship or doctrine of faith taught by man; and to this, in a great degree, is due the freedom of thought, independence of feeling and action, chivalrous bearing, and high honor of the Southern people. Inculcating as it does the simple teachings of the gospel of Christ, — to live virtuously — do no wrong — love thy neighbor as thyself, and unto all do as you would be done by, — a teaching easy of comprehension, and which, when sternly enforced by a pure and elevated public sentiment, becomes the rule of conduct, and society is blessed with harmony and right. This moral power is omnipotent for good, concentrating communities into one without divisions or dissensions, to be wielded for good at once and at all times. Nothing evil can result from such concentration of opinions being directed by the vicious and wicked, so long as the moral of this faith shall control the mind and heart.

Camp-meetings, an institution of this church, and which were first commenced in Georgia, are a tradition there now. Here and there through the country yet remains, in ruinous decay, the old stand or extemporized pulpit from which the impassioned preacher addressed the assembled multitude of anxious listeners; and around the square now overgrown with brush-wood and forest-trees, prostrate and rotten, the remains of the cabin tents may be seen, where once the hospitality of the owners and worshippers was dispensed with a heartiness and sincerity peculiar to the simple habits, and honest, kindly emotions of a rude and primitive people.

How well do I remember the first of these meetings I ever witnessed! I was a small lad, and rode behind my father on horseback to the ground. It was sixty-five years ago. The concourse was large, consisting of the people of all the country around — men, women, and children, white and black. Around a square enclosing some six acres of ground, the tents were arranged — arbors of green boughs cut from the adjoining forest formed a shelter from the sun's rays. In front of all of these, shading the entrance to the tent, under this friendly sheltering from the heat of the sun, assembled the owners and the guests of each, in social and unceremonious intercourse. This was strictly the habit of the young people; and here, in evening's twilight, has been plighted many a vow which has been redeemed by happy unions for life's journey, and to be consummated when the cold weather came. In the rear of the tents were temporary kitchens, presided over in most instances by some old, trusted aunty of ebon hue, whose pride it was to prepare the meals for her tent, and to hear her cooking praised by the preachers and the less distinguished guests of master and mistress. The sermons were preached in the morning, at noon, and at twilight, when all the multitude were summoned to the grand central stand in the square of the encampment by sounding a tin trumpet or ox-horn. My childish imagination was fired at the sight of this assemblage. My wonder was, whence come all these people? as converging from the radius around came the crowding multitude, without order and without confusion — the farmer and his brusque wife side by side, leading their flock and friends: he with an ample chair of home manufacture slung by his side for the wife's comfort as she devoutly listened to the pious brother's comforting sermon — the guests and the young of the family following in respectful silence, and at a respectful distance, all tending to the great arbor of bushes covering the place of worship. Over all the space of the encampment the under-brush had been carefully removed; but the great forest-trees (for these encampments were always in a forest) were left to shade as well as they might the pulpit-stand and grounds. All around was dense forest, wild and beautiful as nature made it.

How well the scene and the worship accorded! There was congruity in all—the woods, the tents, the people, and the worship. The impressions made that day upon my young mind were renewed at many a camp-meeting in after years; and so indelibly impressed as only to pass away with existence.

The preacher rose upon his elevated platform, and, advancing to the front, where a simple plank extending from tree to tree, before him, formed a substitute for a table or desk, where rested the hymn-book and Bible, commenced the service by reading a hymn, and then, line by line, repeating it, to be sung by all his congregation.

Whoever has listened, in such a place, amidst a great multitude, to the singing of that beautiful hymn commencing, "Come, thou fount of every blessing," by a thousand voices, all in accord, and not felt the spirit of devotion burning in his heart, could scarcely be moved should an angel host rend the blue above him, and, floating through the ether, praise God in song. In that early day of Methodism, very few of those licensed to preach were educated men. They read the Bible, and expounded its great moral truths as they understood them. Few of these even knew that it had been in part originally written in the Hebrew tongue, and the other portion in that of the Greeks; but he knew it contained the promise of salvation, and felt that it was his mission to preach and teach this way to his people, relying solely for his power to impress these wonderful truths upon the heart by the inspiration of the Holy Spirit. For this reason the sermons of the sect were never studied or written, and their excellence was their fervor and impassioned appeals to the heart and the wild imaginations of the enthusiastic and unlearned of the land. Genius, undisciplined and untutored by education, is fetterless, and its spontaneous suggestions are naturally and powerfully effective, when burning from lips proclaiming the heart's enthusiasm. Thus extemporizing orations almost daily, stimulated the mind to active thought, and very many of these illiterate young Methodist preachers became in time splendid orators.

It was the celebrated Charles James Fox who said to a young

man just entering Parliament, if he desired to become a great orator, and had the genius and feeling from nature, all he had to do was to speak often and learn to think on his feet. It is to this practice the lawyer and the preacher owe the oratory which distinguish these above every other class of men. And yet, how few of them ever attain to the eminence of finished orators. Eloquence and oratory are by no means identical: one is the attribute of the heart, the other of the head; and eloquence, however unadorned, is always effective, because it is born of the feelings; and there is ever a sympathy between the hearts of men, and the words, however rude and original, which bubble up from the heart freighted with its feelings, rush with electrical force and velocity to the heart, and stir to the extent of its capacities. Oratory, however finished, is from the brain, and is an art; it may convince the mind and captivate the imagination, but never touches the heart or stirs the soul. To awaken feelings in others, we must feel ourselves. Eloquence is the volume of flame, oratory the shaft of polished ice; the one fires to madness, the other delights and instructs.

Religion is the pathos of the heart, and must be awakened from the heart's emotions. The imagination is the great attribute of the mind, gathering and creating thought and inspiring feeling. Hence, the peculiar system of the Methodists in their worship is the most efficient in proselyting, and especially with a rude, imaginative people.

The camp-meeting was an admirable device for this purpose, and its abandonment by the sect is as foolish as would be that of a knight who would throw away his sword as he was rushing to battle. Fashion is omnipotent in religion, as in other things, and with the more general diffusion of education, camp-meetings have come to be considered as vulgar and unfashionable. To be vulgar, is to be common; to be common, is to be natural. The masses, and especially in democratic communities, must always be vulgar or common—must always be, in the main, illiterate and rude; and it is for the conversion and salvation of these multitudes the preacher should struggle, and in his efforts his most efficient means should be used.

The camp-meeting, at night, when all the fire-stands are ablaze, and the multitude are assembled and singing, is beyond description picturesque: when, too, some eloquent and enthusiastic preacher is stimulating to intense excitement the multitude around him with the fervor of his words, and the wild, passionate manifestations ot his manner, to see the crowd swaying to and fro, to hear the groans and sobs of the half-frenzied multitude, and, not unfrequently, the maddened shriek of hysterical fear, all coming up from the half-illuminated spot, is thrillingly exciting. And when the sermon is finished, to hear all this heated mass break forth into song, the wild melody of which floats, in the stillness of night, upon the breeze to the listening ear a mile away, in cadences mournfully sweet, make the camp-meeting among the most exciting of human exhibitions. In such a school were trained those great masters of pulpit oratory, Pierce, Wynans, Capers, and Bascomb. Whitfield was the great exemplar of these; but none, perhaps, so imitated his style and manner as John Newland Maffit and the wonderful Summerfield.

Like all that is great and enduring, the Methodist Church had its beginning among the humble and lowly. Rocked in the cradle of penury and ignorance, it was firmly fixed in the foundations of society, whence it rose from its own purity of doctrine and simplicity of worship to command the respect, love, and adoption of the highest in the land, and to wield an influence paramount in the destinies of the people and the Government. Its ministers are now the educated and eloquent of the Church militant. Its institutions of learning are the first and most numerous all over the South, and it has done for female education in the South more than every other sect of Christians, excepting, perhaps, the Roman Catholic. In the cause of education its zeal is enlisted, and its organization is such as to bring a wonderful power to operate upon the community in every section of the South and West. That this will accomplish much, we have only to look to the antecedents of the Church to determine. Like the coral insect, they never cease to labor: each comes with his mite and deposits it; and, from the humblest beginning, this assiduity and contribution builds up great islands in the sea of ignorance—rich in soil, salubrious in climate, and, finally, triumphant in the conceptions of the chief architect—completing for good the work so humbly begun.

CHAPTER IX.

PEDAGOGUES AND DEMAGOGUES.

EDUCATION — COLLEGES — SCHOOL-DAYS — WILLIAM AND MARY — A SUBSTITUTE — BOARDING AROUND — ROUGH DIAMONDS — CASTE — GEORGE M. TROUP — A SCOTCH INDIAN — ALEXANDER MCGILVERY — THE MCINTOSH FAMILY — BUTTON GWINNETT — GENERAL TAYLOR — MATTHEW TALBOT — JESSE MERCER — AN EXCITING ELECTION.

THE subject of education engaged the attention of the people of Georgia at a very early day subsequent to the Revolution. Public schools were not then thought of; probably because such a scheme would have been impracticable. The population was sparse, and widely separated in all the rural districts of the country; and to have supplied all with the means of education, would have necessitated an expense beyond the power of the State. A system was adopted, of establishing and endowing academies in the different counties, at the county-seat, where young men who intended to complete a collegiate education might be taught, and the establishment and endowment of a college, where this education might be finished, leaving the rudimental education of the children of the State to be provided for by their parents, as best they could. Primary schools were gotten up in the different neighborhoods by the concentrated action of its members, and a teacher employed, and paid by each parent at so much per capita for his children. In these schools almost every Georgian — yes, almost every Southerner — commenced his education. It was at these schools were mingled the sexes in pursuit of their A, B, C, and the incidents occurring here became the cherished memories of after life. Many a man of eminence has gone out from these schools with a better education with which to begin life and a conflict with the world, than is obtained now at some of the institutions called colleges.

Young men without means, who had acquired sufficient of the rudiments of an English education, but who desired to pursue their studies and complete an education to subserve the purposes of the pursuit in life selected by them, frequently were the teachers in the primary schools. From this class arose most of those men so distinguished in her earlier history. Some were natives, and some were immigrants from other States, who sought a new field for their efforts, and where to make their future homes. Such were William H. Crawford, Abram Baldwin, and many others, whose names are now borne by the finest counties in the State — a monument to their virtues, talents, and public services, erected by a grateful people.

These primitive schools made the children of every neighborhood familiar to each other, and encouraged a homogeneous feeling in the rising population of the State. This sameness of education and of sentiment created a public opinion more efficacious in directing and controlling public morals than any statutory law, or its most efficient administration. It promoted an *esprit du corps* throughout the country, and formed the basis of that chivalrous emprise so peculiarly Southern.

The recollections of these school-days are full of little incidents confirmatory of these views. I will relate one out of a thousand I might enumerate. A very pretty little girl of eight years, full of life and spirit, had incurred, by some act of childish mischief, the penalty of the switch — the only and universal means of correction in the country schools. She was the favorite of a lad of twelve, who sat looking on, and listening to the questions propounded to his sweetheart, and learning the decision of the teacher, which was announced thus: "Well, Mary, I must punish you."

All eyes were directed to William. Deliberately he laid down his books, and, stepping quickly up to the teacher, said, respectfully: "Don't strike her. Whip me. I'll take it for her," as he arrested with his hand the uplifted switch. Every eye in that little log school-house brightened with approbation, and, in a moment after, filled with tears, as the teacher laid down his rod and said: "William, you are a noble boy, and, for your sake, I will excuse Mary." Ten years after, Mary was the wife — the dutiful, loving, happy wife of William; and William, twenty years after, was a member of the Legislature, and then a representative in Congress, (when it was an honor to a gentleman to be such,) and afterwards was for years a Senator in the same body — one of Georgia's noblest, proudest, and best men.

Can any one enumerate an instance where evil grew out of the early association of the sexes at school? In the neighborhoods least populous, and where there were but few children, the pedagogue usually divided the year into as many parts as he had pupils, and boarded around with each family the number of days allotted to each child. If he was a man of family, the united strength of the neighborhood assembled upon a certain day, and built for him a residence contiguous to the school-house, which was erected in like manner.

These buildings were primitive indeed—consisting of poles cut from the forest, and, with no additional preparation, notched up into a square pen, and floored and covered with boards split from a forest-tree near at hand. It rarely required more than two days to complete the cabin—the second being appropriated to the chimney, and the chinking and daubing; that is, filling the interstices with billets of wood, and make these air-tight with clay thrown violently in, and smoothed over with the hand. Such buildings constituted nine-tenths of the homes of the entire country sixty years ago; and in such substitutes for houses were born the men who have moved the Senate with their eloquence, and added dignity and power to the bench of the Supreme Court of the nation, startled the world with their achievements upon the battle-field, and more than one of them has filled the Presidential chair.

Men born and reared under such circumstances, receive impressions which they carry through life, and their characters always discover the peculiarities incident to such birth and rearing—rough and vigorous, bold and daring, and nobly independent, without polish or deceit, always sincere, and always honest.

However much the intellect may be cultivated in youth—however much it may be distinguished for great thoughts and wonderful attainments, still the peculiarities born of the forest cling about it in all its roughness—a fit setting to the unpolished diamond of the soul.

The rural pursuits of the country, and the necessities of the isolated condition of a pioneer population, which necessities are mainly supplied by ingenuity and perseverance on the part of each, creates an independence and self-reliance which enter largely into the formation of the general character. The institution of African slavery existing in the South, which came with the very first pioneer, and which was continually on the increase, added to this independence the habit of command; and this, too, became a part of Southern character. The absolute control of the slave, placed by habit and law in the will of the master, made it necessary to enact laws for the protection of the slave against the tyrannical cruelties found in some natures; but the public sentiment was in this, as in all other things, more potent than law. Their servile dependence forbade resistance to any cruelty which might be imposed; but it excited the general sympathy, and inspired, almost universally, a lenient humanity toward them.

They were mostly born members of the household, grew up with the children of each family, were companions and playmates, and naturally an attachment was formed, which is always stronger in the protecting than the protected party. It was a rare instance to find a master whose guardian protection did not extend with the same intensity and effect over his slave as over his child: this, not from any motive of pecuniary interest, but because he was estopped by law from self-defence; and, too, because of the attachment and the moral obligation on the master to protect his dependants. Besides, the community exacted it as a paramount duty. It is human to be attached to whatever it protects and controls; out of this feeling grows the spirit of true chivalry and of lofty intent — that magnanimity, manliness, and ennobling pride which has so long characterized the gentlemen of the Southern States.

Caste, in society, may degrade, but, at the same time, it elevates. Where this caste was distinguished by master and slave, the distinction was most marked, because there was no intermediate gradation. It was the highest and the lowest. It was between the highest and purest of the races of the human family, and the lowest and most degraded; and this relation was free from the debasing influences of caste in the same race. An improper appreciation of this fact has gone far to create with those unacquainted with negro character the prejudices against the institution of African slavery, and which have culminated in its abolition in the Southern States.

The negro is incapacitated by nature from acquiring the high intelligence of the Caucasian. His sensibilities are extremely dull, his perceptive faculties dim, and the entire organization of his brain forbids and rejects the cultivation necessary to the elimination of mind. With a feeble moral organization, and entirely devoid of the higher attributes of mind and soul so prominent in the instincts of the Caucasian, his position was never, as a slave, oppressive to his mind or his sense of wrong. He felt, and to himself acknowledged his inferiority, and submitted with alacrity to the control of his superior. Under this control, his moral and intellectual cultivation elevated him: not simply to a higher position socially, but to a higher standard in the scale of being, and this was manifested to himself at the same time it demonstrated to him the natural truth of his inferiority. This gratified him, promoted his happiness, and he was contented. The same effect of the relation of master and servant can never follow when the race is the same, or even when the race is but one or two degrees inferior to the dominant one.

The influence of this relation upon the white race is marked in the peculiarities of character which distinguish the people of the South. The habit of command, where implicit obedience is to follow, ennobles. The comparison is inevitable between the commander and him who obeys, and, in his estimation, unconsciously elevates and degrades. This between the white man and negro, is only felt by the white. The negro never dreams that he is degraded by this servility, and consequently he does not feel its oppression. He is incapable of aspiring, and manifests his pride and satisfaction by imitating his master as much as is possible to his nature. The white man is conscious of the effect upon the negro, and has no fear that he is inflicting a misery to be nursed in secret and sorrow, and to fill the negro's heart with hate. This, however, is universally the effect of the domination of one man over another of the same race. The relation was for life, and the master was responsible for the moral and physical well-being of his slave. His entire dependence makes him an object of interest and care, and the very fact of this responsibility cultivates kindness and tenderness toward him. But this is not all; it carries with it a consciousness of superiority, and inspires a superior bearing. These influences are more potent in the formation of female than male character. The mistress is relieved absolutely from all menial duties, and is served by those who are servants for life, and compulsorily so. She is only under the obligations of humanity in her conduct toward them. They must do her bidding. She is not afraid to offend by giving an order, nor is she apprehensive of being deserted to discharge her household labor herself by offending them. It is their duty to please—it is their interest—and this is the paramount desire. The intercourse is gentle, respectful, and kind; still, there is no infringement of the barrier between the mistress and the servant. This habit is the source of frankness and sincerity, and this release from the severity of domestic labor the fruitful source of female delicacy and refinement, so transcendently the attributes of character in the ladies of the South. It gives ease and time for improvement; for social and intellectual intercourse; creates habits of refinement, and a delicacy seen and heard in all that is done or said in refined female society in the South. Something, too, I suppose, is due to blood. There are many grades in the Caucasian race. The Anglo-Norman or Anglo-Celtic is certainly at the head. They rule wherever left to the conflict of mind and energy of soul. Sometimes they are conquered for a time, but never completely so. The great constituents of their natures continue to resist, and struggle up, and when the opportunity comes, they strike for control and supremacy—

> "And freedom's battle, once begun,
> The cause bequeathed from sire to son,
> Though baffled oft, is ever won."

The Southern woman's soul is chivalry. From the highest to the humblest, the same lofty purpose, pride, and energy animate them. They have contrasted the free and noble with the mean and servile. Its magic has entered their natures and quickened their souls. In all there is a lofty scorn for the little and mean. The same withering contempt for the cringing and cowardly is met in every one of them. Their impulses are generous, and their aspirations noble, with hearts as soft and tender as love, pity, and compassion can form. Yet in them there is, too, the fire of chivalry, the scorn of contempt, and the daring of her who followed her immortal brother, the great Palafox, at the defence of Saragossa, her native city, and, standing upon the dead bodies of her countrymen, snatched the burning match from the hand of death, and fired the cannon at the advancing foe, and planted Spain's standard, in defiance of the veterans of Soult—a rallying point for her countrymen—and saved Saragossa. They were born to command, and can never be slaves, or the mothers of slaves.

The same influences powerfully operate in producing that bearing of chivalrous distinction, which is seen everywhere in the deportment of the Southern gentlemen toward ladies. They are ever polite, respectful, and deferential. This, however, is only one of many elements in the peculiar character of Southern people. Their piety is Christian in its character. The precepts of the Bible are fashioned into example in the conduct of the older members of society, and especially in the female portion. This is, perhaps, the predominant element. The Bible is the guide, not the fashion, in religious duty. Its doctrines are taught in purity, and in their simplicity enter into the soul, as the great constituent of character.

The chivalrous bearing of man toward woman inspires her with elevated and noble sentiments — a pride and dignity conservative of purity in all her relations — and, reflecting these back upon society, producing most salutary influences. It is woman's pride to lean on man — to share his love and respect — to be elevated by his virtues, and appreciated by the world because of his honors — to be a part of his fame. The mother, the wife, the sister, the relative should share with the husband, the son, the brother, the kinsman, in the world's honors, in the sufferings, sorrows, and miseries incidental to all. They are part and parcel of man, and partake of his nature and his position, as of his fortune. When man shall cease to view woman, and so deport himself toward her as a purer, more refined, and more elevated being than himself, that moment she will sink to his level, and then her prestige for good is gone forever. That delicacy, refinement, and chasteness, so restraining and so purifying to man in her association, is the soul of civilization — the salt of the earth. In its absence, no people are ever great; for, as it is the spirit of man's honor, so is it a nation's glory. It must be cherished, for it inspires man's honor by man's chivalry. Thus she becomes a people's strength; for their crown of glory is her chastity and angelic purity.

These virtues distinguished the pioneer women of Middle Georgia sixty years ago. As their husbands were honest and brave, they were chaste and pious; and from such a parentage sprang the men and women who have made a history for her pre-eminent among all her sister States. Her sons have peopled the West, and are distinguished there for their high honor and splendid abilities; and yet at home she boasts Toombs, Colt, Stephens, Hill, Johnson, Campbell, and a host of others, who are proud specimens among the proudest of the land. They have measured their strength with the proudest minds of all the Union, and won a fame unequalled, adorning her councils, its Cabinet, its Bench, and were the first everywhere.

George Michael Troup, one of the most distinguished of Georgia's sons, was the son of an English gentleman, who emigrated to Georgia anterior to the Revolution. He married Miss McIntosh, of Georgia, sister of General John McIntosh, of McIntosh County. He took no part in the Revolution. England was his mother country; to her he was attached, and in conscience he could not lift his hand in wrath against her. This course did not meet the approval of the McIntoshes, and he retired from the State and country. First, he went to England, but not contented there, he came to the Spanish town of Pensacola. Here he met the celebrated Indian chief, Alexander McGilvery, who was hostile to the Americans, and who invited him to take refuge in his country. McGilvery was a remarkable man; his father was a Scotchman, his mother a half-breed; her father was the celebrated French officer who was killed by his own men in 1732 at Fort Toulouse—his name was Marchand,—and her mother a full-blooded Creek woman.

McGilvery supposed him an English emissary, and invited him to go into the Creek nation and reside with his people. From Pensacola he went to Mobile, and thence to a bluff on the Tombigbee, where he remained during the war. This bluff he named McIntosh's Bluff, and it bears the name yet. Here George M. Troup was born. At the close of the war he returned to Georgia, and fixed his residence among the relatives of his wife. The McIntosh family were Highland Scotch, and partook of all the intrepidity of that wonderful people. They immigrated to Georgia with General Oglethorpe in company with a number of their countrymen, and for one hundred and thirty years have continued to reside in the county named for the first of their ancestors who settled and made a home in the colony of Georgia. It is a family distinguished for chivalry as well in Europe as in Georgia. At the commencement of the Revolution they at once sided with the colonists. Lachlin and John McIntosh became distinguished as leaders in that protracted and doubtful conflict, meeting in battle their kinsman in high command in the British army. On one occasion, when John McIntosh had surrendered at the battle of Brier Creek, a British officer, lost to every sentiment and feeling of honor, attempted to assassinate him, and was only prevented from doing so by Sir Æneas McIntosh, the commander of the English army, whose promptness arrested the blow by interposing his own sword to receive it.

Lachlin McIntosh was the commander of the first regiment raised in Georgia to aid in the Revolution. In 1777, a difficulty arose between Button Gwinnett (who, upon the death of Governor Bullock, had succeeded him as Governor,) and McIntosh. A duel was the consequence, in which Gwinnett was killed. Tradition says this difficulty grew out of the suspicions of McIntosh as to the fidelity of Gwinnett to the American cause. He was an Englishman by birth, and, upon the breaking out of the war, hesitated for some time as to the course he should pursue. This was a time when all who hesitated were suspected, and Gwinnett shared the common fate. Eventually he determined to espouse the revolutionary party, and was elected to the Convention, and was one of the immortal band who signed the Declaration of Independence emanating from that Convention. Until his death he was faithful and active. McIntosh doubted him, and he was not a man to conceal his opinions. McIntosh was severely wounded in the conflict.

This family was one of remarkable spirit; and this has descended to the posterity of the old cavaliers even unto this day. Colonel McIntosh, who fell at Molino del Rey, in our recent war with Mexico, was one of this family. He had all the spirit and chivalry of his ancestors. I remember to have heard Generals Taylor and Twiggs speaking of him subsequently to his death, and felt proud, as a native of the State of Georgia, of the distinguished praise bestowed on him by these gallant veterans. General Taylor was not generally enthusiastic in his expressions of praise, but he was always sincere and truthful. On this occasion, however, he spoke warmly and feelingly of the honor, the gallantry, and intrepidity of his fellow-soldier —his high bearing, his pride, his proficiency as an officer in the field, and the efficiency of his regiment, its perfection of drill and discipline, and coolness in battle — and, with unusual warmth, exclaimed: "If I had had with me at Buena Vista, McIntosh and Riley, with their veterans, I would have captured or totally destroyed the Mexican army."

Captain McIntosh, of the navy, was another of this distinguished family. He had no superior in the navy. So was that ardent and accomplished officer, Colonel McIntosh, who fell at Oak Hill, in the late war in Missouri. In truth, there has not been a day in one hundred and thirty years, when there has not been a distinguished son of this family to bear and transmit its name and fame to posterity. Through his mother, to George M. Troup descended all the nobler traits of the McIntosh family. He was educated, preparatory to entering college, at Flatbush, Long Island. His teacher's name I have forgotten, but he was a remarkable man, and devoted himself to the instruction of the youth intrusted to his care. He seems to have had a peculiar talent for inspiring a high order of ambition in his pupils, and of training them to a deportment and devotion to principle which would lead them to distinguished conduct through life. Governor Troup, in speaking to the writer of his early life, and of his school-days on Long Island, said: "There were twenty-one of us at this school fitting for college, and, in after life, nineteen of us met in Congress, the representatives of fourteen States."

Troup, after leaving this school, went to Princeton, and graduated at Nassau Hall, in his nineteenth year. Returning to Savannah, he read law; but possessing ample fortune, he never practised his profession. His talents were of an order to attract attention. James Jackson, and most of the leading men of the day, turned to him as a man of great promise. The Republican party of Savannah nominated him to represent the county of Chatham, in the Legislature of the State, before he was twenty-one years of age. Being constitutionally ineligible, he, of course, declined; but as soon as he became eligible, he was returned, and, for some years, continued to represent the county. From the Legislature he was transferred to Congress, where he at once became distinguished, not only for talent, but a lofty honor and most polished bearing. While a member of Congress, he married a Virginia lady, who was the mother of his three children. Soon after the birth of her third child, there was discovered aberration of mind in Mrs. Troup, which terminated in complete alienation. This was a fatal blow to the happiness of her husband. She was tenderly beloved by him; and his acute sensibility and high nervous temperament became so much affected as not only to fill him with grief, but to make all his remaining life one of melancholy and sorrow. He had been elected to the United States Senate, but, in consequence of this terrible blow, and the constant care of his afflicted lady, to which he devoted himself, he lost his health, and resigned. He retired to his home, and to the sad duties of afflicted love.

About this time the people of Georgia became divided upon the political issues of the day. William H. Crawford was nominated by his friends for the Presidency. This aroused his enemies' hatred, who organized an opposition to him in his own State. This opposition was headed by John Clarke, his old enemy, and was aided by every old Federalist and personal enemy in the State. Crawford's friends were too confident in the popularity which had borne him to so many triumphs, and were slow to organize. The election of Governor devolved, at that time, upon the Legislature, and Clarke, upon the death of Governor Rabun, was announced as the candidate. The event of Rabun's death occurred only a very short time before the meeting of the Legislature. Matthew Talbot, the President of the Senate, assumed, under the Constitution, the duties of Governor, but sent the message already prepared by Rabun to the Legislature, and immediately an election took place, whereupon Clarke was elected. Troup had been solicited to oppose him, but was loath to embark anew in political life. Ultimately he yielded, and was defeated by thirteen votes. The friends of Crawford were now alarmed, and the contest was immediately renewed. The canvass was one of the most rancorous and bitter ever known in the State, but of this I have spoken in a former chapter. At the ensuing election, Troup was again a candidate. Again the contest was renewed, and, if possible, with increased violence and vigor. Clarke, in obedience to usage, had retired, and his party had put forward Matthew Talbot, of Wilkes County, as the competitor of Troup. This contest had now continued for four years, and Troup was elected by two votes.

The memory of this election will never fade from the minds of any who witnessed it. At the meeting of the Legislature it was doubtful which party had the majority. Two members chosen as favorable to the election of Troup, were unable from sickness to reach the seat of Government, and it was supposed this gave the majority to Talbot. There was no political principle involved in the contest. Both professedly belonged to the Republican party. Both seemed anxious to sustain the principles and the ascendency of that party. There were no spoils. The patronage of the executive was literally nothing; and yet there was an intensity of feeling involved for which there was no accounting, unless it was the anxiety of one party to sustain Mr. Crawford at home for the Presidency, and on the other hand to gratify the hatred of Clarke, and sustain Mr. Calhoun.

During the period intervening between the meeting of the Legislature and the day appointed for the election, every means was resorted to, practicable in that day. There was no money used directly. There was not a man in that Legislature who would not have repelled with scorn a proposition to give his vote for a pecuniary consideration; but all were open to reason, State pride, and a sincere desire to do what they deemed best for the honor and interest of the State. The friends of either candidate would have deserted their favorite instantly upon the fact being known that they had even winked at so base a means of success. Every one was tenaciously jealous of his fame, and equally so of that of the State. The machinery of party was incomplete, and individual independence universal. There were a few members, whose characters forbade violence of prejudice, and who were mild, considerate, and unimpassioned. These men were sought to be operated upon by convincing them that the great interests of the State would be advanced by electing their favorite. The public services of Troup, and his stern, lofty, and eminently pure character, were urged by his friends as reasons why he should be chosen. The people of the State were becoming clamorous for the fulfilment of the contract between the State and General Government for the removal of the Indians from the territory of the State, and Troup was urged upon the voters as being favorable in the extreme to this policy, and also as possessing the talents, will, and determination to effect this end. Finally the day of election arrived. The representative men of the State were assembled. It was scarcely possible to find hotel accommodations for the multitude. The judges of the different judicial districts, the leading members of the Bar, men of fortune and leisure, the prominent members of the different sects of the Christian Church, and especially the ministers of the gospel who were most prominent and influential, were all there. The celebrated Jesse Mercer was a moving spirit amidst the excited multitude, and Daniel Duffie, who, as a most intolerant Methodist, and an especial hater of the Baptist Church and all Baptists, was there also, willing to lay down all ecclesiastical prejudice, and go to heaven even with Jesse Mercer, because he was a Troup man.

The Senate came into the Representative chamber at noon, to effect, on joint ballot, the election of Governor. The President of the Senate took his seat with the Speaker of the House, and in obedience to law assumed the presidency of the assembled body. The members were ordered to prepare their ballots to vote for the Governor of the State. The Secretary of the Senate called the roll of the Senate, each man, as his name was called, moving up to the clerk's desk, and depositing his ballot. The same routine was then gone through with on the part of the House, when the hat (for a hat was used) containing the ballots was handed to the President of the Senate, Thomas Stocks, of Greene County, who proceeded to count the ballots, and finding only the proper number, commenced to call the name from each ballot. Pending this calling the silence was painfully intense. Every place within the spacious hall, the gallery, the lobby, the committee-rooms, and the embrasures of the windows were all filled to crushing repletion. And yet not a word or sound, save the excited breathing of ardent men, disturbed the anxious silence of the hall. One by one the ballots were called. There were 166 ballots, requiring 84 to elect. When 160 ballots were counted, each candidate had 80, and at this point the excitement was so painfully intense that the President suspended the count, and, though it was chilly November, took from his pocket his handkerchief, and wiped from his flushed face the streaming perspiration. While this was progressing, a wag in the gallery sang out, "The darkest time of night is just before day." This interruption was not noticed by the President, who called out "Troup!" then "Talbot!" and again there was a momentary suspension. Then he called again, "Troup—Talbot!" "82—82," was whispered audibly through the entire hall. Then the call was resumed. "Troup!" "A tie," said more than a hundred voices. There remained but one ballot. The President turned the hat up-side down, and the ballot fell upon the table. Looking down upon it, he called, at the top of his voice, "Troup!" The scene that followed was indescribable. The two parties occupied separate sides of the chamber. Those voting for Troup rose simultaneously from their seats, and one wild shout seemed to lift the ceiling overhead. Again, with increased vim, was it given. The lobby and the galleries joined in the wild shout. Members and spectators rushed into each others' arms, kissed each other, wept, shouted, kicked over the desks, tumbled on the floor, and for ten minutes this maddening excitement suspended the proceedings of the day. It was useless for the presiding officer to command order, if, indeed, his feelings were sufficiently under control to do so. When exhaustion had produced comparative silence, Duffie, with the full brogue of the County Carlow upon his tongue, ejaculated: "O Lord, we thank Thee! The State is redeemed from the rule of the Devil and John Clarke." Mercer waddled from the chamber, waving his hat above his great bald head, and shouting "Glory, glory!" which he continued until out of sight. General Blackshear, a most staid and grave old gentleman and a most sterling man, rose from his seat, where he, through all this excitement, had sat silent, folded his arms upon his breast, and, looking up, with tears streaming from his eyes, exclaimed: "Now, Lord, I am ready to die!" Order was finally restored, and the state of the ballot stated, (Troup, 84; Talbot, 82,) when President Stocks proclaimed George M. Troup duly elected Governor of the State of Georgia for the next three years.

This was the last election of a Governor by the Legislature. The party of Clarke demanded that the election should be given to the people. This was done, and in 1825, Troup was re-elected over Clarke by a majority of some seven hundred votes. It was during this last contest that the violence and virulence of party reached its acme, and pervaded every family, creating animosities which neither time nor reflection ever healed.

CHAPTER X.

INDIAN TREATIES AND DIFFICULTIES.

The Creeks — John Quincy Adams — Hopothleyoholo — Indian Oratory — Sulphur Spring — Treaties Made and Broken — An Independent Governor — Colonels John S. McIntosh, David Emanuel Twiggs, and Duncan Clinch — General Gaines — Christianizing the Indians — Cotton Mather — Expedient and Principle — The Puritanical Snake.

During the administration of Troup, a contest arose as to the true western boundary of the State, and the right of the State to the territory occupied by a portion of the Creek tribe of Indians. In the difficulty arising out of the sale by the Legislature of the lands belonging to the State bordering upon the Mississippi River, a compromise was effected by Congress with the company purchasing, and Georgia had sold to the United States her claim to all the lands in the original grant to General Oglethorpe and others by the English Government, west of the Chattahoochee River. A part of the consideration was that the United States should, at a convenient time, and for the benefit of Georgia, extinguish the title of the Indians, and remove them from the territory occupied by them, east of the Chattahoochee River, to a certain point upon that stream; and from this point, east of a line to run from it, directly to a point called Neckey Jack, on the Tennessee River. The war of 1812 with Great Britain found the Creek or Alabama portion of this tribe of Indians allies of England. They were by that war conquered, and their territory wrested from them. Those of the tribe under the influence of the celebrated chief William McIntosh remained friendly to the United States, and were active in assisting in the conquest of their hostile brethren. The conquered Indians were removed from their territory and homes, into the territory east of Line Creek, which was made the western boundary of the Creek Nation's territory. Many of them came into the territory claimed by Georgia as her domain.

This war was a war of the Republican party of the United States, and the State of Georgia being almost unanimously Republican, her people felt it would be unpatriotic, at this juncture, to demand of the Government the fulfilment of her obligations in removing the Indians from her soil. The expenses of the war were onerous, and felt as a heavy burden by the people, and one which was incurred by Republican policy. That party felt that it was its duty to liquidate this war debt as speedily as possible. To this end the sale of those conquered lands would greatly contribute; relieving, at the same time, the people to some extent, from the heavy taxation they had borne during the progress of the war. Consequently, they had not pressed the fulfilment of this contract upon the Government. But now the war debt had been liquidated — the United States treasury was overflowing with surplus treasure — Indian tribes were being removed by the purchase of their lands in the northwest, and a tide of population pouring in upon these lands, and threatening a powerful political preponderance in opposition to Southern policy and Southern interests. Under these circumstances, and the recommendation of Governor Troup, the Legislature of the State, by joint resolution and memorial to Congress, demanded the fulfilment of the contract on the part of the United States, and the immediate removal of the Indians.

John Quincy Adams was at that time President of the United States, and, as he had ever been, was keenly alive to Northern interests and to Federal views. Though professing to be Republican in political faith, he arrayed all his influence in opposition to the rights of the States. In this matter he gave the cold shoulder to Georgia. He did not recommend a repudiation of the contract, but interposed every delay possible to its consummation. After some time, commissioners were appointed to negotiate a treaty with the Indians for the purchase of their claim to the lands within the boundaries established by the sale to the United States — or so much thereof as was in possession of the Creek tribe. To this there was very serious opposition, not only from that portion of the tribe which formerly allied themselves to Great Britain, but from missionaries found in the Cherokee country, and from Colonel John Crowell, who was United States agent for the Creek Indians. These Indians were controlled by their chief, Hopothleyoholo, a man of rare abilities and great daring. He was a powerful speaker, fluent as a fountain, and extremely vigorous in his expressions: his imagery was original and beautiful, apposite and illustrative; and his words and manner passionate to wildness. To all this he added the ferocity of his savage nature.

Crowell was an especial friend of Governor Clarke, and was influenced by his party feelings of hatred to Troup — in his opposition to a treaty, openly declaring that Georgia should never acquire the land while Troup was Governor. He was an unscrupulous man, of questionable morals, and vindictive as a snake.

The persevering energy of Troup, however, prevailed. A treaty was negotiated, and signed by Crowell, as agent, and a number of the chiefs headed by McIntosh. No sooner was this done, than Crowell, with a number of chiefs, hurried to Washington to protest against the ratification and execution of the treaty, charging the United States commissioners with fraud in the negotiation, under the influence of Troup, prompted by W. H. Crawford and friends. The fraud charged was in giving presents to the chiefs, and a couple of reservations of land to McIntosh — one where he resided, and the other around and including the famous Sulphur Spring, known as the Indian Spring, in Butts County.

This habit of giving presents to the chiefs when negotiating treaties has always been the custom of the Government. They expect it; it is a part of the consideration paid for the treaty of sale, for they are universally the vendors of territory and the negotiators of treaties for their tribes. This charge was simply a subterfuge, and one that was known would be influential with the mawkish philanthropists of the North, Mr. Adams, and the senators and representatives from New England. Upon the assumption of fraud, based upon these charges alone, the treaty was set aside by the action of the President and Cabinet alone; and by the same authority a new one made, with a change of boundary, involving a loss of a portion of territory belonging to Georgia under the stipulations of the contract between the State and United States. The previous or first treaty had been submitted to the United States Senate, and duly ratified, thereby becoming a law, under which Georgia claimed vested rights.

It was under these trying circumstances that the stern and determined character of Troup displayed itself. Holding firmly to the doctrine of State rights, he notified the President that he should disregard the latter treaty, and proceed to take possession of the territory under the stipulations of the former one. Upon the receipt of this information, General Gaines was ordered to Georgia to take command of the troops stationed along the frontier of the State, and any additional troops which might be ordered to this point, with orders to protect the Indians, and prohibit taking possession of the territory, as contemplated by Governor Troup. A correspondence ensued between General Gaines and Governor Troup of a most angry character. It terminated with an order to General Gaines to forbear all further communication with the Government of Georgia. This was notified to the President, (if my memory is correct, for I write from memory,) in these terms:

"JOHN QUINCY ADAMS, President of the United States:

"SIR: I have ordered General Gaines to forbear all further communication with this Government. Should he presume to infringe this order, I will send your major-general by brevet home to you in irons. GEORGE M. TROUP, Governor of Georgia."

The surveyors previously appointed by the Legislature were

directed to be on the ground, in defiance of United States authority, on the first day of September succeeding, and at sunrise to commence the work of surveying the lands. A collision was anticipated as certain between the troops of the United States and the authorities of Georgia. But there was a difficulty in the way not previously contemplated. Colonels John S. McIntosh, David Emanuel Twiggs, and Duncan Clinch, each commanded regiments in the South. Twiggs and McIntosh were native Georgians. Clinch was a North Carolinian, but was a resident of Florida. Zachary Taylor was the lieutenant-colonel of Clinch's regiment. He was a Virginian by birth, but resided in Mississippi. All were Southern men in feeling, as well as by birth, and all Jeffersonian Republicans, politically. McIntosh and Twiggs were fanatical in their devotion to the State of their birth. The ancestors of both were among the first settlers, and both were identified with her history. The three wrote a joint letter to the President, tendering their commissions, if ordered to take arms against Georgia. This letter was placed in the hands of one who was influential with Mr. Adams, to be delivered immediately after the order should be issued to General Gaines to prevent by force of arms the survey ordered by Governor Troup. Troup had classified the militia, and signified his intention to carry out, if necessary, the first-negotiated treaty, by force of arms, as the law of the land.

It was, unquestionably, the prudence of this friend which prevented a collision. He communicated with Mr. Adams confidentially, and implored him not to issue the order. He assured him that a collision was inevitable if he did, and caused him to pause and consult his advisers, who declared their conviction that the first treaty was the law of the land, and that Georgia held vested rights under it. In obedience to this advice, Mr. Adams made no further effort to prevent the action of Georgia, and the lands were surveyed and disposed of by the State, under and according to the terms of the first treaty, and she retains a large strip of territory that would have been lost to her under the last treaty. My information of these facts was derived from Twiggs, Clinch, and Henry Clay. Who the friend was to whom the letter was intrusted, I never knew. I mentioned to Mr. Clay the facts, and he stated that they were true, but no knowledge of them ever came to him until the expiration of Mr. Adams' Administration. General Taylor stated to me that long after these events had transpired, and after the resignation of Colonel

Clinch, General Twiggs had made the communication to him. As nearly as I can remember, Twiggs made the statement to me in the language I have used here. On returning from the ratification meeting, at Canton, of the nomination of Mr. Clay for the Presidency, in 1844, before we reached Baltimore, I was in a carriage with General Clinch and Senator Barrow, of Louisiana, and stated these facts, and Clinch verified them.

General Gaines was, of all men, the most unfit for a position like that in which he was placed. He was a good fighter, a chivalrous, brave man; but he was weak and vain, and without tact or discretion. His intentions were, at all times, pure, but want of judgment frequently placed him in unpleasant positions. The condition of the minds of the people of Georgia, at this time, was such, that very little was necessary to excite them to acts of open strife, and had Mr. Adams been less considerate than he was, there is now no telling what would have been the consequence. He was extremely unpopular at the South, and this, added to the inflamed condition of public opinion there, would assuredly have brought on a collision. Had it come, it might have resulted in a triumph of Southern principles, which, at a later day, and under less auspicious circumstances, struggled for existence, only to be crushed perhaps forever.

It was universally the wish of the people of Georgia to have possession of the land properly belonging to her, and but for their factious divisions, the hazards of a conflict between the troops of the United States and those of Georgia would have been more imminent. It was believed by both these factions, that whoever should, as Governor of the State, succeed in obtaining these lands, would thereby be rendered eminently popular, and secure to his faction the ascendency in the State for all time. The faction supporting Clarke believed he would certainly triumph in the coming contest before the people, and assumed to believe that then the matter of acquisition would be easy, as the Administration of Mr. Adams supposed that faction could, by that means, be brought into the support of the party now being formed about it. Clarke and many of his leading friends were coquetting with the Administration. He was — as was his brother-in-law, Duncan G. Campbell — a strong friend of Mr. Calhoun, who was then the Vice-President. National parties were inchoate, and many politicians were chary of choosing, and seemed to wait for the development of coming events, ere they gave shape and direction to their future courses. It was certain that Mr. Clay was identified with the American System, and that would, in a great degree, be the leading policy of the Administration. Mr. Calhoun, when Secretary of War, under Mr. Monroe, had made a strong report in favor of internal improvements by the General Government, within the limits of the States, and, while a member of Congress, had made an equally strong one in favor of a national bank. These were two of the prominent features of the American system, and it was generally believed that this policy would be too popular to combat. It had originated during the Administration of Monroe, and if it had the opposition of any member of his Cabinet, it was unknown to the country. Mr. Crawford and Mr. Calhoun, as well as Mr. Adams, were members of that Cabinet, and were all, in some degree, committed to this policy; for Mr. Crawford, as a Senator from Georgia, during the Administration of Mr. Madison, had sustained the doctrine of the constitutionality and the policy of a national bank, in one of the very ablest speeches ever made upon the subject, saying everything which could or can be said in favor of such a government financial agent, and refuting every objection of its opponents. From this speech is derived every argument and every idea of both the reports of Calhoun and McDuffie, which were heralded to the nation as greater even than that of Mr. Dallas, who, with Robert Morris, may be said to be the fathers of this institution. Mr. Clay had, in one of his ablest speeches, opposed the bank at a former time, and his change of opinion was now well known.

It was very well understood that the coming men were Clay, Jackson, and Calhoun. Clarke and his friends were ardent supporters of Calhoun, and it was thought they had won the favor of the Administration. Mr. Clay was strongly opposed to the execution of the old treaty, and had, by this means, drawn upon himself the opposition of the Crawford, or Troup party. These facts show the condition of public opinion in the State, and conclusively establish the fact, that but for this division of the people, and the check held by this upon the action of the masses and their leaders, fearful consequences would assuredly have ensued.

The reasons influencing the joint action of Mr. Adams and Mr. Clay in opposition to the execution of the old treaty were very different. Mr. Clay was honest and patriotic. He had no ulterior views to subserve. His policy was national. He desired the prosperity and advancement of his country to greatness and power among the nations of the earth. His fame was that of the nation; already it was identified with it. His ambition was a noble and a grand one. He wished his name identified with his acts, and these to constitute the fame and glory of the nation. He ever felt what subsequently he so nobly expressed, "That he would rather be right than be President." He had no petty selfishness—no pitiful revenges to exhaust with the hand of power—no contemptible motives for elevating or advancing the interests of one section of his country by oppressing another. "All his aims were his country's," and his whole country's. He desired that every act of that country should bear the broadest light, and challenge the closest and most searching scrutiny; that each should be a new and brighter gem in the diadem of her glory, and that her magnanimity should be most conspicuous in her transactions with the weakest. This he especially desired, and labored to effect, in all her transactions with the Indians. He viewed these as the primitive proprietors of the soil, and possessors of the entire country. He knew they were fading away before a civilization they were by nature incapacitated to emulate, and this, he felt, was in obedience to the inexorable laws of Divine Providence; and, in the wonderfully capacious compassion of his nature, he desired, in the accomplishment of this fate, that no act of national injustice to them should stain the nation's escutcheon, and determined to signalize this desire in every act of his when giving form and shape to national policy. He had generously lent a listening ear to the protests of the chiefs, seconded by that of their agent, and sincerely believed the treaty had been effected by fraud, and was wrong and oppressive, and, therefore, he opposed its execution, and was the main instrument in forming a new one. The draft of this was from his own pen, and he was solicitous that it should supersede the old one, as an expression of the Indians' desire.

Mr. Adams was, equally with Mr. Clay, opposed to the treaty as ratified, though, as was his constitutional duty, he had sent the instrument for the action of the Senate. In heart he was opposed to any treaty which would remove the aborigines from this territory at this time, and, in consequence of the action of Georgia, it was anticipated that, at no very distant day, the entire Indian population east of the Mississippi River, in the South, would be removed, unless some policy of the Government should be adopted which would prevent it; and those of the North, who felt desirous of crippling the territorial progress of the South, and, of consequence, her augmentation of population, supposed the most effectual means of accomplishing this would be to educate and Christianize the Indian. To do this, they insisted he must remain upon the territory he now occupied. This would bring him into immediate contact with the civilized white, where he could be most readily approached by missionaries and schoolmasters, and be instructed by the force of example. At the same time, he was to remain under the sole protection of the United States Government, without any of the privileges of civil government to be exercised as a citizen of the United States or the State upon whose soil he was located. This was ennobled as the sentiment of Christian benevolence, while its real intention was to withhold the land from the occupancy of the people of Georgia, and in so much retard the growth and increase of the white population of the State. To carry out this scheme, missionary establishments sprang up among the Indians in every part of the South, but especially within the limits of the State of Georgia, filled with Northern fanatics, who employed themselves most actively in prejudicing the minds of the savages against the people who were their neighbors, and preparing them to refuse to treat for the sale of any of their territory.

It has ever been the practice of the Puritan to propagate the vilest heresies, and for the vilest purposes, under the name of philanthropy and religion. It has burned its enemy at the stake, as, assembled around, they sang psalms, and sanctified the vilest cruelties with the name of God's vengeance. It was their great prototype, Cotton Mather, who blasphemously proclaimed, after the most inhuman massacre of several hundred Indians, that they, the Puritans of Massachusetts, "had sent, as a savory scent to the nostrils of God, two hundred or more of the reeking souls of the godless heathen."

This, ostensibly, was deemed a pious act, and a discharge of a pious duty, when, in truth, the only motive was to take his home and country, and appropriate it to their own people. It seems almost impossible to the race to come squarely up to truth and honesty, in word or act, in any transaction, as a man or as a people. Sinister and subtle, expediency, and not principle, seems to be their universal rule of action. Cold and passionless, incapable of generous emotions, he is necessarily vindictive and cruel. Patient and persevering, bigoted and selfish, eschewing as a crime an honorable resentment, he creeps to his ends like a serpent, with all his cunning and all his venom.

John Quincy Adams, in his nature, was much more like his mother than his father. His features were those of his mother, and the cold, persevering hatred of his nature was hers. From his boyhood he was in the habit of recording, for future use, the most confidential conversations of his friends, as also all that incautiously fell from an occasional interview with those less intimate. Had this been done for future reference only to establish facts in his own mind, there could have been no objection to the act; but this was not the motive. These memoranda were to rise up in vengeance when necessary to gratify his spleen or vengeance. He was naturally suspicious. He gave no man his confidence, and won the friendship of no one. Malignant and unforgiving, he watched his opportunity, and never failed to gratify his revengeful nature, whenever his victim was in his power. The furtive wariness of his small gray eye, his pinched nose, receding forehead, and thin, compressed lips, indicated the malignant nature of his soul. Unfaithful to friends, and only constant in selfishness — unconscious of obligation, and ungrateful for favors — fanatical only in hatred — pretending to religious morality, yet pursuing unceasingly, with merciless revenge, those whom he supposed to be his enemies, he combined all the elements of Puritan bigotry and Puritan hate in devilish intensity. He deserted the Federal party in their greatest need, and meanly betrayed them to Mr. Jefferson, whom, from his boyhood, he had hated and reviled in doggerel rhymes and the bitterest prose his genius could suggest.

The conduct of Mr. Adams, after he had been President, as the representative of Massachusetts in Congress, is the best evidence of the motives which influenced his conduct in the matter of these two treaties. He never lost an opportunity to assail the interests and the institutions of the South. He hated her, and to him, more than to any other, is due the conduct of the Northern people toward the South which precipitated the late war, and has destroyed the harmony once existing between the people.

His father had been repudiated by the South for a more trusted son of her own. This was a treasured hatred; and when he shared his father's fate, this became the pervading essence of his nature.

He returned to Congress, after his defeat for the Presidency, for no other purpose than to give shape and direction to a sentiment which he felt must ultimately result in her ruin, and to accomplish this he was more than willing to hazard that of the Government. He felt, should this follow, his own people would be in a condition to dictate and control a government of their own creation, and which should embody their peculiar views, rather than the pure and unselfish principles enunciated in the Declaration of Independence, and preserved in the Constitution of the United States.

The sagacity of George M. Troup was the first to discover this in his conduct as President, and to sound the alarm as Governor of Georgia. He came directly in contact with him, and determined he should be defeated in one of his means for injury to the South. Troup knew and felt the right was with him, and maintained it with the honest boldness of a true man. He triumphed, and the doctrine of State rights was rescued from a fatally aimed blow, and reaffirmed, gave renewed popularity and strength to its supporters. The election of General Jackson soon after followed, and, as the embodiment of the principle, rallied around him its supporters from every section. With these, and his immense popularity personally, he scotched, for a time, the Puritan snake; but, true to its instincts, it struggled to bite, though its head was off.

Mr. Adams saw in Troup a strong and uncompromising foe; he knew, too, the right was with him, and that if pushed to extremities the result would be damaging to his fame, as having, in persevering for the wrong, destroyed the Government, and at a time, too, when every benefit from such destruction would inure to the South. Under the circumstances his course was taken: he dared not consult or trust Mr. Clay with the real motives which influenced him to yield, and made a virtue of patriotism and magnanimity which cloaked his pusillanimity, and shielded from public view his envenomed chagrin.

It was doubtless this triumph which secured the second election of Troup. Personally he was unpopular with the masses. His rearing had been in polished society, and though he was in principle a democrat, in his feelings, bearing, and associations he was an aristocrat. He accorded equality to all under the law and in political privilege, but he chose to select his associates, and admitted none to the familiarity of intimacy but men of high breeding and unquestioned honor. In many things he was peculiar and somewhat eccentric. In dress, especially so — often appearing in midwinter in light, summer apparel; and again, in summer, with a winter cloak wrapped carefully about him. When he appeared first before the assembled Legislature, and many of the first citizens of the State, to take the oath of office, it was a raw, cold day in November: his dress was a round jacket of coarse cotton, black cassimere vest, yellow nankeen pantaloons, silk hose, and dancing-pumps, with a large-rimmed white hat, well worn. In his address, which was short and most beautiful, he made his hat conspicuous by holding it in his right hand, and waving it with every gesture. In person, he was below the middle size, slender, though finely formed; his hair was red, and his eyes intensely blue and deeply set beneath a heavy brow; his nose was prominent and aquiline; his mouth, the great feature of his face, was Grecian in mould, with flexible lips, which, while in repose, seemed to pout. His rabid opposition to those engaged in the Yazoo frauds, and his hatred for those who defended it, made him extremely obnoxious to them, and prompted Dooly to say: "Nature had formed his mouth expressly to say, 'Yazoo.'" Its play, when speaking, was tremulous, with a nervous twitching, which gave an agitated intonation to his words very effective.

The form of his head, and especially his forehead, indicated an imaginative mind, while the lines of his face marked deep thought. He was strictly honest in everything; was opposed to anything which wore the appearance of courting public favor, or seemed like a desire for office. His private life was exemplary, kind, and indulgent to his children and servants, and full of charity; severe upon nothing but the assumptions of folly, and the wickedness of purpose in the dishonest heart. In every relation of life he discharged its duties conscientiously, and was the enemy only of the vicious and wicked. He continued to reside upon his plantation in Lawrence County with his slaves, carefully providing for their every want until his death. He had attained the patriarchal age of threescore years and ten, and sank to rest in the solitude of his forest-home, peacefully and piously, leaving no enemies, and all the people of his State to mourn him.

CHAPTER XI.

POLITICAL CHANGES.

Aspirants for Congress — A New Organization — Two Parties — A Protective Tariff — United States Bank — The American System — Internal Improvements — A Galaxy of Stars — A Spartan Mother's Advice — Negro-Dealer — Quarter Races — Cock-Pitting — Military Blunders on both Sides — Abner Green's Daughter — Andrew Jackson — Gwinn — Poindexter — Ad Interim — Generals as Civil Rulers.

THE remarkable excitement of the political contest between Troup and Clarke had the effect of stimulating the ambition of the young men of education throughout the State for political distinction. For some time anterior to this period, all seemed content to permit those who had been the active politicians in the Republican struggle with the Federal party to fill all the offices of distinction in the State without opposition. It would have been considered presumptuous in the extreme for any young man, whatever his abilities, to have offered himself as a candidate for Congress in opposition to Mr. Forsyth, R. H. Wild, Thomas W. Cobb, Edward F. Tatnal, and men of like age and political faith. The members of Congress were elected by general ticket; and the selection of candidates was not by a convention of the people or party. The names of candidates were generally recommended by influential parties, and their consent to become candidates obtained through solicitations addressed to them, and then published to the people. The State was so unanimous in political sentiment, that for many years no opposition to the Republican party was thought of.

But now parties were organizing upon principles, or rather policies, entirely new; there was a fusion of the old elements of party, and Federalists and Republicans were side by side in this new organization. Men who had been under the ban, for opinion's sake, were coming into public view and public favor, and disclosing great abilities. At the head of these was John McPherson Berrien, who, to the end of his life, was so distinguished in the councils of the nation. At the same time, in every part of the State, young men were rising up as men of promise for talent and usefulness. These men arrayed themselves with either of the two parties, as inclination or interest prompted. Active and assiduous, they were soon prominent before the people, and a new era was commencing. With the election of John Quincy Adams, the State was in a blaze and politics a furor. Opposition immediately commenced to the leading measures of the Administration, and the Legislature of 1825 was filled with young men of talent, who were enthusiastic and fierce in their sentiments and feelings. They had been divided as partisans of Troup and Clarke, and met as antagonists in the Legislature; but really without any defined policy in opposition to that of the administration of the General Government of the nation. A suspicion filled every one that this policy was disastrous to Southern interests, and sectional in its character, although designated as national.

Few men of the South had given much attention to the effect a tariff for revenue had upon the commercial and manufacturing interests of the North. The war with England had created a debt, and this tariff had been imposed solely for the purpose of securing, not only a sufficient revenue for the current necessities of the Government, but a surplus, which should in a short time liquidate the public debt. It was sufficient to afford protection to the manufacturing interests of the North, to increase this into a formidable revenue, and to enlist a national party in its support. It was now, when the public debt was liquidated, that another reason was necessary for continuing a policy which had grown up from the necessities of the nation — consequently it was assumed to be a national policy to promote national independence, and protection was claimed for national industry against European competition. This policy in the Government would encourage extravagance, waste, and corruption — such a bane to republics — because it would create an immense surplus in the national treasury, unless some scheme for its expenditure could be devised which should seem to promote the national interest. To this end, the party of the Administration claimed a constitutional power in Congress to carry on a system of internal improvements; and heavy appropriations were made for this purpose, not only absorbing the surplus revenue, but creating a necessity for more — and this necessity was an excuse for increasing the tariff.

The Bank of the United States was the depository of the moneys of the nation and her disbursing agent. The constitutionality of this institution had been a mooted question from the day it was first proposed by Robert Morris. Mr. Madison, who was a Republican, had at one time vetoed it; at another, approved it. Mr. Crawford, a most inveterate States-rights man and strict constructionist of the Constitution, had uniformly supported it. Mr. Clay had both supported and opposed it. The question was finally adjudicated by the Supreme Court, and, so far as that decision could make it, was decided to be constitutional. This, however, did not satisfy the Republican or States-rights party; a large majority of whom always insisted upon its unconstitutionality. At the time of its creation, a necessity existed for some such institution, to aid the Government in its financial operations, and at the time of the renewal of its charter the Government had just emerged from a war; every State was creating banks, and the country was flooded with an irredeemable and worthless currency, disturbing commerce, unsettling values, and embarrassing the Government. A power was wanted somewhere to control these State banks, and to give a redeemable and uniform currency to the country.

The State banks had proved destructive to the public interest; with no power to restrain their issues except that imposed by their charters and the honesty of their officers — a frail security for the public, as experience had attested. The example of Washington was pleaded by the advocates of the bank. At the very outset it had been opposed for want of constitutionality. Washington had doubted it, and submitted the question to two of his Cabinet — Mr. Jefferson and Mr. Hamilton. They were divided in opinion — Mr. Jefferson opposing, and Mr. Hamilton sustaining the constitutionality of the measure. The opinion and argument of Hamilton prevailed, and the act creating a bank received the Executive approval.

It answered admirably the object of its creation, and the Republican party (then in embryo) acquiesced. Indeed, at this time, there could scarcely be said to be a party separate from the Government. Mr. Hamilton and Mr. Jefferson were the leaders of the parties which divided the people upon the adoption of the Constitution, and these parties, though at this time inchoate, were concreting about these two wonderful men. Upon the renewal of the charter of the United States Bank, during the Administration of Mr. Madison, the Republican party again mooted its constitutionality; but its undisputed usefulness had won for it immense popularity, and there were many who, though acting with the Republicans, were willing (as Washington had approved it, and the Supreme Court had pronounced it constitutional) to view the question as settled, and vote to renew the charter.

It was subsequent to the veto of Mr. Madison (when he had reconsidered his action, and recommended the re-chartering of the bank,) that debates ensued, in which the question was exhausted. In these debates, Mr. Crawford, Mr. Clay, Felix Grundy, William B. Giles, and Mr. Calhoun led. They were continued through several sessions, up to 1816, when they ultimated in the chartering of the last bank of the United States. This charter expired during the Administration of General Jackson, and by him the bank was finally crushed.

Three great measures constituted what was then termed the American System — the United States Bank, a protective tariff, and internal improvements within the States by the General Government. An opposition to this party was formed at the very outset of the Adams Administration. This opposition denied the constitutional power of Congress to create or sustain either.

The South, at the commencement of this opposition, was almost alone. The North was a unit in its support of the Administration, because its policy was vital to her interests. The West, influenced by Mr. Clay, was greatly in the majority in its support. The Southern opposition seemed almost hopeless; and to this cause may, in a great degree, be ascribed the bringing forth to public view the transcendent abilities of the young men aspiring for fame in Georgia, and in the South generally. McDuffie, Hamilton, Holmes, and Waddy Thompson, of South Carolina; Colquett, Cobb, Toombs, Stephens, Johnson, Nesbit, and John P. King, of Georgia; Wise, Bocock, Hunter, Summers, Rives, and others of Virginia; Mangum, Badger, and Graham, of North Carolina; Bell, Foster, Peyton, Nicholson, and James K. Polk, of Tennessee; King and Lewis, of Alabama; Porter, Johnston, White, and Barrow, of Louisiana; Ashley, Johnson, and Sevier, of Arkansas; Chase, Pugh, Pendleton, and Lytell, of Ohio; and Douglas, Trumbull, and Lincoln, of Illinois, were all men of sterling talent, and were about equally divided in political sentiment. Kentucky had Tom and Humphrey Marshall, Crittenden, Menifer, Letcher, Breckinridge, and Preston.

General Jackson was now the avowed candidate of the States-rights party, which soon after assumed the name of Democratic, and his political principles and great personal popularity were not only dividing the West, but the Middle States, and even those of New England.

During the entire administration of Adams, there was a majority in Congress supporting his policy. It was then and there that the great battle for supremacy was fought. Berrien and Forsyth, from Georgia, in the Senate; McDuffie and Preston, from South Carolina; Cass, from Michigan, and Van Buren and Silas Wright, from New York — all giants in intellect. But there were Webster and John Davis, from Massachusetts, George Evans, from Maine, and others of minor powers, but yet great men. Between these great minds the conflict was stupendous. Every means were put into requisition to sustain the Administration and its policy, but all were unavailing — General Jackson was elected by an overwhelming majority. Mr. Clay was immediately returned by Kentucky to the Senate, and organized an opposition upon the policy of the late Administration, led on by himself and Webster. The memory of those days, and the men who made them memorable, flits vividly before me; but I am not writing a history, and can attempt no order, but shall write on as these memories of men and events shall seem to me most interesting in their character to the general reader.

General Jackson was one of those rare creations of nature which appear at long intervals, to astonish and delight mankind. It seems to be settled in the public mind that he was born in South Carolina; but there is no certainty of the fact. His early life was very obscure, and he himself was uncertain of his birth-place, though he believed it was South Carolina. He remembered the removal of his family from South Carolina, and many of the incidents of the war of the Revolution transpiring there; but more especially those occurring in North Carolina, to which the family removed. Judge Alexander Porter, of Louisiana, was an Irishman, and from the neighborhood where were born and reared the parents of Jackson. His own father was brutally executed at Vinegar Hill, by sentence of a drum-head court martial, in 1798, and his family proscribed by the British Government. With his uncle, the Rowans, the Jacksons, and some others, he emigrated to America, and settled at Nashville, Tennessee. The Jacksons were of the same family, and distantly connected with General Jackson. Great intimacy existed between this family and General Jackson for many years.

Judge Porter, of whom I shall hereafter have something to say, visited Europe a short time before his death, and made diligent search into the history of the Jackson family, without ascertaining anything positively: he learned enough to satisfy his own mind that Andrew Jackson was born in Ireland, and brought to the United States by his parents when only two years old. This was also the opinion of Thomas Crutcher, who came with General Jackson to Nashville, and it was also the opinion of Dr. Boyd McNary and his elder brother, Judge McNary, who believed he was four years older than he supposed himself to be.

The McNarys came with him from North Carolina. On the trip a difficulty occurred between Boyd McNary and Jackson, which never was reconciled — both dying in extreme old age. Boyd McNary stopped at Lexington and read medicine, forming there the acquaintance of Mr. Clay and Felix Grundy. The intimacy which sprang up between Clay and McNary was as ardent and imperishable as the hatred between himself and Jackson, enduring until death. Jackson was enterprising and eminently self-reliant; in all matters pertaining to himself, he was his own counsellor; he advised with no man; cool and quick in thought, he seemed to leap to conclusions, and never went back from them. An anecdote relative to his parting from his mother in his outset in life, illustrates this as prominent in the attributes of his nature at that time. The writer heard him narrate this after his return from Washington, when his last term in the Presidential office had expired.

When about to emigrate to Tennessee, the family were residing in the neighborhood of Greensboro', North Carolina.

"I had," said he, "contemplated this step for some months, and had made my arrangements to do so, and at length had obtained my mother's consent to it. All my worldly goods were a few dollars in my purse, some clothes in my saddle-bags, a pretty good horse, saddle, and bridle. The country to which I was going was comparatively a wilderness, and the trip a long one, beset by many difficulties, especially from the Indians. I felt, and so did my mother, that we were parting forever. I knew she would not recall her promise; there was too much spunk in her for that, and this caused me to linger a day or two longer than I had intended.

"But the time came for the painful parting. My mother was a little, dumpy, red-headed Irish woman. 'Well, mother, I am ready to leave, and I must say farewell.' She took my hand, and pressing it, said, 'Farewell,' and her emotion choked her.

"Kissing at meetings and partings in that day was not so common as now. I turned from her and walked rapidly to my horse.

"As I was mounting him, she came out of the cabin wiping her eyes with her apron, and came to the getting-over place at the fence. 'Andy,' said she, (she always called me Andy,) 'you are going to a new country, and among a rough people; you will have to depend on yourself and cut your own way through the world. I have nothing to give you but a mother's advice. Never tell a lie, nor take what is not your own, nor sue anybody for slander or assault and battery. *Always settle them cases yourself!*' I promised, and I have tried to keep that promise. I rode off some two hundred yards, to a turn in the path, and looked back — she was still standing at the fence and wiping her eyes. I never saw her after that." Those who knew him best will testify to his fidelity to this last promise made his mother.

The strong common sense and unbending will of Jackson soon made him conspicuous in his new home, and very soon he was in active practice as a lawyer. His prominence was such, that during the last year of the last term of General Washington's Administration, a vacancy occurring in the United States Senate from Tennessee, General Jackson was appointed to fill it. He was occupying this seat when General Washington retired from the Presidency, and, with William B. Giles, of Virginia, voted against a resolution of thanks tendered by Congress to Washington, for his services to the country. For this vote he gave no reason at the time; and if he ever did, it has escaped my knowledge.

The career of General Jackson, as a public man, is so well known, that it is not my purpose to review it in this place; but many incidents of his private history have come to my knowledge from an association with those who were intimate with him, from his first arrival in Tennessee. These, or so many of them as I deem of interest enough to the public, I propose to relate.

Jackson was a restless and enterprising man, embarking in many schemes for the accumulation of fortune, not usually resorted to by professional men, or men engaged in public matters. In business he was cautious. He was a remarkable judge of human character, and rarely gave his confidence to untried men. Notwithstanding the impetuosity of his nature, upon occasion he could be as cool and as calculating as a Yankee. The result was, that though he had many partners in the various pursuits he at different times resorted to, he rarely had any pecuniary difficulty with any of them. He was in the habit of trading with the low country, that is, with the inhabitants of Mississippi and Louisiana.

Many will remember the charge brought against him pending his candidacy for the Presidency, of having been, in early life, a negro-trader, or dealer in slaves. This charge was strictly true, though abundantly disproved by the oaths of some, and even by the certificate of his principal partner. Jackson had a small store, or trading establishment, at Bruinsburgh, near the mouth of the Bayou Pierre, in Claiborne County, Mississippi. It was at this point he received the negroes, purchased by his partner at Nashville, and sold them to the planters of the neighborhood. Sometimes, when the price was better, or the sales were quicker, he carried them to Louisiana. This, however, he soon declined; because, under the laws of Louisiana, he was obliged to guarantee the health and character of the slave he sold.

On one occasion he sold an unsound negro to a planter in the parish of West Feliciana, and, upon his guarantee, was sued and held to bail to answer. In this case he was compelled to refund the purchase-money, with damages. He went back upon his partner, and compelled him to share the loss. This caused a breach between them, which was never healed. This is the only instance which ever came to my knowledge of strife with a partner. He was close to his interest, and spared no means to protect it.

It was during the period of his commercial enterprise in Mississippi that he formed the acquaintance of the Green family. This family was among the very first Americans who settled in the State. Thomas M. Green and Abner Green were young men at the time, though both were men of family. To both of them Jackson, at different times, sold negroes, and the writer now has bills of sale for negroes sold to Abner Green, in the handwriting of Jackson, bearing his signature, written, as it always was, in large and bold characters, extending quite half across the sheet. At this store, which stood immediately upon the bank of the Mississippi, there was a race-track, for quarter-races, (a sport Jackson was then then very fond of,) and many an anecdote was rife, forty years ago, in the neighborhood, of the skill of the old hero in pitting a cock or turning a quarter-horse.

This spot has become classic ground. It was here Aaron Burr was first arrested by Cowles Mead, then acting as Governor of the Territory of Mississippi, and from whom he made his escape, and it was at this point that Grant crossed his army when advancing against Vicksburg. It is a beautiful plateau of land, of some two thousand acres, immediately below the mouth of the Bayou Pierre, and bordered by very high and abrupt cliffs, which belong to the same range of hills that approach the river's margin at Vicksburg, Grand Gulf, Rodney, Natchez, and Bayou Sara. At this point they attain the height of three hundred feet, and are almost perpendicular. The summit is attained by a circuitous road cut through the cliffs, and this is the summit level of the surrounding country.

This plateau of land, where once stood the little village of Bruinsburgh, has long been a cotton plantation, and a most valuable one it was before the late war. A deep, and, to an army, impassable swamp borders it below, and the same is the case above the Bayou Pierre. To land an army at such a place, when its only means of marching upon the country was through this narrow cut, of about one hundred feet in width, with high, precipitous sides, forming a complete defile for half a mile, and where five thousand men could have made its defence good against fifty thousand, is certainly as little evidence of military genius as was the permission of them to pass through it without an effort to prevent it.

To a military eye, the blunders of Grant and Pemberton are apparent in their every movement—and the history of the siege and capture of Vicksburg, if ever correctly written, will demonstrate to the world that folly opposed to folly marked its inception, progress, and finality.

The friends formed in this section of country by Jackson were devoted to him through life, and when in after life he sent (for it is not true that he brought) his future wife to Mississippi, it was to the house of Thomas M. Green, then residing near the mouth of Cowles Creek, and only a few miles from Bruinsburgh.

Whatever the circumstances of the separation, or the cause for it, between Mrs. Jackson and her first husband, I am ignorant; I know that Jackson was much censured in the neighborhood of his home. At the time of her coming to Green's, the civil authority was a disputed one; most of the people acknowledging the Spanish. A suit was instituted for a divorce, and awarded by a Spanish tribunal. There was probably little ceremony or strictness of legal proceeding in the matter, as all government and law was equivocal, and of but little force just at that time in the country. It was after this that Jackson came and married her, in the house of Thomas M. Green.

That there was anything disreputable attached to the lady's name is very improbable; for she was more than fifteen months in the house of Green, who was a man of wealth, and remarkable for his pride and fastidiousness in selecting his friends or acquaintances. He was the first Territorial representative of Mississippi in Congress —was at the head of society socially, and certainly would never have permitted a lady of equivocal character to the privileges of a guest in his house, or to the association of his daughters, then young. During the time she was awaiting this divorce, she was at times an inmate of the family of Abner Green, of Second Creek, where she was always gladly received, and he and his family were even more particular as to the character and position of those they admitted to their intimacy, if possible, than Thomas B. Green. This intimacy was increased by the marriage of two of the Green brothers to nieces of Mrs. Jackson.

In 1835, when Jackson was President, the writer, passing from Louisiana to New York with his family, spent some days at Washington. His lady was the youngest daughter of Abner Green; he was in company with a daughter of Henry Green and her husband; her mother was niece to Mrs. Jackson. We called to see the President, and when my lady was introduced to the General, he was informed she was the daughter of his old friend, Abner Green, of Second Creek. He did not speak, but held her hand for some moments, gazing intently into her face. His feelings overcame him, and clasping her to his bosom, he said, "I must kiss you, my child, for your sainted mother's sake;" then holding her from him, he looked again, "Oh! how like your mother you are—she was the friend of my poor Rachel, when she so much needed a friend—I loved her, and I love her memory;" and then, as if ashamed of his emotion, he continued: "You see, my child, though I am President through the kindness or folly of the people, I am but a weak, silly old man."

We spent the evening with him, and when in his private sitting-room his pipe was lighted and brought to him, he said: "Now, my child, let us talk about Mississippi and the old people." I have never in all my life seen more tenderness of manner, or more deep emotion shown, than this stern old man continually evinced when speaking of his wife and her friends.

The character of General Jackson is yet greatly misunderstood. This has been caused by the fact that his words and actions, when in command, or when enraged, as a man, have been the main data upon which the estimate of his bearing and character has been predicated. He was irascible and quick in his temper, and when angered was violent in words and manner. It was at such moments that the stern inflexibility of his will was manifest; and his passion towered in proportion to provocation. But in private life and social intercourse he was bland, gentle, and conciliating. His manner was most polished and lofty in society, and in a lady's parlor, in urbanity and polish of manners, he never had a superior. This high polish was nature's spontaneous gift. He had never been taught it in courts, or from association with those who had. It was the emanation of his great soul, which stole out through his every word and movement in the presence of ladies, and which erupted as a volcano at insult or indignity from man.

That evening at the White House is marked in my memory with a white stone. The playful simplicity of his conversation and manner, and the particularity of his inquiries about matters and things so insignificant, but which were links in the chain of his memories, I well remember.

"Is old papa Jack and Bellile living?" he asked, after a pause, of my wife, accompanied with a look of eager anxiety.

These were two old Africans, faithful servants of her father; and then there was an anecdote of each of them — their remarks or their conduct upon some hunting or fishing excursion, in which he had participated forty years before.

I was an interested spectator in the presence of one of nature's wonderful creations — one who had made, and who was making, history for his country, and whose name was to descend to future times as one of her noblest sons and greatest historical characters. I watched every motion of his lips, every expression of his features, and every gleam of his great gray eyes, and I could but wonder at the child-like naturalness of everything about him. Is not this an attribute of greatness — to be natural? Yes; to be natural in all things belongs to truth, and a truthful exhibition of nature, without assumption or deceit, is greatness. Here was one who could, with natural simplicity, amuse a child; and the same one could command and successfully wield a great army, and, with equal success, direct the destinies of a great nation; whose genius was tempered with simplicity and tenderness, and when towering most in its grandeur, was most truthful to nature.

General Jackson's early opportunities were extremely limited. His education was so very defective, that his orthography was almost ludicrous, and his general reading amounted to almost nothing. At no time was he a respectable county-court lawyer, so far as legal learning was concerned, and it is wonderful how the natural vigor of his mind supplied this defect. On the bench, his greatest aim was to get at the facts in every case, and to decide all points upon the broad principles of equity; and in all his charges to the jury, his principal aim was to direct their attention to the simple justice of the case, and a favorite phrase of his in these charges was: "Do right between the parties, and you will serve the objects of the law."

He was an enemy to all unnecessary forms in all matters. His manner was to go directly to the kernel, and he was very indifferent as to how the shell was cracked, or the husk removed. He never seemed to reason. Upon the presentation of any subject to his mind, it seemed, with electrical velocity, to cut through to a conclusion as if by intuition. He was correct in his conclusions more frequently than any man of his age. His knowledge of human nature was more consummate than that of any of his compeers who were remarkable for greatness of mind. In this, as in all other matters, his opinion was formed with the first glance. His intimacy with every sort of character, in his extended intercourse with the world, seemed so to have educated his faculties and whetted his perception, that he only wanted to look at a man for five minutes to know his inmost nature. Yet he was sometimes deceived, and, ascertaining this, nothing enraged him more.

In his friendships he was almost fanatical. The humblest individual, who was his friend, and who had proven it, could command him in any manner, and to the full extent of his capacity to serve him.

A remarkable instance of this trait was manifested in his conduct as President, toward a young friend, Mr. Gwinn, who was reared in the neighborhood of the Hermitage, and whose father had long been a trusted friend of Jackson. In 1832, when the lands obtained from the Choctaws in Mississippi were being brought into market, the office of register in the land-office in that State was an important one. It was given to Gwinn by Jackson, who was then President.

When the nomination was sent to the Senate, opposition was made to its confirmation by George Poindexter, a senator from Mississippi. It had always been the practice of all preceding Presidents, when suitable persons could be had, to nominate them from the State in which the United States office to be filled was located. Poindexter insisted that this custom, from long usage, had become law; and to send a citizen from one State into another, there to fill a national office, was an indignity to her citizens, and a manifestation, to say the least of it, of distrust and suspicion as to the capacity or honesty of the people of the State. This opposition was successful, and Gwinn was rejected. The nomination was renewed, and again rejected. Jackson wrote to Gwinn, who was already by executive appointment discharging the duties of the office, to continue to do so. I was present when the letter was received, and permitted to read it. "Poindexter has deserted me," he said, "and his opposition to your nomination is to render, as far as he can, my Administration unpopular with the people of Mississippi; and a majority of the Senate are more than willing to aid him in this. They are only destroying themselves, not me, and some of them will soon find this out. Do you hold on to the office; I will make no more nominations; but commission you *ad interim* as soon as Congress adjourns, which will be in a few weeks at farthest. Very soon my friends will be in a majority in the Senate — until then, I will keep you in the office, for I am determined you shall have it, spite of Poindexter." The result was as he had promised.

This is but one of a thousand instances which might be enumerated to attest the same fact. Such traits are always appreciated as they deserve to be; they address themselves to the commonest understanding, and are esteemed by all mankind. It is a mistake the world makes, that Jackson's popularity was exclusively military. Those great qualities of mind and soul which constituted him a great general, were not only displayed in his military career, but in all his life; and to them he was indebted for the friends of his whole life;

they made him a man of mark before he was twenty-five years of age. His courage, intrepidity, frankness, honor, truth, and sincerity were all pre-eminent in his conduct, and carried captive the admiration of all men. His devotion to his wife, to his friends, to his duty, was always conspicuous; and these are admired and honored, even by him who never had in his heart a feeling in common with one of these. All these traits were so striking in Jackson's character as to make them conspicuous. They were more marked in his than in that of any other man of his day, because the impulses of his temperament were more prompt and potent. They were natural to him, and always naturally displayed. There was neither assumption of feeling nor deceit in its manifestation; all he evinced, bubbled up from his heart, naturally and purely as spring-water, and went directly to the heart. These great and ennobling traits were not unfrequently marred by passion, and acts which threw a cloud over their brilliancy; but this, too, was natural: the same soul which was parent to this violence and extravagance of passion, was, too, the source of all his virtues, and all were equally in excess. The consequence of this violence were sometimes terrible. They were evanescent, and, like a thunder-storm, seemed only to clear the atmosphere for the display of beautiful weather.

The triumphs of mind, unaided by education, sometimes are astonishing,—in the case of General Jackson, perhaps, not more so than in many others. The great Warwick of England, the putter-up and the puller-down of kings, did not know his letters; Marshal Soult, the greatest of Napoleon's marshals, could not write a correct sentence in French; and Stevenson, the greatest engineer the world ever saw — the inventor of the locomotive engine—did not know his letters at twenty-one years of age, and was always illiterate. It is a question whether such minds would have been greatly aided by education, or whether they might not have been greatly injured by it — nature seeming to have formed all minds with particular proclivities. These are more marked in the stronger intellects. They direct to the pursuit in life for which nature has designed the individual: should this idiosyncrasy receive the proper education from infancy, doubtless it would be aided to the more rapid and more certain accomplishment of the designs of nature. To discover this in the child, requires that it should be strongly developed, and a close and intelligent observation on the part of the parent or guardian who may have the direction of the child's education. But this, in the system of education almost universally pursued, is never thought of; and the avocation of the future man is chosen for him, without any regard to his aptitudes for it, and often in disregard of those manifested for another. Consequently, nature is thwarted by ignorance, and the individual drags on unsuccessfully in a hated pursuit through life. Left alone, these proclivities become a passion, and where strongly marked, and aided by strength of will, they work out in wonderful perfection the designs of nature. Julius Cæsar, Hannibal, Attila, Yengis Khan, Prince Eugène, Marlborough, Napoleon, and Wellington were all generals by nature — and so were Andrew Jackson and "Stonewall" Jackson. The peculiarities of talent which make a great general make a great statesman; and all of those who, after distinguishing themselves as great generals, were called to the administration of the civil affairs of their respective Governments, have equally distinguished themselves as civilians.

The proposing of General Jackson as a candidate for the Presidency was received, by most of those who were deemed statesmen, as a burlesque; and many of those most active in his support only desired his election to further their own views, and not for the country's benefit. It was supposed he was so entirely unacquainted with state-craft, that he would be a pliant tool — an automaton, to dance to their wire-pulling. How little they understood him, and how well he understood them! At once he let them know he was President, and was determined to take the responsibility of administering the Government in the true spirit of its institutions. The alarm, which pervaded all political circles so soon as this was understood, is remembered well. It was a bomb exploded under the mess-table, scattering the mess and breaking to fragments all their cunningly devised machinations for rule and preferment — an open declaration of war against all cliques and all dictation. His inaugural was startling, and his first message explicit. His policy was avowed, and though it gathered about him a storm, he nobly breasted it, and rode it out triumphantly. His administration closed in a blaze of glory. He retired the most popular and most powerful man the nation had ever seen.

CHAPTER XII.

GOSSIP.

UNREQUITED LOVE — POPPING THE QUESTION — PRACTICAL JOKING — SATAN LET LOOSE — RHEA, BUT NOT RHEA — TEACHINGS OF NATURE — H. S. SMITH.

THIS must be a gossiping chapter, of many persons and many things, running through many years.

I love to dwell upon the years of youth. They are the sweetest in life; and these memories constitute most of the happiness of declining life. Incidents in our pilgrimage awaken the almost forgotten, and then how many, many memories flit through the mind, and what a melancholy pleasure fills the soul! We think, and think on, calling this and that memory up from the grave of forgetfulness, until all the past seems present, and we live over the bliss of boyhood with a mimic ecstasy of young life and its gladdening joys.

Like every young man, I suppose, I loved a fair girl with beautiful blue eyes, and lips so pouting and plump, so ruddy and liquid, that the words seemed sweetened as they melted away from them; but my love was unpropitious, and another was preferred to me. I have ever been curious to know why. Vanity always in my own soul made me greatly the superior of the favored one, in all particulars. But she did not think so, and chose as she liked. I saw her but once a bride. I went away, and found, as others do, another and dearer love. Sitting on my horse by her side, as she held in her beautiful palfrey, upon the summit of a cliff, which rises grandly above, and brows the drab waters of the great Mississippi, she pointed to the river, which resembled a great, white serpent, winding among green fields and noble forests, for twenty miles below. Her eyes were gray, and large, and lovely; her form was towering, and her mien commanding. She grew with the scene. She was born only a mile away, in the midst of a wild forest of walnut and magnolia, amid towering hills, and cherished them and this mighty river in childhood, until she partook of their grandeur and greatness. I thought she was like the love of my youth, and I loved her, and told her of it. The sun was waning — going down to rest, and, like a mighty monarch, was folding himself away to sleep in gorgeous robes of crimson and gold. In his shaded light, outstretching for fifty miles beyond the river, lay, in sombre silence, the mighty swamp, with its wonderful trees of cypress, clothed in moss of gray, long, and festooning from their summits to the earth below, and waving, like banners, in the passing wind. The towering magnolia, in all the pride of foliage and flower, shaded us. The river, in silent and dignified majesty, moved onward far below, and evening breezes bathed, with their delicious touch, our glowing cheeks. The scene was grand, and my feelings were intense. In the midst of all this beauty and grandeur, she was the cynosure of eye and heart. I loved her; and yet, my conscience rebuked me for forgetting my first love, and I asked myself if, in all this wild delirium of soul, there was not some little ingredient of revenge. No, it was for herself — all for herself; and, chokingly, I told her of it, when she drooped her head, and, in silence, gave me her hand. We went away in silence. There was too much of feeling to admit of speech. Delicious memory! Of all our ten children, four only remain: The willow's tears bedew her grave, and her sons fill the soldier's grave, and, wrapped in the gray, sleep well.

Yesterday I met her who first kindled in my bosom affection for woman — a widowed woman, withered and old. She smiled: the lingering trace of what it was, was all that was left. The little, plump hand was lean and bony, and wrinkles usurped the alabaster brow. Fifty years had made its mark. But memory was, by time, untouched. We parted. I closed my eyes, and there she was, in her girlhood's robes and her girlhood's beauty. The lip, the cheek, the glorious eye, were all in memory garnered still; and I loved that memory, but not the woman now. Another was in the niche she first cut in my heart, whose cheek and eye and pouting lip were young and lovely. Still these memories awoke out of this meeting, and, for hours, I forgot that I was wrinkled, old, and gray.

I wonder how many's history I am writing now? The history of the heart, at last, is all the endearing history of waning life. Recur as we may to every success, to every sorrow, and they whisper a chapter of the heart. We struggle to make happy those we love. The gratifications of wealth, ambition, and feeling, all refer to the heart. There could be no pleasure from these memories if those we loved had not participated in them. We build a home for her we love, and those who sprout around us. We win wealth and a name for these, and but for them, all that is innate would be only alloy. They must reflect the bliss it brings, or it has no sweetness. Can there be a soul so sordid as to riot in pleasure and triumphs all alone — to shun companionship, and hate participation in the joys that come of successful life?

I am in the midst of the scenes of my childhood, with here and there one friend left, who shared with me the school-hours, Saturday rambles, and sports of early boyhood. With these the memories come fresh and vigorous of the then occurring incidents — the fishings, the Saturday-night raccoon hunts, the forays upon orchards and melon-patches, and the rides to and from the old, country church on the Sabbath; the practical jokes of which I was so fond, and from which even my own father was not exempt. Kind reader, indulge the garrulity of age, and allow me to recount one of these. There are a few who will remember it; for they have laughed at it for fifty years. I never knew my father to tell a fib but upon one occasion in my life. Under the circumstances, I am sure the kindly nature will, at least, allow it to be a white one.

I am near the old mill my father built, and, if I remember all connected with my boyhood there, I trust there will be few or none to sneer or blame. The flouring-mill, or mill for grinding grain, and the saw-mill were united under the same roof; and it was the business of father to give his attention, as overseer, not only to the mills, but to his planting interest. He employed a North Carolina Scotchman — that is, a man descended of Scotch parents, but born in North Carolina — to superintend his saw-mill, who had all the industry, saving propensities, and superstitions of his ancestry. He was a firm believer in spells, second-sights, and ghosts. Taking advantage of these superstitions, my brother and myself made him the sufferer in many a practical joke. Upon one occasion, we put into circulation, in the neighborhood, a story full of wonder. A remarkable spectre had been seen near the mill on dark nights, and especially on those misty nights of murky gloom, common in early spring to this latitude. Its form was unique and exaggerated, with flaming eyes, and mouth of huge proportions, with long, pointed teeth, white and sharp. For weeks, this gorgon of my imagination constituted the theme of neighborhood gossip. Several negroes had seen it, and fled its fierce pursuit, barely escaping its voracious mouth and attenuated claws, through the fleetness of fear. The old hardshell Baptist preacher, of the vicinage, had proclaimed him from the pulpit as Satan unchained, and commencing his thousand years of wandering up and down the earth.

I had procured from a vine in the plum-orchard a gourd of huge dimensions, such as in that day were used by frugal housewives for the keeping of lard for family use. It would hold in its capacious cavity at least half a bushel. This was cut one-third of its circumference for a mouth, and this was garnished with teeth from the quills of a venerable gander, an especial pet of my mother. The eyes were in proportion, and were covered with patches of red flannel, purloined from my mother's scrap-basket. A circle, an inch in diameter, made of charcoal, formed an iris to a pupil, cut round and large, through the flannel. A candle was lighted, and introduced through a hole at the bottom of the gourd, and all mounted upon a pole some ten feet long. In the dark it was hideous, and, on one or two occasions, had served secretly to frighten some negroes, to give it reputation. It was designed for Rhea, the Carolinian. On Saturday night it was his uniform practice to come up to the house, cleanly clad, to spend the evening. There was a canal which conveyed the water from the head above to the mill. This ran parallel with the stream, and was crossed, on the public road, by a bridge, one portion of which was shaded by a large crab-apple bush. Though fifty years ago, it still remains to mark the spot. Beyond the creek (which was bridged, for foot-passengers, with the trunk of a large tree,) was a newly cleared field, in which the negroes were employed burning brush on the Saturday night chosen for my sport. Here, under this crab-tree, I awaited the coming of Rhea. It was misty, and densely dark. Presently the footsteps of my victim were heard approaching; he was on the bridge. He came on cautiously, to be secure of a safe footing in the dark. Suddenly I turned the grinning monster full in his face. A scream and a leap followed. Down the muddy creek-bank rushed my victim, plunged through the tumbling waters waist-deep, and, as soon as the opposite shore was reached, a vociferous call was made for Tom, the negro foreman. Horror of horrors! it was my father's voice. In an instant my candle was out, and I was running.

I passed unconcernedly through the house and took a seat in the back passage, and awaited events. It was not long before the sloppy noise of shoes full of water, heard in walking, came through the yard, and into the house. It was my dear old frightened father, all reeking from his plunge into the creek. "Why, husband," asked mother, "how did you get so wet?" He slung the damp from his hat as he cleared his throat, and said: "I slipped off that cursed log, in crossing the creek." Reflection had told him he had been foolishly frightened, and he was ashamed to acknowledge it. My conscience smote me, but I laughed, and trembled — for had he made discovery of the trick, it would have been my time to suffer.

Memory brings back the features, the kind and gentle look of that dear and indulgent parent, and the unbidden tear comes. The last time I ever saw him was at the terminus of the railroad, on the banks of Lake Pontchartrain; he placed his aged arms about my shoulders, and, pressing me to his bosom, bid me "Farewell," as, trembling with emotion, he continued: "we are parting forever, my child." He had met misfortunes in his latter days, and was poor, but I had filled his purse with the means which smoothed his way the remnant of his life. The prediction was but too true; in less than one year after that parting, he slept in death.

And now, when war and death have swept from me children, fortune, all, and I am old and needy, it is a consolation known only to my own bosom that I plucked the thorn from my parent's path.

These are childish memories, and may be too puerile for record; but I am sure most of my readers will find in them something of their own childhood's memories. It is my memories of men and things, I am writing, and I would be faithful to them.

Boyhood's memories crowd the after-life with half the joys its destiny demands; associations which revive them come as pleasant showers to the parched herbage when autumn's sun withers its flush, and yellows the green of spring-time. Oh! the zest of early sports — of boyhood's mischief; so free from selfishness, so untouched with meanness, so full of joyous excitement, so loved for itself. Every man has been a boy; every woman has been a girl; and all alike have felt and enjoyed the sweets of young life; and when years and cares and tears have stolen away the green from the soul, and the blossoms of the grave whiten about the brow, and the unbidden sigh breaks away from the grief of the heart, and memory startles with what was when we were young, the contrast would be full of misery did not a lingering of the joys which filled our frolics and our follies come to dull the edge of sorrow.

When the cravings of the mind, taught by time to be unrealizable, are driven from hope; when the purity of youthful feelings are soiled by contact with the world's baseness; when the world's passing interests harden the sensibilities, and we have almost forgotten that we were ever young, or had a youthful joy, some little story, some little incident will startle the memory, and touch and tone the heart to the music of its spring, and the desert waste which time has made green again with memories which grew from bliss budding in our youth; and, though they never come to fruitage, are cherished with a joy.

Oh! the heart, the heart—what are all its joys of youth, and all its griefs of age? Is it that youth has no apprehensions, and we enjoy its anticipations and its present without alloy? or does its *all* belong to love and joy when life and the world is new? Are these too bright, too pure for time? and the griefs of later life the Dead Sea apples which grow from them. And is it so with all? Is there one, whose years have brought increase of happiness, and who has lived on without a sorrow?

In God's economy must all experience misery, to dull the love of life, and kindle hope for a blissful future, to steal from the heart its cherished *here*, to yield it all in its *hereafter*. Ah! we know what a world this is, but what a world is to come we know not. Is it not as reasonable to believe we lived before our birth into this, as to hope we shall live after death in another world? Is this hope the instinct of the coming, or does it grow from the baser instinct of love for the miserable life we have? It is easy to ask, but who shall answer? Is it the mind which remembers, and is the mind the soul? or is the soul independent of the mind, surviving the mind's extinction? and do the memories of time die with time? or,

Do these pursue beyond the grave?
Must the surviving spirit have
Its memories of time and grief?
Then, surely, death is poor relief.
Shall it forget the all of time,
When time 's with all her uses gone,
And be a babe in that new clime?
Then death is but oblivion.

Youth's happiness is half of hope; all that of age is memory—

and yet these memories more frequently sadden than gladden the heart. Then what is life to age? Garrulity, and to be in the way. Our household gods grow weary of our worship, and the empty stool we have filled in gray and trembling age in the temple we have built, when we are gone is kicked away, and we are forgotten; our very children regret (though they sometimes assume a painful apprehension) we do not make haste to die — if we have that they crave, and inherit when we shall have passed to eternity. But if the gift of raiment and food is imposed by poverty on those who gave them birth, they complain, and not unfrequently turn from their door the aged, palsied parent, to die, or live on strangers' charity. Sad picture, but very true, very true; poor human nature! And man, so capable in his nature of this ungodliness, boasts himself made after God's own image. Vanity of vanities!

Nature's harmony, nature's loveliness, nature's expansive greatness and grandeur teaches of God, and godliness. The inanimate and unthinking are consistently harmonious and beautiful; man only mars the harmony, and makes a hell for man in time. Then, is time his all? or, shall this accursed rabidness be purged away with death, and he become a tone in accord with inanimate things? or, shall this but purify as fire the yielding metal, the inner man, which hope or instinct whispers lives, and animates its tenement of time, to view, to know, and to enjoy creation through eternity? Wild thoughts are kindling in my brain, wild feelings stir my heart.

This is a beautiful Sabbath morning, the blazing sun wades through the blue ether, and space seems redolent of purity and beauty. The breeze is as bland as the breath of a babe, coming through my casement with the light, and bathing my parched cheek; and the sere summer is warming away the gentle, genial spring. This is her last day; and to how many countless thousands is it the last day of life? Oh! could I die as gently, as beautifully as dies this budding season of the year, and could I know my budding hopes, like these buds of spring, would, in their summer, grow to fruit as these are growing, how welcome eternity! But I, as well, have my law, and must wait its fulfilment. It is the Sabbath wisely ordained to rest, and in its quiet and beauty obliviating care and sorrow. Would it were to the restless mind as to the weary limbs, and as to these, to this give ease and repose!

I have been dreaming, and my boyhood days revive with busy

memories. My gentle mother, ever tender and kind, seems busy before me; the old home, the old servants, as they were; the old school-house in the woods by the branch, and many a merry face laughing and beaming around; and my own old classmate, my solitary classmate, so loved, ah! so loved even unto this day. It was only yesterday I saw him, old and care-worn, yet in all the nobility of his soul, bearing with stern philosophy the miseries of misfortune inflicted by the red hand of merciless war, yielding with dignity and graceful resignation to the necessities imposed by unscrupulous power, conscious of no wrong, and sustained by that self-respect the result of constant and undeviating rectitude which has marked his long life. From childhood our hearts have been intertwined, and death only has the power to tear them apart. We sat together long hours, and talked of the past — alternately, as their memories floated up, asking each other, "Where is this one? and this?" and to each inquiry the sad monosyllable, "Dead!" was the reply, of all who were with us at school when we were boys. We alone are left!

In my strife with the world, I can never forget
The scenes of my childhood, and those who were there
When I was a child. I remember them yet;
Their features, their persons, to memory so dear,
Are present forever, and cling round my heart —
On the plains of the West, in the forest's deep wild,
On the blue, briny sea, in commerce's mart,
'Mid the throngs of gay cities with palaces piled.

The bottle of milk, and the basket of food,
Prepared by my mother, at dawning of day,
For my dinner at school; and path through the wood:
How well I remember that wood and that way,
The brook which ran through it, the bridge o'er the brook,
The dewberry-briers which grew by its side,
My slate, and my satchel, and blue spelling-book,
And little white pony father gave me to ride!

The spring by the hill, where our bottles were placed
To bathe in its waters, so clear and so cool,
Till dinner-time came! Oh! then how we raced
To get them, and dine in the shade by the pool!
The spring, and the pool, and the shade are still there,
But the dear old school-house has rotted and gone,
And all who were happy about it are — where?
Go — go to the church-yard, and ask the grave-stone!

A few there are left, old, tottering, and gray,
Apart and forgotten, as those who are dead;
Yet sometimes they meet on life's thorny way,
And talk, and live over the days that have fled.
Oh! how I remember those faces so bright,
Which beamed in their boyhood with honesty's ray!
And oft, when alone, in the stillness of night,
We're all at the school-house again, and at play!

Of all those who were there with me, the best loved was H. S. Smith, now of Mobile; and he, with perhaps one or two more, are all that are now living. Our ages are the same, within a week or two, I am sure; and we are of the same height and same weight; and our attachment was mutual: it has never been marred through three-score years and ten, and to-day we are, as brothers should be, without a secret hidden in the heart, the one from the other. As a friend, as a husband, as a father, as a man, I know none to rival H. S. Smith. He never aspired to political distinction: content to pursue, through life, the honorable and responsible business of a merchant, he has distinguished himself for energy, capacity, probity, and success; and in his advanced years enjoys the confidence and esteem of all honest men. Our years have been, since 1826, spent apart—communication, however, has never ceased between us, and the early friendship, so remarked by all who knew us, continues, and will until one is alone in life.

I know this narrative will not be interesting to those unacquainted with Smith and myself. To such I say, close the book, nor read on, but turn to that which may interest more, because more known. I could not pen the memories of fifty years, and forbear those the sweetest now, because their fruit to me has ever been the sweetest; and the noble virtues of the private gentleman cannot be the less appreciated because they have only adorned a circle where they shone in common with those around him. These are the men who preserve the public morals, and purify the atmosphere polluted by the corruptions of men prominent before the world for distinguished abilities, and equally distinguished immoralities. From these radiate that open-hearted honesty which permeates society, and teaches by example, and which so often rebukes the laxity of those who, from position, should be an example and an ornament. The purling stream murmuring its lowly song beneath the shading forest and modest shrubs may attract less attention than the turbid, roaring river, but is always purer, sweeter, more health-giving and lovely.

The romance of youth is the sugar of life, and its sweets to memory, as life recedes, augment as "distance lends enchantment to the view." We make no account of the evanescent troubles which come to us then but for a moment, and are immediately chased away with the thickening delights that gild young life and embalm it for the memories of age. The gravity of years delights to recount these; and few are indisposed to listen, for it is a sort of heart-history of every one, and in hearing or reading, memory awakes, and youth and its joys are back again, even to tottering, palsied age. Then, gentle reader, do not sneer at me: these are all I have left; my household gods are torn away, my boys sleep in bloody graves, my home is desolate, I am alone, with only one to comfort me — she who shares the smiles and tears which lighten and soothe the weary days of ebbing life.

CHAPTER XIII.

INFLUENCE OF CHILDHOOD.

First Impressions — Fortune — Mirabeau B. Lamar — Dr. Alonzo Church — Julius Cæsar — L. Q. C. Lamar — Texan Independence — Colquitt — Lumpkin — What a Great Man Can Do in One Day — Charles J. Jenkins.

THE memories of childhood cling, perhaps, more tenaciously than those of any after period of life. The attachments and antipathies then formed are more enduring. Our school-companions at our first school — the children of our immediate neighborhood, who first rolled with us upon the grass, and dabbled with us in the branch — we never forget. Time, absence, protracted separation, all fail to obliterate the features, the dispositions, or anything about them, which so unconsciously fastens upon the mind, and grows into the tender soul of childhood. These memories retain and bring back with them the feelings, the likes and dislikes, which grew with them. These feelings are the basis of lifetime loves, and eternal antipathies.

The boy is father to the man, as the girl is mother to the woman. Who that has lived seventy years will not attest this from his own life's experience? The generous, truthful boy will be the noble, honorable man; the modest, timid, truthful girl will be the gentle, kind, and upright woman. Nature plants the germ, and education but cultivates the tree. It never changes the fruit. The boy who, when dinner-time comes, happens to have a pie, when his fellows have none, and will open his basket before his companions, and divide with them, will carry the same trait to the grave. His hand will open to assist the needy, and he will seek no reward beyond the consciousness of having done right. And he who, with the same school-boy's treasure, will steal away, and devour it behind the school-house, and alone, will, through life, be equally mean in all his transactions. From motives of interest, he may assume a generosity of conduct, but the innate selfishness of his heart will, in the manner of his dispensing favors, betray itself. Education, and the influences of polished society, may refine the manners, but they never soften the heart to generous emotions, where nature has refused to sow its seed. But where her hand has been liberal in this divine dispensation, no misfortune, no want of education or association, will prevent their germination and fructification. Such hearts divide their joys and their sorrows, with the fortunate and afflicted, with the same emotional sincerity with which they lift their prayers to Heaven.

The school-room is an epitome of the world. There the same passions influence the conduct of the child, which will prompt it in riper years, and the natural buddings of the heart spring forth, and grow on to maturity with the mind and the person. College life is but another phase of this great truth, when these natural proclivities are more manifest, because more matured. It is not the greatest mind which marks the greatest soul, and it is not the most successful who are the noblest and best. The shrewd, the mean, and the selfish grow rich, and are prosperous, and are courted and preferred, because there are more who are mean and venal in the world than there are who are generous and good. But it is the generous and good who are the great benefactors of mankind; and yet, if there was no selfishness in human nature, there would be no means of doing good. Wealth is the result of labor and economy. These are not incompatible with generosity and ennobling manliness. The proper discrimination in the application of duties and donations toward the promotion of useful institutions, and the same discrimination in the dispensation of private charities, characterize the wise and good of the world. These attributes of mind and heart are apparent in the child; and in every heart, whatever its character, there is a natural respect and love for these, and all who possess them. Such grow with their growth in the world's estimation, and are prominent, however secluded in their way of life, or unpretending in their conduct, with all who know them, or with whom, in the march of life, they come in contact.

It is to but few that fortune throws her gifts, and these are rarely the most deserving, or the goddess had not been represented with a bandage over her eyes. She is blind, and though her worshippers are many, she kisses but few, and cannot see if they be fair and beautiful or crooked and ugly. Hence most of those who receive her favors conceal them in selfishness, and hoard them to be despised; while hundreds, slighted of her gifts, cultivate the virtues which adorn and ennoble, and are useful and beloved.

Will you, who yet live, and were children when I was a child, turn back with me in memory to those days, and to those who were your school-fellows and playmates then? Do you remember who were the brave and generous, kind and truthful among them? and do you recall their after lives? Answer me; were not these the true men in that day? Do you remember William C. Dawson, Joseph H. Lumpkin, Lucius Q. C. Lamar, and his brother Mirabeau B. Lamar, Eugenius Nesbit, Walter T. Colquitt, and Eli S. Shorter? How varied in temperament, in character, in talent; and yet how like in the great leading features of the soul! Love for their country, love for their kind, love for the good was common to them all; unselfish beyond what was necessary to the wants of their families, generous in the outpourings of the soul, philanthropic, and full of charity. They hoarded no wealth, nor sought it as a means of power or promotion. Intent upon the general good, and content with an approving conscience and the general approbation, their lives were correct, and their services useful; and they live in the memory of a grateful people as public benefactors.

There are others who rise to memory, who were at school with these, who were men with these, but they shall be nameless, who struggled, and successfully, to fill their coffers to repletion, and for nothing else; who have been courted by the mercenary, and flattered by the fawning sycophant; who, with their hoardings, have passed away, and no grateful memory remains of their lives; their hoards are dissipated, and they are only remembered to be despised. And yet others, who swam in the creek and sported on the play-ground with all of these, whose vicious propensities were apparent then — whose after lives were as their boyhood promised, a curse to society in evil deeds and evil example — have gone, too, unwept, unhonored, and luckily unhung.

Mirabeau B. Lamar was the son of John Lamar, of Putnam County, Georgia, and received his education principally at Milledgeville and at Putnam. From his earliest boyhood, he was remarkable for his genius and great moral purity. His ardent, poetical temperament was accompanied with exquisite modesty, and a gentle playfulness of disposition; with an open, unaffected kindness of heart, which as a boy rendered him popular with his fellows at school, and beloved by his teachers. There was in him a natural chivalry of character, which characterized him above all of his early compeers, and made him a model in conduct. Truthful and manly, retiring and diffident, until occasion called out the latent spirit of his nature; then the true greatness of his soul would burst forth in an impetuous eloquence, startlingly fierce and overwhelming. Nor was this excitement always wasted in words — not a few, when yet a boy, have regretted the awakening of his wrath. It was upon occasions like this, that his eye assumed an expression which I have never seen in the eye of any other human being. His eyes were beautifully blue, large, and round, and were always changing and varying in their expression, as the mind would suggest thought after thought; and so remarkable were these variations, that, watching him in repose, one who knew him well could almost read the ideas gathering and passing through his mind. There was a pleasant vein of satire in his nature, sometimes expressed, but always in words and in a manner which plucked away its sting:

> An abstract wit of gentle flow,
> Which wounds no friend, and hurts no foe.

He was my school-fellow and companion in childhood, my friend and associate in early manhood; our intimacy was close and cordial, and in after life this friendship became intense — and I knew him perhaps better than any man ever knew him.

All the peculiarities of the boy remained with the man, distinguishing him in all his associations. The refined purity of his nature made him naturally to despise and scorn all meanness and vice, and so intensely as to render an association with any man distinguished by these, however exalted his intellect, or extensive his attainments, impossible. Falsehood, or the slightest dishonorable conduct in any man, put him at once beyond the pale of his favor or respect. In all my association with him, I never saw an indelicate act in his conduct, or heard an obscene word in his conversation. In youth, he was fond of the society of ladies — fond of this society not for a pastime, but because of his high appreciation of the virtues of those he selected for society. In his verse, "Memoriam," he has embalmed the memory of those of our early female friends he most esteemed. He rather courted this association in the individual than in the collective assembly — for he was not fond of crowds, either in society, or the ordinary assemblages of men and women.

The love of fame, more than any other passion, fired his ambition; but it was not the love of notoriety — the fame he courted was not that which should only render his name conspicuous among men, that he might receive the incense of hypocritical flattery, or be pointed at by the fickle multitude — for such, his contempt was supreme; but it was the desire of his heart, and the struggle of his life, to be embalmed in men's memories as the benefactor of his race, to be remembered for his deeds as the great and the good. This was the spontaneous prompting of his heart, and for this he labored with the zeal of a martyr.

Much of his early life was devoted exclusively to literature. His reading, though without order, was select and extensive. He was well versed in ancient history. The heroic characters of Greece and Rome were his especial admiration, and that of Brutus above all others. Of the nations of modern Europe, and their history, he knew everything history could teach. His imagination was fired with the heroic in the character of those of modern times, as well as those of antiquity, and seemed the model from which was formed his own. The inflexible integrity, the devoted patriotism, the unselfish heroism of these were constantly his theme when a school-boy, and the example for his imitation in manhood.

When a school-boy, and at a public examination and exhibition, (then common at the academies throughout the State,) our teacher, that paragon of good men, Dr. Alonzo Church, selected the tragedy of Julius Cæsar for representation by the larger boys, and, by common consent, the character of Brutus was assigned to Lamar. Every one felt that the lofty patriotism and heroic virtues of the old Roman would find a fit representative in Lamar. I remember, in our rehearsals, how completely his identity would be lost in that of Brutus. He seemed to enter into all the feelings and the motives which prompted the great soul of the Roman to slay his friend for his country's good. Time has left but one or two who participated in the play. The grave has closed over Lamar, as over the others. Those who remain will remember the bearing of their companion, on that occasion, as extraordinary—the struggle between inclination and duty—the pathos with which he delivered his speech to the people after the assassination, but especially his bearing and manner in the reply to Cassius' proposition to swear the conspirators—the expansion of his person to all its proportions, as if his soul was about to burst from his body, as he uttered:

"No, not an oath."

And again, when the burning indignation burst from him at the supposition of the necessity of an oath to bind honorable men:

"Swear priests, and cowards, and men cautelous,
Old, feeble, carious, and such suffering souls
That welcome wrongs, unto bad causes. Swear
Such creatures as men doubt, but do not stain
The even virtue of our enterprise,
Nor the unsuppressive mettle of our spirits,
To think that our cause, or our performance,
Did need an oath; when every drop of blood
That every Roman bears, and nobly bears,
Is guilty of a several bastardy
If he do break the smallest particle
Of any promise that hath passed from him."

Though a boy, the effect upon the audience was electrical. The nature of his boy representative was the same as that which animated

Rome's noblest son. From his soul he felt every word, and they burned from his lips, with a truth to his soul and sentiments, that went home· to every heart in that assembly of plain farmers, and their wives and daughters. There were not ten, perhaps, who had ever witnessed a theatrical entertainment, but their hearts were mortal and honest, and they saw in the mimic youth the impersonation of the nobility of soul, and mighty truth, and the spontaneous burst of applause was but the sincerity of truth. The exclamation of one I shall never forget: "He is cut out for a great man." There was no stage-trick; he had never seen a theatre. There was no assumption of fictitious feeling; but nature bubbled up in his heart, and the words of Shakspeare, put into the mouth of Brutus, were but the echo of the deep, true feelings of his soul. Through all his life this great nature adorned his conversation, and exemplified his conduct.

The soul of Brutus was born in Lamar. All the truth and chivalry illustrative of the conduct of the one, was palpable in the other. Let those who saw him, at San Jacinto, at the head of his sixty horsemen, ride upon the ranks of Santa Anna's hosts, tell of his bearing in that memorable charge, when he rose in his stirrups, and, waving his sword over his head, exclaimed: "Remember, men, the Alamo! Remember Goliad, Fannin, Bowie, and Travis! Charge! and strike in vengeance for the murdered of our companions." Resistless as the tempest, they followed his lead, and swept down upon the foe, charging through, and disordering their ranks, and, following in their flight for miles, made many a Mexican bite the dust, or yield himself a prisoner to their intrepidity. To this charge was solely attributable the capture of Santa Anna, Almonte, and the principal portion of the Mexican army, and the establishment of Texan independence.

As a poet, he was above mediocrity, and his "Sully Riley," and many of his fugitive pieces, will long survive, to perpetuate the refined delicacy of his nature, when, perhaps, his deeds as a soldier and as President of Texas shall have passed away. In stature he was below the medium height, but was stout and muscular. His face was oval, and his eyes blue, and exceedingly soft and tender in their expression, save when aroused by excitement, when they were blazing and luminous with the fire of his soul, which enkindled them. He was free from every vice, temperate in living, and remarkable for his indifference to money — with a lofty contempt for the friends and respectability which it alone conferred. If there ever lived four men insensible to fear, or superior to corruption, they were the four brothers Lamar. They are all in eternity, and their descendants are few, but they wear unstained the mantle of their ancestry.

L. Q. C. Lamar, the elder brother of the four, was educated at Franklin College, and studied law in Milledgeville. Very soon after, he was admitted to the Bar. He became distinguished for attention to business, and for talent, as well as legal attainments. Like his brother, M. B. Lamar, he was remarkable for his acute sense of honor and open frankness, a peerless independence, and warm and noble sympathies. He married, while young, the daughter of D. Bird. The mother of his lady was one of the Williamson sisters, so remarkable for their superiority, intellectually, and whose descendants have been, and are, so distinguished for talent.

The character of L. Q. C. Lamar as a man, and as a lawyer, prompted the Legislature of the State to elevate him to the Bench of the Superior Court when very young; and at thirty-two years of age, he was known throughout the State as the great Judge Lamar. This family had contributed perhaps a greater number of men of distinguished character than any other family of the State. Zachariah Lamar, the uncle of Judge Lamar, was a man of high order of mind, distinguished for his love of truth, stern honesty, and great energy. He was the father of Colonel John B. Lamar, who fell in the service of the South, in the recent conflict. He was one of Georgia's noblest sons, and his memory is cherished by all who knew him. Henry G. Lamar, a former member of Congress, and Judge of the Superior Court of the State, was a cousin of both John B. and M. B. Lamar; and the eminent and eloquent Lucius Lamar, of Mississippi, who was considered, when young, the best orator of the House of Representatives of the United States Congress, is the son of Judge L. Q. C. Lamar.

The name of Lamar has long been a synonym for talent and chivalrous honor in Georgia. They have been distinguished in every pursuit, and no stain has ever rested upon the name — in whatever avocation employed, conspicuous for capacity, honesty, and energy. They are of French extraction, and to their latest posterity they continue to exhibit those traits peculiar to the French

— chivalry, intense sensibility, love of truth, refinement of manner, lofty bearing, and a devotion to honor which courts death rather than dishonor.

The name of M. B. Lamar is identified with the history of Texas, as a leader among that band of remarkable men who achieved her independence of Mexican rule — Houston, Sidney Johnson, Bowie, Travis, Crockett, and Fannin. He was twice married; his first wife, Miss Jordan, died young, leaving him a daughter. This was a bitter blow, and it was long ere he recovered it. His second wife was the daughter of the distinguished Methodist preacher John Newland Moffitt, and sister of Captain Moffitt, late of the service of the Confederacy. He died at Richmond, Fort Bend County, Texas, beloved and regretted as few have been.

Perhaps among the most remarkable men of the State, contemporaneous with the Lamars, was Walter T. Colquitt, Joseph H. Lumpkin, Charles J. Jenkins, William C. Dawson, and Charles J. McDonald: all of these were natives of the State — Colquitt, Eugenius A. Nesbit, and McDonald, of Hancock County; Lumpkins, Oglethorpe, Dawson, Green, and Jenkins, of Richmond; Nesbit, of Greene. At the period of time when these men were young, education was deemed essential, at least to professional men. They all enjoyed the benefits of a classical education. Lumpkin and Colquitt received theirs at Princeton, New Jersey, and I believe were classmates, at least they were college-mates. Colquitt returned home before graduating; Lumpkin received the second honor in his class. Returning to Georgia, Lumpkin read law in the town of Lexington, the court-house town of his native county; and commenced, as soon as admitted, its practice in the northern circuit of the State. At the time he came to the Bar, it was ornamented with such men as Thomas W. Cobb, Stephen Upson, George R. Gilmer, John A. Herd, and Duncan G. Campbell. He rose rapidly to eminence in the midst of this galaxy of talent and learning. The great John M. Dooly was upon the bench of this circuit, and was the intimate friend of Wilson Lumpkin, an elder brother of Joseph H. Lumpkin.

Wilson Lumpkin and Joseph H. Lumpkin were politically opposed. The former was an especial friend of Dooly; the latter, of William H. Crawford. Mr. Crawford, soon after Lumpkin's admission to the Bar, returned to his home, near Lexington, and gave his countenance and support to him, and at the same time his bitterest opposition to the political aspirations of his brother. The forensic abilities of young Lumpkin were winning for him in the State a proud eminence. His exalted moral character, studious habits, and devotion to business attracted universal observation and general comment. He had been from his birth the favorite of all his acquaintances, for the high qualities of his head and heart — the model held up by mothers for the example of their sons. Scarcely any boy in the county was ever reprimanded for a wild frolic or piece of amusing mischief, who was not asked, "Why can't you be like Joe Lumpkin?"

All this favoritism, however flattering, did not spoil him, as is too frequently the case with precocious youth. His ambition had fixed a lofty mark, and he availed himself of this universal popularity to reach it; at the same time, he left no effort neglected to deserve it, and maintain it, once acquired.

The State was teeming with young men of talent, scarcely a county without at least one of great promise. Lumpkin saw and knew the rivalry would be fierce, and success only to be obtained by superior abilities and eminent attainments. The Legislature was the first step to fame, and political fame then the most desired and the most sought. Party was rancorous in its spirit, producing intense excitement, pervading every bosom, male and female, to the extremes of the State — an excitement which so stamped itself upon the hearts of the entire people as to endure, and to mark their character and opinions even until to-day.

Lumpkin was very decided in his opinions, and open in their expression, yet there was none of that empoisoned bitterness in these expressions so characteristic of political aspirants in that day. Such was alien to his kindly nature; and if it had not been, there were other causes to estop him from any such indulgence. His family was large. There were eight brothers; only one of these was younger than himself; these were about equally divided in political sentiment, and they, at least some of them, less amiable or less considerate than himself. He was the favorite of all, and was continually in communication with all of them, and was really the moderator of the family, and the healer of its feuds. At this time, too, the deep morality of his nature was growing into piety, and this sentiment was mellowing from his heart even the little of unkindness that had ever found a place there.

At twenty-five years of age he was sent, by an almost unanimous vote, to the Legislature from his county. He came with an exaggerated reputation for talent, especially for oratorical talent, and many of his friends feared he would not be able to sustain it in that body, where there were many of age and experience, with characters already long established for learning and eloquence, and also many young men from different parts of the State, who, like himself, had already won fame for high talent. Among these was Robert Augustus Bell, in sight of whose grave I write these lines. He passed away in early life, but Georgia never produced a brighter or a nobler spirit. There were also Charles Dougherty, (who died young, but not without making his mark,) William Law, Hopkins Holsey, and others, who have honored themselves and the State by eminent services on the Bench and at the Bar, and in the councils of their native and other States to which many of them emigrated.

At the very opening of the session, Lumpkin took position with the first on the floor of the House of Representatives. His first speech was one of thrilling eloquence, and, before its conclusion, had emptied the Senate chamber; many of its oldest and most talented members crowding about him, and listening with delight.

The memory of that day revives with the freshness of yesterday. Two or three only remain with me now, to recall the delight with which all hearts were filled who acted, politically, with Lumpkins, as the beautiful and cogent sentences thrilled from his lips, with a trembling fervor, which came from an excitement born of the heart, and which went to the heart. Bell, Brailsford, Dougherty, Rumbert, and Baxter, who, with myself, grouped near him, all are in the grave, save only I, and, standing a few weeks since by the fresh mould that covers Joseph H. Lumpkin, and yesterday by the grave of Bell, my mind wandered back to the old State House, and to those who were with me there. Separated for more than forty years from the home of my birth, being with, and becoming a part of another people — a noble, generous, and gallant people — and almost forgetting my mother tongue, these had faded away almost into forgetfulness; but, tottering with years, and full of sorrows, I am here amid the scenes made lovely and memorable by their presence, when we were all young and hopeful. They come back to me, and now, while I write, it seems their spirits float in the air of my chamber, and smile at me. Why is my summons delayed so long? All that made life lovely is gone — youth, fortune, and household gods. My children are in bloody graves — she who bore them preceded them to eternity; yet I live on, and sigh, and remember, while imagination peoples with the past the scenes about me. The faces, the jest, and merry laugh come again; I see and hear them again. Oblivion veils away the interval of forty-five years, and all is as it was. Oh, could the illusion last till death shall make it truth! It is, I feel, but a foretaste of the reality soon to be, when hearts with hearts shall group again, and the reunion of sundered ties be eternal.

Lumpkin served a few sessions in the Legislature, and retired from public life to devote his entire attention to his profession. He had married, almost as soon as he was admitted to the Bar, one to whom he had been attached from boyhood, and the cares of a family were increasing and demanding his attention and efforts. No man ever more faithfully discharged these duties.

The judiciary of Georgia had consisted of two courts only — the superior, and inferior or county court — from the organization of the State. The country had long felt the want of a supreme court, for the correction of errors, and to render uniform the decisions upon the law throughout the State, which, under the prevailing system, had become very diverse, and which was becoming grievously oppressive. Finally it was determined by the Legislature to establish a supreme court. After the passage of the law, however, its organization was incomplete for the want of judges. Party was distracting the councils of the State, and was carried into everything, and each party desired a controlling influence in this court, and their united co-operation in selecting judges could only be effected by the dominant party consenting to Joseph H. Lumpkin's accepting the chief-justiceship. He consented to do so, and the organization of the court was completed. This position, under repeated elections, he continued to hold until the day of his death, which occurred in the spring of 1867.

No man, perhaps, ever had the confidence of a people in the discharge of a high judicial duty more than had Joseph H. Lumpkin. His public duties were discharged with the most scrupulous conscientiousness, as were all of those pertaining to his private life and relations. He died in the neighborhood of his birth, and where he had continued to live through his whole life, passing through time with the companions of his childhood, and preserving their confidence and affection to the last. His death was sudden, and deeply mourned throughout the State, which had delighted so long to honor him. His name is identified with her history, as one of her brightest and best men.

The talents of Judge Lumpkin were of a high order, and though he distinguished himself as a jurist, they were certainly more fitted for the forum than the bench. Those who knew him best, and who were best fitted to judge, unite in the opinion that his eminence in political life would have been greater than that which distinguished him as a judge. He was a natural orator, and his oratory was of the highest order. His ideas flowed too fast for the pen, and he thought more vividly when on his feet, and in the midst of a multitude, than when in the privacy of his chamber. His language was naturally ornate and eloquent, and the stream of thought which flowed on in declamation, brightened and grew, in its progress, to a mighty volume. This, with the fervor of intense feeling which distinguished his efforts, made them powerfully effective. In toning down these feelings, and repressing the ornate and beautiful to the cold, concise legal opinion, his delivery lost not only its beauty, but much of its strength and power. He might have been less useful, but certainly he would have been more distinguished, had he pursued the bent of his genius. Abilities like Lumpkin's must succeed respectably, if directed to any pursuit; and even should they be prostituted to base and dishonorable purposes, they will distinguish the possessor above the herd.

His temperament was nervous, his sensibility acute, and his sentiments exalted. Fluent, with great command of language, he was peculiarly gifted for display in debate, and it was supposed, when he first came into the Legislature, that he would soon rise to the first position in the national councils. But he determined for himself a different field; and, in view of his eminent services as an able and conscientious judge, who shall say he did not choose wisely?

In an almost adjoining county to that of the residence of Judge Lumpkin, was coming forward, in the profession of law, another gifted son of Georgia — Walter T. Colquitt. He was a compeer, at the Bar, of Chief-Justice Lumpkin. They were admitted to practice about the same time. He was a native of the county of Hancock. His mother was the only sister of the eight brothers Holt, every one of whom was distinguished for probity and worth. They all lived and died in the State, and every one of them was a representative man. They have all left descendants but one, and none yet have stained the name. As their ancestors, they are energetic, honest, and most worthy citizens.

Colquitt gave evidence, when very young, of his future career. As a boy, he was wild and full of mirth, but little inclined to study. He was fond of sport of every kind, and in everything to which his mind and inclinations turned, he would be first. Compelled, by parental authority, to apply himself, he at once mastered his task, and was ready, then, for fun or frolic. Remarkable for physical powers, he fondly embarked in all athletic sports, and in all excelled. Bold and fearless, he was the leader in all adventures of mischief, and always met the consequences in the same spirit. It was remarked of him, when a boy, by one who knew him well, that in all he did he played "high, game," never "low, Jack."

In the wildness of his mischief there was always discoverable boldness and mind. At school and at college, though rarely winning an honor, he was always admitted by his fellows to possess superior abilities. These abilities were manifest more in the originality of his ideas, and their peculiar exemplification in his conduct, than in the sober, every-day manner of thought and action. His mind was versatile, and seemed capable of grasping and analyzing any subject. Quick to perceive and prompt to execute, yielding obedience to no dogma, legal or political, he followed the convictions of his mind, without regard to precedent or example. His knowledge of human nature seemed intuitive, and his capacity of adaptation was without limit. At the period when he commenced the practice of law, the successful abilities in the profession were forensic. Every case was tried by a jury, and the law made juries judges of law and fact. The power to control and direct these was the prime qualification of a lawyer, and nature had bestowed this, in an eminent degree, upon Colquitt. There were few more eminent as advocates, or more successful as practitioners, though his legal attainments were never of a very high order. He was elevated to the bench, where he remained but a short time, feeling that this was no situation for the display of his peculiar powers, nor the proper or successful course for the gratification of his ambition. He had, at a previous time, united himself with the Methodist Church, and was licensed to preach. It was his habit to open his court, each morning, with prayer, and not unfrequently, during the week of his court, in each county of his circuit, to preach two or three sermons. He was a general of the militia, and would come down from the bench to review a regiment or brigade. It was this discharge of his multifarious duties which prompted an aged sister of his church, when the great men of the State were being discussed by the venerable ladies of a certain neighborhood, to claim the palm for Colquitt.

"Ah! you may talk of your great men, but none on 'em is equal to brother Colquitt; for he, in our county, tried a man for his life, and sentenced him to be hung, preached a sermon, mustered all the men in the county, married two people, and held a prayer-meeting, all in one day. Now, wa'n't that great?"

Before a jury he was unequalled. His knowledge of men enabled him to determine the character of every juror, and his versatility to adapt his argument or address to their feelings and prejudices so effectually as to secure a verdict in mere compliment to the advocate. He left the bench to enter the political arena. It was here he found the field nature designed him for. Before the people he was omnipotent. At this period Dawson, Cooper, Colquitt, Cobb, Stephens, and Toombs were before the people — all men of talent, and all favorites in the State. This was especially true of Dawson, Cobb, and Stephens, and no men better deserved the public favor.

Very soon after he went into Congress, he, with Cooper and Black, abandoned the Whig party. At the approaching election they canvassed the State, and justified their course before the people. There was no middle ground on which to stand. To abandon one party, was to go over, horse, foot, and dragoons, to the other, which was always ready to welcome new converts of talent and popularity. These three became, in the canvass, the champions of Democracy, and fiercely waged the war in antagonism with their former allies. In this contest were made manifest the great abilities of Colquitt, Toombs, Stephens, Cobb, and Herschel V. Johnson.

Subsequently, Colquitt was elected to the United States Senate, where he was distinguished as a debater and leading man of the Democratic party; but his talents and peculiar manner were better suited for the debates of the House of Representatives, and the hustings.

Lumpkin was ardent and persuasive. Colquitt was equally ardent, but more aggressive. Where Lumpkin solicited with a burning pathos, Colquitt demanded with the bitterest sarcasm. Lumpkin was slow and considerate; Colquitt was rapid and overwhelming. The one was the sun's soft, genial warmth; the other, the north wind's withering blast. Colquitt was remarkable for daring intrepidity; Lumpkin for collected firmness. Lumpkin persuaded; Colquitt frightened. Both were brave, but Colquitt was fiercely so. Lumpkin was mild, but determined. Unaggressive himself, the dignity and gentleness of his character repelled it in others. The consequence was, that he passed through life without strife with his fellow-man, while Colquitt was frequently in personal conflict with those as impetuous as himself. The open frankness and social nature of Colquitt won him many friends, and of that description most useful to politicians — friends who were devoted, who felt for, and preferred him to any other man. His features were versatile, and variable as an April day, betraying every emotion of his mind — especially his eyes, which were soft or fierce, as the passion of the heart sprang to view in them, and spoke his soul's sensations. His oratory was playful, awakening wild mirth in his auditors, and again it was impetuous and sarcastic, overwhelming with invective and denunciation.

Charles J. Jenkins, a compeer of Lumpkin and Colquitt, was essentially different from both in many of the features of his character. His mind was more logical, more analytical, and capable of deeper research. He had little ambition, and whenever he was before the people, it was when his friends thrust him there. The instinctive morality of his nature, like that of Lumpkin, would never permit the compromise of conscience or dignity of character so often the case with men of ardent natures and intense ambition. Eminently cool in debate, he never made any attempt at forensic display, but confined himself exclusively to the logic of his subject. He clearly saw his way, and carefully went along, spurning ornament or volubility, and only compelling into service words which clearly and succinctly conveyed his ideas, and these only elucidated the subject-matter he was discussing. Strictly honest, and equally truthful, he never deviated, under any circumstances, from what he believed his duty. Only for a short time was he in the Legislature, and then he displayed in most exciting times the great virtues of his nature.

Upon one occasion, the party with which he acted determined, to defeat a certain measure, to leave the chamber in a body, and break the quorum. It was the only means in their power to prevent a measure which they deemed wrong in principle and injurious to the public interest. Jenkins thought such extreme measures wrong, and entirely unjustifiable. Though as much opposed to the views of the majority as any member of his party, he refused to participate in their action, and was the only member of the party who persistently remained in his seat. This conduct was censured by his party friends, and he immediately resigned his seat and returned to his constituency, who, knowing and appreciating the great worth of the man, returned him at once to his seat under a new election. In all the relations of life the same traits of character have distinguished him. While at the Bar, his rank was the first; this, combined with his integrity and great firmness, made him so conspicuous before the people of the State, that he was placed on the bench of the Supreme Court — a position he distinguished by his great legal attainments, dignity, and purity.

The political opinions of Judge Jenkins were in many of their features unpopular. He was always opposed to universal suffrage, and made no secret of his sentiments. He was opposed to an elective judiciary, and to mob-rule in every shape. He despised alike the arts and the humiliation of party politicians, and was never a man to accept for public trust any man whose only recommendation to public favor was his availability, because of his popularity with the masses. He was taken from the supreme bench to fill the gubernatorial chair of the State, and no man, not even Jackson, Early, or Troup, ever more dignified this elevated position — none ever had the same trying difficulties to encounter. Chosen by the people at a period when civil war had distracted the government and uprooted all the landmarks so long the guide for those who preceded him — when a manifest determination of the so-called Congress, representing but two-thirds of the States, was apparent to usurp all power — when the State governments of ten States, though that of their people, were threatened with military usurpation, Jenkins remained firm to his convictions of duty. The credit of the State had never suffered while under his guardianship; a large amount was in her treasury; this was an objective point for the usurpers. He met the military satrap, and was assured of his intentions. Satisfied of his insincerity and dishonesty, knowing he held the power of the bayonet, and would be unscrupulous in its use, calm as a Roman senator he defied the power of this unprincipled minion of a base, corrupt, and unconstitutional power, and deliberately removed the treasure of the State, and applied it to the liquidation of her obligations. Hurled from the office bestowed by his fellow-citizens, so far as he could he protected their interests, at the hazard of the horrors of Fort Pulaski and the sweat-box — the favorite instruments of torture of this infamous defendant of an irresponsible Congress, and now for personal safety, exiled from home and country, finds protection under a foreign flag. This one act alone will be sufficient to immortalize the name of Charles J. Jenkins, and to swell with pride the heart of every true Georgian who aided to place such a man in such a position, at such a time. Governor Jenkins still lives, and if the prayers of a virtuous and oppressed people may avail on high, will be spared to reap in better days his reward in their gratitude.

An exalted intellect, unaccompanied with exalted virtue, can never constitute greatness. In whatever position placed, or whatever inducements persuade, virtue and a conscientious conviction of right must regulate the mind and conduct of man to make him great. The tortuous course of politics, made so by unprincipled men, renders the truly upright man usually a poor politician. He who possesses the capacity to discern the true interests of a country, and who will virtuously labor to secure and promote those interests, defying opposition and fearlessly braving the calumnies of interested, corrupt men, organized into parties — which so often lose sight of the interests of their country, in promoting party ends, or from inflamed passions — is the great man. He whose pedestal is virtue, and whose action is honest, secures the respect of his own age, and becomes the luminary of succeeding ages. Stern honesty often imposes unpleasant duties — strict obedience to its behests, not unfrequently involves apparent inconsistencies of conduct; but the conscientious man will disregard these in doing what his judgment determines right — the only real consistency which sustains a man in his own estimation, and leaves no bitter reflections for the future. To subserve the cause of right, is always a duty — not so the cause of party or selfish interest. All men respect the right, but many have not the virtue to resist wrong. Ambition prompts for success the expedient: and hence the laxity of political morals. This is slipping the cable that the ship may swing from her anchorage and drift with the tide; any minnow may float with the current, but it requires a strong fish to stem and progress against the stream. A man, to brave obloquy and public scorn, requires strong moral courage ; but when his judgment convinces him that he is right, and when he feels that his intentions are pure, conscientious, and sincere, this may ruffle him for a time, but never permanently disturbs his peace or injures his reputation. The truly great are only known by nobly resisting every temptation to wrong, and braving the world's condemnation in pursuing and sustaining the right. It is the soul to which greatness belongs, not the mind. This latter is too often, in its transcendent greatness, coupled with a mean and degraded soul, which stimulates the mind's power to the corruption of the masses, and the destruction of public morals, undermining the very basis of society and government.

The combination of a great mind and a great soul constitutes the truly great, and the life of such a man creates a public sentiment which, like an intense essence, permeates all it touches, leaving its fragrance upon all. Such a man was George M. Troup, such a man is Charles J. Jenkins; and the incense of his character will be a fragrance purifying and delighting the land when he shall have passed away. The exalted abilities of his mind, the great purity of his heart, the noble elevation of his sentiments, and his exquisite conscientiousness, will be an honor and an example to be remembered and emulated by the coming generations of his native land.

CHAPTER XIV.

A REVOLUTIONARY VETERAN.

Tapping Reeve — James Gould — Colonel Benjamin Talmage — The Execution of Major Andre — Character of Washington — A Breach of Discipline — Burr and Hamilton — Margaret Moncrief — Cowles Meade.

FIFTY years ago, the only law-school in the United States was taught by Tapping Reeve and James Gould, at Litchfield, Connecticut. The young men of the South, destined for the profession of law, usually commenced their studies in the office of some eminent practitioner at home, and, after a year or so spent in reading the elementary authors, they finished by attending the lectures at this school. A course of lectures occupied a year. Then they were considered prepared to commence the practice.

Many of the young men of Georgia, at that day, received their education at the North. Most of those who selected law as a profession, finished at the school in Litchfield. Few remain in life at this day who graduated there. Thomas Flornoy and Nicholas Ware were among the first, who read law there, who were natives of Georgia. William Cumming succeeded them. Then followed L. Q. C. Lamar, William C. Dawson, Thaddeus Goode Holt, and many others of less distinction, all of whom are gone save Judge Holt, who remains a monument and a memory of the class and character of the Bar of Georgia fifty years ago, when talent and unspotted integrity characterized its members universally, and when the private lives and public conduct of lawyers were a withering rebuke to the reiterated slanders upon the profession — when Crawford, Berrien, Harris, Cobb, Longstreet, the brothers Campbell, and a host of others, shed lustre upon it.

1820 was spent by the writer at the law-school at Litchfield, in company with William Crawford Banks, Hopkins Holsey, Samuel W. Oliver, and James Clark, from Georgia. All are in the grave except Clark, who, like the writer, lives in withered age. His career has been a successful and honorable one, and I trust a happy one.

During this probation it was my fortune to form many acquaintances among the young and the old whom I met there, and from them to learn much, especially from the old. At that time there resided in the pleasant little village, Governor Oliver Wolcott, Benjamin Talmage, and my distinguished preceptors, Tapping Reeve and James Gould.

Colonel Benjamin Talmage was a distinguished officer in the American army of the Revolution, and was a favorite aide of Washington. It was he who was charged with the painful duty of superintending the execution of Major Andre, who suffered as a spy. He was a tall, venerable man, and though cumbered with years, when I knew him, was active and energetic in attending to his business. The first time I ever met him, he was standing in front of his yard-gate, shaping a gate-pin with a small hatchet, which he used as a knife, to reduce it to the desired size and form. One end he held in his left hand; the other he rested against the trunk of a sycamore-tree, which grew near by and shaded the sidewalk. I knew his character and his services. As I approached him, my feelings were sublimated with the presence of a man who had been the aide to and confidant of George Washington. He was neatly attired in gray small-clothes. His white hair was carefully combed over the bald portion of his head, as, hatless, he pursued his work. His position was fronting me, and I caught his brilliant gray eyes as he looked up from his work to know who was passing. Involuntarily I stopped, and, lifting my hat from my head, bowed respectfully to him, and passed him uncovered, as he returned my salutation with that ease and dignity characteristic of the gentleman of the old school. To-day that towering, manly form is present to my view, as it stood before me then. He inquired of Judge Gould, his immediate neighbor, who I was, and was pleased to mention my respectful demeanor toward him. My reply, when told of this, was: "I should have despised myself, could I have acted otherwise toward one so eminent, and who was the confidential friend of Washington." This was reported to the venerable colonel, who showed his appreciation of my conduct by extending to me many kindnesses during my stay in the village.

By his own hearth-stone I have listened with eager interest to the narration of Andre's capture and execution. He was opposed, with Alexander Hamilton, to the hanging of Andre, and always contended that it was not clearly established that he had come into the American lines as a spy. Andre, when captured, wore his uniform under an overcoat, which concealed it, and the papers found on his person only proved that he sought to deliver them to Arnold. The day before his execution he solemnly declared his only object was an interview with Arnold, or, should he fail in this, to contrive to send him the papers which had been found upon him. When he knew the commander-in-chief had refused him clemency, through Colonel Talmage he appealed to Washington to let him be shot, and die a soldier's death — not to permit him to perish as a felon upon the gallows. Colonel Talmage, when he stated this wish to him, assured him it would be granted. Every effort was made, by his officers and aides, to induce the granting of the request, but in vain. "And never in my life," said Colonel Talmage, "have I had imposed upon me so painful a duty as communicating this fact to the young and gallant officer. He saw my embarrassment and feelings, and, rising from his seat, said: 'Colonel, I thank you for the generous interest you have taken in my case. It has proved of no avail; yet I am none the less grateful.' He paused a moment, when he continued: 'It is hard to die, and to die thus. My time is short, and I must employ it in writing to my family, and must request that you will see my letters forwarded to headquarters.' I promised; when he extended his hand, and, grasping mine, asked: 'Is this our last parting, or shall I see you to-morrow?' I told him it had been made my duty to superintend his execution. 'We will part at the grave,' he said, and, covering his face with his hands, sank, sobbing, into his chair.

"I went away sorrowing, and spent a sleepless night. When the hour had arrived, I waited on him in his prison, and found him cool and prepared for the sacrifice. We both felt too much for words, and there was little said. I remember he asked me to procure his watch, which had been taken from him, if possible, and send it to headquarters. He desired his family to have it."

"Did you ever get it?" I asked.

The colonel bit his lip in shame for him who had it, and only answered: "Never."

"The grave was prepared near the gallows, and the open coffin was by it. As Andre approached, he saw it, and a shudder ran through his frame. Turning to me, he said: 'I am to be buried there. One more request, colonel. Mark it; so that when this cruel conflict shall have ended, my friends may find it!' He then shook hands with me, and, with unfaltering steps, went to the scaffold."

I heard this narrative many times, and with its ending the white kerchief about the old man's neck was loosed, and the moisture from his eyes told that the feelings as well as the memory of that day still survived. He would a moment after continue: "Washington was a stern man — he was a hard man — slow to form opinions or resolutions; but once formed, there was no power under heaven to move him. He never formed either until his judgment was convinced of the right. There was less of impulse in his nature than in that of any man I ever knew. I served by his side for years, and I never saw the least manifestation of passion or surprise. He received the information of Arnold's treachery with the same apparent indifference that he would an orderly's report; and with the same indifference of manner signed the death-warrant of Andre.

"This indifference was marked with a natural sternness, which forbid all familiarity to all men. Even Colonel Hamilton, who was naturally facetious, never ventured, during his long service, the slightest intimacy. Hamilton, whom he esteemed above all men, and to whom he gave his entire confidence, always observed in his private intercourse, as in his public, the strictest etiquette. This cool sternness was natural to him, and its influence was overwhelming. The humblest and the highest felt it alike; inspiring a respectful awe, commanding a dignified demeanor. He was best beloved at a distance, because the qualities of the man were only present, and these were purer and more lofty than those given to any other man. There is no character of ancient or modern times so consistent as that of Washington. He was always cool, always slow, always sincere. There is no act of his life evincing the influence of prejudice. He decided all matters upon evidence, and the unbiassed character of his mind enabled him impartially to weigh this evidence, and the great strength of his judgment to analyze and apply it. He seemed to understand men instinctively, and if he was ever deceived in any of those in close association with him, it was Tom Jefferson. Burr had not been on his staff ten days before he understood him perfectly, and he very soon got rid of him. Of all the officers of the Continental army, General Greene was his favorite; and he was right, for Greene was a great military man — far superior to Washington himself, and none knew it better than he. I remember to have heard him say that Greene was the only man in the army who could retrieve the mistakes of Gates and save the Southern country. The result verified the statement.

"Washington's lenity never extended to the excusing of any palpable neglect of duty. The strict regularity of his own private character was carried into everything connected with his public duties. However much he esteemed any man, it was for his worth in his especial position, and not because of any peculiarity of bearing or properties of heart. That he appreciated the higher qualities of the heart, is certainly true — but for what they were worth always — and neither quality of head or heart created a prejudice which would lead him to excuse any neglect of duty or laxity of morals. He was not without heart, but it was slow to be moved, and never so moved as to warp or obscure his judgment, or influence the discharge of his duty.

"Mrs. Washington was less amiable than her husband, and at times would sadly tax his patience — she never forgot that she was wealthy when she married him, and would sometimes allude to it in no very pleasant manner to her husband; who, notwithstanding, bore with her with remarkable patience. I do not remember ever to have seen General Washington laugh; sometimes a faint smile would tinge his features; but very soon they returned to the sedateness and gravity of expression common to them; and though they rarely brightened with a smile, they were never deformed with a frown. There was in their expression a fixity indicative of his character, a purpose settled and unalterable. Of all the men I have ever known, Washington was the only one who never descended from the stilts of his dignity, or relaxed the austerity of his bearing. It has been said that he swore at General Charles Lee at the battle of Brandywine — I could never have it authenticated. He asked excitedly of General Lee, by what ill-timed mistake the disaster had occurred, which was forcing his retreat. Lee was a passionate, bad man, and disliked to serve under Washington's command. He had served with distinction in the British army in Europe, and felt, in adopting the cause of the colonies, he should have been proffered the chief command. There had been an intrigue at Philadelphia, headed by Dr. Rush, aided by others, to prejudice Congress against the commander-in-chief, to have him displaced, that Lee might succeed him. If Washington was aware of this, it never escaped him to any of his military family; and certainly never influenced his conduct toward Lee — for he had confidence in his military abilities, and always gave him the position where the most honor was to be won. Lee's reply to Washington was violent, profane, and insolent. He said to General Lafayette that his reply was: 'No man can boast of possessing more of that damned rascally virtue than yourself.' He was arrested, court-martialed, and by its decision, suspended for one year from command. He never returned to the service, but retired to the interior of Virginia, and lived in great seclusion until his death.

"Toward the young officers Washington was more indulgent than to the older and more experienced. He would not see the smaller improprieties of conduct in these, unless brought officially to his notice. Then they were uniformly punished. He frequently counselled and advised them, but was ever severe toward intemperance, with old and young.

"Upon one occasion, a certain Maryland colonel came suddenly and quite unexpectedly upon the General, who was taking a walk. The colonel attempted to salute, but in doing so, disclosed his inebriety. 'You are intoxicated, sir,' said the General, with a humorous twinkle of the eye. The colonel replied: 'I am glad you informed me, General; I will go to my quarters before I make an ass of myself;' turned and walked away. Without the slightest movement of feature the General continued his walk. Nothing more was heard of it until the battle of Monmouth, in which the colonel distinguished himself. The day after, in going the grand-rounds, he approached the colonel, and remarked: 'Your gallantry of yesterday excuses your late breach of discipline;' and saluting him, passed on.

"In a conversation over the mess-table, at West Point, some severe remarks upon the conduct of Washington, in hanging Andre, escaped Hamilton. He said, warmly, that it was cruelly unjust, and would assuredly sully the future fame of the General; that he felt aggrieved that the ardent solicitations of his staff, and most of the field-officers, in the unfortunate young man's behalf, had been so little regarded. These remarks reached the ears of the General. We were not aware of this, until some weeks subsequently he summoned his staff to his presence, and stated the fact.

"'You will remember, gentlemen, that Captain Asgill, who was a prisoner, and sentenced, by lot, to die, in retaliation for the cold-blooded murder of Captain Huddy, by the orders of a British officer. You, and many of the officers of the army, interceded to save his life. His execution was, in consequence, respited. The heart-rending appeal of his mother and sisters, communicated to me in letters from those high-bred and accomplished women, determined me to lenity in his case, and he was pardoned. Immediately upon the heels of this pardon comes an intrigue to seduce from his duty and allegiance a major-general, distinguished for services and capacity; and Major Andre is the instrument to carry out this intrigue — to communicate their plans to the traitor, and to consummate the arrangement. These plans were to seize, treacherously, the person of the general commanding the American forces, and carry him a prisoner to the enemy's headquarters. Lenity to this man would have been a high crime against Congress, the army, and the country, which could not have been justified. I regretted the necessity as much as any of you; but mine was the responsibility, not yours. Its being a painful duty did not make it less a duty. Not mine alone, but the safety of the army depended upon the discharge of this duty — a duty recognized by all nations in civilized warfare. I felt it such; I discharged it, and am satisfied with it. I hope I am superior to any apprehension of future censure for a faithful discharge of an imperative duty.' Waving his hand, he bade us 'Good evening.'

"General Washington, upon all important movements, sought the opinions of his staff, as well as those of the general officers of his command. This was not for want of reliance upon his own judgment, but from a desire to see the matter through every light in which it could be presented. These opinions were not unfrequently asked in writing. They were always carefully studied, and due weight given to them, especially when they differed from his own. His mind was eminently analytical, and always free from prejudice, and to these facts is to be attributed the almost universal correctness of his judgment upon all subjects which he had examined. With regard to men, I never knew him to ask another's opinion; nor was he ever the man to give utterance to his own, unless it became necessary as a duty. I knew, from the time I entered his military family, of his high appreciation of Hamilton's abilities; and the frequent concurrence of opinion between them sometimes (and especially with those not entirely acquainted with him) induced a belief that Hamilton formed his opinions, or, as Arnold once expressed it, was his thinker. Yet there were many occasions upon which they differed, and widely differed; and never did Washington surrender his own opinion and adopt that of Hamilton. I never thought the feelings of Washington toward him were more than respect for his exalted abilities. I do not believe a kinder or more social attachment ever was felt by him, and I am positively sure these were the feelings of Hamilton for Washington.

"His respect for the abilities of Colonel Burr was quite as exalted as for those of Hamilton; but he had no confidence in his honesty or truth, and, consequently, very soon got rid of him. Burr's liaison with Margaret Moncrief destroyed entirely the little regard left for him in the mind of Washington. I asked Colonel Talmage if Burr and Hamilton ever were friends. They were very close friends apparently; but it was palpable that each entertained a jealousy of the other, however much they strove to conceal it. They were both ambitious, and felt the way to preferment was through the favor of the commander-in-chief. Burr was the more sensitive and the more impulsive of the two. They knew the abilities of each other, and they knew these were highly appreciated by the General; and at the moment when this jealousy was likely to interfere with this friendship, Burr left the position of aide to the General. He knew he had forfeited the confidence of Washington, and he figured in the army very little after this. The rivalry, however, did not cease here, nor did the secret enmity in their hearts die. The world is not aware of the true cause of the hatred between them, and it may never be.

"You are aware," continued the colonel, "that your preceptor, Judge Reeve, is the brother-in-law of Colonel Burr. If I speak freely of him, it is because I know him, and because you seem curious to pry into these secret histories of national men. It is not to be repeated to offend Judge Reeve, or disturb our relations as friends; for we are such, and have been for fifty years.

"Colonel Burr has ever been remarkable for abilities from his boyhood. Reeve and the celebrated Samuel Lathrop Mitchell were his classmates, and agree that he had no equal in college. They were educated at Princeton. Burr showed not only talent, but application, and a most burning ambition. He showed, too, that he was already unscrupulous in the use of means to accomplish his object. There are stories told of his college-life very discreditable to his fame. He was as remarkable in his features as in his mind. His capacious forehead, aquiline nose, and piercingly brilliant eyes, black as night, with a large, flexible mouth, Grecian in form, made him extremely handsome as a youth. His manners were natural and elegant, and his conversational powers unequalled. They are so to-day. Think of these gifts in a man uninfluenced by principle, and only obedient to the warmer passions. He ever shunned collective society, and seemed (for the time, at least) totally absorbed by one or two only. The eloquence of manner, as the persuasion of words, was in him transcendent. The whispered sophisms of his genius burned into the heart, and it was remarked of him, by one wise and discreet, that he could, in fewer words, win the sympathy and start to tears a female auditor, than any preacher in the land. From boyhood he seemed to have the key to every heart he desired to unlock. Fatal gift! and terribly fatal did it prove to many a victim, and especially to that gifted but frail girl — Margaret Moncrief.

"Margaret Moncrief was the daughter of an officer of the British army, and had been left with that old veteran, Putnam, after this officer was a prisoner of war. Hamilton formed an attachment for her, and Burr, more from vanity than any other feeling, determined to win her away from him. She was, for her sex, as remarkable as Burr for his; her education was very superior, her reading as extensive as most professional men, and entirely out of the line of ordinary female reading; she was familiar with the entire range of science — her person in form was perfect, in features exquisitely beautiful. She, too, possessed the art to steal away the affections of any one around whom she threw her spell. Apparently unconscious of her natural gifts, she displayed them without reserve, and so artlessly, as to lure and beguile almost to frenzy such temperaments as those of Burr and Hamilton. Never before had Burr met his equal, and his vanity and ambition were equally stimulated to triumph in her conquest, and ere he was aware of it, what had been commenced in levity, had become a passion which held him in chains. The sequel was the ruin of both. Here commenced the heart-hatred which terminated in the duel and the death of Hamilton.

"I know there was a romantic story, that gained credit with many, that the influence of Miss Moncrief had corrupted Burr, and that she was acting as a spy, and from Burr obtained all the information she desired of the movements of the American army. Such was the credit attached to this story, that General Putnam was questioned rather closely on the subject of the intercourse between them. It was his opinion that it was without foundation, and that it was simply a love affair. It was also stated, and this Hamilton credited, that Burr was preparing to leave the country with the lady, and there were some circumstances which seemed to warrant such suspicion. To this day, there are ladies who were at that time in communication with Miss Moncrief, who mention that every preparation had been made, that her wardrobe had been removed from her apartment, and that it was carried to those of Colonel Burr, and that they had been turned back in the harbor by a sentry-boat, when striving with a solitary oarsman to reach a British man-of-war, in the lower harbor of the bay of New York. There was never any proof of this, however, and I imagine it was only a gossiping story of Madame Rumor.

"Of the sincerity of the attachment on the part of the lady, her subsequent confessions are the only proof; and at the time of making these confessions, such was her position that little credit could be given them. But that Colonel Burr was ever seriously attached to her, those who knew him best scarcely believed. Men of his character rarely, if ever, have serious and sincere attachment for any woman. To gratify his vanity he would court the affections of any woman whose beauty and accomplishments had attracted him. It was always for base purposes Burr professed love. Such men too frequently win upon the regards of women, and occupy high and enviable positions in female society; but their love is diffusive, and for the individual only for a time. In truth, they are incapable of a deep and sincere affection. The suspicion of woman's purity forbids an abiding love; it is a momentary passion, and not an elevated and enduring sentiment — not the embalming with the heart's riches a pure and innocent being who yields everything to love.

"Colonel Burr was an indifferent husband toward one of the most accomplished and lovable women I ever knew, and who was devoted to him, and whose heart he broke. She was the widow of a British officer named Provost, I believe, who died in the West Indies; and a more deserving woman, or one more lovely, never went to the arms of a *roué*, to be kissed and killed.

"Burr hated Washington, and united himself politically with his enemies. There was a close political intimacy between him and Jefferson, but never anything like confidence. In their party they were rivals; and after the election which made Jefferson President, there was no semblance of intimacy or friendship between them.

"Burr believed he was really elected President, and that Jefferson had defrauded him in the count of the ballots. He was disappointed and dissatisfied with his position and with his party, and immediately commenced an intrigue to separate the Western States from the Union, and on the west of the mountains and along the waters of the Mississippi to establish a separate government, where he hoped to fill the measure of his ambition, and destroy the power of the Union — thus at the same time to crush both the Federal and Republican parties, for now he hated both alike.

"Hamilton had been his early rival; he had, as he believed, destroyed him with Washington, and that he had been mainly instrumental in defeating him with Jefferson for the Presidency. There can be no doubt of the fact, that Jefferson had been voted for by the colleges for President, and Burr for Vice-President; but they were not so designated on the ballots. They received an equal number of votes, and had to be elected, owing to a defect in the law at that time, by the House. The balloting continued several days. There were sixteen States, and each received eight. Jefferson was especially obnoxious to the hatred of the Federal party; Burr, though belonging to the Republican party, less so; and many of the leading men in Congress of the Federal party determined to take Burr in preference. The strength of this party was mainly in the North, and Burr was a Northern man; and they felt more might be expected of him, from Northern interest, than from Jefferson. But the main cause of the effort was the animosity to Jefferson. Washington was viewed as the representative man of the Federal party. Jefferson, though he had been a Cabinet minister in his Administration, had made no secret of his opposition to the views of Washington; and had aided a clerk in his department to establish a newspaper, especially to attack Washington, and to oppose the Administration, which he did, in the most bitter and offensive manner.

"Jefferson was an unscrupulous man — a man of wonderful intellect and vast attainments, but entirely unprincipled. This editor and clerk of Jefferson's, sent daily to the President two copies of his paper, filled with the vilest abuse of him personally, and of his Administration. Much of this was, doubtless, written by Jefferson himself. This supposition is the more to be relied on from the fact that Washington remonstrated with Jefferson upon the matter, and requested the removal of the offending clerk, which was refused by Jefferson. His declining to remove Jefferson himself, is conclusive of the considerate forbearance of this truly great man. These were reasons operating upon the minds and feelings of those men who had not only sustained Washington through the Revolution, but had stood to the support of his Administration, and who concurred with him in political opinion and principle.

"Mr. Adams had made this party unpopular by the course pursued by him in conducting the Government. The Alien Law, and the Sedition Law, which obtained his signature, (though I know he was opposed personally to both,) and the prosecutions which arose, especially under the latter, were very offensive, and entirely at variance with the spirit of our people, and indeed of the age, and had so damaged the Federal party, as to render it odious to a large majority of the people.

"The more considerate of the party believed in the election of Burr — the Southern and Northern Democracy would become divided. Jefferson was known to be specially the favorite of this party, South, and would naturally oppose, himself, and lead his party in opposition to the Administration of Burr, and the Federal party, uniting in his support, with the Republicans, North, would ultimately succeed in recovering the control of the Government. During the ballotings this was fully discussed in the secret meetings of the Federalists. The balloting continued from the 11th to the 17th of February, and only eight States could be carried for Mr. Jefferson, six for Burr, and two were divided. It was supposed Hamilton's influence would be given to Burr, and he was sent for, but to the astonishment of his political friends, it was thrown in opposition to Burr. This influenced those controlling the vote of the divided States. Burr had entered heartily into the scheme of defeating Jefferson. Had Hamilton co-operated with his party, there is now no telling what might have been the future political destiny of the country. Burr was sworn in as Vice-President, and there is no doubt but that the will of the people was substantially carried out.

"The restlessness of Burr was manifested; he seemed to retire from the active participation in politics which had previously been his habit — still, however, adhering to the Republican party, and opposing strenuously every view or opinion advanced by Hamilton. Burr did not take his seat as presiding officer of the Senate, and in February, after the election of Jefferson, Hillhouse was chosen to fill his place *pro tem.* After the inauguration of Jefferson, Abraham Baldwin was elected to preside as President *pro tem.* of the Senate. It had not then become the habit of the Vice-President to preside over the Senate; nor was it the custom for the Vice-President to remain at the seat of Government during the sessions of Congress. Burr, disgusted with the Republican party, ceased to act with it, and went to New York. Here he resumed the practice of law. He was never considered a deeply read lawyer, nor was he comparable with his rival, Hamilton, in debate, or as an advocate at the Bar. He was adroit and quick, and was rather a quibbler than a great lawyer.

"You ask me if I thought, or think, he ever deserted the Republican party in heart? I answer, no; for I do not think he ever had any well-defined political or moral principle, and was influenced always by what he deemed would subserve his own ambitious views; and you ask me, if I ever thought him a great man? Men greatly differ, as you will find as you grow older, and become better acquainted with mankind, as to what constitutes a great man. I think Colonel Burr's talents were eminently military, and he might, in command, have shown himself a great general. His mind was sufficiently strong to make him respectable in any profession he might have chosen; but his proclivity, mentally, was for arms — he loved to direct and control. In very early life he showed much skill and tact as an officer in the Canadian campaign; but he wanted those moral traits which give dignity and decision to character, and confidence to the public mind. His vacillation of opinion, as well as of conduct, was convincing proof that he acted without principle, and was influenced by his own selfish views. Man, to be great, must act always from principle. Principle, like truth, is a straight edge, will admit of no obliquity, is always the same, and under all circumstances: conduct squared by principle, and sustained by truth, inspires respect and confidence, and these attributes, though they may and do belong to very ordinary minds, are nevertheless great essentials to the most powerful in making greatness. Great grasp of intellect, fixity of purpose, strong will, high aims, and incorruptible moral purity, make a great man. They are rare combinations, but they are sometimes found in one man — they certainly were not in Colonel Burr. A great general, a great statesman, a great poet, a great astronomer, may be without morals; and he is consequently not a great man. My young friend, a great man is the rarest creation of Almighty God. Time has produced few. Washington, perhaps, approaches the standard nearest, of modern men; but he was selfish to some extent.

"After Colonel Burr's return to New York, he was nominated by the Federal party for Governor of the State; this was the first open announcement of his having deserted the Republican party. Hamilton threw all his influence against him, and he was defeated. This defeat sublimated his hatred for Hamilton. He made an excuse of

17*

certain words Hamilton had used in relation to him for challenging him. They met, and Hamilton fell. The death of Hamilton overthrew the little remaining popularity left to Burr. The nation, the world, turned upon him, and he became desperate.

"Burr's term as Vice-President terminated on the fourth of March, 1805. The odium which attached to his name found universal utterance after the duel. It was not simply the killing of Hamilton; this merely gave occasion for the outburst of public indignation. His private character had always been bad. As a member of the Legislature, he had so conducted himself as to excite general suspicion of his integrity. His desertion of the party elevating him to the Vice-Presidency, and lending himself to the opposition party to defeat the clearly expressed views of his own party, all combined to make him extremely odious to the populace.

"In the canvass for the Presidency, he had been mainly instrumental in carrying the State of New York for the Republican party. In this he had triumped over Hamilton; but in the more recent contest for Governor of the State, he found that the Republican party adhered to principle, and refused to be controlled by him, repudiating his every advance; and learned, also, that the Federal party would not unite in accepting him. Defeated on every side, in all his views, and mainly through the instrumentality of Hamilton, he determined, after killing his rival, if possible, to destroy the Government.

"There was nothing unfair, or out of the ordinary method of conducting such affairs, in this duel. Hamilton's eldest son, but a little while before, had been slain, in a duel, on the very spot where his father fell, and the event created little or no excitement; and when Burr saw himself met with universal scorn, he knew it was the eruption of an accumulated hatred toward himself, and that all his ambition for future preferment and power was at an end. Immediately he left for the West, and commenced an abortive effort to break up the Union.

"The Allegheny Mountains opposed, at that time, an obstacle to free communication with the East. The States west were politically weak, and, supposing their interests were neglected by Congress, were restless and dissatisfied. This was especially true of Western Pennsylvania. There were very many young and ambitious men in all the Western States and Territories. Tennessee, Kentucky, and Ohio were rapidly populating from the Eastern and Middle

States. Their commercial communication with the East was attended with so many difficulties as to force it almost entirely to New Orleans.

"Geographically, it seemed that the valley of the Mississippi was, by nature, formed for one nation. The soil and climate promised to enterprise and industry untold wealth. The territorial dimensions were fabulous. The restless and oppressed multitudes of overstocked Europe had already commenced an emigration to the United States, which promised to increase to such an amount as would soon fill up, to a great extent, this expanded and promising region. The Mississippi furnished an outlet to the ocean, and a navigation, uninterrupted throughout the year, for thousands of miles, and New Orleans, a market for every surplus product. Burr saw all this, and determined to effect its separation from the Union, and there to establish a new empire, which should, ere long, control the destinies of the continent. It was the conception of genius and daring, but required an administrative ability which he had not, to consummate this conception. He miscalculated his material. The people of the West were vastly more intelligent than he had supposed them. They were not so simple as to receive his views, and blindly adopt and act upon them. They canvassed them, and concluded for themselves. At Pittsburgh he found a number of adventurous young men (who had nothing to lose, and who were ripe for any enterprise which promised fame or fortune,) to unite with him.

"He found Henry Clay in Kentucky, and Andrew Jackson in Tennessee, young, enterprising, and full of spirit and talent. He supposed them to be the men he sought, and approached both, cautiously revealing his views; but, to his astonishment, the grievances of the West had not so warped their patriotism as to dispose them to engage in any schemes which threatened the dismemberment of the Union. Clay listened and temporized, but never, for a moment, yielded assent. Jackson, more ardent, and a military man by nature, was carried away with the idea for a time. He was well acquainted with the people of the West, and especially with the population on the Lower Mississippi, and was the man who recommended Burr to make first a descent upon Mexico, as I have been confidentially informed, and sincerely believe. I have also been informed that he dissuaded Burr from any attempt to excite a war of the West with the East; but first to make Mexico secure, which they and Wilkinson believed would be an easy matter. It was when Burr, having abandoned his first enterprise, descended the Mississippi, that he was arrested. This arrest was made by the acting Governor of Mississippi, and at some point in that Territory, where Jackson had a store or trading establishment. He was, with three of his aides, on his way to meet Wilkinson, for the purpose of arranging matters. He escaped, and finding things prepared for his interception, he made his way across the country; but was finally arrested, on the Tombigbee, by an officer of the United States army. When on his trial at Richmond, Jackson went there, and was found on the street haranguing the people in Burr's favor, and denouncing the prosecution and the President. Subsequently, however, he denounced Burr, and pretended that he had deceived him. Humphrey Marshall, Pope, Grundy, and Whitesides united with Clay in condemning the entire scheme. There was a crazy Irishman, an adventurer, named Blannerhasset, residing on the Ohio, who at once entered into his views, embarked all his fortune in the enterprise, and, with Burr, was ruined. He was tried for treason, and acquitted. Soon after, he left the country, and remained away for many years, returning to find himself a stranger, and almost forgotten."

Some months subsequent to this conversation, Colonel Burr came up from New York to visit his brother-in-law, Judge Reeve, and an opportunity was thus afforded me to see and converse with him; but no allusion was made to the past of his own life, save an account of some suffering he underwent in the Canadian campaign, with General Montgomery. He had contracted, he said, a rheumatism in his ankle, during the winter he was in Canada, and that he had occasional attacks now, never having entirely recovered. He was not disposed to talk, and still he seemed pleased at the attentions received from the young gentlemen who visited him occasionally during his short stay. I do not remember ever having seen him on the street, or in the company of any one, except some of the young men who were reading with Judge Reeve. Some years after this, I met Colonel Burr in the city of New York, and spent an evening with him. At this time he alluded to his trip down the Mississippi, and made inquiry after several persons whom he had known. There were then living three men who, as his aides, had accompanied him upon his expedition. I knew the fact, and expected he would allude to them, but he did not. He seemed to desire to know more of those who had been active in procuring his arrest.

It was Cowles Mead (who was acting Governor of the Territory of Mississippi at the time) who arrested Burr at Bruensburgh, a small hamlet on the banks of the Mississippi, immediately below the mouth of the Bayou Pierre. "Mead," he said, "was a great admirer of Jefferson, because, I suppose, when he had been unseated by the contestant of his election, (a Mr. Spaulding,) Jefferson, to appease his wounded feelings, had appointed him secretary to the Mississippi Territory. He was a vain man of very small mind, and full of the importance of his official station." I remarked that he was a brother-in-law of mine. "I was not aware of that, but I am sure you are too well acquainted with the truth of the statement to be offended at my stating it." I remarked: "Colonel, I am thoroughly acquainted with General Mead, and equally as well acquainted with all the circumstances connected with your acquaintance with him. The adventure of Bruensburgh has been, through life, a favorite theme with the General, and I doubt if there is living a man who ever knew the General a month, who has not heard the story repeated a dozen times." He dryly remarked: "I should have supposed the episode to that affair would have restrained him from its narration;" and the conversation ceased.

I shall have much more to say of these two in a future chapter. At this time Colonel Burr was old and slightly bent, very unlike what he was when I first met him; still his eyes and nose, brow and mouth, wore the same expression they did fifteen years before. About the mouth and eye there was a sinister expression, and he had a habit of looking furtively out of the corner of his eye at you, when you did not suppose he was giving any attention to you.

CHAPTER XV.

CHANGE OF GOVERNMENT.

GOVERNOR WOLCOTT — TOLERATION — MR. MONROE — PRIVATE LIFE OF WASHINGTON — THOMAS JEFFERSON — THE OBJECT AND SCIENCE OF GOVERNMENT — COURT ETIQUETTE — NATURE THE TEACHER AND GUIDE IN ALL THINGS.

DURING the year 1820 I was frequently a visitor at the house of Governor Oliver Wolcott, who then resided in Litchfield, Connecticut. Governor Wolcott was a remarkable man in many respects. He was originally a Federalist in politics, and enjoyed the confidence of that party to an unlimited extent. His abilities were far above ordinary, and his family one of great respectability. He was a native of Connecticut, and after Alexander Hamilton retired from the Treasury bureau in the Cabinet of Washington, he succeeded to that position. He filled the office with credit to himself, and to the satisfaction of his chief. He had, after considerable time spent in public life, left Connecticut, to reside in New York. Subsequent to the war, and when the Federal party had abandoned its organization under the Administration of Mr. Monroe, there grew up in his native State a party called the Toleration party. In reality it was a party proscriptive of the old Federal leaders, and it grew out of some legislation in connection with religious matters, in which, as usual, the Puritan element had attempted to oppress, by special taxation, for their own benefit, all others differing from them in religious creed. Governor Wolcott favored this new organization, and he was invited to return to the State and give his aid to its success. He did so, and in due time was made Governor by this party. At the time of which I write, he was as bitterly and sincerely hated by the old Federal party as ever Jefferson was, or as Andy Johnson now is by the Radical party, which is largely constituted of the *débris* of that old and intolerant organization, and which is now eliminating every principle of the Constitution to gratify that thirst for power, and to use it for persecution, that seems inherent in the nature of the Puritan. By the hour I have listened to the abuse of him, from the mouths of men whose lives had been spent in his praise and support, simply because he had interposed his talents and influence to arrest the oppressor's hand. They said he had deserted his party, that he would live to share the fate of Burr, and that he was as great a traitor.

The bitterness and injustice of party is proverbial, and its want of reason is astonishing. Men who are cool and considerate on all other subjects, are frequently the most violent and unreasonable as partisans. It seems akin to religious fanaticism, and proscribes with the same bigotry all who will not, or conscientiously cannot, act or think with them. It prescribes opinions, and they must be obeyed by all who belong to the organization, and without reservation or qualification. Its exactions are as fierce and indisputable as the laws and regulations of the Jesuits. These are changed with party necessities, and not unfrequently are diametrically antagonistic to the former creed; yet you must follow and sustain them, or else you are a traitor, and denounced and driven from the party, and often from intercourse socially with those who have been your neighbors and friends from boyhood. In this method party compels dishonesty in politics, and is eminently demoralizing, for it is impossible to familiarize the conscience with political dishonesty without tainting the moral man in ordinary matters pertaining to life. Once break down the barrier which separates the right from the wrong, that success may come of it, and every principle of restraint to immoral or dishonest conduct is swept away. For this reason men of stern integrity never make good politicians. They are very often the reliable statesmen, never the reliable politicians.

Governor Wolcott had through his life sustained an unimpeached reputation. He had filled to the full his political ambition. Again and again he had been honored by his people who had grown up with him. He had been honored by the confidence of Washington, and the nation. He was wealthy, was old, and only aspired to do, and to see done, justice to the whole people of his native State. In doing this he came in conflict with the unjust views and iniquitous conduct of an old, crushed party, and he was denounced as a traitor, and ostracized because he would be just.

This was the disruption forever of the Federal party in Connecticut; for though it had ceased to exist as a national organization, it still was sufficiently intact to control most of the New England States. Mr. Monroe's Administration had been so popular that in his second election he received every vote of every State in the

Union, save New Hampshire: one man in her electoral college, who was appointed to vote for him, refused to do so, and gave as his reason that he was a slave-owner. New interests had supervened, old issues were dead — they had had their day — their mission was accomplished; old men were passing away, the nation was expanding into great proportions, and men of great talents were growing with and for the occasion; old party animosities were dimming out, and the era of good feelings seemed to pervade the national heart. Even John Adams and Thomas Jefferson were amicably corresponding and growing affectionate at eighty. It was but the lull which precedes the storm — the sultry quiet which augurs the earthquake.

Upon one occasion I ventured to ask Governor Wolcott to tell me something of Washington. We were strolling in his garden, where he had invited me to look at some melons he was attempting to grow under glass. He stopped, and turning round, looked me full in the face, and asked me if I had not read the "Life of Washington."

"Not the private life," was the reply.

"Ah! a very laudable curiosity in one so young. I knew him well, and can only say his private was very much like his public life. I do not suppose there ever lived a man more natural in his deportment than Washington. He did nothing for effect. He was more nearly the same man on the street that he was in his night-gown and slippers, than any man I ever knew; I can't say I was intimate with Washington; no man can or ever could have said that. His dignity was austere and natural. It was grand, and awed and inspired a respect from every one alike. You breathed low in his presence — you felt uneasy in your seat, before him. There was an inspiring something about him, that made you feel it was a duty to stand in his presence, uncovered, and respectfully silent. I have heard this sternness attributed to his habit of command; not so — it was natural, and he was unconscious of it. Most men, however stern, will unbend to woman. There is in woman's presence a divinity which thaws the rigor of the heart and warms the soul, which manifests itself in the softening of the eye, in the glow upon the cheek, and the relaxation of manner. It was not so with Washington. In his reception-rooms he was easily polite and courteously affable; but his dignity and the inflexibility of his features never relaxed.

"I remember to have heard Mrs. Adams say 'she did not think

he was ever more than polite to Mrs. Washington.' With all this he was very kind, and if he ever did let himself down it was to children, and these never seemed to feel his austerity, or to shrink away from it. It is said that it is the gift of childhood to see the heart in the eye and the face. It is certain they never approach an ill-natured or bad man, and never shrink from a kind and good one. In his intercourse with his Cabinet, he was respectful to difference — consulted each without reserve or concealment, and always weighed well their opinions, and never failed to render to them his reasons for differing with them. He was very concise and exact in stating a case, and never failed to understand well every question before acting. He had system and order in everything. In his private affairs, in his household, as well as in his public conduct, he observed strict rules, and exacted their obedience from all about him. In nothing was he demonstrative or impulsive; but always considerate and cool.

"I know nothing of his domestic matters. There were malicious persons who started many reports of discord between Washington and his lady. These I believe were all false. Mrs. Washington was a high-bred woman, a lady in everything; and so far as my observation or acquaintance extended, was devoted and dutiful. Of one thing I am very sure: she was a proud woman, and was proud of her husband. She certainly had not the dignity of her husband; no one, male or female, ever had. She was less reserved, more accessible, and not indifferent to the attentions and flatteries of her husband's friends. In fine, she was a woman. Washington's deportment toward his wife was kind and respectful, but always dignified and courteous. Toward his servants he was uniformly kind.

"He was an enemy to slavery, and never hesitated to avow his sentiments. His black servants were very much attached to him. The peculiar nature of Washington forbade those heart-friendships demanded by a narrower and more impulsive nature. He kept all the world too far from him ever to win that tenderness of affection which sweetens social life in the blending of hearts and sympathy of souls. But he commanded that esteem which results from respect and appreciation of the great and commanding attributes of his nature, which elevated him so far above the men of his age. He wanted the softness and yielding of the heart that so wins upon the affections of associates and those who are in close and constant intercommunication. Are not these incompatible with the stern and towering traits essential to such a character as was Washington's? Like a shaft of polished granite towering amid shrubs and flowers, cold and hard, but grand and beautiful, he stood among the men and the women who surrounded him when President.

"General Washington was cautious and reserved in his expressions about men. He rarely praised or censured. At the time I was in the Cabinet, he had abundant cause for dislike to Mr. Jefferson, who, in his Mazéi letter, had represented him as laboring to break up the Government, that upon its ruins a monarchy might arise for his own benefit. He spoke of this letter more severely than I had ever heard him speak of anything, and said no man better knew the charge false, than Mr. Jefferson. Some correspondence, I believe, took place between them on the subject. I believe they never met after this. Upon one occasion I heard him say that it was unfortunate that Jefferson had been sent to France at the time that he was, when morals and government alike were little less than chaos, for he had been tainted in his ideas of both."

"You knew Mr. Jefferson?" I asked.

"Come into the house, and I will show you something," said the venerable man, then tottering to the grave. I went, and he showed me some letters addressed to him by persons in Virginia, presenting, in no very enviable light, the character of Jefferson. When I had read them, he remarked: "You must not suppose I am anxious to prejudice your youthful mind against the great favorite of your people. It is not so. You seem solicitous to learn something of the men who have had so much agency in the establishment of the Government and the formation of the opinions of the people, that I am willing you should see upon what my opinions have, in a great degree, been formed. Mr. Jefferson is still living, and still writing. His pen seems to have lost none of its vigor, nor his heart any of its venom. You will hear him greatly praised, and greatly abused. I knew him at one time, but never intimately, and may be said only to know him as a public man; what of his private character I know, comes from the statements of others, and general report. You have just seen some of these statements. I knew the writers of these letters well, and know their statements to be entitled to credit, and I believe them. They assure me that Mr. Jefferson is without moral principle. His public conduct must convince every one of his want of political principle. His whole life has been a bundle of contradictions. He has had neither chart nor compass by which to regulate his course, but has universally adopted the expedient.

"That he has a great and most vigorous intellect is beyond all question; but most of its emanations have been the *ad captandum* to seize the current, and sail with it. He saw the democratic proclivity of the people, he concentrated it by the use of his pen, and he has aided its expansion, until it threatens ruin to the Government. He knows it, and he still perseveres. Under the plea of inviting population, he advocated the extension of the franchise to aliens, and was really the parent from whose brain was born the naturalization laws, making citizens of every nationality, and giving them all the powers of the Government, extending suffrage to every pauper in the land, increasing to the utmost the material for the demagogue, and thus depriving the intelligence of the country of the power to control it. The specious argument that if a man is compelled to serve in the militia and defend the country, he should be entitled to vote, was his. Its sophistry is as palpable to Jefferson as to every thinking mind. Government is the most abstruse of the sciences, and should, for the security of all, be controlled by the intelligence of the country. During the world's existence, all the intelligence it has ever afforded, has not been competent to the formation of a government approximating perfection.

"The object of government is the protection of life, liberty, and property. The tenure of property is established and sustained by law; it is the basis of government; it is the support of government; in proportion to its extent and security, it is the strength and power of government, and those who possess it should have the control of government. In a republic, there can be no better standard of intelligence than the possession of property, and to give the greatest security to the government, none should, in a republic, be intrusted with the ballot, but the native, and the property-holder, or the native property-holder. The complications of our system are scarcely understood by our own people, and to suppose that ignorant men (for such constitute the bulk of our emigrant population) shall become so intimate with it, and so much attached to it, as to constitute them, in a few years, persons to be intrusted with its control, is supposing human intelligence to be of much higher grasp than I have ever found it. Most of these emigrants come here with preconceived prejudices toward the institutions of their native lands. This is natural. Most of them speak a foreign language. This has to be overcome, before they can even commence to learn the nature and operation of our system, which is so radically dissimilar to any and all others. These men, as the ignorant of our own people, naturally lean on some one who shall direct them, and they will blindly do his bidding. This is an invitation to the demagogue; these are his materials, and he will aggregate and control them. Such men are always poor, and envy makes them the enemies of the rich. This creates an antagonism, which we see existing in every country.

"The poor are dependent for employment upon the rich; the rich are dependent upon the poor for labor. This mutual dependence, it would be supposed, would tend to create mutual regard; but experience teaches the reverse. The poor have nothing to sell but their labor, and there are none to buy but the rich. Each, naturally, struggles to make the best bargain possible, and take advantage of every circumstance to effect this. Very few are satisfied with fair equivalents, and one or the other always feels aggrieved. Here is the difficulty. Well, endow the laborer with the ballot, and he usurps the government; for to vote is to govern. What is to be the consequence? We now have, with all the means of expansion and facilities a new country of boundless extent gives to the poor for finding and making homes, many more without property than with it. This disproportion will go on to increase until it assimilates to every old country, with a few rich and many poor. These many will control; they will send of their own men to legislate; they will favor their friends; they will levy the taxes, which the property-holders of the country must pay; they will make the laws appropriating these taxes; all will be for the benefit of their constituency, and the property, the government, and the people are all at their mercy. Jefferson sees this, and is taking advantage of it, and has indoctrinated the whole unthinking portion of our people with these destructive notions. It made him President. His example has proven contagious, and I see no end to its results short of the destruction of the Government, and that speedily. Mr. Jefferson's fame will be co-existent with the Government. When that shall perish, his great errors will be apparent. The impartial historian, inquiring into the cause of this destruction, with half an eye will see it, and then his true character will be sketched, and this great, unprincipled demagogue will go naked down to posterity. He has always been unprincipled, immoral, and dissolute. These, accompanying his great intellect, have made it a curse, rather than a blessing, to his kind.

"The world has produced few great statesmen — Washington and Hamilton were the only ones of any pretensions this country has produced. It was a great misfortune that Hamilton did not succeed Washington. Mr. Adams, now lingering to his end at Braintree, was a patriot, but greatly wanting in the attributes of greatness. He was suspicious, ill-tempered, and full of unmanly prejudices — was incapable of comprehending the great necessities of his country, as well as the means to direct and control these necessities. He had animosities to nurse, and enemies to punish — was more concerned about a proper respect for himself and the office he filled, than the interest and the destiny of his country. He quarrelled with Washington, was jealous of him, who never had a thought but for his country. Adams was all selfishness, little selfishness, and earned and got the contempt of the whole nation. Jefferson was turning all this to his own advantage; and the errors and follies of Adams were made the strength and wisdom of Jefferson. He had but one rival before the nation, Burr — he whom you saw yesterday, the crushed victim of the cunning and intrigue of his friend Jefferson.

"Washington had died — despondent of the future of his country. The prestige of his name and presence was gone. He had committed a great error in bringing Jefferson into his Cabinet and before the nation with his approbation. He knew every Cabinet secret, and took advantage of every one, and had placed himself prominently before the people, and with Burr was elected. The defect in the law as existing at the time, enabled Burr, when returned with an equal number of electoral votes, to contend with Jefferson for the Presidency. It was in the power of Hamilton, at this time, to elect. The States were divided, six for Burr, eight for Jefferson, and two divided. There was one State voting for Jefferson, which by the change of one vote would have been given to Burr: the divided States were under his control. He was, during the ballotings, sent for, with a view to the election of Burr; but he preferred Jefferson — thought him less dangerous than Burr, and procured his election. It was a terrible alternative, to have to choose between two such men. The consequences to Burr and the country have been terrible — the destruction of both.

"I suppose much I have said cuts across your prejudice, coming from the South. I have sought to speak sincerely to you, because you are young, impressible, and anxious for knowledge; and it is better to know an unwelcome truth, than to find out by-and-by you have all your life been believing an untruth. Nothing is more sickening to the candid and sincere heart, than to learn its cherished opinions and dearest hopes have been nothing but fallacies; and when you are old as I am, you will have been more fortunate than I have been, if you do not find much that you have loved most, and most trusted, a deceit—a miserable lie. Come and see me at your leisure: I shall always be glad to see you, and equally as glad to answer any of your questions, if these answers will give you information."

Governor Oliver Wolcott was short in stature and inclined to corpulency; his head was large and round, with an ample forehead; his eyes were gray and very pleasant in their expression; his mouth was voluptuous, and upon his lips there usually lurked a smile, humorous in its threatening, provoking a pleasing dimple upon his cheek. In society, in his extreme old age, for I only knew him then, he was less gay than the general expression of his features would have indicated. He was a man of strong will and most decided character. His individuality was marked and striking, and his tenacity of purpose made his character one of remarkable consistency.

Governor Wolcott was one of the old-school Federalists, a thorough believer in Federal principles. He believed in the capacity of the people for self-government, if the franchise of suffrage was confined to the intelligence and freeholds of the country, but reprobated the idea of universal suffrage as destructive of all that was good in republican institutions. Succeeding Alexander Hamilton as Secretary of the Treasury, he found all matters of finance connected with the Government in so healthy a condition and arranged upon such a basis as only required that he should be careful to keep them there. During the four last years of the Administration of Washington, this prevented any display on his part of any striking financial ability. The administration of his office was entirely satisfactory to the country, though it seemed he was only there to superintend the workings of the genius of Hamilton. Once in my hearing he remarked, he had only to work up to the scribings of Hamilton to make everything joint up and fit well.

He held Washington in higher esteem even than Colonel Talmage;

and differed from him in many particulars relative to his character. It was my good fortune to sit and listen, more than once, to discussions between these venerable men. It was always amicable and eminently instructive. Wolcott was an admirer of Mrs. Washington, Talmage was not. Talmage was a military man, and saw a healthy discipline only in obedience to superiors, and exacted in his own family what he deemed was proper in that of every man. Accustomed himself to a strict obedience to the commands of his superiors, and deeming Washington almost incapable of error, he thought hardly even of Mrs. Washington when she manifested a disposition the slightest to independence of her husband. Wolcott did not see her in the camp, but only as the wife of the President of the United States — mistress of the Presidential mansion, and affably dispensing the duties of hostess there — receiving, entertaining, and socially intermingling in the society admitted to the Presidential circle.

At that period there was more of ceremony and display in the higher circles of official society than at this time. The people had seceded from a monarchical government, and established a democratic one; but the prestige of titular and aristocratic society still lingered with those high in office, of distinguished position, and wealth. Many of those most prominent about the Government had spent much time in Europe, and had imported European manners and customs, and desired to see the court etiquette of the mother country prevail at the court of the new Government. Time and the institutions of democracy had not effected that change in the practices of the people, which the Revolution and the determination to control and direct their own government had in their sentiments.

Mr. Jefferson affected to despise this formal ceremony, and the distinctions in society encouraged by monarchical institutions, and sustained by authority of law — though coming from a State and from the midst of a people whose leading and wealthiest families had descended directly from the nobility and gentry of England, and who affected an aristocracy of social life extremely exclusive in its character, while professing a democracy in political organization of the broadest and most comprehensive type. His sagacity taught him that the institutions of a democratic government would soon produce that social equality which was their spirit, in the ordinary intercourse of the people — that he who enjoyed all and every privilege, politically and legally, given under its Constitution and laws, possessed a power which ultimately would force his social equality with the most pretentious in the land. In truth, the government was in his hands, and he would mould it to his views, and society to his status.

The institutions of government everywhere form the social organization of society. Men are ambitious of distinction in every government, and aspire to control in directing the destinies of their country — are justly proud of the respect and confidence of their fellow-men, and will court it in the manner most likely to secure it. Now and then, there are to be found some who are insensible to any fame save that given by wealth — who will wrap themselves up in a pecuniary importance, with an ostentatious display of their wealth, and an exclusiveness of social intercourse, and are contented with this, and the general contempt. Such men, and such social coteries, are few in this country. Fortunately, wealth which is only used as a means of ostentatious display is worthless to communities, and its possessor is contemptible. "Wealth is power" is an adage, and is true where it is used to promote the general good. Without it no people can be prosperous or intelligent, and the prosperity and intelligence of every people is greatest where there is most wealth, and where it is most generally diffused. This is best effected by democratic institutions, where every preferment is open to all, and where the division of estates follows every death. No large and overshadowing estates, creating a moneyed aristocracy, can accumulate, to control the legislation and the people's destinies under such institutions. No privileged class can be sustained under their operation; for such a class must always be sustained by wealth hereditary and entailed, protected from the obligations of debt, and prohibited from division or alienation.

Mr. Jefferson had studied the effects of governments upon their people most thoroughly, and understood their operation upon the social relations of society, and the character and minds of the people. He was wont to say there was no hereditary transmission of mind; that this was democratic, and a Cæsar, a Solon, or a Demosthenes was as likely to come from a cottage and penury as from a palace and wealth; that virtue more frequently wore a smock-frock than a laced coat, and that the institutions of every government should be so modelled as to afford opportunity to these to become what nature designed they should be — models of worth and usefulness to the country. Every one owes to society obligations, and the means should be afforded to all to make available these obligations for the public good. Nature never designed that man should hedge about with law a favored few, until these should establish a natural claim to such protection, by producing all the intellect and virtue of the commonwealth. This was common property, and wherever found, in all the gradations and ranges of society, should, under the operations of law, be afforded the same opportunities as the most favored by fortune. "In all things nature should be teacher and guide."

These doctrines are beautiful in theory, and are well calculated to fasten upon the minds of the many. They have been, time and again, incorporated into the constitution of governments, and have uniformly produced the same disastrous results. They are equally as fallacious as the declaration "that all men are born free and equal," which, with those above, has won the public approbation in spite of experience. The equality of intellect is as certainly untrue as the equality of stature; the one is not more apparent than the other. Transcendent intellect is as rare as an eclipse of the sun. It manifests itself in the control of all others—in forming the opinions and shaping the destinies of all others. This is a birthright—is never acquired, admits of great cultivation, receives impressions, generates ideas, and makes wonderful efforts. Cultivation and education gives it these, but never its vigor and power. In whatever grade or caste of society this is born, it soon works its way to the top, disrupts every band which ties it down, and naturally rises above the lower strata, as the rarefied atmosphere rises above the denser. This higher order of intellect will naturally control, and as naturally protect its power. From such, a better government may always be expected; and without this control, none can be wholesome or permanent.

CHAPTER XVI.

PARTY PRINCIPLES.

Origin of Parties — Federal and Republican Peculiarities — Jefferson's Principles and Religion — Democracy — Virginia and Massachusetts Parties — War with France — Sedition Law — Lyman Beecher — The Almighty Dollar — "Hail Columbia" and "Yankee Doodle."

THE Federal and Republican parties of the nation had their rise and formation out of the two principles of government — the one descending, as by inheritance, from the mother-country, and the other growing out of the formation of the governments established in the early organization of the colonies. A republican form of government was natural to the people. It had become so from habit. They had, in each colony, enjoyed a representative form; had made their own laws, and, with the exception of their Governors and judicial officers, had chosen, by ballot, all their legislative and ministerial officers. Most of the principles and practices of a democratic form of government, consequently, were familiar to them. The etiquette of form and ceremony preserved by the Governors, conformed to English usage. This was only familiar to those of the masses whose business brought them in contact with these ministerial officers and their appendages.

These were continued, to some extent, for a time; but Jefferson saw that they must soon cease, and yield to a sensible, simple intercourse between the officials of the Government and the people. This was foreshadowed in the Declaration of Independence, drafted by him. Immediately upon the success of the Revolution, and the organization of the General Government, he enunciated the opinions and principles now known as Jeffersonian or democratic. It has been charged upon him, that he borrowed his principles from the leaders of the French Revolution, as he did his religion from Voltaire and Tom Paine.

Jefferson was an original thinker, and thought boldly on all subjects. He had studied not only the character and history of governments, but of religions, and from the convictions of his own judgment were formed his opinions and his principles. His orthodoxy was his doxy, and he cared very little for the doxy of any other man or set of men. His genius and exalted talents gave him a light which shines in upon few brains, and if his religious opinions were fallacious, there are few of our day who will say that his social and political sentiments were or are wrong. As to his correctness in the former, it is not, nor will it ever be, given to man to demonstrate. This is the only subject about which there is no charity for him who differs from the received dogmas of the Church, and to-day his name is an abomination only to the Federalists and the Church.

Jefferson was made Secretary of State by General Washington, and was at once the head and representative man of the democracy of the country. There was, however, no organized opposition to the Administration of Washington. But immediately upon the election of Adams it begun to take shape and form, under the leadership of Jefferson. The two parties were first known as the Virginia and Massachusetts parties. Jefferson had been elected Vice-President with Adams, and before the termination of the first year of the Administration the opposition was formidable in Congress. Governor Wolcott was of opinion that Adams destroyed the Federal party by the unwise policy of his Administration. He said he was a man of great intellect, but of capricious temper, incapable from principle or habit of yielding to the popular will. He certainly saw the palpable tendency of public feeling, and must have known its strength: instead of attempting to go with it, and shape it to the exigencies his party required, he vainly attempted to stem the current, defy it, and control it by law. He disregarded the earnest entreaties of his best friends, counselling only with the extremists of the Federal party: the result was the Alien and Sedition Laws. Pickering warned him, and he quarrelled with him. He would not conciliate, but punish his political foes. He loved to exercise power; he did it unscrupulously, and became exceedingly offensive to many of his own party, and bitterly hated by his political enemies. The Alien and Sedition Laws emanated from the extremists of the Federal party, and were in opposition to the views of Adams himself — yet he approved them, and determined to execute them. He knew these laws were in direct opposition to the views and feelings of an immense majority of the people; and with these lights before him, and when he had it in his power to have conciliated the masses, he defied them.

Mr. Adams was unaccustomed to seek or court public favor; his associations had never been with the masses, and he understood very little of their feelings; when these were forced upon him, he received their manifestations with contempt, and uniformly disregarded their teachings. All these defects of character were seized upon by the opposition, to render odious the Federal party.

Mr. Jefferson placed himself in active opposition, and was known at an early day as the candidate of the opposition to succeed Adams. Our difficulties with France, and the action of Congress in appointing Washington commander-in-chief of the American forces, brought Washington into contact with Adams on several occasions; and especially when Washington made his acceptance of the office conditional upon the appointment of Hamilton as second in command, Adams thought he had not been respectfully treated, either by Congress or Washington; and there were some pretty sharp letters written by Washington in relation to the course of Adams.

Jefferson was opposed to the French war. The aid afforded by France in our Revolution had made grateful the public heart, and the people were indisposed to rush into a war with her for slight cause. The pen of Jefferson was never idle: he knew the general feeling, and inflamed it, and what the consequences to the country might have been, had not the war come to an abrupt and speedy end, there are no means of knowing. The trial and conviction of Lyon and Cooper under the Sedition Law, aroused a burst of indignation from the people. Still it taught no wisdom to Mr. Adams. He was urged to have their prosecutions abandoned, but he refused. After conviction, he was seriously pressed to pardon these men, in obedience to the popular will, but he persistently refused, and Lyon was continued in prison until liberated by the success of the Republican party, and the repeal of the offensive and impolitic laws soon after.

Adams professed great veneration for the character of Washington, and he was doubtless sincere. Yet he never lost sight of the fact that it was he who had seconded the motion when made in Congress by Samuel Adams to appoint Washington commander-in-chief of the armies of the Revolution, or that it was he who suggested it to Samuel Adams, and that he sustained the motion in a speech of burning eloquence. He felt that this conferred an obligation and that Washington was at times unmindful of this. He was more exacting than generous, and more suspicious than confiding In truth, Adams had more mind than soul; more ambition than patriotism, and more impulse than discretion. Yet the country owes him much. He was a great support in the cause of the Revolution, and his folly was to charge too high for his services. The people honored him — they have honored his family, and will yet make his son President. He received all they could give, and his littleness crept out in his desire for more.

General Washington's estimate of men was generally correct. He understood Adams, Jefferson, Hamilton, and Burr. I do not think he was personally attached to any one of them ; yet he appreciated them as the public now do. He had need of the talents of Hamilton and Jefferson. The organization of the Government required the first minds of the country; and Washington was the man to call them to his side. In nothing did he show more greatness than in this. He knew Jefferson was without principle, but he knew that he was eminently talented; he could forget the one, and call to his aid the other. His confidence in the integrity of Hamilton was stronger, as well as in his ability. Upon all matters of deep concern to the country he consulted both, and these consultatations often brought these two men into antagonistical positions before him, and upon important public matters — one of which was the constitutionality of a United States Bank. To each of these, when the charter of the bank was before him, he addressed a note requesting their opinions upon its constitutionality. Jefferson replied promptly in a short, written opinion, not well considered or ably argued, as was his wont; denying the constitutionality of such an institution. This opinion was handed to Hamilton, who pleaded public duties as the cause of delay on his part, for not furnishing an opinion. It came at last, and was able and conclusive, as to its constitutionality. But it was terrible in its slashing and exposure of the dogmatical sophisms of Jefferson. From that time forward there were bitter feelings between these two eminent men.

Intellectually, Hamilton had no equal in his day. It is ridiculous to compare him with Burr, which is often done by persons who should know better, because they have all the evidence upon which to predicate a conclusion. The occasion was open to both, equally, to discover to the world what abilities they possessed. They equally filled eminent positions before the nation, and at a time when she demanded the use of the first abilities in the land. What each performed is before the world.

Men having talent will always leave behind some evidence of this, whether they pass through life in a public or private capacity. Flippant pertness, with some wit, is too often mistaken for talent — and a still tongue with a sage look, will sometimes pass for wisdom. But wherever there is talent or wisdom, it makes its mark.

The evidences of Hamilton's abilities are manifested in his works. They show a versatility of talent unequalled by any modern man. He was conspicuous for his great genius before he was fifteen years of age; he was chief-of-staff for General Washington before he was twenty, and before he was thirty, was admitted to be the first mind of the country. As a military man, every officer of the army of the Revolution considered him the very first; as a lawyer, he had no equal of his day; as a statesman, he ranked above all competition; as a financier, none were his equal, and an abundance of evidence has been left by him to sustain this reputation in every particular.

What has Burr left? Nothing. He still lives, and what his posthumous papers may say for him, I cannot say; but I know him well, and consequently expect nothing. As a lawyer, he was mediocre; as a statesman, vacillating and without any fixed principles; as an orator, (for some had claimed him to be such,) he was turgid and verbose — sometimes he was sarcastic, but only when the malignity of his nature found vent in the bitterness of words. His private conduct has, in every situation, been bad. He was one of the Lee and Gates faction to displace Washington from the command of the army. He decried the abilities of Washington. He violated the confidence of General Putnam, when his aide, in seducing Margaret Moncrief, (whose father had intrusted her to Putnam's care.) He violated his faith to the Republican party, in lending himself to the Federal party to defeat the known and expressed will of the people, and the Republican party, by contesting the election before Congress of Mr. Jefferson. In the Legislature of New York, his conduct was such as to draw on him the suspicion of corruption, and universal condemnation. Contrast his public services with his public and private vices, and see what he is — the despised of the whole world, eking out a miserable existence in hermitical seclusion with a woman of ill-fame.

There resided as minister of the Congregational Church, at that time, in Litchfield, Lyman Beecher. He was a man of short stature; remarkable dark complexion, with large and finely formed head; his features were strong and irregular, with stern, ascetic expression. He was naturally a man of great mind, and but for the bigoted character of his religion, narrowing his mind to certain contemptible prejudices and opinions, might have been a great man. Reared in the practice of Puritan opinions, and associated from childhood with that strait-laced and intolerant sect, his energies, (which were indomitable) and mind, more so perverted as to become mischievous, instead of useful. He was a propagandist in the broadest sense of the term—would have made an admirable inquisitor—was without any of the charities of the Christian; despised as heretical the creed of every sect save his own, and had all of the intolerant bitterness and degrading superstitions of the Puritans, and persecutors of Laud, in the Long Parliament. In truth, he was an immediate descendant of the Puritans of the seventeenth century, and was distinguished for the persecuting and intolerant spirit of that people. He seemed ever casting about for something in the principles or conduct of others to abuse, and delighted to exhaust his genius in pouring out his venom upon those who did not square their conduct and opinions by his rule. At this time, 1820, the admission of Missouri into the Union gave rise to the agitation of the extension of slavery. This was a sweet morsel under and on his tongue. He at once commenced the indulgence of his persecuting spirit, in the abuse of slavery, and slave owners. His own immediate people had committed no sin in the importation of the African, and the money accumulated in the traffic was not blood-money. The institution had been wiped out in New England, not by enfranchisement, but by sale to the people of the South, when no longer useful or valuable at home; and all the sin of slavery had followed the slave, to barbarize and degrade the people of the South. The fertility of his imagination could suggest a thousand evils growing from slavery, which concentrating in the character of those possessing them, made them demons upon earth, and fit heritors of hell, deserving the wrath of God and man.

It was palpable to the scrutinizing observer, that it was not the sin of slavery which actuated the zeal of Beecher. The South had held control of the Government almost from its inception. The Northern, or Federal party, had been repudiated for the talents and energy of the South. Its principles and their professors were odious — the conduct of its leading representatives, during the late war, had tainted New England, and she was offensive to the nostrils of patriotism everywhere. Her people were restless and dissatisfied under the disgrace. They were anxious for power, not to control for the public good the destinies of the country; but for revenge upon those who had triumphed in their overthrow. Their people had spread over the West, and carried with them their religion and hatred — they were ambitious of more territory, over which to propagate their race and creed; yet preparatory to the great end of their aims, and the agitation necessary to the education of their people upon this subject, they must commence in the pulpit to abolish some cursing sin which stood in their way. They had found it, and a fit instrument, too, in Lyman Beecher, to commence the work. It was the sin of slavery. It stood in the way of New England progress and New England civilization. New England religion must come to the rescue. There was nothing good which could come from the South; all was tainted with this crying sin. New England purity, through New England Puritanism, must permeate all the land, and effect the good work — and none so efficient as Beecher. The students of the law-school had a pew in his little synagogue — it was after the fashion of a square pew, with seats all around, and to this he would direct his eye when pouring out his anathemas upon the South, Southern habits, and Southern institutions; four out of five of the members of the school were from the South.

It was his habit to ascribe the origin and practice of every vice to slavery. Debauchery of every grade, name, and character, was born of this, and though every one of these vices, in full practice, were reeking under his nose, and permeating every class of his own people; when seven out of every ten of the bawds of every brothel, from Maine to the Sabine, were from New England, they were only odious in the South. I remember upon one occasion he was dilating extensively upon the vice of drunkenness, and accounting it as peculiar to the South, and the direct offshoot of slavery, he exclaimed, with his eyes fixed upon the students' pew: "Yes, my brethren, it is peculiar to the people who foster the accursed institution of slavery, and so common is it in the South, that the father who yields his daughter in wedlock, never thinks of asking if her intended is a sober man. All he asks, or seems desirous to know, is whether he is good-natured in his cups." Before him sat his nest of young adders, growing up to inherit his religion, talents, and vindictive spirit. Instilled into those from their cradles were all the dogmas of Puritanism, to stimulate the mischievous spirit of the race to evil works. Admirably have they fulfilled their destiny. To the preaching and writings of the men and women descended from Lyman Beecher has more misery ensued, than from any other one source, for the last century. "Uncle Tom's Cabin" has slain its hundreds of thousands, and the sermons of Henry Ward Beecher have made to flow an ocean of blood.

The example of Pymm, Cromwell, Whaley, and Goff, and their fate, has taught the Puritans no useful lesson. They seem to think to triumph in civil war, as their ancestors did, regardless of the danger that a reaction may bring to them, is all they can desire. The fate of these men has no warning. Reactions sometimes come with terrible consequences. They cannot see Cromwell's dead body hanging in chains. They will not remember the fate of Whaley and Goff, whose bones are mouldering in their own New Haven, after flying their country and, for years, hiding in caves and cellars from the revengeful pursuit of resentful enemies. The Pymms and the Praise-God-bare-bones of the thirty-ninth Congress may and (it is to be hoped) will yet meet the merited reward of their crimes of persecution and oppression.

At the time of which I write, there were many remaining in Connecticut who participated in the conflicts and perils of the Revolution. These men were all animated with strong national sentiments, and felt that every part of the Union was their country. They idolized Washington, and always spoke with affectionate praise of the Southern spirit, so prominent in her troops during the war. The conduct of the South (and especially that of Georgia toward General Greene, in donating him a splendid plantation, with a palatial residence, upon the Savannah River, near the city of Savannah, to which he removed, lived, and in which he died,) was munificent, and characteristic of a noble and generous people.

But these were passing away, and a new people were coming into their places. The effects of a common cause, a common danger, and a united success, were not felt by these. New interests excited new aspirations. The nation's peril was past, and she was one of the great powers of the earth, and acknowledged as such. She had triumphantly passed through a second war with her unnatural mother, in which New England, as a people, had reaped no glory. In the midst of the struggle, she had called a convention of her people, with a view of withdrawing from the Union. Her people had invited the enemy, with their blue-light signals, to enter the harbor they were blockading, and where the American ships, under the command of one of our most gallant commanders, had sought refuge. They were sorely chagrined, and full of wrath. They hated the South and her people. It was growing, and they were nursing it. Even then we were a divided people, with every interest conserving to unite us — the South producing and consuming; the North manufacturing, carrying, and selling for, and to, the South. The harmony of commerce, and the harmony of interest, had lost its power, and we were a divided people. The breach widened, war followed, and ruin riots over the land. The South was the weaker, and went down; the North was the stronger, and triumphed — and the day of her vengeance has come.

In that remote time, the chase after the almighty dollar had commenced, and especially in New England, where every sentiment was subordinate to this. Patriotism was a secondary sentiment. Hypocritical pretension to the purity of religion was used to cover the vilest practices, and to shield from public indignation men who, praying, pressed into their service the vilest means to make haste to be rich. The sordid parsimony of ninety-hundredths of the population shut out every sentiment of generosity, and rooted from the heart every emotion honorable to human nature. Neighborhood intercourse was poisoned with selfishness, and the effort to overreach, and make money out of, the ignorance or necessities of these, was universal. These degrading practices crept into every business, and petty frauds soon became designated as Yankee tricks. There was nothing ennobling in their pursuits. The honorable profession of law dwindled into pettifogging tricks. Commerce was degraded in their hands by fraud and chicanery. The pernicious and grasping nature everywhere cultivated, soon fastened upon the features. Their eyes were pale, their features lank and hard, and the stony nature was apparent in the icy coldness of manner, in the deceitful grin, and lip-laugh, which the eye never shared, and which was only affected, when interest prompted, or the started suspicions of an intended victim warned them to be wary. The climate, and the inhospitable and ungenerous soil, seemed to impart to the people their own natures.

The men were all growing sharp, and the women, cold and passionless; the soul appeared to shrivel and sink into induration, and the whole people were growing into a nation of cheats and dastards. Such was the promise for the people of New England, in 1820. Has it not been realized in the years of the recent intestine war? The incentive held out to her people to volunteer into her armies, was the plunder of the South. The world has never witnessed such rapacity for gain as marked the armies of the United States in their march through the South. Religion and humanity were lost sight of in the general scramble for the goods and the money of the Southern people. Rings were snatched from the fingers of ladies and torn from their ears; their wardrobes plundered and forwarded to expectant families at home; graves were violated for the plates of gold and silver that might be found upon the coffins; the dead bodies of women and men were unshrouded after exhumation, to search in the coffins and shrouds to see if valuables were not here concealed; and, in numerous instances, the teeth were torn from the skeleton mouths of the dead for the gold plugs, or gold plates that might be found there. Nor was this heathenish rapacity confined to the common soldier; the commanders and subalterns participated with acquisitive eagerness, sharing fully with their commands the hellish instincts of their race.

They professed to come to liberate the slave, and they uniformly robbed or swindled him of every valuable he might possess — even little children were stripped of their garments, as trophies of war, to be forwarded home for the wear of embryo Puritans, as an example for them in future. Such are the Yankees of 1863–4, and '67. They now hold control of the nation; but her mighty heart is sore under their oppression. She is beginning to writhe. It will not be long, before with a mighty effort she will burst the bonds these people have tied about her limbs, will reassert the freedom of her children, and scourge their oppressors with a whip of scorpions.

Such men as Talmage, Humphries, and Wolcott are no more to be found in New England. The animus of these men is no longer with these people. The work of change is complete. Nothing remains of their religion but its semblance — the fanaticism of Cotton Mather, without his sincerity — the persecuting spirit of Cotton, without the sincerity of his motives. Every tie that once united the descendants of the Norman with those of the Saxon is broken. They are two in interest, two in feeling, two in blood, and two in hatred. For a time they may dwell together, but not in unison; for they have nothing in common but hatred. Its fruit is discord, and the day is not distant, when these irreconcilable elements must be ruled with a power despotic as independent, whose will must be law unto both. It is painful to look back fifty years and contrast the harmony then pervading every class of every section with the discord and bitterness of hate which substitutes it to day. Then, the national airs of "Hail Columbia" and "Yankee Doodle" thrilled home to the heart of every American. To-day, they are only heard in one half of the Union to be cursed and execrated. To ask a lady to play one of these airs upon the harp or piano, from the Rio Grande to the Potomac, would be resented as an insult. The fame of Washington and John Hancock mingled as the united nations; but the conduct of the sons of the Puritan fathers has stolen the respect for them from the heart of half of the nation; and now, even the once glorious name of Daniel Webster stirs no enthusiasm in the bosoms which once beat joyfully to his praise, as it came to them from New England. Those who from party purposes proclaim peace and good will, only deceive the world, not themselves, or the people of the South. Peace there is; but good will, none. When asked to be given, memory turns to the battle-fields upon Southern soil, the bloody graves where the chosen spirits of the South are sleeping, and the heart burns with indignant hatred. Generations may come and pass away, but this hatred, this cursed memory of oppressive wrong will live on. The mothers of to-day make for their infants a tradition of these memories, and it will be transmitted as the highlander's cross of fire, from clan to clan, in burning brightness, for a thousand years. The graveyards will no more perish than the legends of the war that made them. They are in our midst, our children, the kindred of all are there — and those who are to come will go there — and their mothers, as Hamilcar did, will make them upon these green graves swear eternal hatred to those who with their vengeance filled these sacred vaults.

We are expected to love those whose hands are red with the blood of our children; to take to our bosoms the murderers and robbers who have slain upon the soil of their nativity our people, and who have robbed our homes and devastated our country; who have fattened Southern soil with Southern blood, and enriched their homes with the stolen wealth of ours. Are we not men, and manly? Do we feel as men? and is not this insult to manliness, and a vile mockery to the feelings of men? We can never forget—we will never forgive, and we will wait; for when the opportunity shall come, as come it will, we will avenge the damning wrong.

This may be unchristian, but it is natural — nature is of God and will assert herself. No mawkish pretension, no hypocritical cant, can repress the natural feelings of the heart: its loves and resentments are its strongest passions, and the love that we bore for our children and kindred kindles to greater vigor in the hatred we bear for their murderers.

CHAPTER XVII.

CONGRESS IN ITS BRIGHTEST DAYS.

MISSOURI COMPROMISE — JOHN RANDOLPH'S JUBA — MR. MACON — HOLMES AND CRAWFORD — MR. CLAY'S INFLUENCE — JAMES BARBOR — PHILIP P. BARBOR — MR. PINCKNEY — MR. BEECHER, OF OHIO — "CUCKOO, CUCKOO!" — NATIONAL ROADS — WILLIAM LOWNDES — WILLIAM ROSCOE — DUKE OF ARGYLE — LOUIS MCLEAN — WHIG AND DEMOCRATIC PARTIES.

IT was at the last session of the fifteenth Congress, in the winter of 1820–21, when the famous Compromise measure, known as the Missouri Compromise, was effected. A portion of that winter was spent by the writer at Washington. Congress was then composed of the first intellects of the nation, and the measure was causing great excitement throughout the entire country.

Missouri, in obedience to a permissory statute, had framed a constitution, and demanded admission into the Union as a State. By this constitution slavery was recognized as an institution of the State. Objection was made to this clause on the part of the Northern members, which led to protracted and sometimes acrimonious debate. At the first session of the Congress the admission of the State had been postponed, and during the entire second session it had been the agitating question; nor was it until the very end of the session settled by this famous compromise.

The debates were conducted by the ablest men in Congress, in both the Senate and the House of Representatives. In the Senate, William Pinckney, of Maryland; Rufus King, of New York; Harrison Gray Otis, of Massachusetts; James Barbor, of Virginia; William Smith, of South Carolina, and Freeman Walker, of Georgia, were most conspicuous. In the House were John Randolph, of Virginia; William Lowndes, of South Carolina; Louis McLean, of Delaware; Thomas W. Cobb, of Georgia, and Louis Williams, of North Carolina, and many others of less note. Henry Clay, of Kentucky, was Speaker of the House during the first session of the Congress; but resigned before the meeting of the succeeding Congress, and John Taylor, of New York, was elected to preside as Speaker for the second session. Mr. Clay was absent from his seat during the early part of this session; and notwithstanding the eminent men composing the Congress, there seemed a want of some leading and controlling mind to master the difficulty, and calm the threatening excitement which was intensifying as the debate progressed. Mr. Randolph was the leader in the debates of the House, and occupied the floor frequently in the delivery of lengthy and almost always very interesting speeches. These touched every subject connected with the Government, its history, and its powers. They were brilliant and beautiful; full of classical learning and allusion, and sparkling as a casket of diamonds, thrown upon, and rolling along, a Wilton carpet. It seemed to be his pleasure to taunt the opposition to enforce an angry or irritable reply, and then to launch the arrows of his biting wit and sarcasm at whoever dared the response, in such rapid profusion, as to astonish the House, and overwhelm his antagonist.

His person was as unique as his manner. He was tall and extremely slender. His habit was to wear an overcoat extending to the floor, with an upright standing collar which concealed his entire person except his head, which seemed to be set, by the ears, upon the collar of his coat. In early morning it was his habit to ride on horseback. This ride was frequently extended to the hour of the meeting of Congress. When this was the case, he always rode to the Capitol, surrendered his horse to his groom — the ever-faithful Juba, who always accompanied him in these rides — and, with his ornamental riding-whip in his hand, a small cloth or leathern cap perched upon the top of his head, (which peeped out, wan and meagre, from between the openings of his coat-collar,) booted and gloved, he would walk to his seat in the House — then in session — lay down upon his desk his cap and whip, and then slowly remove his gloves. If the matter before the House interested him, and he desired to be heard, he would fix his large, round, lustrous black eyes upon the Speaker, and, in a voice shrill and piercing as the cry of a peacock, exclaim: "Mr. Speaker!" then, for a moment or two, remain looking down upon his desk, as if to collect his thoughts; then lifting his eyes to the Speaker would commence, in a conversational tone, an address that not unfrequently extended through five hours, when he would yield to a motion for adjournment, with the understanding that he was to finish his speech the following day.

He had but few associates. These were all from the South, and very select. With Mr. Macon, Mr. Crawford, Louis Williams, and Mr. Cobb, he was intimate. He was a frequent visitor to the family of Mr. Crawford, then Secretary of the Treasury, where occasionally he met Macon and Cobb, with other friends of Crawford. Macon and Crawford were his models of upright men. He believed Mr. Crawford to be the first intellect of the age, and Mr. Macon the most honest man. The strict honesty of Macon captivated him, as it did most men. His home-spun ideas, his unaffected plainness of dress, and primitive simplicity of manner, combined with a wonderful fund of common sense, went home to the heart of Randolph, and he loved Macon in sincerity.

Macon and Crawford humored his many eccentricities, and would always deferentially listen to him when the humor was on him to talk. It was at such times that Randolph was most interesting. He had read much, and to great advantage; he had travelled, and with an observant eye; he knew more, and he knew it more accurately, than any other man of his country, except, perhaps, that wonderful man, William Lowndes. In his talking moods all the store-house of his information was drafted into service. His command of language was wonderful. The antithetical manner of expressing himself gave piquancy and *vim* to his conversation, making it very captivating. He was too impatient, and had too much nervous irritability and too rapid a flow of ideas, to indulge in familiar and colloquial conversation. He would talk all, or none. He inaugurated a subject and exhausted it, and there were few who desired more than to listen when he talked. Two or three evenings in the week there would assemble at Mr. Crawford's a few gentlemen, members of Congress. This was especially the case pending the Missouri question, when Mr. Randolph, Mr. Macon, Mr. McLean, Mr. Holmes, of Maine, (a great admirer of Mr. Crawford,) Mr. Lowndes, and sometimes one or two gentlemen from Pennsylvania, would be present. At these meetings this question was the first and principal topic, and Mr. Randolph would engross the entire conversation for an hour, when he would almost universally rise, bid good-night, and leave. At other times he would listen attentively, without uttering a word, particularly when Crawford or Lowndes were speaking. These, then, almost universally, did all the talking. The diversity of opinion scarcely ever prompted reply or interruption. In these conversations the great powers of Crawford's mind would break out, astonishing and convincing every one.

It was upon one of these occasions, when discussing in connection with the Missouri question, the subject of slavery, its influences, and its future, that Mr. Crawford remarked: "If the Union is of more importance to the South than slavery, the South should immediately take measures for the gradual emancipation of the slaves, fixing a period for its final extinction. But if the institution of slavery is of more vital importance than the perpetuation of the Union to the South, she should at once secede and establish a government to protect and preserve this institution. She now has the power to do so without the fear of provoking a war. Her people should be unanimous, and this agitation has made them so — I believe. I know the love of the Union has been paramount to every other consideration with the Southern people; but they view, as I do, this attempt to arrest the further spread of slavery as aggressive on the part of Congress, and discover an alarming state of the Northern mind upon this subject. This with an increasing popular strength may grow into proportions which shall be irresistible, and the South may be ultimately forced to do, what she never will voluntarily do — abolish at once the institution." It was urged by Mr. Holmes that the Constitution guaranteed slavery to the States, that its control and destiny was alone with the States, and there was no danger that the North would ever violate the Constitution to interfere with what they had no interest in.

"Never violate the Constitution!" said Randolph, in an excited and querulous tone. "Mr. Holmes, you perhaps know the nature of your people better than I do. But I know them well enough not to trust them. They stickle at nothing to accomplish an end; and their preachers can soon convince them that slavery is a sin, and that they are responsible for its existence here, and that they can only propitiate offended Deity by its abolition. You are a peculiar people, Holmes, prone to fanaticism upon all subjects, and this fanaticism concentrated as a religious duty — the Constitution will only prove a barrier of straw. No, sir; I am unwilling to trust them. They want honesty of purpose, have no sincerity, no patriotism, no principle. Your dough-faces will profess, but at a point will fly the track, sir; they can't stand, sir; they can't stand pressing. Interest, interest, sir, is their moving motive. Do you not see it in their action in this matter? Missouri is a fertile and lovely country; they want it for the purpose of settlement with their own people. Prohibit slavery to the inhabitants, and no Southern man will go there; there will be no competition in the purchase of her land. Your people will have it all to themselves; they will flock to it like wild geese, and very soon it is a Northern State in Northern interest; and, step after step, all the Western territory will be in your possession, and you will create States *ab libitum*. You know the Constitution permits two-thirds of the States to amend or alter it: establish the principle that Congress can exclude slavery from a territory, contrary to the wishes of her people expressed in a constitution formed by them for their government, and how long will it be, before two-thirds of the States will be free? Then you can change the Constitution and place slavery under the control of Congress — and, under such circumstances, how long will it be permitted to remain in any State?

"Your people are too religious, sir; eminently practical, inventive, restless, cold, calculating, malicious, and ambitious; invent curious rat-traps, and establish missions. I don't want to be trapped, sir; I am too wary a rat for that; and think with Mr. Crawford, now is the time for separation, and I mean to ask Clay to unite with us. Yet, sir, I have not spoken to the fellow for years, sir; but I will to-morrow; I will tell him I always despised him, but if he will go to his people, I will to mine, and tell them now is the time for separation from you; and I will follow his lead if he will only do so, if it leads me to perdition. I never did follow it, but in this matter I will. I bid you good night, gentlemen." He waited for no reply, but taking his hat and whip, hurriedly left the room.

"Can Mr. Randolph be in earnest?" asked several.

"Intensely so," replied Mr. Crawford. "Mr. Holmes, your people are forcing Mr. Randolph's opinions upon the entire South. They will not permit Northern intermeddling with that which peculiarly interests themselves, and over which they alone hold control."

There was a pause, the party was uneasy. There were more than Mr. Holmes present who were startled at both Crawford's and Randolph's speculation as to the value of the Union. They had ever felt that this was anchored safely in every American breast, and was paramount to every other consideration or interest. It was a terrible heresy, and leading to treason. This was not said, but it was thought, and in no very agreeable mood the party separated for the night.

Mr. Clay had just arrived from Kentucky. There had been many speculations as to what course he would pursue in this delicate matter. Many had suspended their opinions awaiting his action. The members from Ohio were generally acting and voting with those of the East and North. Some seemed doubtful, and it was supposed Mr. Clay would exercise great influence with all the West, and those from Ohio, especially. Hence, his coming was universally and anxiously awaited. But now he was in Washington, all were on the *qui vive*.

Randolph's declaration was whispered about in the morning, and little coteries were grouped about the hall of the House of Representatives. Randolph was in conversation, near the Speaker's chair, with the clerk, who was pointing and calling his attention to something upon the journal of the House. The hour of meeting was at hand, and the crowd was increasing upon the floor. Mr. Taylor was in conversation, near the fire-place, on the left of the Speaker's chair, with Stratford Canning, the British Plenipotentiary, Harrison Gray Otis, and Governor Chittenden, of Vermont. Mr. Clay entered in company with William S. Archer, a man whose only merit and sole pride was the having been born in Virginia; whose pusillanimous arrogance was only equalled by the poverty of his intellect, and who always foisted himself upon the presence of eminent men, deeming he was great because of his impudence and their association. All eyes were turned to Clay, and the members flocked about him. Releasing himself from these he came up the aisle toward the

Speaker's chair. Mr. Randolph stepped into the aisle immediately in front of the chair. At this moment Clay discovered him and, towering to his full height, paused within a few feet of him whose eye he saw fixed upon his own.

Randolph advanced and, without extending his hand, said: "Good morning, Mr. Clay." Clay bowed, and Randolph immediately said: "I have a duty to perform to my country; so have you, Mr. Clay. Leave your seat here, sir, and return to your people, as I will to mine. Tell them, as I will mine, that the time has come: if they would save themselves from ruin, and preserve the liberties for which their fathers bled, they must separate from these men of the North. Do so, sir; and, though I never did before, I will follow your lead in the effort to save our people, and their liberties." Mr. Clay listened, and without apparent surprise remarked, with a smile: "Mr. Randolph, that will require more reflection than this moment of time affords," and bowing passed on.

But a bomb had fallen on the floor, and consternation was on every face. All turned to Mr. Clay. All saw a crisis was at hand, and that this matter must be settled as speedily as possible. Archer filed off with Randolph, who affected to pet him, as some men do foils for their wit, in the person of a toady.

A few days after this occurrence the famous Compromise measure was reported, and the first speech I ever listened to from Mr. Clay was in its advocacy. About him was gathered the talent of the Senate and the House. The lobbies and galleries were filled to overflowing. Mr. Pinckney, of Maryland; Landman, of Connecticut; Rufus King, William Lowndes, Otis, Holmes, Macon, and others, all manifested intense interest in the speech of Mr. Clay. How grandly he towered up over those seated about him! Dressed in a full suit of black, his hair combed closely down to his head, displaying its magnificent proportions, with his piercing, gray eyes fixed upon those of the Speaker, he poured out, in fervid words, the wisdom of his wonderful mind, and the deep feelings of his great heart. All accorded to him sincerity and exalted patriotism; all knew and confided in his wisdom; all knew him to be a national man, and into the hearts of all his words sank deep, carrying conviction, and calming the storm of angry passions which threatened not only the peace, but the existence of the Government. All the majesty of his nature seemed as a halo emanating from his person and features, as, turning to those grouped about him, and then to the House, his words, warm and persuasive, flowing as a stream of melody, with his hand lifted from his desk, he said:

"I wish that my country should be prosperous, and her Government perpetual. I am in my soul assured that no other can ever afford the same protection to human liberty, and insure the same amount. Leave the North to her laws and her institutions. Extend the same conciliating charity to the South and West. Their people, as yours, know best their wants — know best their interests. Let them provide for their own—our system is one of compromises—and in the spirit of harmony come together, in the spirit of brothers compromise any and every jarring sentiment or interest which may arise in the progress of the country. There is security in this; there is peace, and fraternal union. Thus we may, we shall, go on to cover this entire continent with prosperous States, and a contented, self-governed, and happy people. To the unrestrained energies of an intelligent and enterprising people, the mountains shall yield their mineral tribute, the valleys their cereals and fruits, and a million of millions of contented and prosperous people shall demonstrate to an admiring world the great problem that man is capable of self-government."

There beamed from every countenance a pleased satisfaction, as the members of the Senate and the House came up to express their delight, and their determination to support the measure proposed, and so ably advocated. There was oil upon the waters, and the turbulent waves went down. Men who had been estranged and angered for many months, met, and with friendly smiles greeted each other again. The ladies in the gallery above rose up as if by a common impulse, to look down, with smiles, upon the great commoner. One whose silvered hair, parted smoothly and modestly upon her aged forehead, fell in two massy folds behind her ears, clasped her hands, and audibly uttered: "God bless him."

The reconciliation seemed to be effected, and the confidence and affection between the sections to be renewed with increased fervor and intensity. There was rejoicing throughout the land. Dissatisfaction only spake from the pulpits of New England, and there only from those of the Puritan Congregationalists. But the public heart had received a shock, and though it beat on, it was not with the healthful tone of former days.

The men of the Revolution were rapidly passing to eternity. The cement of blood which bound these as one was dissolving, and the fabric of their creation was undermined in the hearts of the people, with corroding prejudices, actively fomented by the bigotry of a selfish superstition. A sectional struggle for supremacy had commenced. The control of the Government was the aim, and patriotism was consuming in the flame of ambition. The Government's security, the Government's perpetuity, and the common good, were no longer prime considerations. All its demonstrated blessings had remained as ever the same. Stimulated by the same motives and the same ambitions, the new world and the new Government were moving in the old groove; and the old world saw repeating here the history of all the Governments which had arisen, lived, and passed away, in her own borders. The mighty genius of Clay and Webster, of Jackson and Calhoun, had, for a time, stayed the rapid progress of ruin which had begun to show itself, but only for a time. They have been gathered to their fathers, and the controlling influence of their mighty minds being removed, confusion, war, and ruin have followed.

The men conspicuous in the debates on the Missouri question were giants in intellect, and perhaps few deliberative assemblies of the world ever contained more talent, or more public virtue. At the head of these stood Henry Clay, Pinckney, Rufus King, William Lowndes, Harrison Gray Otis, William Smith, Louis McLean, the two Barbors, John Randolph, Freeman Walker, Thomas W. Cobb, and John Holmes, of Maine.

James Barbor was a member of the Senate; Philip P. Barbor, of the House. They were brothers, and both from Virginia. They were both men of great abilities, but their style and manner were very different. James was a verbose and ornate declaimer; Philip was a close, cogent reasoner, without any attempt at elegance or display. He labored to convince the mind; James, to control and direct the feelings. A wag wrote upon the wall of the House, at the conclusion of a masterly argument of Philip P. Barbor,

> "Two Barbers to shave our Congress long did try.
> One shaves with froth; the other shaves dry."

Of the Senate Mr. Pinkney was the great orator. His speech upon this most exciting question has ever been considered the most finished for eloquence and power, ever delivered in the United States Senate. The effect upon the Senate, and the audience assembled in the galleries and lobbies of the Senate, was thrilling. Mr. King was old, but retained in their vigor his faculties, was more tame perhaps than in his younger years; still the clearness and brilliancy of his powerful mind manifested itself in his every effort. Mr. Pinkney had all the advantages which a fine manly person and clear, musical voice gives to an orator. He spoke but rarely and never without great preparation. He was by no means a ready debater, and prized too much his reputation to hazard anything in an impromptu, extemporaneous address. He listened, for weeks, to King, Otis, and others who debated the question, and came at last prepared in one great effort to answer and demolish the arguments of these men. Those who listened to that wonderful effort of forensic power will never forget his reply to King, when he charged him with uttering sentiments in debate calculated to incite a servile war. The picture he drew of such a war: the massacring by infuriated black savages of delicate women and children; the burning and destroying of cities; the desolating by fire and sword the country, was so thrilling and descriptively perfect, that you smelt the blood, saw the flames, and heard the shrieks of perishing victims. Mr. King shuddered as he looked on the orator, and listened to his impassioned declamation. But when Pinkney turned from the President of the Senate and, flashing his eye upon King, continued in words hissing in whispers, full of pathos as of biting indignation, Mr. King folded his arms and rested his head upon them, concealing his features and emotion from the speaker and the Senate. For two hours the Senate and galleries were chained as it were to their seats. At times so intense was the feeling, that a pause of the speaker made audible the hard and excited breathing of the audience, catching their breath as though respiration had been painfully suspended and relief had come in this pause. When he had finished and resumed his seat, there was profound silence for many seconds, when a Senator in seeming trepidation rose and moved an adjournment.

Mr. Pinkney was in every respect a most finished gentleman, highly bred, only associating with the first men and minds of the country; courteous and polished in his manners, and scrupulously neat in his dress, which was always in the height of fashion and always of the finest and most costly materials. He never came to the Senate but in full dress, and would have been mortified to find a mite of lint upon his coat, or a dash of dust upon his boots.

At that time the United States Senate was the most august and dignified body in the world. What is it to-day? *O tempora, O mores!* In the House, the palm of oratory was disputed between Mr. Clay and Mr. Randolph. Their styles were so different, and both so effective, that it was difficult to distinguish by comparison, to which belonged the distinction of being first. Mr. Clay was always collected and self-possessed—he was, too, always master of his subject; and though he was a ready debater, he never made a set speech upon any important subject without careful preparation. He was not easily disconcerted; courageous, with a strong will, he feared no intemperate opposition, and was never restrained from uttering his sentiments and opinions of men or measures. He was kind and generous, until aroused or offended and, then, was merciless. His sarcasm and invective upon such occasions was withering, and his vehemence daring and terrible. No man of his day had a mind better balanced than Mr. Clay. His judgment was almost always correct; his imagination brilliant, but always under the control of his judgment; his memory and preceptive faculties were wonderful; his education was defective, and the associations of the West had not given that polish to his manners which distinguishes men of education, reared in educated communities, and associating always with polished society. Mr. Clay had been at the most polished courts of Europe, and was familiar with their most refined society; but these he visited in mature life, after the manners are formed, and habit made them indurate. He had long been familiar, too, with the best society in his own country and, by this, had been much improved. Still the Kentuckian would sometimes come through the shell, but always in a manner more to delight than offend; besides, Mr. Clay set little value upon forms and ceremony. There was too much heart for such cold seeming, too much fire for the chill, unfeeling ceremony of what is termed first society.

Mr. Clay's manners partook much of the character of his mind and soul. They were prompt, bold, and easy; his eloquence was bold, rough, and overwhelming.

Like all men of genius, will, and self-reliance, Mr. Clay was impatient of contradiction. The similarity in this regard, between Jackson, Clay, and Crawford was wonderful. They were equally passionate, equally impetuous, and equally impatient — all being natural men of great powers and limited education. To say they were self-made, would be paying the Almighty a left-handed compliment. But to say they assiduously cultivated His great gifts without much aid from the schoolmaster, would only be doing them unbiased justice.

Randolph was clasically educated. He had enjoyed every advantage of cultivation. Socially, he had never mingled with any but refined society. The franchise of suffrage in Virginia was confined to the freeholders, thus obviating in the public man the necessity of mingling with, and courting the good opinion of the multitude. The system, too, of electioneering was to address from the hustings the voters, to declare publicly the opinions of candidates, and the policy they proposed supporting. The vote was given *viva voce*. All concurred to make representative and constituent frank and honest. While this system existed, Virginia ruled the nation. These means secured the services of the first intellects, and the first characters of her people. The system was a training for debate and public display. Eloquence became the first requisite to the candidate, and was the most powerful means of influence and efficiency in the representative. Randolph had been thus trained; he had listened to, and been instructed by the eloquence of Patrick Henry, in his early youth, and in later life had met him as a competitor on the hustings. He had grown up by the side of Edmonds, Peyton Randolph, George Mason, and Thomas Jefferson. In his very youth he had excited the wonder and admiration of these great minds. He was sent into the Congress of the United States almost before he was qualified by age to take his seat; and at once took position by the side of such men as William B. Giles, William H. Crawford, James A. Byard, and Littleton W. Tazwell. His style of speaking was peculiar; his wit was bitter and biting; his sarcasm more pungent and withering than had ever been heard on the floor of Congress; his figure was *outre;* his voice, fine as the treble of a violin; his face, wan, wrinkled, and without beard; his limbs, long and unsightly, especially his arms and fingers; the skin seemed to grow to the attenuated bone; and the large, ill-formed joints were extremely ugly. But those fingers, and especially the right fore-finger, gave point and *vim* to his wit and invective.

In his manner he was at times deliberate, and apparently very considerate, and again he was rapid and vehement. When he would demolish an adversary, he would commence slowly, as if to collect all his powers, preparatory to one great onset. He would turn and talk, as it were, to all about him, and seemingly incongruously. It was as if he was slinging and whirling his chain-shot about his head, and circling it more and more rapidly, to collect all his strength for the fatal blow. All knew it would fall, but none knew where, until he had collected his utmost strength, and then, with the electrical flash of his eye, he would mark the victim, and the thundering crash of his vengeance, in words of vehemence, charged with the most caustic satire, would fall upon, and crush the devoted head of his scarce suspecting foe. I remember, upon one occasion, pending the debate upon the Missouri question, and when Mr. Randolph was in the habit of almost daily addressing the house, that a Mr. Beecher, of Ohio, who was very impatient with Randolph's tirades, would, in the lengthy pauses made by him, rise from his place, and move the previous question. The Speaker would reply: "The member from Virginia has the floor." The first and second interruption was not noticed by Randolph, but upon the repetition a third time, he slowly lifted his head from contemplating his notes, and said: "Mr. Speaker, in the Netherlands, a man of small capacity, with bits of wood and leather, will, in a few moments, construct a toy that, with the pressure of the finger and thumb, will cry 'Cuckoo! Cuckoo!' With less of ingenuity, and with inferior materials, the people of Ohio have made a toy that will, without much pressure, cry, 'Previous question, Mr. Speaker! Previous question, Mr. Speaker!'" at the same time designating Beecher, by pointing at him with his long, skeleton-looking finger. In a moment the House was convulsed with laughter, and I doubt if Beecher ever survived the sarcasm.

At the time Mr. Clay came into Congress, Randolph had no rival upon the floor of the House. He had become a terror to timid men. Few ventured to meet him in debate, and none to provoke him. Mr. Clay's reputation had preceded him. He had before, for a short time, been in the Senate. He was known to be the first orator in the West, and the West boasted Doddridge, Humphrey Marshall, John Rowan, Jesse Bledsoe, John Pope, and Felix Grundy.

It was not long, before these two met in debate upon the subject of the national road. Randolph opposed this measure as unconstitutional, denying to the General Government any power to make any improvements within the limits of any State, without the consent of the State. Mr. Clay claimed the power under that grant which constituted Congress competent to establish post-offices and post-roads. The discussion was an excited one. Mr. Clay was a Virginian, but not of Randolph's class; besides, he was not now from Virginia, and Randolph chose to designate him a degenerate, renegade son of the Old Dominion. He had been reared, as Randolph, a Democrat of the Jeffersonian school. In this he was an apostate from the ancient faith. Randolph fully expected an easy victory, and no man upon the floor was more surprised than himself, at the bold, eloquent, and defiant reply of Clay. Between them the combat was fierce and protracted. Randolph had the mortification of seeing Western Virginia moving with Clay, and the entire representation of the Western States joining with them. Clay was triumphant. The measure became a law, the road was built, and a monument was erected to Mr. Clay in Western Virginia, and by Virginians. It stands in a beautiful valley, immediately on the road's side. From that time until, as old men, they met in mortal combat upon the banks of the Potomac, they were rivals and enemies.

Randolph was rancorous in his hatred of Clay. In proportion as Clay rose in the estimation of his countrymen, did Randolph's hate increase. Clay sprang from the plebeian stock of his native Virginia. He had come as the representative of the rustics of Kentucky. He was not sanctified by a college diploma. He boasted no long line of ancestry, and yet he had met, and triumphed over, the scion of a boasted line — had bearded the aristocrat upon the field of his fame, and vanquished him. This triumph was followed up, in quick succession, with many others. He was now the cynosure of the nation, and the star of Randolph was waning. His disregard of Randolph's proposition, to withdraw from Congress and denounce the Union, and his success in effecting this compromise, sublimated Randolph's hatred, and no opportunity was permitted to pass unimproved for abuse of him as a politician, and as a man.

William Lowndes, after Clay, exercised more influence in the House than any other man. He was a South Carolinian, and of distinguished family. His health, at this time, was failing: it had always been delicate. Mr. Lowndes was comparatively a young man. He was remarkably tall: perhaps six feet six inches. He stood a head and shoulders above any man in Congress. His hair was golden ; his complexion, clear and pale, and his eyes were deep blue, and very expressive. He had been elaborately educated, and improved by foreign travel, extensive reading, and research. As a belles-lettres scholar, he was superior even to Mr. Randolph. Very retiring and modest in his demeanor, he rarely obtruded himself upon the House. When he did, it seemed only to remind the House of something which had been forgotten by his predecessors in debate. Sometimes he would make a set speech. When he did, it was always remarkable for profound reasoning, and profound thought. He was suffering with disease of the lungs, and his voice was weak : so much so that he never attempted to elevate it above a conversational tone. So honest was he in his views, so learned and so unobtrusive, that he had witched away the heart of the House. No man was so earnestly listened to as Mr. Lowndes. His mild and persuasive manner, his refined and delicate deportment in debate and social intercourse captivated every one; and at a time when acrimonious feelings filled almost every breast, there was no animosity for Mr. Lowndes. His impression upon the nation had made him the favored candidate of every section for the next President ; and it is not, perhaps, saying too much, that had his life been spared, he, and not John Quincy Adams, would have been the President in 1824. He would have been to all an acceptable candidate. His talents, his virtues, his learning, and his broad patriotism had very much endeared him to the intelligence of the country. At that time these attributes were expected in the President, and none were acceptable without them.

Mr. Lowndes in very early life gave evidence of future usefulness and distinction. His thirst for knowledge, intense application, and great capacity to acquire, made him conspicuous at school, and in college. He entered manhood already distinguished by his writings. While yet very young he travelled in Europe, and for the purpose of mental improvment. Knowledge was the wife of his heart, and he courted her with affectionate assiduity. An anecdote is related of him illustrative of his character and attainments. While in London, he was left alone at his hotel, where none but men of rank and distinction visited, with a gentleman much his senior ; neither knew the other. A social instinct, (though not very prominent in an Englishman,) induced conversation. After a time the gentleman left the apartment and was returning to the street, when he encountered the

Duke of Argyle. This gentleman was William Roscoe, of Liverpool, and author of "The Life of Leo the Tenth."

"I have been spending a most agreeable hour," he said to the Duke, "with a young American gentleman, who is the tallest, wisest, and best bred young man I have ever met."

"It must have been Mr. Lowndes, of South Carolina," replied the Duke. "He is such a man, I know him and I know no other like him. Return and let me make you his acquaintance." He did so, and the acquaintance then commenced, ripened into a friendship which endured so long as they both lived.

Blue eyes, of a peculiar languid expression; yellow hair, lank and without gloss; with a soft sunny sort of complexion, seems ever to indicate physical weakness. Indeed, pale colors in all nature point to brief existence, want of stamina and capacity to endure. All of these combined in the physical organization of Mr. Lowndes, and served to make more conspicuous the brilliancy of his intellect. It has been said, consumption sublimates the mind, stealing from the body, etherealizing and intensifying the intellect. This was peculiarly the case in the instance of Mr. Lowndes. As the disease progressed, attenuating and debilitating the physical man, his intellectual faculties grew brighter, and brighter, assuming a lucidity almost supernatural. At length he passed from time while yet young, leaving a vacuum which in South Carolina has never been filled. His death was at a time his services were most needed, and as with Clay, Jackson, and Webster, his death was a national calamity.

Conspicuous among the remarkable men of that era was Louis McLean, of Delaware. He belonged to the Republican school of politics, and was a very honest and able man. He combined very many most estimable traits in his character; open and frank, without concealment; cheerful and mild, without bitterness, and with as few prejudices as any public man. Yet he was consistent and firm in his political opinions and principles, as he was devoted and tenacious in his friendships. He was extremely considerate of the feelings and prejudices of other people — had a large stock of charity for the foibles and follies of his friends and political antagonists. In social intercourse he was quite as familiar and intimate with these as with his political friends. Difference of political principles did not close his eyes to the virtues and worth of any man, and his respect for talent and uprightness was always manifest in his public and private intercourse with those who differed with him in opinion. His was a happy constitution, and one well fitted to win him friends. Personally, with the exception of Mr. Lowndes, he was perhaps the most popular man upon the floor of the House of Representatives. The influence of his character and talent was very great, and his geographical position added greatly to these in his efforts upon the Missouri question. His speech was widely read, and no one found fault with it. It was a masterly effort and added greatly to his extended fame.

In the character of Mr. McLean there was a very happy combination of gentleness with firmness. He carried this into his family, and its influence has made of his children a monument to his fame; they have distinguished, in their characters and conduct, the name and the virtues of their father. It may be said of him what cannot be said of many distinguished men, his children were equal to the father in talent, usefulness, and virtue.

The Administration of Mr. Monroe saw expire the Federal and Republican parties, as organized under the Administration of John Adams. It saw also the germ of the Democratic and Whig parties planted. It was a prosperous Administration, and under it the nation flourished like a green bay-tree. He was the last of the Presidents who had actively participated in the war of the Revolution. To other virtues and different merits, those who now aspire to the high distinction of the Presidency must owe their success. There must always be a cause for distinction. However great the abilities of a man or exalted his virtues, he must in some manner make a display of them before the public eye, or he must of necessity remain in obscurity. War developes more rapidly and more conspicuously the abilities of men than any other public employment. Gallantry and successful conflict presents the commander and subalterns at once prominently before the country; besides military fame addresses itself to every capacity, and strange as it may seem, there is no quality so popular with man and woman, too, as the art of successfully killing our fellow-man, and devastating his country. It is ever a successful claim to public honors and political preferments. No fame is so lasting as a military fame. Cæsar and Hannibal are names, though they lived two thousand years ago, familiar in the mouths of every one, and grow brighter as time progresses. Philip and his more warlike son, Alexander, are names familiar to the learned and illiterate, alike; while those who adorned the walks of civil life with virtues, and godlike abilities, are only known to those who burrow in musty old books, and search out the root of civilization enjoyed by modern nations. They who fought at Cannæ and Marathon, at Troy and at Carthage, are household names; while those who invented the plough and the spade, and first taught the cultivation of the earth, the very base of civilization, are unknown — never thought of. Such is human nature.

The war of 1812 had developed one or two men only of high military genius, and the furor for military men had not then become a mania. Abilities for civil government were considered essential in him who was to be elevated to the Presidency. Indeed, it was not so much a warrior's fame which had controlled in the election of the previous Presidents, as their high intellectual reputations. Washington had rendered such services to the country, both as a military man and a civilian, that his name was the nation. He had been everywhere designated as the father of his country, and such was the public devotion, that he had only to ask it, and a despot's crown would have adorned his brow. John Adams, Jefferson, and Madison had no military record; but in the capacity of civilians had rendered essential service to the cause of the Revolution. Their Administrations had been successful, and the public mind attributed this success to their abilities as statesmen, and desired to find as their successors, men of like minds, and similar attainments. Crawford, Calhoun, Clay, John Quincy Adams, and Lowndes, had all of them given evidences of eminent statesmanship, and the public mind among these was divided. At the time of the death of Lowndes, this mind was rapidly concentrating upon him, as more eminently uniting the desired qualifications than any other.

It was about this very time that General Jackson's name began to attract the public as a prominent candidate. Mr. Calhoun was ready to retire from the contest, and it is very probable his friends would have united in the support of Lowndes, but he being out of the way, they united upon Jackson. When Jackson was first spoken of as a candidate, most men of intelligence viewed it as a mere joke, but very soon the admiration for his military fame was apparent in the delight manifested by the masses, when he was brought prominently forward. That thirst for military glory, and the equally ardent thirst to do homage to the successful military man, was discovered to be as innate and all-pervading with the American people, as with any other of the most warlike nations. Had the name of Jackson been brought before the people six months earlier than it was, he would, most assuredly, have been triumphantly elected by the popular vote. It would be fruitless to speculate upon what might have been the consequences to the country had he been then chosen. Besides, such is foreign to my purpose. I mean merely to record memories of men and things which have come under my eye and to my knowledge, for the last fifty years, and which I may suppose will be interesting to the general reader, and particularly to the young, who are just now coming into position as men and women, and who will constitute the controlling element in society and in the Government. To those of my own age, it may serve to awaken reminiscences of a by-gone age, and enable them to contrast the men and things of now and then.

CHAPTER XVIII.

FRENCH AND SPANISH TERRITORY.

Settlers on the Tombigbee and Mississippi Rivers — La Salle — Natchez — Family Apportionment — The Hill Country — Hospitality — Benefit of African Slavery—Capacity of the Negro—His Future.

ABOUT the year 1777, many persons of the then colonies, fearful of the consequences of the war then commencing for the independence of the colonies, removed and sought a home beyond their limits. Some selected the Tombigbee, and others the Mississippi River, and, braving the horrors of the wilderness, made a home for themselves and posterity, amid the rude inhospitalies of uncultivated nature.

There were, at that time, small settlements of French and Spanish adventurers upon these streams, in different localities. La Salle descended upon Canada, and, taking possession of Louisiana in the name of the French king, had created among many of the chivalrous and adventurous spirits of France a desire to take possession of the entire country, from the mouth of the Saint Lawrence to that of the Mississippi. Nova Scotia, called Acadia by its first settlers, and the provinces of Canada, were his already, and France desired to restrict the further expansion of the English colonies, now growing into importance along the Atlantic coast.

The vast extent of the continent and its immense fertility, with its mighty rivers, its peculiar adaptation to settlement, and the yielding of all the necessaries and luxuries of human wants, had aroused the enterprise of Europe. Spain had possessed herself of South America, Mexico, and Cuba, the pride of the Antilles. The success of her scheme of colonization stimulated both England and France to push forward their settlements, and to foster and protect them with Governmental care. After some fruitless attempts, the mouth of the Mississippi had been discovered, and approached from the Gulf. The expedition under La Salle had failed to find it. The small colony brought by him for settlement upon the Mississippi, had been landed many leagues west of the river's mouth, and owing to disputes between that great and enterprising man and the officer commanding the two ships which had transported them across the Atlantic, they were mercilessly left by this officer, without protection, and almost without provisions, upon the coast of what is now Texas. La Salle had started with a small escort, by land, to find the great river. These men became dissatisfied, and not sharing in the adventurous and energetic spirit of their leader, remonstrated with him and proposed to return to their companions; but, disregarding them, he pressed on in his new enterprise. In wading a small stream, one of the men was carried off by an alligator, and a day or so after, another was bitten and killed by a rattle-snake. Terror seized upon his men, and all their persuasions proving fruitless, they determined to assassinate him and return. They did so, only to find the colony dispersed and nowhere to be found. After many hazardous adventures they reached the Arkansas River, and descended it to its mouth, where they proposed preparing some means of ascending the Mississippi, and thus return to Canada. Fortunately they had been there but a few hours, when a small boat or two, which had been dispatched from Canada to look after the colony so long expected, arrived, and, learning the unfortunate issue of the enterprise, took on board the party, and returned up the river. They reported the colony destroyed, and it was not until many years after, that it was discovered that those left on the sea-side had been found, and conveyed to the Jesuit Mission, at San Antonio, where they had been cared for and preserved by the pious and humane missionaries.

Subsequently a colony was located at Boloxy, on the shore of the lake, and thence was transferred to New Orleans. Mobile, soon after, was made the nucleus of another colony, and from these two points had proceeded the pioneers of the different settlements along these rivers — the Tombigbee and the Mississippi. It was to these settlements or posts, or their neighborhoods, that these refugees from the Revolutionary war in the colonies had retired. Natchez and St. Francisville, on the Mississippi, and St. Stephen's and McIntosh's Bluff, on the Tombigbee, were the most populous and important.

About these, and under the auspicious protection of the Spanish Government, then dominant in Louisiana and Florida, commenced the growth of the Anglo-Norman population, which is now the almost entire population of the country. There proceeded from South Carolina, about the time mentioned above, a colony of persons which located near Natchez. They came down the Holston, Tennessee, and Mississippi Rivers, on flat-boats; and after many escapes from the perils incident to the streams they navigated, and the hostility of the savages who dwelt along their shores, they reached this Canaan of their hopes. They had intended to locate at New Madrid. The country around was well suited for cultivation, being alluvial and rich, and the climate was all they could desire; but they found a population mongrel and vicious, unrestrained by law or morals, and learning through a negro belonging to the place of an intended attack upon their party, for the purpose of robbery, they hastily re-embarked what of their property and stock they had debarked. Under pretense of dropping a few miles lower down the river for a more eligible site, they silently and secretly left in the night, and never attempted another stop until reaching the Walnut Hills, now Vicksburg. A few of the party concluded to remain here, while the larger number went on down; some to the mouth of Cole's Creek, some to Natchez, and others to the cliffs known by the name of one of the emigrants whose party concluded to settle there.

These cliffs, which are eighteen miles below Natchez, have always been known as Ellis' Cliffs. In their rear is a most beautiful, and eminently fertile country. Grants were obtained from the Spanish

Government of these lands, in tracts suited to the means of each family. A portion was given to the husband, a portion to the wife, and a portion to each child of every family. These grants covered nearly all of that desirable region south of St. Catharine's Creek and west of Second Creek to the Mississippi River, and south to the Homochitto River. Similar grants were obtained for lands about the mouth, and along the banks of Cole's Creek, at and around Fort Adams, ten miles above the mouth of Red River, and upon the Bayou Pierre. The same authority donated to the emigrants lands about McIntosh's Bluff, Fort St. Stephens, and along Bassett's Creek, in the region of the Tombigbee River. Here the lands were not so fertile, nor were they in such bodies as in the region of the Mississippi. The settlements did not increase and extend to the surrounding country with the same rapidity as in the latter country. Many of those first stopping on the Tombigbee, ultimately removed to the Mississippi. Here they encountered none of the perils or losses incident to the war of the Revolution. The privations of a new country they did, of necessity, endure, but not to the same extent that those suffer who are deprived of a market for the products of their labor. New Orleans afforded a remunerative market for all they could produce, and, in return, supplied them with every necessary beyond their means of producing at home. The soil and climate were not only auspicious to the production of cotton, tobacco, and indigo — then a valuable marketable commodity — but every facility for rearing without stint every variety of stock. These settlements were greatly increased by emigration from Pennsylvania, subsequently to the conclusion of the war, as well as from the Southern States.

Very many who, in that war, had sided with the mother country from conscientious, or mercenary views, were compelled by public opinion, or by the operation of the law confiscating their property and banishing them from the country, to find new homes. Those, however, who came first had choice of locations, and most generally selected the best; and bringing most wealth, maintained the ascendency in this regard, and gave tone and direction to public matters as well as to the social organization of society. Most of them were men of education and high social position in the countries from which they came. Constant intercourse with New Orleans, and the education of the youth of both sexes of this region in the schools of that city, carried the high polish of French society into the colony.

Louisiana, and especially New Orleans, was first settled by the nobility and gentry of France. They were men in position among the first of that great and glorious people. Animated with the ambition for high enterprise, they came in sufficient numbers to create a society, and to plant French manners and customs, and the elegance of French learning and French society, upon the banks of the Mississippi.

The commercial and social intermingling of these people resulted in intermarriages, which very soon assimilated them in most things as one people, at least in feeling, sentiment and interest. From such a stock grew the people inhabiting the banks of the Mississippi, from Vicksburg to New Orleans. In 1826, young men of talent and enterprise had come from Europe, and every section of the United States, and, giving their talents to the development of the country, had created a wealth, greater and more generally diffused than was, at that time, to be found in any other planting or farming community in the United States. Living almost exclusively among themselves, their manners and feelings were homogeneous; and living, too, almost entirely upon the products of their plantations, independent of their market-crops, they grew rich so rapidly as to mock the fable of Jonah's gourd. This wealth afforded the means of education and travel; these, cultivation and high mental attainments, and, with these, the elegances of refined life. The country was vast and fertile; the Mississippi, flowing by their homes, was sublimely grand, and seemed to inspire ideas and aspirations commensurate with its own majesty in the people upon its borders.

In no country are to be found women of more refined character, more beauty, or more elegance of manners, than among the planters' wives and daughters of the Mississippi coast. Reared in the country, and accustomed to exercise in the open air, in walking through the shady avenues of the extensive and beautifully ornamented grounds about the home or plantation-house; riding on horseback along the river's margin, elevated upon the levee, covered with the green Bermuda grass, smoothly spreading over all the ground, save the pretty open road, stretching through this grass, like a thread of silver in a a cloth of green; with the great drab river, moving in silent majesty, on one side, and the extended fields of the plantation, teeming with the crop of cane or cotton, upon the other. Their exercise, thus surrounded, becomes a school, and their ideas expand and grow with the sublimity of their surroundings. The health-giving exercise and the wonderful scene yields vigor both to mind and body. Nor is this scene, or its effects, greater in the development of mind and body than that of the hill-country of the river-counties of Mississippi.

These hills are peculiar. They are drift, thrown upon the primitive formation by some natural convulsion, and usually extend some twelve or fifteen miles into the interior. They consist of a rich, marly loam, and, when in a state of nature were clothed to their summits with the wild cane, dense and unusually large, a forest of magnolia, black walnut, immense oaks, and tulip or poplar-trees, with gigantic vines of the wild grape climbing and overtopping the tallest of these forest monarchs. Here among these picturesque hills and glorious woods, the emigrants fixed their homes, and here grew their posterity surrounding themselves with wealth, comforts, and all the luxuries and elegances of an elevated civilization. Surrounded in these homes with domestic slaves reared in them, and about them, who came at their bidding, and went when told, but who were carefully regarded, sustained, and protected, and who felt their family identity, and were happy, served affectionately, and with willing alacrity, the master and his household. In the midst of scenes and circumstances like these grew women in all that constitutes nobility of soul and sentiment, delicacy, intelligence, and refined purity, superior to any it has ever been my fortune to meet on earth.

Here in these palatial homes was the hospitality of princes. It was not the hospitality of pride or ostentation, but of the heart; the welcome which the soul ungrudgingly gives, and which delights and refines the receiver. It is the welcome of a refined humanity, untainted with selfishness, and felt as a humane and duly bound tribute to civilization and Christianity; such hospitality as can only belong to the social organization which had obtained in the community from its advent upon this great country.

The independence of the planter's pursuit, the institution of domestic slavery, and the form and spirit of the Government, all conduce to this. The mind is untrammelled and the soul is independent, because subservient neither to the tyrannical exactions of unscrupulous authority, or the more debasing servility of dependence upon the capricious whims of petty officials, or a monied aristocracy. Independently possessing the soil and the labor for its cultivation, with only the care necessary to the comforts and necessities of this labor, superadded to those of a family, they were without the necessity of soliciting or courting favors from any one, or pandering to the ignorant caprices of a labor beyond their control. Independence of means is the surest guarantee for independence of character. Where this is found, most private and most public virtues always accompany it. Truth, sincerity, all the cardinal virtues are fostered most where there is most independence. This takes away the source of all corruption, all temptation. This seeks dependence, and victimizes its creatures to every purpose of corruption and meanness.

Under the influences of the institutions of the South, as they were, there was little of the servile meanness so predominant where they were not, and the lofty and chivalrous character of the Southern people was greatly owing to these institutions, and the habits of the people growing out of them. The slave was a class below all others. His master was his protector and friend; he supplied his wants and redressed his wrongs, and it was a point of honor as well as duty to do so; he was assured of his care and protection, and felt no humility at his condition. The white man, without means, was reminded that, though poor, he was above the slave, and was stimulated with the pride of position as contrasted with that of the slave; his political, legal, and social rights were unrestrained and equal with those of the wealthiest. This was the only distinction between him and the wealthiest in the land, and this wealth conferred no exclusive privilege, and its acquisition was open to his energy and enterprise, and he gloried in his independence. He could acquire and enjoy without dependence, and his pride and ambition were alike stimulated to the emulation of those who shared most fortune's favors.

The beneficial influences of the institution of African slavery were not only apparent in the independent and honorable bearing and conduct of the Southern people, growing from the habit of command, and involuntary contrast of condition, but upon the material advancement and progress of the country. The product of slave labor, when directed by a higher intelligence than his own, is enormous, and was the basis of the extended and wealth-creating commerce of the entire country. These products could be obtained in no other manner, and without this labor, are lost to the world. The African negro, in osseous and muscular developments, and in all the essentials for labor, is quite equal to those of the white race ; in his cerebral, greatly inferior. The capacities of his brain are limited and incapable of cultivation beyond a certain point. His moral man is as feeble and unteachable as his mental. He cannot be educated to the capacity of self-government, nor to the formation and conducting of civil government to the extent of humanizing and controlling by salutary laws a people aggregated into communities. He learns by example which he imitates, so long as the exampler is present before him ; but this imitation never hardens to fixed views or habits, indicating the design of Providence, that these physical capacities should be directed and appropriated for good, by an intelligence beyond the mental reach of the negro.

Why is this so? In the wisdom and economy of creation every created thing represents a design for a use. The soil and climate of the tropical and semi-tropical regions of the earth produce and mature all, or very nearly all of the necessaries and luxuries of human life. But human beings of different races and different capacities fill up the whole earth. The capacity to build a fire and fabricate clothing is given only to man. Was the element of fire and the material for clothing given for any but man's use? This enables him to inhabit every clime. But the capacity to produce all the necessaries and luxuries of life is given only to a certain portion of the earth's surface; and its peculiar motions give the fructifying influences of the sun only to the middle belt of the planet. The use of this organization is evidenced in the production of this belt, and these productions must be the result of intelligently directed labor.

The peculiarity of the physical organization of the white man makes it impossible for him to labor healthfully and efficiently for the greatest development of this favored region. Yet his wants demand the yield and tribute of this region. His inventive capacity evolved sugar from the wild canes of the tropics, than which nothing is more essential to his necessities, save the cereals and clothing. He fabricated clothing from the tropical grass and tropical cotton, found the uses of cassia, pimento, the dye woods, and the thousand other tropical products which contribute to comfort, necessity, and luxury; advancing human happiness, human progress, and human civilization.

The black man's organization is radically different. He was

formed especially to live and labor in these tropical and semi-tropical regions of the earth; but he is naturally indolent, his wants are few, and nature unaided supplies them. He is uninventive, and has always, from creation down, lived amid these plants without the genius to discover, or the skill and industry to develope their uses. That they are used, and contribute to human health and human necessities, is abundant evidence of Divine design in their creation.

The black man's labor, then, and the white man's intelligence are necessary to the production and fabrication, for human use, of these provisions of Providence. This labor the black man will not yield without compulsion. He is eminently useful under this compulsion, and eminently useless, even to himself, without it. That he was designed to obey this authority, and to be most happy when and where he was most useful, is apparent in his mental and moral organization. By moral I mean those functions of the nervous system which bring us in relation with the external world. He aspires to nothing but the gratification of his passions, and the indulgence of his indolence. He only feels the oppression of slavery in being compelled to work, and none of the moral degradation incident to servility in the higher or superior races. He is, consequently, more happy, and better contented in this, than in any other condition of life. His morals, his bodily comforts, and his status as a man, attain to an elevation in this condition known to his race in no other.

All the results of his condition react upon the superior race, holding him in the condition designed for him by his Creator, producing results to human progress all over the world, known to result in an equal ratio from no other cause. The institution has passed away, and very soon all its consequences will cease to be visible in the character of the Southern people. The plantation will dwindle to the truck-patch, the planter will sink into the grave, and his offspring will degenerate into hucksters and petty traders, and become as mean and contemptible as the Puritan Yankee.

In the two hundred years of African slavery the world's progress was greater in the arts and sciences, and in all the appliances promotive of intelligence and human happiness, than in any period of historical time, of five centuries. Why? Because the labor was performed by the man formed for labor and incapable of thinking, and releasing the man formed to think, direct, and invent, from labor, other than labor of thought. This influence was felt over the civilized world. The productions of the tropics were demanded by the higher civilization. Men forgot to clothe themselves in skins when they could do so in cloth. As commerce extended her flight, bearing these rich creations of labor, elaborated by intelligence, civilization went with her, expanding the mind, enlarging the wants, and prompting progress in all with whom she communicated. Its influence was first felt from the Antilles, extending to the United States. In proportion to the increase of these products was the increase of commerce, wealth, intelligence, and power. Compare the statistics of production by slave-labor with the increase of commerce, and they go hand in hand. As the slave came down from the grain-growing region to the cotton and sugar region, the amount of his labor's product entering into commerce increased four-fold. The inventions of Whitney and Arkwright cheapened the fabric of cotton so much as to bring it within the reach of the poorest, and availed the world in all the uses of cloth.

The shipping and manufacturing interests of England grew; those of the United States, from nothing, in a few years were great rivals of the mother country, and very soon surpassed her in commercial tonnage. Every interest prospered with the prosperity of the planter of the Southern States. His class has passed away; the weeds blacken where the chaste, white cotton beautified his fields; his slave is a freedman — a constitution-maker — a ruler set up by a beastly fanaticism to control his master, and to degrade and destroy his country.

This must bear its legitimate fruit. It is the beginning of the end of the negro upon this continent. Two races with the same civil, political and social privileges cannot long exist in harmony together. The struggle for supremacy will come, and with it a war of races — then God have mercy on the weaker! The mild compulsion which stimulated his labor is withdrawn, and with it the care and protection which alone preserved him. He works no more; his day of Jubilee has come; he must be a power in the land. Infatuated creature! I pity you from my heart. You cannot see or calculate the inevitable destiny now fixed for your race. You cannot see the vile uses you are made to subserve for a time, or deem that those who now appear your conservators, are but preparing your funeral pyre.

CHAPTER XIX.

THE NATCHEZ TRADITIONS.

NATCHEZ — MIZEZIBBEE; OR, THE PARENT OF MANY WATERS — INDIAN MOUNDS — THE CHILD OF THE SUN — TREATMENT OF THE FEMALES — POETIC MARRIAGES — UNCHASTE MAIDS AND PURE WIVES — WALKING ARCHIVES — THE PROFANE FIRE — ALAHOPLECHIA — OYELAPE — THE CHIEF WITH A BEARD.

THE little city of Natchez is built upon a bluff some three hundred feet in elevation above the Mississippi River, and immediately upon its brink. It receives its name from a tribe of Indians once resident in the country; and who were much further advanced in civilization than their more warlike neighbors, the Choctaws and the Chickasaws. The country around is hilly and beautiful, fertile and salubrious. The population was intelligent and refined, and was remarkable for having more wealth than any community outside of a large city, in the United States, of the same amount of population. The town of Natchez (for, properly speaking, it is no more) consists of some three or four thousand inhabitants, and has not increased to any considerable extent, for many years.

Beyond the river, in Louisiana, is an alluvial plain extending for fifty miles, through which meander many small streams, or bayous, as they are termed in the language of the country. Upon most of these the surface of the soil is slightly elevated above the plane of the swamp, and is remarkably fertile. Most of these were, at the commencement of the late war, in a high state of cultivation as cotton plantations. As in many other places, the river here has changed its bed by cutting off a large bend immediately opposite the town, creating what is known as Lake Concordia. This lake was formerly the bed of the river, and describes almost a complete circle of some twelve miles in diameter. On both sides of this lake beautiful plantations, with splendid improvements, presented a view from the bluff at Natchez extremely picturesque when covered with luxuriant crops of corn and cotton. The fertility of the soil is such that these crops are immensely heavy; and when the cotton-plant has matured its fruit, and the pent-up lint in the large conical balls has burst them open, exposing their white treasure swelling out to meet the sun's warm rays, and the parent stock to the first frost of autumn has thrown off her foliage, and all these broad fields are one sheet of lovely white, as far as the eye can view — the scene is lovely beyond description; and when the same rich scene was presented extending along the banks of the great river, with the magnificent steamers resting at the wharf below, and others cleaving the current in proud defiance of the mighty volume of hurrying waters — the splendor and magnificence of the whole sublimated the feelings as we viewed it in wonder.

The river, the bluff, and the lake are there; but waste and desolation frown on these, and the fat earth's rich fruits are yielded no more. Fanaticism's hot breath has breathed upon it, and war's red hand (her legitimate offspring) has stricken down the laborer; tillage has ceased, and gaunt poverty and hungry want only are left in her train.

When the great La Salle moored his little fleet at the foot of this bluff, ascended to its summit, and looked over this then forest-clad plain, did he contemplate the coming future of this beautiful discovery of his genius and enterprise? When he looked upon the blue smoke curling above the tall tree-tops along the lake, in the far distance, as it ascended from the wigwams of the Natchez, the wild denizens of this interminable forest, did his prophetic eye perceive these lovely fields, happy homes, and prosperous people, who came after him to make an Eden of this chosen spot of all the earth? and did it stretch on to contemplate the ruin and desolation which overspreads it now? How blest is man that he sees not beyond to-day!

Here he first met the Natchez, and viewed with wonder the flat heads and soft, gazelle eyes of this strange people. They welcomed his coming, and tendered him and his people a home. From them he learned the extent of the great river below, and that it was lost in the great water that was without limit and had no end. These Indians, according to their traditions, had once inhabited, as a mighty nation, the country extending from near the city of Mexico to the Rio Grande, and were subjects of the Aztec empire of Mexico. They had been persecuted and oppressed, and determined, in grand council, to abandon the country and seek a home beyond the Mizezibbee, or Parent-of-many-waters, which the word signifies.

Their exodus commenced in a body. They were many days in assembling upon the east bank of the Rio Grande; and thence commenced their long march. They abandoned their homes and the graves of their ancestors for a new one in the lovely region they found on the hills extending from the mouth of the Yazoo to Baton Rouge. Their principal town and seat of empire was located eleven miles below Natchez, on the banks of Second Creek, two miles from the Mississippi River. It is a delightful spot of high table-land, with a small strip of level low-land immediately upon the margin of the dimpling little stream of sweet water. Upon this flat they erected the great mound for their temple of the Sun, and the depository of the holy fire, so sacred in their worship. At each point of the compass they erected smaller mounds for the residences of their chief, or child of the Sun, and his ministers of state. In the great temple upon the principal mound they deposited the fire of holiness, which they had borne unextinguished from the deserted temple in Mexico, and began to build their village. Parties went forth to establish other villages, and before a great while they were located in happy homes in a land of abundance. They formed treaties of amity with their powerful but peaceable neighbors, the Choctaws, and ere long with the Chickasaws and other minor tribes, east, and below them, on the river, the Tunicas, Houmas, and others; for the country abounded with little bands, insignificant and powerless.

These Indians revered, as more than mortal, their great chief, whom they called the child of the Sun. They had a tradition that when they were a great nation, in Mexico, they were divided into parties by feuds among their chiefs, and all their power to resist the aggressions of their enemies was lost; consequently they had fallen under the power of the Aztecs, who dominated them, and destroyed many of their people. Upon one occasion, when a common enemy and a common suffering had made them forget their quarrels, they were assembled for council. Suddenly there appeared in their midst a white man and woman, surrounded with a halo of light coming directly from the sun. They were all silent with awe when this man spoke, and with such authority as to make every chief tremble with fear. They bowed to him with reverence, and he professing to be weary with his long journey, they conducted him with his wife to a lodge, and bade them repose and be rested. The chiefs, in the darkness of the night and in silence, assembled, while the celestial pair slept, conscious of security. After long and close council, they determined to proffer the supreme authority of the nation to this man, sent to them by the sun. When this determination had been reached, the chiefs, in a body, repaired to the house occupied by their mysterious visitors and, arousing them from sleep, they formally tendered to the man the crown and supreme authority over the chiefs, all their villages, and all their people. At first he refused, asserting that he knew their hearts; they carried hatred of one another, and that they would come to hate him; then they would disobey him, and this would be death to all the Natchez. Finally yielding to the importunities and earnestly repeated protestations of a determination to obey him and follow his counsels implicitly, he agreed to accept the crown upon certain conditions. These were: first and paramount, that the Natchez should abandon their homes and country, and follow him to a new home which he would show them; and that they should live and conform strictly to the laws he would establish. The principal of these were: the sovereign of Natchez should always and forever be of his race, and that if he had sons and daughters, they should not be permitted to intermarry with each other, but only with the people of the Natchez. The first-born of his sons should be his successor, and then the son of his eldest daughter, and should he have no daughter, then the son of his eldest sister, or in default of such an heir, then the eldest son of the nearest female relative of the sovereign, and so in perpetuity.

So soon as he was inaugurated chief and supreme ruler, he went out in the midst of the assembled multitude and called down in their presence fire from the sun; blessed it and made it holy. He created a guard of eight men, made them priests and gave them charge of the fire, and bid them, under pain of death, to preserve and keep alive this holy fire. They must tend it day and night and feed it with walnut wood, and in their charge it went before the moving host to where he had promised they should find a new and better home than the one they were leaving.

Another tradition says, they were aiders of the Spaniards in the conquest of Mexico, and that these became as great persecutors of their people as the Aztecs. But from many of their traditions connected with their new home which extended back far beyond the conquest of Mexico, it is thought by historians that this tradition alludes to some other war in which they took part against their oppressors. They were remarkable for their size and symmetry of form of their men; but like all the race, they made slaves of their women, imposing every burden from the cultivation of their fields to the duties of the household — the carrying of heavy burdens and the securing of fuel for winter. These labors served to disfigure and make their women to appear prematurely aged and worn, and they seemed an inferior race when compared with the men.

The laws imposed by their chief of the sun were strictly obeyed. They compelled the telling of truth on all occasions; never to kill, but in self-defence; never to steal, and to preserve inviolate the marriage-vow. The marriage ceremony was poetic and impressive. No girl ever dreamed of disobeying her parents in the choice of a husband; nor was elopement ever heard of among them; nor did the young man presume to thrust himself upon a family to whom, or to any member of whom, he was not acceptable. But when the marriage was agreeable to the families of both parties and was consequently determined upon, the head of the family of the bride went with her and her whole family to the house of the bridegroom, who there stood with all his family around him, when the old man of the bridegroom's family welcomed them, by asking: "Is it thou?" "Yes," answered the other ancient. "Sit down," continued the other. Immediately all were seated, and a profound silence for many minutes ensued. Then the eldest man of the party bid the groom and bride to stand up, when he addressed them in a speech in which he recapitulated all the duties of man and wife; informed them of the obligations they were assuming, and then concluded with a lecture of advice as to their future lives.

When this ceremony was concluded, the father of the bridegroom handed to his son the present he was to make to the family of the bride. Then the father of bride stepped up to the side of his daughter, when the groom said to the bride: "Wilt thou have me for thy husband?" The bride answered: "With all my heart; love me as I will love thee; for thou art my only love for all my life." Then holding the gift above her head, the groom said: "I love thee; therefore I take thee for my wife, and this is the present with which I buy thee," and then he handed the present to her parents. Upon his head he wore a tuft of feathers, and in his hand a bow, emblematic of authority and protection. The bride held in one hand a green twig of the laurel-tree, and in the other an ear of corn — the twig indicated she would preserve her fame ever fair and sweet as the laurel leaf; the corn was to represent her capacity to grow it and prepare it for his food, and to fulfil all the duties of a faithful wife. These ceremonies completed, the bride dropped the ear of corn which she held in her right hand, and tendered that hand to the bridegroom, who took it and said: "I am thy husband." She replied: "I am thy wife." The bridegroom then went round and gave his hand to every member of the family of his wife. He then took his bride by the arm and led her around and she took the right hand of all the family of the bridegroom. This done, he walked with her to his bed, and said: "This is our bed, keep it undefiled."

There obtained among these primitive beings a most curious and most disgusting custom. The young marriageable females were permitted to prostitute themselves for gain, in order to provide a marriage portion; and she who could thus enrich herself was the most distinguished and the most sought. But after marriage, she was compelled to purity, both by their laws and by public sentiment; and in all the intercourse of the French with them, no instance of infidelity was ever known in a wife.

The great sun was indeed their Lycurgus. If before his advent among them they had any laws, these had become obsolete, and his edicts adopted universally. Their traditions represent him as living to extreme old age, seeing his desendants of the fourth generation. These were all little suns, and constituted the nobility of their nation, which extended at one time to the country above, as far as St. Louis and across to the Wabash. These traditions were carefully kept. Every two years there were selected from the most intelligent boys of the nation ten, to whom these traditions were carefully taught by the depositories of them who had kept them best for the greatest time. They were careful to exact that no word or fact should be withheld, and this lesson was daily taught until the boy was a man, and every legend a familiar memory. These he was compelled to repeat daily lest the memory should rust, and for this purpose they went forth to all the villages repeating all of these legends to all the people.

There were others selected in like manner to whom the laws were taught as the traditions, and in like manner these were taught the people. In every community there was a little sun to administer these laws, and every complaint was submitted to him, and great ceremony was observed at every trial, especially criminal trials. The judge, or little sun, purified himself in the forest, imploring the enlightenment of the Good Spirit, and purging away the influence of bad spirits by his purification; and when he felt himself a fitted tabernacle of pure justice, he came forward and rendered his judgment in the presence of all the villagers of his jurisdiction, whose attention was compulsory.

It was one of the laws established in the beginning of the reign of the Great Sun, that his posterity should not marry *inter se*, but only with the common people of the nation. This custom was expelling the pure blood of royalty more and more every generation, and long after the arrival of the Natchez upon the Mississippi, the great and little suns were apparently of the pure blood of the red man. Their traditions, however, preserved the history of every cross, and when Lasalle found these at Natchez and the White Apple village, nearly every one could boast of relationship to the Great Sun. At that time they had diminished to an insignificant power, and were overawed by their more numerous and more powerful neighbors, the Choctaws and Muscagees or Alabamas. Their legends recorded this constant decline, but assigned no reason for it. They could now not bring more than two thousand warriors into the field. Gayarie says not more than six hundred; but those contemporaneous with planting the colony of Orleans say, some two thousand, some more, and some estimate them as low as the number stated in that admirable history of Louisiana whose author is so uniformly correct. And here let me acknowledge my obligations to that accomplished historian, and no less accomplished gentleman, for most of the facts here stated, and if I have used his own language in portraying them to a great extent, it was because it was so pure and beautiful I could not resist it, the excuse the Brazilian gave for stealing the diamond.

With regard to these people, their mode of life was that of most of the other tribes. They lived principally by the chase; their only cultivation was the Indian corn, pumpkins, and a species of wild beans or peas, perfectly black, until their intercourse with the French, and then they only added a few of the coarser vegetables. From whom they derived the pumpkin is not known.

Their wars were not more frequent or more destructive than those of their neighbors; and their general habits were the same. Still they were going on to decay, and they contemplated with stolid calmness their coming extinction. They felt it a destiny not to be averted or avoided by anything they could do, and were content with the excuse of folly for all its errors and sins. *It is the will of God, or the Great Spirit, as the Indian phrases it.* They were more enlightened than their neighbors, as historians have stated, because, I suppose, they were more superstitious. They bowed to fate, the attribute of superstition everywhere, and made no effort at relief from the causes of decay.

Their religion, like all the aborigines of the continent, consisted in the worship of the Great Spirit typified in the sun, to whom was addressed their prayers and all their devotion. The sacred fire was the emblem on earth; their Great Sun had brought it from the sun and given it as holy to them to be forever preserved and propitiated by watching and prayer. In every village and settlement they erected mounds upon which the temple of the sun was built, and where was deposited the sacred fire. Mounds, too, were built for burying-places, and in these are now to be found in great abundance the flat heads and other bones of this remarkable people.

They had a tradition that an evil spirit was always tempting them to violate the laws, and the regulations of their religious belief. That at one time he had so nearly extinguished the holy fire in their temples, and the love of the sun in their hearts, that the Great Spirit came and fought with them against him, until finally he was conquered and chained in a deep cave, whence he still continued to send out little devils to tempt and torment their people. It was these who brought disease and death; these who tempted to lie, steal, and kill; disobedience in their wives when they refused to perform their duties or became bellicose, as wives sometimes will, of every people on earth. It was a trite saying, shut up the cave in your heart and smother or put out the bad spirit. It was a belief that these imps or little devils found much more easy access to the caves in the hearts of women than into those of men, and that they encouraged them to come and nestle there. Is the belief alone the Indian's? There are some within my knowledge whose experience at home might readily yield belief to this faith of the savage.

Their traditions, too, told them of the great waters coming over all the land, and destroying all the inhabitants except those who had boats; and that the latter were carried away by the waters and left by them on all the land that was permitted again to come above the waters; and that by that means people were planted everywhere. These traditions are quite as rational as most of the speculations as to how the earth was populated, especially that which we learn in the cradle, of Adam and Eve's mission.

It was death, by their law, to permit the holy fire to become extinguished in the temples. To prevent such a calamity, it was preserved in two temples at different points; when accidentally extinguished in one, it was to be obtained from the other; but not peacefully. The keepers must resist and blood must be spilt in order to obtain it. Soon after they became acquainted with the French, the fire was extinguished in the great temple at the White Apple village by the lazy watcher. Knowing his fate, he stealthily lighted it from profane fire. Great misfortunes following this, and shortly thereafter the loss of the holy fire in the other temple near the Grindstone ford, on the Bayou Pierre, in Claiborne County, Mississippi, they sought after the legal and holy manner to procure fire from the White Apple village. Yet the calamities continued. The watch who had suffered the fire to fail in the first temple, conscience smitten, confessed his sin and paid its penalty.

They now had only profane fire, and the whole nation was in the agonies of despair. The cause of all their calamities was now no longer a secret. They extinguished the profane fire, and in prayer, fasting, and continued oblations, they propitiated the sun to send them fire that was holy, to protect and preserve them. It was the folly of ignorance and superstition, and availed nothing; but, like all prayer, was considered a pious duty, though nothing was ever known to result therefrom, and nature moved steadily and undeviatingly forward in obedience to the fixed, immutable, and eternal laws affirmed by the all-wise Creator. There was gloom upon every brow and despair in every heart. The curse pronounced by the first Great Sun had come — destruction and death to all the Natchez — because of the extinction of the holy fire. At length a tree was stricken by lightning near the White Apple village temple, and set on fire. The men of the temple saw the answer to their prayers in this, and hastened to re-kindle the holy flame from this fire, so miraculously sent them from heaven. It was to them a miracle, because, though perfectly in obedience to natural laws, they did not comprehend them, and like unto all people under similar circumstances, all in nature is a miracle which they do not understand, and cannot satisfactorily explain. But there was no efficiency found in this, and the trouble went forward.

The French had come among them, and taught them the value and corrupting influence of money. Boats had ascended and descended the Great River, and communication, through this channel, had been established with Canada. They were grasping, by degrees, the lands, building forts and peopling the country. They had introduced the black man, and the wiser of the Natchez saw in the future the doom of their race. They saw the feuds fomented between the numerous tribes along the coast of the Mississippi by the French, and the destruction of these by bloody wars. They saw, too, to offend the French was sure to bring destruction upon the offending party. Their neighbors were made, through French influence, to fall upon and destroy them. The Chickasaws and Choctaws — great nations, having multitudes of warriors — were under the dominion of these pale-faced intruders, and they feared they might be turned upon them in an unsuspecting hour.

There was among the Natchez a mighty chief and warrior. He was of great stature and fame, being seven feet high and powerfully proportioned. He had a large beard, and was called the chief of the Beard, because he was the only man of all the tribe who had this facial ornament or incumbrance. He was a mighty warrior and was wise in counsel. He believed he saw great evil to the Natchez in the increase of the French and the extension of French power. He knew, and told his people, this was the foreboding of the extinction of the holy fire. He went forth with the chief of the Walnut Hills, named Alahoplechia, and the chief of the White Clay, Oyelape, among their neighbors of other tribes, the Chicasaws and Choctaws, preaching a crusade against the French; urging them to unite with the Natchez, the Homochittas, and the Alabamas, and to attack and destroy the last man of the French settlements at Mobile, Boloxy, Ship Island, and New Orleans, as they were mischievous intruders from across the Salt Lake, whence they were yearly bringing their people to rob them of their homes and appropriate them.

There had come to them red men from the Wabash and Muskingum, who bore to them the sad news of the encroachments of the pale-faces upon their people and their hunting-grounds. "Soon," said the bearded chief, who was the leading spirit of the mission, "these white faces will meet along the Great River. They will forget the arrow of truth and the tomahawk of justice. They will only know power and oppression. Then they will be mighty as the hurricane when the Great Sun hides his face in wrath and the tempest tears the forest. Who can resist him then? The holy fire has been sent again from heaven, from the Great Spirit, our God, the Great Sun. It tells us to save our people from this fearful destruction which comes with the white man. These pale-faces are cunning; they must not know of our union. We must not counsel long, or they will learn our intentions. We must strike at once. The Choctaws must strike at Mobile. At the same moment, Homochittas, Boloxies, and Homas, you must strike at Boloxi. The Chickasaws and the Natchez will fall upon New Orleans and Rosalie." (The latter is the Indian name for what is now Natchez.) His advice was startling, but unheeded. In order to precipitate a war, on his return with the chiefs who accompanied him and two warriors, they murdered a trading-party of French, at the hills where is now Warrenton, in Warren County, Mississippi.

This murder was communicated to the French who, under Bienville, were sent by Cordelac, then Governor of Louisiana, to take revenge, by waging war upon the Natchez. Bienville was hated by Cordelac, because he had refused the hand of his daughter, formally tendered him by her father. He only gave the young and sagacious commander a small force with which to wage this war — such an one as would have been overwhelmed at once had he attempted open field movements. Knowing this, he proceeded to an island opposite the village of the Tunicas, where he entrenched himself and invited a conference. Three spies were sent by the Natchez to reconnoitre; but they were baffled by Bienville with superior cunning. They were sent back as not the equals of Bienville, and with a message to the Great Sun that he must come with his chiefs, that he desired to establish trading-posts among them, and would only treat with the first in authority. They came with a consciousness that the French were ignorant of these murders, and were immediately arrested and ironed. Bienville told them at once of the murder, and of his determination to have the murderers and to punish them. He had the Great Sun, the Stung Serpent, and the Little Sun. The latter was sent to bring the heads of the murderers, and he returned with three heads; but Bienville, after examining these, told the chiefs they had treacherously deceived him, and that those were not the heads of the murderers. After a night's consultation they concluded it was impossible to deceive him, and in the morning confessed the whole truth, proposing to send Stung Serpent to bring the real murderers. But knowing the wily character of this chief and his influence with his tribe, he was not permitted to go. The young Sun was dispatched, and succeeded in bringing the chief of the Beard and the chief of the Walnut Hills, with the two warriors; but Oyelape had fled and could not be had. He had probed to the truth of the French expedition; and being guilty, cunningly and wisely made his escape.

The death sentence was passed upon these, and the two warriors were shot at once; but the two chiefs were reserved for execution to another day. Upon the sentence being communicated to them they commenced to chant the death-song of their people, which they continued to do throughout all the time, night and day, until led forth for execution.

The Great Sun, Stung Serpent, his brother, and all the other Indians were brought out to witness the execution. When the two condemned chiefs were brought forward, these witnesses of their death sang the death-song; but the chief of the Beard looked sternly at them, and defiantly at the executioners; and taking his positon, turned to his people and, addressing them, said:

"'Let there be joy in the hearts of the Natchez. A child is born to them of the race of their Suns. A boy is born with a beard on his chin. The prodigy still works on from generation to generation.' So sang the warriors of my tribe when I sprang from my mother's womb, and the shrill cry of the eagle, in the heavens, was heard in joyful response. Hardly fifteen summers had passed over my head when my beard had grown long and glossy. I looked around, and saw I was the only red man that had this awful mark on his face, and I interrogated my mother and she said:

"'Son of the chiefs of the Beard,
Thou shalt know the mystery
In which thy curious eye wishes to pry,
When thy beard from black becomes red.'

"Let there be joy in the hearts of the Natchez! A hunter is born to them — a hunter of the race of the Suns. Ask of the bears, of the buffaloes, of the tigers, and of the swift-footed deer, whose arrows they fear most! They tremble and cower when the footstep of the hunter with the beard on his chin is heard on the heath. But I was born with brains in my head as well as a beard on my chin, and I pondered on my mother's words. One day, when a panther which

I slaughtered had torn my breast, I painted my beard with my own blood, and I stood smiling before her. She said nothing; but her eye gleamed with wild delight, and she took me to the temple when, standing by the sacred fire, she thus sang to me:

"'Son of the chiefs of the Beard,
Thou shalt know the mystery,
Since, true to thy nature, with thine own blood
Thy black beard thou hast turned to red.'

"'Let there be joy in the hearts of the Natchez; for a mighty chief, worthy of the race of their Suns, has been born to them in thee, my son — a noble chief with a beard on his chin. Listen to the explanation of this prodigy. In days of old a Natchez maid of the race of their Suns was on a visit to the Mobelians. There she soon loved the youthful chief of that nation, and her wedding-day was nigh, when there came from the big Salt Lake on the south a host of bearded men, who sacked the town, slew the red chief with their thunder, and one of those accursed evil spirits used violence to the maid when her lover's corpse was hardly cold in death. She found in sorrow her way back to the Natchez hills, where she became a mother, and lo! the boy had a beard on his chin, and when he grew old enough to understand his mother's words she whispered in his ear:

"'Son of the chiefs of the Beard,
Born from a bloody day,
Bloody be thy hand, and bloody be thy life
Until thy black beard with blood becomes red.'

"Let there be joy in the hearts of the Natchez. In my first ancestor a long line of the first of hunters, chiefs, and warriors of the race of their Suns had been born to them with beards on their chins. What chase was ever unsuccessful over which they presided? When they spoke in the council of the wise men of the nation, did it not always turn out that their advice, whether adopted or rejected, was the best in the end? In what battle were they ever defeated? When were they known to be worn out with fatigue — with hardship, hunger or thirst, heat or cold, either on land or water? Who ever could stem as they the rushing current of the Father of rivers? Who can count the number of scalps which they brought from distant expeditions? Their names have always been famous in the wigwams of all the red nations. They have struck terror into the breasts of the boldest enemies of the Natchez; and mothers, when their sons paint their bodies in the colors of war, say to them:

"'Fight where, and with whom you please;
But beware, oh! beware of the chiefs of the Beard.
Give way to them as you would to death,
Or their black beards with your blood will be red.'

"Let there be joy in the hearts of the Natchez. When the first chief of the Beard first trimmed the sacred fire in the temple, a voice was heard which said: 'As long as there lives a chief of the race of the Suns with a beard on his chin, no evil can happen to the Natchez nation; but if the white race should ever resume the blood which it gave in a bloody day, woe, three times woe, to the Natchez! Of them nothing will remain but the shadow of a name.' Thus spake the invisible prophet. Years rolled on, years thick on years, and none of the accursed white-faces were seen; but they appeared at last, wrapped up in their pale skins like shrouds of the dead, and the father of my father, whom tradition had taught to guard against the predicted danger, slew two of the hated strangers, and my father, in his turn, killed four.

"'Praise be to the chiefs of the Beard,
Who knew how to avenge their old ancestral injury,
When with the sweet blood of a white foe
Their black beards they proudly dyed red.'

"Let there be joy in the hearts of the Natchez. When I saw the glorious light of day there was born to them a great warrior of the race of their Suns — a warrior and a chief with a beard on his chin. The pledge of protection, of safety, and of glory stood embodied in me. When I shouted my first war-whoop the owl hooted and smelt the ghosts of my enemies, the wolves howled, and the carrion vultures shrieked with joy; for they knew their food was coming, and I fed them with Chickasaws' flesh and with Choctaws' flesh until they were gorged with the flesh of the red man. A kind master and purveyor I was to them — the poor, dumb creatures that I loved. But lately I have given them more dainty food. I boast of having done better than my father. Five Frenchmen have I killed, and my only regret in dying is, that it will prevent me from killing more.

"'Ha! ha! ha! that was game worthy of the chief of the Beard!
How lightly he danced. Ho! ho! ho!
How gladly he shouted. Ha! ha! ha!
Each time with French blood his beard became red.'

"Sorrow in the hearts of the Natchez! The great hunter is no more. The wise chief is going to meet his fathers. The indomitable warrior will no more raise his hatchet in defence of the children of the Sun. O burning shame! He was betrayed by his brother-chiefs, who sold his blood. If they had followed his advice they would have united with the Choctaws, Chickasaws, and all the other red nations, and they would have slain all the French dogs that came prowling and stealing over the beautiful face of our country. But there was too much of the woman in their cowardly hearts. Well and good! Let the will of fate be accomplished. The white race will soon resume the blood which it gave, and then the glory and the very existence of the Natchez nation will have departed forever with the chief of the Beard; for I am the last of my race, and my blood flows in no other human veins. O Natchez, Natchez! remember the prophet's voice! I am content to die; for I leave no one behind me but the doomed, while I go to revel with my brave ancestors.

"'They will recognize their son in the chief of the Beard;
They will welcome him to their glorious homestead
When they see so many scalps at his girdle,
And his black beard with French blood painted red.'"

He stood up in proud defiance before the admiring French; his noble form expanded to its full proportions, hatred in his heart and triumph in his eyes. Facing his foes, he viewed the platoon selected to deal him his death, and lifted his eyes and hands to the sun. The officer gave the command, the platoon fired as one man, and the great chief of the Beard passed away.

This was the beginning of difficulties with the French, and also the commencement of the utter destruction of the Natchez. War succeeded war, until the last of this people, few in number, broke up from the Washita, whither they had fled for security years before, and went, as they fondly hoped, too far into the bosom of the deep West to be found again by the white-skins. But Clarke and Lewis found them high up on the Missouri, still preserving the holy fire, the flat heads, and their hatred of the white race. Their bones are even now turned up by the plough near the mounds of their making, and soon these mounds will be all that is left to speak of the once powerful Natchez. I have stood upon the great mound of their temple at the White Apple village, forty years ago, then covered with immense forest-trees, at the graves of the great grandfather and mother of my children. To these was donated, in 1780, by the Spanish Government, the land on which the temple and the village stood. It is a beautiful spot in the centre of a lovely and most picturesque country. It was here these Indians feasted the great La Salle and his party when descending the Mississippi. They were the first white men that had descended the river, and the first white men the Natchez had ever seen.

CHAPTER XX.

EXPLORATION OF THE MISSISSIPPI VALLEY.

Chicago — Crying Indians — Chickasaws — De Soto — Feast of the Great Sun — Cane Knives — Love-Stricken Indian Maiden — Rape of the Natchez — Man's Will — Subjugation of the Waters — The Black Man's Mission — Its Decade.

LA SALLE, who first discoverd the mouth of the Mississippi River, was a man of most remarkable energy and enterprise. He had been engaged in commercial pursuits for some time in Canada; but, seized with the spirit of adventure — very probably inspired by the reports of the Jesuit missionaries, who were going and returning from the vast wilderness — and inspired with the belief (then common) that the rivers west, and particularly the great river found by De Soto, debouched into the Pacific Ocean, he determined to learn the truth, and projected and commenced the ascent of the St. Lawrence and the navigation of the lakes as a means of reaching the Mississippi. It required almost superhuman daring to undertake such an enterprise; but there was enough in La Salle to accomplish anything possible to human capacity. His followers, like himself, were fearless and determined and, with a few small boats, or skiffs, he commenced his perilous adventure. It was like walking in the dark over uncertain ground; for every step was over unexplored territory, the moment he passed the establishments of the Jesuits, who were then pioneering to propagate their creed among the aborigines of the new continent.

His first winter was spent on the spot, or in the immediate neighborhood of where Chicago now stands. Here he invited to his camp the neighboring Indians, and endeavored to learn as much as possible of the geography of the country he was about to explore. Parties were sent out with these Indians to ascertain if there was any stream or water-communication leading from Lake Michigan to the West, and which might connect it with the Mississippi. Sufficient of the language of the tribes about him had been acquired to establish a means of intelligent intercourse with them. They were curious to know the objects of the visit of the white strangers to their country. Always suspicious of strangers — supposing all, like themselves, treacherous and cruel — they kept on the alert and were chary of giving any information they might possess as to this, or any other matters about which the white men asked; but, watchful of their movements, and seeing from their explorations their intentions, they became convinced of the sincerity of their inquiries, and readily pointed out the portage dividing the waters of Chicago Creek and those of the Illinois River.

When the spring came, and the snows had melted away, and the boats were all over the portage, with the assistance of the savages, the expedition was renewed in the descent of the Illinois. The Indians had been so kindly treated, and so sincerely dealt with, that every suspicion that made them fear the whites was dissipated, and they were loath to part from them, and many accompanied the party until they were about entering the territory of hostile neighbors. Of these they seemed to entertain great fears, and every means of persuasion and warning were used to prevent their white friends hazarding themselves to the power of these enemies. When the last were to leave, they manifested more emotion than is usual with the savage, and one of La Salle's party more facetious than the Indian designated them the Crying Indians.

La Salle was a wise as well as a bold adventurer. His policy with all the tribes he encountered was kindness and truth. These were human beings, and he correctly judged influenced by the motives and impulses of men. They had never seen white men before, and there could be no cause of quarrel, and there was little in the possession of the whites, the use of which was known to the Indian to tempt his cupidity. He manifested no fears in approaching them. Their curiosity tempted them to come to him, and once met, his kindness and gentleness won them; and he experienced no opposition or trouble from any he met; but succeeded in gaining much information from his communications with them. When he reached the Mississippi he began to doubt the accepted theory of its discharging its waters into the Pacific, and upon reaching the mouth of the Missouri and counseling with the chief of the tribe he met there, he at once determined the speculation a delusion, and decided to prosecute his journey to the mouth of the mighty stream, now with almost irresistible impetuosity hurrying on his little flotilla. This chief by many signs and diagrams marked with his finger upon the sand of the beach, described the country out of which flowed the Missouri, and into which went the Mississippi, and seemed to comprehend at least the extent of its constantly accumulating waters and great length. Like all the other savages, he represented the dangers below as being too formidable for the small party of La Salle. He described the Natchez Indians and gave them a terrible character; then the monsters of the woods and the waters. He marked the form of the tiger, the bear, and the alligator and described them as aggressive and ferocious. Taking a handful of sand he scattered it on the boat's floor or bottom, and pointing to the separate particles, attempted to explain by this means the countless numbers of these Indians, and monsters of the country below. Here was his first information of the existence of the Natchez, but his information augmented as he descended the river. At the bluffs, where now is Memphis, he encountered the Chickasaws and learned of the visit of De Soto to that point, and of his death. These Indians warned him of the dangers he had to encounter. They had had trouble with De Soto and were chary of their intercourse with the whites, but manifested no hostility.

The next tribe of Indians seen was at the Walnut Hills, now Vicksburg. Their flat heads told him he had reached the country of that formidable nation, but he held no communication with them. Landing at the great bluff or Natchez, he found there quite a village.

The natives approached him manifesting the kindest and most hospitable intentions. For some days he delayed, to learn as much as possible from these people in the observation of their character and the topography and peculiarities of the country they were inhabiting. Runners had been dispatched to the Great Sun at the White Apple village, to inform him of the advent of these pale-faced strangers, with beard on their chins. Like information was communicated to the towns on Cole's Creek and further in the interior. La Salle was furnished with pilots and requested to drop down to the White Cliffs, now known as Ellis' Cliffs, eighteen miles below Natchez, where a delegation would meet and conduct him to the White Apple village. These pilots caused the landing of the party at the mouth of St. Catharine's Creek, a point much nearer the village than the cliffs, and from whence it was much more easily approached. Thence they conducted them to the village and temple of the Great Sun. They came by surprise, and there was manifested some suspicions of the motive. But being informed it was the work of the pilots, all were satisfied and a messenger dispatched for the great escort awaiting the party at White Cliffs.

There were great preparations made for a solemn feast. Game in abundance had been collected: the meat of the deer and the bear and every variety of the wild-fowl peculiar to the country and season. These were spread out upon tables made of the wild-cane, placed upon poles sustained by posts driven into the ground, and covered with neatly dressed skins of the bear, elk, and buffalo. There were fish in abundance, the paupaw and the berries which grew abundantly in the forest. The Great Sun led La Salle to the centre of the square formed by the tables, where one had been prepared for him and the great ruler of the Natchez. Rude seats were arranged only for these two. The Little Suns, or smaller chiefs of surrounding villages, assembled with the great warriors and whites accompanying the expedition at the tables forming the square. These Indians had knives formed from the wild cane of the country and hardened in the fire, which were used for carving their meats and other like purposes, one of these was placed in the hand of every white man. The Great Sun standing up, looked reverently upon the sun for a few moments. Then lifting his hands, placed them on the head of La Salle. This was imitated by the Little Suns placing their hands upon the heads of all the whites, and when the chief or Great Sun removed his hands, and said, "Eat," the Little Suns did likewise, and the feast commenced. These cane knives, however, were comparatively useless in the hands of the French, and laying them down, they took from the belts at their sides the large hunting-knives they carried. This movement was so simultaneous, that alarm was apparent in every Indian face and a movement was made by the Indians as if to leave the table; but they were soon reassured when they saw the use to which they were applied. They watched the ease with which these cut through the flesh and cleaved the smaller bones of their repast, and expressed their astonishment in asking where the canes grew from which they were made — indicating conclusively that they had never before seen a metallic knife, and probably never before had seen iron or steel. When the feast had concluded, La Salle was led to a lodge prepared for him, and all his party were shown to places prepared for them, to repose after the meal. Upon the males retiring, the women came forth cleanly clad and removed everything from the tables.

This was the first view the whites had of the Natchez women. When their work was completed, they commenced to chant a song in slow and measured tones; soon, however, it quickened into merry cadences and the young females commenced a wild, fantastic dance. The older sang on, keeping time by slapping their hands and a swinging movement of the head and body right and left. Apparently, at the termination of a stanza, they would stoop suddenly forward and slap the hands upon each thigh, uttering at the same moment a shrill cry, when the dancers would leap with astonishing agility high in the air and, alighting, stand perfectly still. This exhibition called the French from their repose, who seemed delighted, and very soon joined in the dance; mirth excited mirth, and in a little while the village was in a complete uproar. The young warriors, however, were seen to scowl whenever the French approached too nigh the women, and especially when they took their hands and turned them around. The French were not slow to perceive this, nor were they mistaken in the delight it afforded the girls. The timidity of the latter soon disappeared and each lass singled out a beau, and was quite familiar with him. The French remained for some days enjoying the hospitality of the Natchez, returning to their boats and to the opposite shore of the river at night for greater security.

Among the French there was one, a stalwart young fellow, who had made the conquest of a heart among the maidens, and was surprised late at night to find she had swum the Mississippi to place herself by his side at the camp-fire. She implored him to remain with the Natchez and become a Great Sun, that her family was one of great influence at the White Clay village of which she was the belle, and she would marry him. She was rich, and the favorite of the Little Sun of her town, who had given her great presents. But Crapaud was aware of the price of these gifts, and though he did not refuse, was not inclined to the union, or to remain with her people. He promised, however, to see her to-morrow, and told her if he could prevail on some of his companions to remain, he would; but insisted if they would not, she must consent to follow him and provide a girl for each of his companions, who would accompany them to their homes, which he made very lovely in his description. They were standing now on the bank of the river and day was approaching. She pointed to the planet just above the horizon, and then to the place in the heavens where it would be in an hour, and said she must then be in her lodge, and plunging into the river swam rapidly to the opposite shore. The next day was the one appointed for the departure of La Salle and party. True to her promise — the Natchez girl had found a maiden for each of the party, who was willing to abandon her people and go with the strangers on their perilous and unknown journey, and to be the wives of the pale-faces.

The French, with much ceremony, were dismissed by the Great Sun, and a strong escort of both sexes followed them to their boats. The ceremony of shaking hands was gone through with; all the men first, and then the women; the last, as previously arranged, were the girls who were to follow their sweethearts. At a signal each was grasped and hurried forward toward the boats. The alarm was given, and in a moment the bows of the warriors were strung, and they rushed yelling to the rescue; overpowered, the French released the women and springing into their boats were soon out of danger of the arrows which were sent in showers after them — nor did they escape unscathed. Several of the men were wounded, and some of them severely. When once away from the shore, the French seized their guns and fired a volley, but were prevented from further demonstrations by La Salle; not wishing to leave behind him an enemy, who might be troublesome to him on his return up the river.

This adventure was the only hostile one of the entire trip. This was provoked by the folly and crime of his men without the knowledge of La Salle. How true it is that man in every condition and of every race will fight for his woman as surely as the game cock for his hen! Long years after, and when the last Natchez had been gone from the land of his love many years, and when threatening war was disturbing the people of the colonies, there came here a band of men, as had come to this land of beauty and plenty, the oppressors of the Natchez, seeking to make a peaceful home upon these hills, where grew in luxuriant profusion the magnolia and great tulip-trees, and where the atmosphere was redolent with the perfume of the wild flowers which clothed and ornamented the trees and grounds so fruitful and rich with nature's gifts.

The country was claimed as part of West Florida and dominated by the Spanish Government. They were anxious to have the country populated, and donated certain quantities or tracts of land to any one who came to settle and remain in the country. These settlements at first were made on the bluffs projecting through the alluvial swamp to the river's brink, and at or near the mouths of the small streams debouching into the river from the eastern shore. The west bank was deemed uninhabitable in consequence of the spring-floods sweeping over the alluvial formation, extending from forty to seventy miles west of the river; and there being no highlands or bluffs approaching the river from the west, below what is now known as Helena, in Arkansas, this vast territory was one interminable swamp, clothed with immense forest-trees, gigantic vines, and jungle-bushes. It was interspersed with lakes, and bayous as reservoirs and drains for the wonderful floods which annually visit this country. Around these were lands remarkable for their fertility—indeed, unsurpassed by any on the face of the earth; but worthless, however, for cultivation, as long as unprotected against these annual floods. The system of leveeing was too onerous and expensive to be undertaken by the people sparsedly populating the eastern bank throughout the hill-country. The levee system which had reclaimed so much of the low country in Louisiana, had not extended above Pointe Coupée, in 1826. Yet there were some settlements on several of the lakes above, especially on Lakes Concordia and St. Joseph.

The immense country in Georgia, Tennessee, Alabama, and Mississippi in possession of the Indians, interposed a barrier to emigration. To think of leaving home and friends to go away beyond these savages, seemed an undertaking too gigantic for any but men of desperate fortunes, or of the most indomitable energy.

Adventurers had wandered into the country and returned with terrible stories of the unhealthiness of the climate as well as the difficulties to be overcome in reaching it; thus deterring the emigrant who desired a new home. When General Jackson was elected to the Presidency a new policy was inaugurated. The Indians were removed beyond the Mississippi; the lands they had occupied were brought into market, and a flood of emigration poured into these new acquisitions. Cotton had suddenly grown into great demand. The increase of population, and the great cheapness of the fabrics from cotton, had increased the demand. In Europe it had rapidly increased, and in truth all over the world. Emigration from Europe had set in to a heavy extent upon the United States, and the West was growing in population so rapidly as to create there a heavy demand for these fabrics. The world was at peace; commerce was unrestricted, and prosperity was everywhere. Europe had recovered from her long war, and the arts of peace had taken hold of every people, and were bearing their fruit. All the lands intermediate between the frontiers west of Georgia and Tennessee and those of the east of Mississippi and Louisiana were soon appropriated; and the more fertile lands of the two latter States were coming rapidly into request for the purpose of cotton cultivation.

The great flood of 1828 had swept over every cultivated field west of the Mississippi, and seemed to demonstrate the folly of ever attempting to reduce these lands to profitable cultivation. But with the increase of population came wealth and enterprise. The levees were continued up the river. A long period of comparatively low water encouraged settlements upon the alluvial bottoms. The levees were continued up the west bank, and in a few years the forests had melted away from the margin of the river. Large fields were in their stead, and were continually increasing in extent. Improvements of a superior character were commencing, and an occasional break in the levee, and partial inundation, did not deter, but rather stimulated the planters to increased exertion, to discipline and control the great floods poured down from the rain-sheds extending from the head-waters of the Ohio to those of the Mississippi, Missouri, Arkansas, and Red Rivers, embracing in extent an area greater than the continent of Europe. It really seemed an attempt to defy the decrees of fate. In 1828, the waters from Cairo to Baton Rouge, a distance of nine hundred miles, averaged fifty miles in width. For months the great river was covered with forests of timber, torn up with the roots by the flood, floating and tumbling wildly along the terrible torrent, making the navigation extremely dangerous for the few steamers then upon the river. How often have I heard old men, who were long resident in the country, when standing on the bluff at Natchez, viewing the extent of that memorable flood, say: "Every man who attempts to cultivate these bottom lands will be ruined. The river demands them as a reservoir for her surplus waters when in flood." But enterprise was undeterred; the levees went up and the settlements went on to increase; and when the spoiler came all the valley was dotted over with pretty villages and magnificent cotton plantations, containing and sustaining a prosperous, rich, intelligent, and happy population. They are swept away, and ruin reigns over this desolated land.

This was but the beginning of the subduing to man's will and cultivation this entire and unparalleled valley. What had been done demonstrated the possibility of redeeming every inch of the alluvial land along the entire valley to the production of the richest staples, with all the necessaries to man's support, comfort, and wealth. It is pleasing to contemplate this immense plain as one extended scene of cultivation — the beautiful lakes of every form, surrounded with palatial homes and fertile fields; lovely towns upon their borders, with the church-spires pointing to heaven, surrounded with shrubs and flowers of every variety and hue; streams meandering among the extended plantations; railroads intersecting it in every direction; and all this mighty field, a thousand miles long by fifty broad, teeming with production, and pouring into the lap of commerce a wealth absolutely incalculable. The work was begun and was rapidly progressing; but now, when and by whom will this great, glorious garden be made?

To do this was the black man's mission; but ere his work was done he was converted into a machine to undo all his work. Inconceivable calamity has followed, and to him is fixed a decade which will soon run to extinction.

CHAPTER XXI.

TWO STRANGE BEINGS.

Romance of Western Life — Met by Chance — Parting on the Levee — Meeting at the Sick-bed — Convalescent — Love-Making — "Home, Sweet Home" — Theological Discussions — Uncle Tony — Wild, Yet Gentle — An Odd Family — The Adventurer Speculates.

IT was in the spring of the year away back in time when there landed at the town of St. Francisville, or Bayou Sara, a small periagua, or canoe, containing two young men clad in skins, with a camp-kettle, guns, some curiously painted skins, Indian bows, quivers, and Indian curiosities. Their hair was long, their unshaven beards were full and flowing, and in all their appearance they were wild and savage. There were but few houses in the hamlet below the hill. Among these was one of more pretensions than the rest. It was a store, and the merchant was an Irishman. There was near it a neat family carriage. One of the young savages went into this store to find materials for writing to his home-friends, from whom he had been separated for many long months. He found in the store three ladies. Two were young, the other was an aged matron. They seemed not only surprised at the novel apparition before them, but alarmed. This surprise seemed to increase when they saw the young savage rapidly filling, upon the counter, a sheet of paper. They desisted from their shopping, and watched intently the wild savage. When his letter was completed, he politely desired the accommodating merchant to send it for him to the post-office. Then lifting his gray wolf-skin cap from his head, he bowed politely to the ladies and turned to leave the store and their presence. The salutation was gracefully acknowledged, and especially by the matron. Very soon they joined the curious crowd who were examining the contents of the canoe, now placed on the land to await the coming of a steamer that was freighting with cotton above. One of the young ladies seemed much interested and made many inquiries. A bow and quiver was given into her hand. The latter was fashioned from the skin of a Mexican tiger, and was filled with arrows. One of these was bloody, and its history was asked of the youth she had met in the store. It was the blood of a Pawnee chief who, by this arrow, had been slain in battle, and was the gift to the youth from the daughter of the fallen chief, together with the bow and quiver of the Indian who had slain her father, and who was in turn killed by a chief of her tribe.

How beautiful she was to this wanderer of the wilderness! Months upon months had passed away, and he had only looked upon the blank and unmeaning features of the desert savage woman. With these his heart had no sympathy. Like the panther of their plains they were swift of foot, symmetrical in form, wild, untamed and untamable, fierce and unfeeling; and were not formed by nature for sympathy or social union with the higher organizations of civilized man. His dream of romance was being realized. The vacuum in his heart was filling. How in contrast were his feelings and appearance! Clad as a savage, his skin was covered with the fabric of an Indian woman, closely fitting, with moccasins on his feet, and a gray wolf-skin cap upon his head — his long, black hair with the luxuriant growth of two years curling over his shoulders, and his beard, like the wing of night fluttering in the breeze, waving down from his chin to his breast in ringlets, glossy and beautiful. He was lithe as a savage, and seemed to be one. In his heart were kindling soft emotions, and memories of maidens he had known — now far, far away — came crowding upon that heart. Before him stood the embodiment of beauty and grace, attired with costly and beautiful fabrics which flowed about her person like the white vapor upon the breezes of spring. Elegance was in her every attitude, and grace in every movement. Her features and her eyes beamed with a curious wish to learn the story of the strange wild being before her. Their two hearts were in sympathy; but to each other it was a secret. How strangely they had met! How strangely they were feeling! How soon they were to part! "Where is he from? Where is he going?" asked her eyes; and he looked: "Who are you; and where is your home, beautiful being, so strangely and so unexpectedly met?"

An arrow was shot from the bow to gratify a request. She followed the quivering thing with her eye, as it sped like a shaft of light to its destined mark. To retrieve it she walked with the youth to where, fixed in a bale of cotton, it trembled, some hundred yards away. Slowly she returned by the youth's side, and drooped her head, listening to the wild mountain adventures he was telling — the chase of the elk, the antelope, and the wild buffalo; the hazardous ride through the wild prairies, expanding away in the distance to kiss the horizon; the stealthy wiles of the revengeful savage; the fierce fight of savage men; the race for very life, when the foe followed; and the bivouac upon the prairie's breast, with the weary horse sleeping and resting by his side. Will he ever forget the speaking of the beaming features of that beautiful creature, when she lifted her head and looked into his face? A frown darkened the matron's features as her *élève* returned to the curious group which was listening to the narrative of the older of the two strangers. It said: "What did you leave me for? Why this indiscretion?" Ah! how often old women forget they were once young!

The steamer is coming. She is here; and the trappings of the wanderers are on board. The young wild man stands alone upon the upper deck. His eyes pierce to where stands the sylph he leaves with reluctance. She is looking at him. He lifts his cap and bows farewell. She waves her kerchief in return. The steamer speeds away. They are parted. Has that brief interview left an impression upon those two young hearts to endure beyond a day? Will she dream of the dark beard, curled and flowing—of the darker eye which looked and spoke? and will the wild story of the western wilderness come in the silent darkness of her chamber, and make her nestle closer to her pillow? Will her heart ask: "Shall I ever meet him again?"

He has gone away; a waif about the land—a feather on the world, driven about, as destiny impels, without fixed intentions; yet buoyant with the ardor of youth, and happy in the excess of youthful hopes, dreamy and wild adventures. He has tasted the savage love of woods and wilds, and the nature—which was born thousands of years ere the teachings of civilization had tamed the wild man into an educated, home-loving being—revives, and the two struggle for mastery in his heart. The bleak mountain-peaks, the wide-extended plain and its wild denizens, and the excitement these give, stirs his bosom, and the wish struggles up to return to them. But the gentler chords of his heart are in tune. The once-loved home, and she, the once-loved and yet-remembered maiden, is there, and it may be she pines for his return. He gazed on the beautiful apparition but a moment gone, and thought of another; and thought begat thought until the loved one he had left rose up to memory's call. He was alone, looking upon the great river through whose turbid waters he was borne away, and he felt he was lengthening a chain linked to his heart which pulled him back — to what, and to whom? It was a vision — a dream with his eyes open: indistinct, unembodied, a very shadow; still it floated about in his imagination, and he was sad. He was in the city — the great Sodom of the West. He was an object of wonder to every curious eye. His wild appearance and gentle manner comported illy, and the thoughtless crowd followed him. Attired now as a civilized being, and feeling that the vagrant life of a savage must lead to grief, he called to mind the tear which stole from the rheumy eyes of the old trapper as he narrated his adventures in the wilderness, and cursed the hour he ever wandered from his home. His life had been a continual danger, his hope had been always to return to his early attachments; but the chain of habit fettered him, and he had learned to love the wild, solitary life, because of its excitements and its dangers. Should he, like this man, come to love the solitude and silence of the wilderness, and find companionship only with his traps and guns?

His resolution was taken, he would renew the strife with the world and go back to busy life. His companion of many dangers and long marches was going to Mexico in search of new adventures. They are alone upon the broad levee — busy men are hurrying to and fro, little heeding the two — a small schooner is dropping and sheeting home her sails; she is up for Tampico, and Gilmanot goes in her; she is throwing off her fastenings. "All aboard," cries the swarthy, whiskered captain — a grasp of the hand — no word was spoken — it was warm and sincere, there was no need of words — each understood that last warm farewell pressure. She is sweeping around Slaughter-house Point — only the topmasts are visible now — and now she is gone. The young adventurer stands alone and the crowd goes hurrying on. How many in desolation of heart have stood alone and unheeded by the busy, passing multitude upon that broad levee! How many tears of misery have moistened its shell-covered summit, when thinking of friends far, far away they should never see again, and when hope had been rooted from the heart!

He wandered to the great square, now so beautifully ornamented with shrubs and flowers which love the sun and the South's fat soil, growing and blooming about the bronze representation of the loved hero who had been her shield and savior in the hour of her peril, Andrew Jackson. Then there were a few trees only, and beneath these, here and there, a rude rural seat or bench. The old, gray cathedral was frowning on the world's sins, so rife around her; and the great, naked square and the mighty muddy river which was hurrying away to the sea. To the most thoughtless will come reflection, and the sweetest face is mellowed by sorrow. Here under these trees, in the midst of a great city, came to the young adventurer reflection and sighing sorrow. His mother and father came up in memory; the home of childhood, his brother, his sister, his friends, all were remembered; his heart flooded over and he wept like a little child. Blessed are they who can cry. It is nature's outlet for grief, and the heart would break if we could not cry. The heart is not desolate when alone in the forest or the boundless grass-clothed plains of the West. Nature is all around you, and her smile is benificent. There is companionship in the breeze, in the waving grass, the rustling leaves, and the moanings of the wind-swayed limbs of the yielding forest. In the city's multitude to move, and be unknown of all; to hear no recognized voice; to meet no sympathizing smile or eye; to be silent when all are speaking, and to know that not one of all these multitudes share a thought or wish with you — this is desolation, the bitterness of solitude.

A year has gone by, and the youth has found a new home and has made new friends. He is one of the busy world and struggling with it. He is in commerce's mart and is one of the multitude who come and congregate there for gain; in the hall of Justice, where litigants court the smiles and favors of the blind goddess, where right contends against wrong, and is as often trampled as triumphant; and where wisdom lends herself for hire, and bad men rarely meet their dues.

Pestilence had come, and the frightened multitude were fleeing from the scourge. There was one who came and proffered the hospitality of his home — where Hygeia smiled and fever never came. Thither he went, but the poison was in his blood, and as he slept it seized upon his vitals. His suffering was terrible, and for days life's uncertain tenure seemed ready to release her hold on time. In his fever-dream there was flitting about him a fairy form; it would come and go, as the moonlight on the restless wave — a moment seen and in a moment gone. He saw and knew nothing for many days distinctly;

he would call for his mother and weep, when only winds would answer. Delirium was in his brain, and wild fancies chased each other; he heard the crowing of cocks and saw his sister; his father would come to him, and he would stretch out his hand and grasp the shadowy nothing. There was a halo of beauty all about him; prismatic hues trembled in the light, and the tones of sweet music floated upon the breeze. He saw angels swimming in the golden light; the blue ether opened, and they came through to greet him and to welcome him to heaven. Then all was darkness, the crisis had come. He slept in oblivious ease — it was long; and awaking, the fever was gone. There was a gentle, sweet, sorrowful face before him — their eyes met; for a moment only he looked — it was she whom he had met and parted from without a hope of ever meeting again when robed as the Indian he stood upon the steamer's deck and waved farewell forever. He reached forth his hand. She took it and approached, saying, "You are better, and will soon be well." He could only press her hand as the tears flooded over his eyes. With a kerchief white as innocence it was wiped away and the hand that held it laid gently on his brow — that touch thrilled his every nerve.

Days went by, and the convalescent was amid the shrubs and flowers of the beautifully ornamented grounds. When he came to the maiden reading in the shade of a great pecan-tree, she bid him to a seat.

"Do you remember our first meeting?" he asked.

"Here, on your sick-bed, yes; you were, oh! so sick, and I little thought you would ever leave it alive. You called in your delirium your mother and your father, and in the frenzy of your mind you saw them by you; how my heart was pained, and how I prayed for you, in my chamber, here, and everywhere — and now you are well, only weak."

"It was not when sick I met you first," he replied; "as a wild man you saw me first, clothed in the skins of the wild beasts of the forest."

She gazed intently; could it be? and clasping her hands she bowed her head and was silent.

"We have met again," he continued; "I had not forgotten you, but I dared not hope we should ever meet any more. It was a painful thought; but I must not tell that —" and there was silence.

Days went by, and the invalid was growing in strength and health.

They only met at the table at the family meals, but they were near each other. It was at dinner when a ride on horseback was proposed for the evening's recreation. They rode in company, and through the forest where the winding road circled the hills, and the great magnolias threw their dark shade and deliciously cooled the vesper breeze.

"Is it romance, or are you the young gentleman with flowing hair and black, curling beard I met, and who shot the arrow into the cotton bale for my amusement? O! how often have I seen you in my dreams; but I shall never see you as I saw you then. What a study you were to me! How could your words be so soft and gentle in the wild costume of the murderous savage? Had you uttered the war-whoop and strode away with the stride and pride of the savage warrior, there would have been euphony in it, and I should have felt and known you were a savage—and you would have passed from my mind. But, ah! look how beautifully bounds away the startled doe we have aroused from her lair in the cave here."

"She seems scarcely more startled than did you when I came so unexpectedly upon you in the store at Bayou Sara. Were you not surprised to see that I could write?"

"You must not question me now. Why have you cut your hair and beard? why doffed the prairie chieftain's robes of state and come forth a plain man? You have dispelled my romance. I have tried to paint you as I saw and remembered you, and made charcoal sketches for the gratification of friends to whom I would describe you. I would so like to see you as you were! O! you were a wonder to me, a very Orson — now, you are simply a —"

"Miserable creature in plain clothes, and by no means a lady's fancy. Why did you not let me die, since all that was to be fancied about me — my hair, my beard, and my buckskin coat, pants, and moccasins are gone and destroyed?"

The maiden laughed wildly; it was not the laugh of mirth or mischief, there was a madness in it that thrilled and awed.

"Do you know you are on the graves of a great nation?" she asked. "This mound and yonder three, were the burial-places of the Natchez Indians. The Suns and Sachems sleep here, and he, the Great Sun, who came from the orbit's self, and was their lawgiver, and in whom and whose divinity they believed as the Jews in that of Moses, or the Christians in the Redeemer. Is it not all a mystery—strange, strange, incomprehensible, and unnatural? What is your faith?"

"To worship where I love; the divinity of my soul's worship is the devotion of my wild heart.'

"Why, you are mysterious! Have you, as had the Natchez, a holy fire which is never extinguished in your heart? Is the flame first kindled burning still? Did your sun come to you with fire in her hand and kindle it in your heart? Your words mean so much. Was she, or is she a red maiden of the wild prairies; or dwells she in a mansion surrounded with the appliances of wealth, reclining on cushions of velvet and sleeping on a bed of down, canopied with a pavilion of damask satin fretted with stars of silver; with handmaids to subserve and minister to every want?" And again the wild laugh rang to the echo among the hills and dense forests all around. "O! I see I have tuned the wrong chord and have made discord, not music in your mind. Shall we return? You are not yet strong, and your weakness I have made weaker, because I have disturbed the fountain of your heart and brought up painful memories?"

"You are strange," said her companion, "and guess wide of the mark. The untutored savage is only a romance at a distance — the reality of their presence a disgusting fact. They are wild, untamable, and wicked, without sentiment or sympathy, cruel and murderous; disgusting in their habits and brutal in their passions."

"And yet, sir, the stories which come down to us of these so quietly sleeping here are full of romance and poetry. Their intercourse with the French impressed that mercurial people with exalted notions of their humanity, chivalry, and nobleness of nature. Can it be that these historians only wrote romances? You must not disturb this romance. If it is an illusion let me enjoy it; do not strip from it the beard, the hair, the hunting-shirt, the bow and quiver — reality or fiction, it is sweet to the memory. How often have I wandered from our home and stood here alone and conjured from the spirit-land the ghosts of the Great Suns, the Stung Serpent, and the chief of the Beard, and hers who warned the French of the conspiracy for their destruction. In my day-dreaming I have talked with these, and learned with delight of their bliss in their eternal hunting-grounds. And as I have knelt here, they in hosts have come to me with all their legends and long accounts against the white man, and I have wept above these dry bones, and felt too it was the fate of the white man, when his mission shall have been completed on earth, and his nation's age bear him into the ground, and only his legends shall live a tradition, like that of the Natchez.

"The hieroglyphics of Thotmes, of Rameses, of Menephthah, and of the host of kings gone before these in Egypt's old life, cannot be read; their language, letters, and traditions, too, sleep beyond the revelations of time, and yet their tombs, like these, give up their bones to the curious, who group through the catacombs, or dig at the base of their monumental pyramids. All besides has passed away and is lost. Not even the color of the great people who filled these monuments, and carved from the solid stone these miles of galleries, now filled to repletion with their mummied dead, and whose capacity is sufficient to entomb the dead of a nation for thousands of years, is known now to those who people the fields reclaimed from the forest beyond the memory of time.

"Nations are born, have their periods of youthful vigor, their manhood of sturdy strength, the tottering of decrepit age, the imbecility of superstitious dotage—and their death is final extinction. Such is man, and such is the world. What we are, we know; what we shall be, we know not, save that we only leave a pile of bones. Come, we are approaching home, and the moon dares to shine, ere yet the sun has gone. Yonder is brother, and I expect a scolding; but let him fret—it is not often I have a toy. Fate threw you in my way and you must not complain if I use you."

"I shall not complain," replied the astonished young man; "but will you ride again to-morrow?"

She checked up her steed (a noble one he was) and seemed to take in his entire man, as slowly her eye went up from his stirrup to his face, when she said: "To-morrow, ah, to-morrow! Who can tell what to-morrow may bring forth? To you and to me, there may come no to-morrow. We may in a twinkling be hurled from our sphere into oblivion. The earth may open to-night, or even now, and we may drop into her bosom of liquid fire, and be only ashes to-morrow.

"'Take no heed for to-morrow,'' is the admonition of wisdom. Look, yonder I was born. Here sleep the Natchez. See yonder tall mound, shaded from base to summit with the great forest trees peculiar to our land. On the top of that mound stood the temple dedicated to the worship of the sun. He smiles on it as the earth rolls up to hide his light away, as he did when the holy fire was watched by the priests in that temple. But the Indian worshipper is gone; to him there comes no morrow. There, on that mound, sleep the parents of my mother; to them comes no morrow. *Allons!* We shall be late for tea. Brother has gone to sister's, and we shall be alone." In a few minutes they were galloping down the avenue to the old Spanish-looking mansion, hid away almost from view in the forest and floral surroundings, which made it so lovely to view.

There had come in their absence another; it was she who was the youthful companion of his fairy at the Bayou Sara — a silent, reserved woman: very timid and very polished. Upon the gallery she was awaiting the return of her cousin. The meeting was (as all meetings between high-bred women should be) quiet, but cordial; without show, but full of heart. They loved one another, and were high-bred women. The stranger was presented, and at tea the cousin was informed that he was the man from the mountains, and there was a curious, silent surprise in her face, when she almost whispered, "I am pleased, sir, to meet you again. I hope you will realize the romance of my cousin's dream with your legends of the West, the woods, and the wild men of the prairies."

Days went by, and still the fever raged in the city. The cerulean was bright and unflecked with a speck of vapor, like a concave mirror of burnished steel. It hung above, and the red sun seemed to burn his way through the azure mass. The leaves drooped as if weighted with lead, and in the shade kindly thrown upon the wilting grass by the tulips, oaks, and pecans about the yard, the poultry lifted their wings and panted with exhaustion in the sickly heat of the fervid atmosphere. The sun had long passed the zenith, dinner was over, and the inmates were enjoying the siesta, so refreshing in this climate of the sun. Here and there the leaves would start and dally with a vagrant puff from vesper's lips, then droop again as if in grief at the vagaries of the little truant which now was fanning and stirring into lazy motion another leafy limb.

There was music in the drawing room. It was suppressed and soft — so sweet that it melted into the heart in very stealth. Ah! it is gone. "Home, sweet home!" Poor Paine! like you, wandering in the friendless streets of England's metropolis and listening to your own sweet song, breathed from titled lips in palatial homes, the listener to-day was homeless. He thought of you and the convivial hours he had passed with you, listening to the narrative of your vagrant life, and how happy you were in the poetry of your own thoughts when you were a stranger to every one, and your purse was empty, and you knew not where you were to find your dinner.

Genius, thou art a fatal gift! Ever creating, never realizing; living in a world of beauty etherialized in imagination's lens, and hating the material world as it is; buffoted by fortune and ridiculed by fools whose conceptions never rise above the dirt.

A little note, sweetly scented, is placed in his hand:

"Cousin and I propose a ride. Shall we have your company? You are aware it is the Sabbath. You must not, for us, do violence to your prejudices."

"Is this," thought he, "a delicate invitation to save my feelings, and is the latter clause meant as a hint that they do not want me? Well, the French always, when a compliment has as much bitter as sweet in it, take the sweet and leave the bitter unappropriated. It is a good example. I will follow it. Say to the ladies I will accompany them."

"The horses are all ready, sir; and the ladies bonneted wait in the drawing-room."

The sun was in the tree-tops and the shadows were long. There was a flirtation going on between the leaves and the breeze. The birds were flitting from branch to branch. A chill was on the air: it was bathing the cheek with its delicious touch, and animated life was rejoicing that evening had come.

Arriving at the great mound of the temple of the sun, with some difficulty they climb to its summit. So dense is the shade that it is almost dark. Here are two graves, in which sleep the remains of the grand-parents of these two beautiful and lovely women. All around are cultivated fields clothed with rich crops, luxuriant with the promise of abundance. At its base flows the little creek, gliding and gabbling along over pure white sand. Sweet Alice! How sad she seems! She stood at the grave's side, and, looking down, seemed lost in pious reverie. Every feature spoke reverence for the dead. Her cousin, too, was silent; and if not reverent, was not gay. He, their gallant, was respectfully silent, when Alice said, without lifting her eyes:

"I wonder if La Salle ever stood here? This is holy ground. No spot on earth has a charm for me like this. I am in the temple. I see the attentive, watchful priest feeding there (as she pointed) the holy fire, and yonder, with upturned eyes, the great lawgiver worshipping his god, as he comes up from his sleep, bringing day, warmth, light, and life. Was not this worship pure? Was it not natural? The sun came in the spring and awoke everything to life. The grass sprang from the ground and the leaves clothed the trees; the birds chose their mates and the flowers gladdened the fields; everything was redolent of life, and everything rejoiced. He went away in the winter, and death filled the land. There were no leaves, no grass, no flowers. All nature was gloomy in death. Could any but a god effect so much? The sun was their god; his temple was the sky, and his holy fire burned on through all time. Beautiful conception! Who can say it is not the true faith?"

"To the unlettered mind, it was," answered the young gentleman; "because the imagination could only be aided by the material presented to the natural eye. Science opens the eye of faith. It teaches that the sun is only the instrument, and faith looks beyond for the Creator. To such the Indian's faith cannot be the true one. The ignorance of one sees God in the instrument, and his thoughts clothe him with the power of the Creator, and his heart worships God in sincerity, and to him it is the true faith. But to the educated, scientific man, who knows the offices of the sun, it appears as it is, only the creature of the unseen, unknown God, and to this God he lifts his adoration and prayers, and to him this is the true faith."

"So, my philosopher, you believe, whatever lifts the mind to worship God is the true faith?"

"You put it strongly, Miss, and I will answer by a question. If in sincerity we invoke God's mercy, can the means that prompt the heart's devotion, reliance, and love, be wrong? His magnitude and perfection are a mystery to the untutored savage: he knows only what he sees. The earth to him, (as it was to the founders and patriarchs of our own faith,) is all the world. He has no idea that it is only one, and a small one of a numerous family, and can conceive only that the sun rules his world; gives life and death to everything upon the earth—but this inspires love and reverence for God. The scientific man sees in the sun only an attractive centre, and sees space filled with self-illuminating orbs, and reasoning from the known to the unknown, he believes these centres of attraction to planetary families, and the imagination stretches away through space filled with centres and revolving worlds, and each centre with its dependents revolving around one great centre, and this great centre he believes is God. His idea is only one step beyond the Indian's, and has only the same effect: it leads the heart to depend on and worship God."

"You are a heretic, and must like a naughty boy be made to read your Bible and go to Sunday-school, and be lectured and taught the true faith. Fy! fy! shall the heathen go to heaven? Where is the provision for him in the Bible? What are we to do with missions? If this be true, there is no need that we should be sending good men and dear, pious women to convert the Chinese, the Feejees, and the poor Africans so benighted that their very color is black, and the Australians, and New Georgians, to be roasted and eaten by the cannibals there. If they worship God in sincerity, you say that is all?"

"No, miss, faith without works is a futile reliance for heaven. It is the first necessity, and perhaps the next and greatest, is, to 'Do unto all what you would have all do unto you.' These are the words of the great Chinese philosopher, Confucius, and were taught four and a half centuries before Christ, yet we see Him teaching the same. This, as Confucius said, was the great cardinal duty of man, and all else was but a commentary upon this. This I fancy is all, at least it is very comprehensive. You tell me the traditions of the people who worshipped here say that this was a cardinal law unto them?"

"You, sir, have lived too long among the heathen, if you are not one already. You are like an August peach in July: you are turning, and in a little while will be ripe. You talk, as Uncle Toney says, like a book, and to me, like a new book, for yours are new thoughts to me. Cousin, does he not astonish you?"

"By no means; true, they are new thoughts; but they are natural thoughts, and I do not fear to listen to them — on the contrary, I could listen to them all day, and, Alice, I have often, very often, heard from you something like this."

"Nonsense, cousin, nonsense; I am orthodox, you know, and a good girl and love to go to church, especially when I have a becoming new dress."

"Here are the bones of our ancestors, if they were once animated with souls; and I guess they were, particularly the old man, for I have heard many stories from old Toney, that convince me that he was a pretty hard one. How do we know that their spirits are not here by us now? Why is it deemed that there shall be no communication between the living and the dead? O! how I want to ask all about the spirit-land. Wake up and reclothe thy bones and become again animated dust, and tell me thou, my great progenitor, the mysteries of the grave, of heaven and hell. How quiet is the grave? No response, and it is impious to ask what I have. O! what is life which animates and harmonizes the elements of this mysterious creation, man! Life how imperious, and yet how kind; it unites and controls these antagonistic elements, and they do not quarrel on his watch. Mingling and communing they go on through time, regardless of the invitation of those from which they came to return. But when life is weary of his trust and guardianship, and throws up his commission, they declare war at once—dissolve, and each returns to his original. Death and corruption do their work, and life returns no more, and death is eternal, and the soul — answer ye dumb graves — did the soul come here? or went it with life to the great first cause? or is here the end of all; here, this little tenement? I shudder — is it the flesh, the instinct of life; or is it the soul which shrinks with horror from this little portal through which it must pass to eternal bliss, or eternal — horrible! Assist me to my horse, if you please. Come cousin, let us go and see old Uncle Toney — and, sir, he will teach you more philosophy than you ever dreamed of."

"Who is Uncle Toney? miss," asked the stranger of the visiting cousin when he returned to aid her descent of the mound.

"He is a very aged African, brought to this country from Carolina by our grandfather, in 1775, or earlier; he says there were remnants of the Natchez in the country at that time, and the old man has many stories of these, and many more very strange ones of the doings of the whites who first came and settled the country. He retains pretty well his faculties, and, like most old people, is garrulous and loves a listener. He will be delighted with our visit."

"Miss Alice, do you frequently visit Uncle Toney?"

"Very nearly every day. I have in my basket, here, something for the old man. Turn there, if you please — yonder by that lightning-scared old oak and those top-heavy pecans is his cabin and has been for more than sixty years. Here was the local of my grandfather's house; here was born my mother; but all the buildings have long been gone save Uncle Toney's cabin. Think of the hopes, the aspirations, the blisses, the sorrows, the little world that once was here — all gone except Uncle Toney. In my childhood I used to come here and go with him to the graves where we have been to-day, and have sat by them for hours listening to the stories he delights to tell of my grandfather and mother, until their very appearance seems familiar to my vision. I know that my grandfather was a small man, and a passionate man, and Toney sometimes tells me I am like him. His eye was gray — so is mine; his face sharper than round — so is mine, and sometimes my temper is terrible — so was his;" and she laughed again that same wild thrilling laugh as she gallopped up to the cabin and leaped down to greet the old man, who was seated at the door of his hut beneath the shade of a catalpa, the trunk of which was worn smooth from his long leaning against it. He was very black and very fat. His wool was white as snow, and but for the seams in both cheeks, cut by the knife in observance of some ridiculous rite in his native land, would have been really fine-looking for one of his age. He arose and shook hands with the cousin, but did not approach the gentleman. He was evidently not pleased with his presence and was chary of his talk.

"Ah! young missus," he said, when he received the basket, "you bring old Toney sometin good. You is my young missus, too; but dis one is de las one. Dey is all married and gone but dis one." (This conversation was addressed to the cousin.) "All gone away but dis one, and when she marry dare will be nobody to fetch dis ole nigger good tings and talk to de ole man."

"Uncle Toney, I don't intend to marry."

"Ha, ha, ha!" laughed the old man, "berry well, berry well! I hear dat from ebery one ob my young misses, and where is dey now? All done married and gone. You gwine to do jus as all on em hab done, byne by when de right one come. Ah! may be he come now."

"You old sinner, I have a great mind to pull your ears for you."

"O no, missus, I don't know! I see fine young man dare; but maybe he come wid Miss Ann, and maybe he belong to her."

"Uncle Toney, don't you remember I told you of a wild man away from the mountains, all clothed in skins, with a long, curly beard and hair over his shoulders as black as a stormy night? This is he."

"Gosh!" said the venerable negro. "I mus shake his hand; but what hab you done wid your beard, your hair, and your huntin-shirt?"

"I have thrown them all into the fire, uncle. People among white people must not dress like Indians."

"Dat 's a fac, young massa; but I tell you Miss Alice was mity taken wid dem tings. She come here soon as she comed home, and told me all about 'em and all about you — how you could shoot de bow and how you could talk, and she said: 'O! what would I not give to see him again?'"

"Toney, if you don't shut up, I won't come to see you, or bring you any more good things. This young gentleman has come with us to see you, and wishes to hear you tell all about the Natchez, and to get you to show him the many things you have dug up on and around these mounds, and have you tell him all about the old people who came here first and made all these big plantations and built all these great houses."

"Well, Miss Alice, dis is Sunday, you know, and dem tings mus not be telled on Sunday, and den you and Miss Ann don't want ole nigger to talk. You go ride and talk wid de young gemman, and maybe to-morrow, or some week-day, young massa can come down from de great house wid de gun to shoot de squirrels along de way, and when he tired, den he can come and rest, and I can tell him all. Yes, young massa, I been live long time here. Me is mity old. All dem what was here when I comed wid ole massa is dead long time. Yes, dare aint one on em livin now, and dare chillin is old."

"I shall be sure to come," said the young man, "and suppose I bring with me these ladies?"

"Neber you do dat, massa. I knows young folks ways too well for dat. Toney may talk, but dey neber will listen. Dey will talk wid one anoder, and Miss Alice been hear all de ole nigger's talk many a time, and she don't want to hear it ober and ober all de time; and beside dat, young massa, sometimes when I tells bout de ole folks, she trimbles and cries. She 's got a mity soft heart bout some tings, and she tells me I mus tell you eberyting."

"There now, Toney, you have said enough about me to make the gentleman think I am a very silly little girl."

"God bress my young missus!" he said as he tenderly patted her head. "I wouldn't hurt your feelins for noffin. You is too good, Miss Alice. Toney lubed your mamma — Toney lubs you, and de day you is married and goes away, I want to go away too. I want to go yonder, Miss Alice, on de top ob dat mound, and lie down wid ole massa and missus. He told your pa to put me dar; but your pa 's gone. O Miss Alice! dey 's all gone but you and me and your brodder, and he don't care for Toney, and maybe he will trow him out in de woods like a dog when he die." Tears stole down the black face of the venerable man, and the eyes of Alice filled — and then she laughed the shrill, fearful laugh, and rode rapidly away.

She was singing and walking hurriedly the gallery, when the stranger and her cousin came leisurely into the yard.

"Your cousin, Miss Ann, has a strange laugh."

"Indeed she has, sir; but we who know her understand it. She never laughs that unearthly laugh when her heart is at ease. I doubt if you have ever met such a person. I think the world has but one Alice. She is very young, very impressible, and some think very eccentric, very passionate and romantic to frenzy. There is something which impels me to tell you — but no, I have no right to do so. But this I must tell you; for you cannot have been in the house here so long without observing it. There is no congeniality between herself and brother; indeed, very little between her and any of her family. She is alone. She is one by herself; yes, one by herself in the midst of many; for the family is a large one. But remember, there is none like Alice. Be gentle to her and pity her; and pity her most when you hear that strange laugh."

There was music in the drawing-room, soft and gentle, and the accompanying voice was tremulous with suppressed emotion. Gradually it swells in volume until it fills the spacious apartment, and the clear notes from the tender trill rose grandly in full, clear tones, full of pathetic melody, and now they almost shriek. They cease — and the laugh, hysterical and shrill, echoes through the entire house. The judge was silent; but a close observer might have seen a slight contraction of the lips, and a slighter closing of the eyes. A moment after Alice entered the room, and there was a glance exchanged between her brother and herself. There was in it a meaning only for themselves.

"You have been riding, sir," he said to his guest, "and my sister tells me to the mound at the White Apple village. To those curious in such legends as are connected with its history, it is an interesting spot. All I know in relation to these, I acquired from a dreamy and solitary man employed by my father to fit myself and brother for college. He read French, and was fond of tracing all he could find in the writings of the historians of the first settlement of Louisiana and Mississippi, and of the history, habits, and customs of the aborigines of the country. He knew something of the adventures of De Soto and La Salle, and something of the traditions of the Natchez. He was a melancholy man, and perished by his own hand in the chamber that you occupy. My sister is curious in such matters, and from her researches in some old musty volumes she has found in the possession of an old European family, she has made quite a history of the Natchez, and from the old servants much of that of the first white or English occupants of this section. For myself, I have little curiosity in that way. My business forbids much reading of that kind, and indeed much of anything else, and I am glad that my tastes and my business accord. I would not exchange one crop of cotton grown on the village-field, for a perfect knowledge of the history of every Indian tribe upon the continent."

"I am no antiquarian, sir. A life on a plantation I suppose must be most irksome and monotonous to a young lady, unless she should have some resource besides her rural employments."

"Our only amusements, sir," said Alice, "are reading, riding, and music, with an occasional visit to a neighbor. I ride through the old forest and consult the great patriarchal trees, and they tell me many strange stories. When the ruthless axe has prostrated one of these forest monarchs, my good palfrey waits for me, and I count the concentric circles and learn his age. Some I have seen which have yielded to man's use or cupidity who have looked over the younger scions of the woods, and upon the waters of the mighty river a thousand years."

"Indeed, miss," replied the guest, "I had not supposed the natural life of any of our forest trees extended beyond three, or at most four centuries."

"The tulip or poplar-tree and the red-oak in the rich loam of these hills live long and attain to giant proportions. The vines which cling in such profusion to many of these are commensurate with them in time. They spring up at their bases and grow with them: the tree performing the kindly office of nurse, lifting them in her arms and carrying them until their summits, with united leaves, seem to kiss the clouds. They live and cling together through tempests and time until worn out with length of days, when they tumble and fall to the earth together, and together die. We all, Flora and Fauna, go down to the bosom of our common mother to rest in death. I love the companionship of the forest. There is an elevation of soul in this communion with incorruptible nature: there is sincerity and truth in the hills and valleys — in the trees and vines, and music — grand orchestral music — in the moaning of the limbs and leaves, played upon by the hurrying winds. I have prayed to be a savage, and to live in the woods."

"You are as usual, sister, very romantic to-night."

"By and by, brother, I shall forget it I presume. I am human, and shall soon die, or live on till time hardens my nature, or sordid pursuits plough from my heart all its sympathies, and old age finds me gloating over the gains of laborious care and penurious meanness.

"'To such vile uses we must come at last.'"

"You draw a sad picture, miss, for old age. Do not the gentler virtues of our nature ever ripen with time? Is it the alchemist who always turns the sweets of youth to the sours of age? There are many examples in every community to refute your position. I would instance the venerable negro we visited to-day. He wept as he placed his trembling hand upon your head. There was surely nothing ascetic or sordid in his feelings."

"Uncle Toney is an exception, sir. The affectionate memories he has of our family, and especially of my mother and father, redeems him from the obloquy of his race. His heart is as tender as his conduct is void of offense. He was a slave. God had ordained him for his situation. He had not the capacity to aspire beyond his lot, or to contrast it with his master's. Contented to render his service, and satisfied with the supply of his wants from the hands of him he served — he had a home, and all the comforts his nature required. He has it still; but I know he is not as contented as when he was my father's slave. God bless the old man! He shall never want while I have anything, and should I see him die, he shall sleep where he wished to-day."

"By our grandfather, I suppose, Alice?"

"Yes, my brother, by our grand-parents. They told him it should be so. Ah! there are no distinctions in the grave; white skin and black skin alike return to dust, and the marl of the earth is composed alike of the bones of all races, and their properties seem to be the same. I, too, wish to sleep there. It is a romantically beautiful spot, and its grand old traditions make it holy ground. How its associations hallow it! Imagination peoples it with those bold old red men who assembled in the temple to worship the holy fire—emblematic of their faith—humbling their fierce natures and supplicating for mercy. I go there and I feel in the touch of the air that it is peopled with the spirits of the mighty dead, surrounding and blessing me for my memory of, and love for, their extinct race."

"Bravo, sister! What an enthusiast! You, sir, have some knowledge of the Indians. Do they stir the romance of your nature as that of my baby sister?"

The glance from her eye was full of scorn: it flashed with almost malignant hate as she rose from her seat, and taking the arm of her cousin she swept from the room, audibly whispering "baby sister" in sneering accents.

"Woman's nature is a strange study, my young friend. I have several sisters and they are all strange, each in her peculiar way. They are remarkable for the love they bear their husbands, and yet they all have a pleasure in tormenting them, and are never so unhappy, as when they see these happy. This younger sister has a nature all her own. I do not think she shares a trait with another living being. Wild, yet gentle; the eagle to some, to some the dove. Quick as the lightning in her temper—as fervid, too; a heart to hate intensely, and yet to melt in love and worship its object; but would slay it, if she felt it had deceived her. Always searching into the history of the past, and always careless of the future."

"You have drawn something of the character of a Spanish woman. Their love and their hate is equally fierce; and both easily excited, they are devoted in all their passions. I have thought that this grew from the secluded life they live. Ardency is natural to the race, and this restrained makes their lives one long romance. Their world is all of imagination. The contacts of real life they never meet outside of their prison-homes, and the influence of experience is never known. They are seen through bars, are sought through bars, they love through bars—and the struggle is, to escape from these restraints; and the moral of the act or means for its accomplishment, or the object to be attained, never enters the mind. Such natures properly reared to know the world, to see it, hear it, and suffer it, tunes all the attributes of the mind and heart to make sweet music. Nothing mellows the heart like sorrow; nothing so softens the obduracy of our natures as experience. None, sir, man or woman, are fitted for the world without the experiences its contact brings. These experiences are teachings, and the bitter ones the best. To be happy, we must have been miserable; it is the idiosyncracy of the mind, to judge by comparison; and the eternal absence of grief leaves the mind unappreciative of the incidents and excitements which bring to him or her who have suffered, such exquisite enjoyment. The rue of life is scarcely misery to those who have never tasted its ambrosia."

"You are young, sir, thus to philosophize, and must have seen and experienced more than your years would indicate."

"Some, sir, in an incident see all of its characters that the world in a lifetime may present. They suffer, and they enjoy with an acuteness unknown to most natures; and in youth gain the experiences and knowledge they impart, while most of the world forget the pain and the pleasure of an incident with its evanescence. With such, experience teaches nothing. These progress in the world blindly and are always stumbling and falling."

"The ladies have retired — shall we imitate their example, sir? This will light you to your chamber; good night."

Alone, and kindly shielded with the darkness, the adventurer lay thoughtful and sleepless. Here are two strange beings. There is in the one angelic beauty animated with a soul of giant proportions, large in love, large in hate, and grandly large in its aspirations; and yet it is chained to a rock with fetters that chafe at every motion. The other cold, emotionless, with a reserved severity of manner, which is the offspring of a heart as malignant and sinister as Satan himself may boast of. They hate each other, but how different that hatred! The one is an emotion fierce and fiery but without malice; the other malicious and revengeful. One is the hatred of the recipient of an injury who can forgive; the other the hatred of one who has inflicted an injury with calculation. Such never forgive. And this I am sure is the relation of this brother and sister. Deprived when yet young of the fostering care of a mother, scarcely remembering her father, she has been the ward of this cold, hard being, whose pleasure it has been to thwart every wish of this lovely being: to hate her because she is lovely, and to aggravate into fury her resentments, and to sour every generous impulse of her extraordinary nature. What a curse to have so sensitive a being subjected to the training of so cold and malignant a one!

There is no natural affection. The heart is born a waste: its loves, its hates are of education and association; and the responsibility for the future of a child rests altogether with those intrusted with its rearing and training. The susceptibilities only are born with the heart, and these may be cultivated to good or evil, as imperceptibly as the light permeates the atmosphere. These capacities or susceptibilities are acute or obtuse as the cranium's form will indicate, and require a system suited to each. Attention soon teaches this: the one grows and expands beautifully with the slightest attention; the other is a fat soil, and will run to weeds, without constant, close, and deep cultivation, and its production of good fruit is in exact proportion with its fertility and care. It gives the most trouble but it yields the greatest product. And here in that warm, impulsive heart is the fat soil. O! for the hand to weed away all that is noxious now rooting there. That look, that whispered bitterness was the fruit of wicked wrong — I know it; the very nature prompting there would give the sweetest return to justice, kindness, and love.

CHAPTER XXII.

THE ROMANCE CONTINUED.

Father Confessor — Open Confession — The Unread Will — Old Toney's Narrative — Squirrel Shooting — The Farewell Unsaid — Brothers-in-Law — Farewell Indeed.

WHEN the morrow came, the clouds were weeping and the damp was dripping from every leaf, and gloomy rifts of spongy vapor floated lazily upon the breeze, promising a wet and very unpleasant day. These misty periods rarely endure many hours in the autumn, but sometimes they continue for days. The atmosphere seems half water, and its warm damp compels close-housing, to avoid the clammy, sickly feeling met beyond the portals. At such times, time hangs heavily, and every resource sometimes fails to dispel the gloom and ennui consequent upon the weather; conversation will pall; music cease to delight, and reading weary. To stand and watch the rain through the window-panes, to lounge from the drawing-room to your chamber, to drum with your fingers upon the table — to beat your brain for a thought which you vainly seek to weave into rhyme in praise of your inamorata — all is unavailing. The rain is slow but ceaseless, and the hours are days to the unemployed mind. We hum a tune and whistle to hurry time, but the indicating fingers of the tediously ticking clock seems stationary, and time waits for fair weather. The ladies love their chambers, and sleeping away the laggard hours, do not feel the oppression of a slow, continuous, lazy rain.

The morning has well-nigh passed, and the drawing-room is still untenanted. The judge was busy in his office, looking over papers and accounts, seemingly unconscious of the murky day; perhaps he had purposely left this work for such a day — wise judge — a solitary man, unloving, and unloved; hospitable by freaks, sordid by habit, and mean by nature. Yet he was wise in his way; devoid of sentiment or sympathy as a grind-stone, his wit was as sharp as his heart was cold. Absorbed in himself, the outside world was nothing to him. He had work, gainful work for all weathers, and therefore no feeling for those who suffered from the weather or the world, if it cost him nothing in pence. He was the guardian of his baby sister; but all of her he had in his heart was a care that she should not marry, before he was ready to settle her estate. The interest he felt in her, was his commissions for administering her property with a legitimate gain earned in the use of her money.

The guest of this strange man was restless, he knew not why; there were books in abundance, and their authors' names were read over and over again as he rummaged the book-cases he knew not for what. First one and then another was pulled out from its companions, the title-page read and replaced again, only to take another. Idly he was turning the pages of one, when a voice surprised him and sweetly inquired at his elbow if he found amusement or edification in his employment. "I must apologize for my rudely leaving you last night. I hope I am incapable of deceit or unnecessary concealments. I was hurt and angry, and I went away in a passion. Yours is a gentle nature, you do not suffer your feelings to torture and master you. I should not, but I am incapable of the effort necessary to their control. It is best with me that they burn out, but their very ashes lie heavily upon my heart. Our clime is a furnace, and her children are flame, at least, strange sir, some of them are a self-consuming flame. I feel that is my nature. Is not this an honest confession? I could explain further in extenuation of my strange nature. It was not my nature until it was burned into my very soul. I am very young, but the bitterness of my experiences makes me old, at least in feeling. But you are not my father confessor — then why do I talk to you as to one long known? Because — perhaps — but never mind the reason. I know my cousin has whispered something to you of me; my situation, my nature — is it not so?"

"Ah! you would be *my* father confessor. You must not interrogate, but if you would know, ask your cousin."

"O! no, I could not. Is it not strange that woman will confide to the strange man, what she will not to the kindred woman? Woman will not sympathize with woman; she goes not to her for comfort, for sympathy, for relief. Is this natural? Men lean on one another, women only on man. Is this natural? Is it instinctive? or an acquired faculty? Do not laugh at me, I am very foolish and very sad; such a day should sadden every one. But my cousin is very cheerful, twitters and flits about like an uncaged canary, and is as cheerful when it rains all day, as when the sun in her glory gladdens all the earth and everything thereon. I am almost a Natchez, for I worship the sun. How I am running on! You are gentle and kind, are you not? You are quick, perceptive — you have seen that I am not happy — sympathize, but do not pity me. That is a terrible struggle between prudence and inclination. There, now I am done — don't you think me very foolish?"

"Miss Alice — (will you allow me this familiarity?)"

"Yes, when we are alone; not before cousin or my *man* brother." (She almost choked with the word.) "Not before strangers — we are not strangers when alone. You read my nature, as I do yours, and we are not strangers when alone. It is not long acquaintance which makes familiar friends. The mesmeric spark will do more than years of intercommunication, where there is no congeniality — and do it in a little precious moment. The bloody arrow we held in common was an electric chain. I learned you at the plucking of that arrow from the cotton bale — in your strange, wild garb; but never mind — what were you going to say?"

"I was going to say that our acquaintance was very brief, but what I have seen or heard, I will not tell to you or to any one. Your imagination is magnifying your sufferings. You want a heart to confide in. You have brothers-in-law, wise and strong men.

"That, for the whole of them," she said, as she snapped her fingers. "Their wives are my sisters, some of them old enough to be my mother, but they and their husbands are alike — sordid. The hope of money is even more debasing than the hoarding. Do you understand me? I must speak or my heart will burst. Are you a wizzard that you have so drawn me on? Dare I speak? Is it maidenly that I should? There is a spell upon me. Go to your chamber—there is a spy upon me; I am seen, and I fear I have been overheard; go to your chamber — here, take this book and read it if you never have — dinner is at hand, and after dinner —, but let each hour provide for itself, — at dinner, — well, well, adieu."

She was in the drawing-room, and again the soft melody of half-suppressed music, scarcely audible, yet every note distinct, floated to his chamber, and the guest scarcely breathed that he might hear. There was something so plaintive, so melting in the tones that they saddened as well as delighted. How the heart can melt out at the finger-points when touching the keys of a sweetly-toned instrument! It is thrown to the air, and in its plaint makes sweet music of its melancholy. Like harmonious spirits chanting in their invisibility, making vocal the very atmosphere, it died away as though going to a great distance, and stillness was in the whole house. He stole gently to the door. There seated was Alice; her elbow on her instrument, and her brow upon her hand. The bell rang for dinner. The repast is over, and a glass of generous wine sent the rose to the cheeks of Alice, but enlivened not her eye. Her heart was sad: the eye spoke it but too plainly, and she looked beautiful beyond comparison. The eye of the stranger was rivetted upon that drooping lid and more than melancholy brow.

His situation was a painful one. More than once had he caught the quick, suspicious glance of the judge flash upon him. He was becoming an object of interest to more than one in the house; but how different that interest! How at antipodes the motives of that interest! He knew too much, and yet he wanted to know more.

He was left alone in the drawing-room with the timid, modest little cousin. It rained on, and the weather seemed melancholy, and their feelings were in unison with the weather.

"I shall leave, I believe, miss, as soon as the rain will permit. I presume I may go down to the city without fear."

"You will find it but a sorry place, sir. All the hotels are closed and everybody is out of town save the physicians, and the poor who are unable to get away. The gloom of the desolated place is enough to craze any one. I hope you do not find your stay disagreeable in this house?"

"I will not attempt to deceive you, miss. I cannot say why; but I feel uncomfortable — not at my ease. It were needless for me to repeat it; I am sure you know the cause."

"Perhaps I do, sir; and still I cannot see in that sufficient cause for your going away. Perhaps, sir, we are not thinking of the same cause," she said with a mischievous twinkle in her eye.

"I particularly allude to what you yourself communicated to me. I perceive Miss Alice is very unhappy, and I also am apprehensive that I may in some way be the cause of this."

"I will tell you, sir, any special attention on your part to Alice will enrage her brother. From motives known to himself, he is very much opposed to her marrying any one. His reasons as given are that she is so peculiar in her disposition that she would only increase her own misery in making her husband miserable, which her eccentric nature would certainly insure. I have heard that he has sometimes had a thought of carrying her to an asylum for the insane. The world, however, is not charitable enough to believe this the true reason. The judge is very grasping, and he has in his hands Alice's fortune. Some of his own family suppose he desires the use of it as long as possible. There are many hard things said of him in relation to his influencing his mother to leave him the lion's share of her estate. This very home was intended for Alice, and though he had not spoken to his mother for years, in her last hours he came with a prepared will and insisted on her signing it. She feared him (most people do) and affixed her name to the fatal document, which report says was never read to her. After that she could not bear the presence of Alice, saying in her delirium: 'My poor baby will hate me; I have turned her from her home.' Alice has learned all this, and she has upbraided him with his conduct; for once provoked she does not even fear him."

"Why do not her brothers-in-law inquire into this? They are equally interested in the matter it seems to me."

"Ah, sir! they are hoping that he may do them justice in his will. I am sure this is the understanding with at least one of them, and neither of them will hazard a loss to protect the rights of Alice. Large expectations are strong inducements to selfishness. I am disclosing family matters, sir; but I have done so from a good motive. It is but half disclosed to you; but the rest I must not tell. You are not so dull as not from what I have said to be able to shape your conduct. Alice is coming."

The rain had ceased, and for two days the genial sun had drank up the moisture from the land, which underfoot was dry again. The autumn had come, and the earth groaned with the rich products of this favored land. The cotton-fields were whitening, and the yellow corn's pendant ears hung heavily from their supporting stocks. Fat cattle in the shade of the great trees switched away the teasing flies as they lazily ruminated. The crows were cawing and stealing from their bursting shells the rich pecan nuts, and the black-birds flew in great flocks over the fields. In the hickory-woods the gray squirrel leaped from tree to tree, hunting for, and storing away for winter's use, his store of nuts and acorns, or running along the rail-fence to find a hiding-place when frightened from his thieving in the corn-fields. The quail whistled for his truant mate in the yellow stubble, and the carrion-bird — black and disgusting — wheeled in circles, lazily, high up in the blue above. There was in everything the appearance of satisfaction; abundance was everywhere, and the yellowing of the leaves and the smoky horizon told that the year was waning into winter.

Under the influences of the scene and the season the visitor of the judge was sober and reflective as he strolled through the woods, gun in hand, little intent upon shooting. The quail whirred away from his feet; the funny little squirrel leaped up the tree-side and peeped around at him passing; but he heeded not these, and went forward to find the cabin of old Toney. He found the old negro in his usual seat at the foot of his favorite tree, upon his well-smoothed and sleek wooden stool.

"Ha! ha! ha!" laughed Toney. "You come dis time widout

Miss Alice. Why she not come wid you? You not want somebody to turn de squirrel for you? May be you bring de ole man more dan one dar?"

"It was too great a walk for her, Uncle Toney, and then she does not like my company well enough to pay so much fatigue for it."

Toney laughed again. "Too much walk, indeed, she walk here most ebery day, wid her little bonnet in her hand and basket too, wid someting good for Toney. When sun yonder and de shade cobber de groun; den she set dare, (pointing to the grass which grew luxuriantly near by) and talk to de ole man and lissen so still like a bird hiding, when I tell her all bout de ole folks, dat is buried dare, and how we all comed away from de States when de ole war driv us off, not General Jackson's war. No, sir, General Washington's war, de ole war of all — and den, young massa, you ought to see her. She 's mity putty den, she is — face red and smove, and she little tired and she look so like ole missus yonder, when she was a gall, and dem English red coats comes out from Charleston, to de ole place to see her. Dat 's a long time ago, young massa."

"Uncle Toney, how old are you?"

"Moss a hundred, young massa; I don 't know zackly — but I great big boy when I comed from de ole country, tudder side ob de sea — my country, massa. When I comed to Charleston, I was so high — (holding his hand some four feet from the earth) yet I was big nuff to plow, when ole massa, de fadder of him burried yonder, bied me and tuck me up to de high hills ob Santee. Den, sir, my massa who brought me here, was gone to de country whar de white folks first comed from, England. I nebber see him till de ole war, when his fadder been dead two year, den he comed home one night and all de family but one had gone to de war. He not talk much, but look mity sorry. My ole missus was a pretty gall, den, live close by us, and it not long afore dey gets married, and den many ob de nabors come and dey hab long talk. Dey 's all comes to de greement to come away from de country, fraid ob de war, and all de fadders ob all de nabors here take all der niggers and der stock and go up de country to de riber dat 's named de Holsten, and dare dey built heep flat boats, and in de spring dey starts down de riber. Some ob de boats hab hogs on 'em, some hosses, some cows, some niggers, some corn and meat, and some de white families. Dar was boff de grandfadder ob Miss Alice, and her fadder. He was small, not grown, and old massa, her modder's fadder, was young wid young wife, but dey all made him captain.

"We was long time comin down de riber, and we had to fite de Injuns long time at de place dey calls Mussel Shoals. Some ob de boats got on de ground, and one on em we had to leave wid de hogs on it. De bullets come from the Injuns so hot dat we all had to get out into de water and go to anudder boat and get away from dar. Dem was the wust Injuns I eber seed. But we got away and we runned all night. Nex day Miss Alice's fadder was on de top ob de boat ob his fadder when Injun shoot him in de back from de woods, and he buried wid dat bullet in him up yonder to de great house. Well, young massa, we comed one day into a big riber, and dar we stopt one hole week, and de massa and some on de ress on em got out and luck at de country, but dey not like him and we started agin, and de nex day we gits into di Massasippi, and in two days more we comed to de place dey called New Madrid, and here stopt agin.

"De land was mity level and rich, and all de men said dey would stop here and live. De people what lived here was Spanish, and some niggers and Injuns, and dey talked a lingo we did'nt know. Dere was a nigger who could talk American, and he comed one night and tuck ole massa out and telled him de Spaniards was gwine to rob dem all, and dat dey would kill all on de white folks, and take all de niggers and stock, and dey was gwine to do it de fus dark night. Dis larmed us all, and dat night we slipt off, and when mornin comed we was way down de riber and gwine ahead I tell you. We nebber stopt any more till we got to de mouth of Cole's Creek. Dare de fadder of Miss Alice's fadder stopt, and said he would stay dare. Ole massa seed an Injun dat tole him ob dis place and dey started true de cane, dey was gone long time, but when dey comed back, ole massa got us all ready and away we went and nebber stopt till we comed to the mouth of St. Catharine's, right ober dar. Dar we landed and unloaded de boats, and in a week we was all camped up dar whare de big percan is, and right dar de ole man raise all his family — and dar he and ole missus died.

"All dis country was full ob deer and Injuns, and dem hills yonder was all covered wid big canes and de biggest trees you ebber seed. Yonder, all round dat mound we cleaned a field and planted corn and indigo; and ober yonder was another settlement; and yonder, down de creek was another; and on de cliffs was another, and den dare comed a heap ob people and stopt at Natchez and St. Catharine, and all us people a most, young massa, about here is come ob dem; but dare was trouble moss all de time twixt em.

"Ole massa was made de Governor, by somebody, and dare was another man made a Governor, too, and he git a company one night and comed down here; but somebody had tole old massa, and dat day he tell me, and we went down to de riber under de cliff war was some cane and he tole me he was gwine to stay dar, and I muss bring him sometin to eat ebery day, but I mus 'nt tell whar he was, not eben to ole missus, for dey would scare her and make her tell on him. Shore nuff, dat night here dey comed, a many a one on em, and dey went right into de great house and serched it and ebery whar, but dey was fooled bad, and den dey tuck me and put a rope round my neck and hung me to de lim of a tree what is dead and gone now, right out dar. But wen I was moss dead, dey let me down and axed me whar was de Governor. I swared I did 'nt know, and dey pulled me up agin; and dis time dey thought dey had killed me, shore nuff. It was a long time before I comed to, and den I tole um I could show um whare he was, and we started.

"De cane was mity thick, and we went up one hill and down another till we comed to dat big hill ober de creek dar. De todder side ob it is mity steep, but de cane was all de way down it. I was a good ways before em and I jumpt down de steepest place and way I went through de cane down de hill, and de way dey made de bullets whistle was curos. But I got away and went round and told de ole man all dey had done. When I went back all de black people was gone and missus said dese men had tuck em off. De nex nite dey cotch me and carried me to whar our black folks was, and den we all started in a boat down de riber, and when we got to New Orleans we got on a skiff and run down de riber to a big ship and went out to sea dat night and landed at Pensacola, and dare dat wicked ole man sold us to de Spanish."

"Uncle Toney, who was that wicked old man?"

"Ah! my young massa, I musn't tell, cause his grandchillen is great folks here now, and Miss Alice telled me I musn't tell all I knows. Dey aint sponsible, she says, for what dere grandfadder did. But I tell you he was a mity bad man. Well, I staid at Pensacola two years wid my ole oman; and we could talk wid de Injuns, and one day two Injuns dat I knowd out here comed to my cabin, and dey telled me dat ole massa was gone way from here and missus was here by herself and had nobody to help her. So I makes a bargain wid dese Injuns to come here wid me and my old oman. One Saturday night we started to go and see some ob our people dat was bout ten miles from whar we was; but we neber stopped. We tuck to de woods, and we killed a deer wheneber we was hungry. De Injuns, you know, can always do dat. We was a mity long time comin; but at last we got here, and den it was moss a year arter dat before ole massa come. Den dar was more trouble. One day dar comed fifty men and tuck ole massa, and dey tied him and den begin to rob de house. Dey had all de silver and sich like, when de captain comed in, and he did cuss mity hard and made em put it every bit down, and march out. Ole missus she thanked him mitily; but dey carried ole massa off to New Orleans.

"Dar was great trouble wid de nabors. Dey comed and talked bout it; and one day when ole massa was gone bout a mont, when dey was all dar, who should step into de house but ole massa. He was fash, I tell you he was. Dar was old Mr. E——, and Mr. O——, and Mr. T——, and a heap more, and dey all put der heads togeder and talked. One day ole massa come to me and sez he: 'Toney, you mus get on my black hoss and go down to de bluffs. Watch down de riber, and when you see two big boats comin up — big keel-boats wid plenty ob men on em — way down de riber, jes come as hard as de hoss can bring you here and let me know it.'

"I knowd dar was trouble comin, young massa; for I seed Miss Alice's papa comin wid plenty ob de nabors wid him. He was a tall man, and neber talk much. Miss Alice's modder was a young oman den, and I knowd dey was gwine to be married. When she seed him wid his gun and so many men she gins to cry. Well, I was gone quick, and moss as soon as I got to de cliff, I see de boats way down de riber, pulling long by de shore. I made dat hoss do his best home, when I told old massa: 'Dey 's comin, sir!' He sorter grin, and git on his hoss and gallop away down toward St. Catharine's. He telled me to come on, and I comed. When we got to de mouth ob de creek dar was fifty men dar, all wid der guns, settin on de ground, and ole massa talkin to em. Way moss night de boats comed in sight. Den all de men hide in de cane, and massa tell me: 'Toney, you call em and tell em to come to de shore.' I called em, and dey comed and tied der boats to de trees, and de captain and some ob de men jumped on de land, and walked out, and comed close to me.

"De fuss ting dey knowd, bang! bang! bang! go de guns, and de captain fall. De men all run for de boats, and de men on de boats gin to shoot too. I runs wid all my might, and ole massa shout to his friends to fire agin, and two men untying de boats fall. Den dey cut de ropes wid an axe, and shove out de boats into de riber, and pull em away wid de oars too far to hit em. Ole massa comes out ob de cane and goes to de men what is lying on the ground. Dar was six on em, and four was dead sure nuff. Two was jus wounded, and one of dese was de captain. Him de same man what make his men put down de silber and tings dey was takin from ole missus. Den dey carry all on em to de grate house and bury de dead ones. De captain and de oder wounded man was tuck into de house, and ole missus she knowd de captain, and she cried mitily bout his bein shot. Well, he talk plenty bout his wife and modder, and Miss Alice's modder nurse him; but he died, and his grave 's yonder wid ole massa and missus. De oder man he got well and went away, and berry soon arter dat Miss Alice's fadder and modder got married. Dar come de judge. He hab seen you, and he ride out ob de road to come see you."

"Toney, I shall come to see you again, and you must tell me more about the family and these people about here; you must tell me everything."

"You musn't tell anybody I tell you anyting. De judge mity quare man; he don't like for people to know all I knows."

The judge rode up, and Toney with great respect arose and saluted him. "Ah!" said he, "you have found this old hermit, have you? Toney is the chronicle of the neighborhood — a record of its history from the day of its first settlement. I hope he has amused you. He is upwards of ninety years old, and retains all his faculties in a remarkable degree."

"I have been quite entertained with his history of the descent of the river with your ancestors. He seems to remember every incident, and says your father was wounded at the Muscle Shoals on the Tennessee River."

"He is quite right, sir. It was a perilous trip. My grandfather was a man of wonderful energy and determination. He pioneered the ancestors of almost every family in this vicinage to this place. There was a large grant of land from the Spanish Government made here and divided among his followers, every foot of which is in the possession of their descendants to-day, except perhaps one thousand acres which were swindled from my family by a most iniquitous decision of a jury, influenced by an artful old Yankee lawyer. This spot here, sir, was the nucleus of the first settlement which in a few years spread over the country."

"This county I believe, sir, was once represented in the State of Georgia as the County of Bourbon, at the time this State with Alabama constituted a part of that State."

"My father was elected to represent the county, but he never took his seat. We continued to be governed by the laws of Spain which we found in force here until the line between Florida and the United States was established — indeed until the American Government extended its jurisdiction in the form of a territorial government over the country. I am riding to my sisters. You will have fine shooting if you will go through yonder piece of woods. Every tree seems to have a squirrel upon it. We will meet again at tea. Adieu, till then."

"He been watchin you. Better go, young massa."

"You don't appear, Toney, to like your young master."

"Him not good to Miss Alice. He got plenty sisters; but he only lub two, and dey don't lub anybody but just him. Him not like his fadder nor ole massa yonder. He bring plenty trouble to massa and to his modder. No, me don't like him. Miss Alice know him all."

"Well, Toney, no one shall ever know you have told me anything. Some of these days I will come and see you again. Good by."

"God bress you, young massa! Kill ole nigger some squirrels. Tell Miss Alice dey is for me, and she will make some on de little ones run down here wid em. Good by, massa."

Slowly the young man wended his way to the mansion; but remembering the negro's request, he shot several squirrels, and gave them as requested:

"Then you have been to see Uncle Toney. Did he give you any of his stories? Like all old persons, he loves to talk about his younger days."

"I was quite interested in his narrative of the trip down the river, when your grandparents and your father emigrated to this part of the country."

"Did he tell you his Indian ghost story?"

"He did not. He was quite communicative; but your brother came and arrested his conversation." A shade fell upon the features of the beautiful creature as she turned away to send the squirrels to Toney.

"These are beautiful grounds, Miss Ann."

"Yes, sir; there has been great care bestowed upon them, and they make a fairy-land for my cousin who in fair weather is almost always found here in these walks and shady retreats afforded by these old oaks and pecans."

"There is something very beautiful, miss, in the attachment of Miss Alice to Uncle Toney. The devotion to her on his part almost amounts to adoration."

"My aunt, the mother of Alice, taught her this attachment. There is a little history connected with it, and indeed, sir, all the family remember his services to our grandfather in a most perilous moment; but you must ask its narration from the old man. He loves to tell it. My cousin's memory of her mother is the cherished of her heart. Indeed, sir, that is a strong, deep heart. You may never know it; but should you, you will remember that I told you there was but one Alice. In all her feelings she is intense; her love is a flame — her hate a thorn; the fragrance of the one is an incense — the piercing of the other is deep and agonizing. Shan't we go in, sir; I see the damp of the dew is on your boot-toe, and you have been ill. The absence of the sun is the hour for pestilence to ride the breeze in our climate, and you cannot claim to be fully acclimated."

The autumn progressed, and the rich harvests were being gathered and garnered. This season is the longest and the loveliest of the year in this beautiful country. During the months of September, October, and November, there ordinarily falls very little rain, and the temperature is but slightly different. The evolutions of nature are slow and beneficent, and it seems to be a period especially disposed so that the husbandman should reap in security the fruits of the year's labor. The days lag lazily; the atmosphere is serene, and the cerulean, without a cloud, is deeply blue. The foliage of the forest-trees, so gorgeous and abundant, gradually loses the intense green of summer, fading and yellowing so slowly as scarely to be perceptible, and by such attenuated degrees accustoming the eye to the change, that none of the surprise or unpleasantness of sudden change is seen or experienced.

The fields grow golden; the redly-tinged leaves of the cotton-plant contrast with the chaste pure white of the lint in the bursting pods, now so abundantly yielding their wealth; the red ripe berries all over the woods, and the busy squirrels gathering and hoarding these and the richer forest-nuts; the cawing of the crows as they forage upon the ungathered corn, feeding and watching with the consciousness of thieves, and the fat cattle ruminating in the shade, make up a scene of beauty and loveliness not met with in a less fervid clime. The entranced rapture which filled my soul when first I looked upon this scene comes over me now with a freshness that brings back the delights of that day with all its cherished memories, though fifty years have gone and their sorrows have crushed out all but hope from the heart — and all the pleasures of the present are these memories kindly clustering about the soul. Perhaps their delights, and those who shared them, will revive in eternity. Perhaps not; perhaps all alike — the pleasant and the painful — are to be lost in an eternal, oblivious sleep. It is all speculation; yet hope and doubt go on to the grave, and thence none return to cheer the one or elucidate the other. But be it eternal life or eternal death, it is wise; for it is of God.

The autumn grew old and was threatening a frost — the great enemy of fever. The falling leaves and the fitful gusts of chill wind presaged the coming of winter. The ear caught the ring of sounds more distant and more distinct now that the languor of summer was gone, and all animal nature seemed more invigorated and more elastic. Health and her inhabitants were returning to the city, and the guests of the hospitable planters were thinning from the country. Business was reviving and commotion was everywhere.

The young stranger was preparing to leave; yet he lingered. Ann had gone; Alice grew more shy and timid, and his walks and rides were solitary, and but that he loved nature in her autumn robes would have been dull and uninteresting. The judge was absent at another plantation beyond the river, and his books and his gun were his only companions. Sometimes he read, sometimes he rode, and sometimes he walked to visit Toney. It was on one of those peculiarly lonely afternoons which come in the last days of October when the stillness persuades to rest and meditation in the woods that, seated on a prostrate tree near the pathway which led down the little creek to the residence of Uncle Toney, the young guest of the judge was surprised by Alice with a small negro girl on their way to visit Uncle Toney. Both started; but in a moment were reassured, and slowly walked to the cabin of the good old negro.

"I have come, Uncle Toney," said the youth, "to see you for the last time. I am going away to-morrow and, as soon as I can, going back to the distant home I so foolishly left."

"I am sorry you tell me so; won't you be sorry, Miss Alice?" asked Toney. Alice bit her lip, and the flush upon her cheek was less ruddy than usual.

"You no find dis country good like yourn, young massa?"

"Yes, Toney, this is a good country, and there is no country more beautiful. But, uncle, it requires more than a beautiful country to make us happy; we must have with us those we love, and who love us; and the scenes of our childhood — our fathers and mothers, and brothers and sisters who are glad with us and who sorrow with us, and the companions of our school-days, to make us happy. I am here without any of these — not a relation within a thousand miles; with no one to care for me or to love me." There was something plaintively melancholly in his words and tones. He looked at Alice, her eyes were swimming in tears and she turned away from his gaze.

"You been mity sick, here, young massa, didn't Miss Alice be good to you? Aunt Ann tell me so. If Miss Alice had not nuss you, you die." Alice stepped into the cabin taking with her the basket the little negro had borne, and placing its contents away, came out and handing it to Rose, bid her run home. "I am coming," she said as she adjusted her bonnet-strings, "the bugaboos won't catch you."

"Yes, Uncle Toney, I am very grateful to Miss Alice. I shall never forget her."

How often that word is thoughtlessly spoken? Never to forget, is a long time to remember. Our lives are a constant change: the present drives out the past, and one memory usurps the place of another. Yet there are some memories which are always green. These fasten themselves upon us in agony. The pleasant are evanescent and pass away as a smile, but the bitter live in sighs, recurring eternally.

Both were silent, both were thoughtful. "Good-by, Uncle Toney," said Alice.

"May I join you in your walk home, miss?" There was something in the tone of this request, which caused Alice to look up into his face and pause a moment before replying, when she said, very timidly, "If you please, sir."

The sun was drooping to the horizon and the shadows made giants as thy grew along the sward. "Farewell, Uncle Toney," said the gentleman, shaking hands with the old negro. Alice had walked on.

"O! you need 'nt say farewell so sorry, you'll come back. I sees him. You 'll come back. Eberybody who comes to dis country if he does go way he 's sure to come back, ticlar when he once find putty gall like Miss Alice, ya! ya!" laughed the old man. "You 'll come back. I knows it."

In a few moments he was by the side of Alice. They lounged lazily along through the beautiful forest a few paces behind Rose, who was too much afraid of bugaboos to allow herself to get far away from her mistress. There was a chill in the atmosphere and now and then a fitful gust of icy wind from the northwest. Winter was coming: these avant-couriers whispered of it; and overhead, swooped high up in the blue, a host of whooping cranes, marching in chase of the sun now cheering the Antarctic just waking from his winter's sleep.

"I believe, sir," said Alice, "that the ancients watched the flight of birds and predicated their predictions or prophecies upon them."

"Yes, the untutored of every age and country observe more closely the operations of nature than the educated. It is their only means of learning. They see certain movements in the beasts and the birds before certain atmospheric changes, and their superstitions influence a belief, that sentient and invisible beings cause this by communicating the changes going on. The more sagacious and observant, and I may add the less scrupulous, lay hold upon this knowledge, to practice for their own pleasure or profit upon the credulity of the masses. There are very many superstitions, miss, which are endowed with a character so holy, that he who would expose them is hunted down as a wretch, unworthy of life. The older and the more ridiculous these, the more holy, and the more sacredly cherished."

"Are you not afraid thus to speak — is there nothing too holy to be profanely assaulted?"

"Nothing which contravenes man's reason. Truth courts investigation — the more disrobed, the more beautiful. Science reveals, that

27

there is no mystery in truth. Its simplicity is often disfigured with unnatural and ridiculous superstitions, and these sometimes are so prominent as to conceal it. They certainly, with many, bring it into disrepute. The more intellectual pluck these off and cast them away. They see and know the truth. Yonder birds obey an instinct: the chill to their more sensitive natures warns them that the winter, or the tempest, or the rain-storm is upon them; they obey this instinct and fly from it. Yet it in due time follows these — the more observant know it, and predict it. Those, with the ancients, were sooth-sayers or prophets; with us, they are the same with the ignorant negroes; with the whites, not quite so ignorant, they are — but, miss, I will not say. I must exercise a little prudence to avoid the wrath of the ignorant — they are multitudinous and very powerful."

"Kind sir, tell me, have you no superstitions? Has nothing ever occurred to you, your reason could not account for? Have no predictions, to be revealed in the coming future, come to you as foretold?"

"Do not press me on that point, if you please, I might astonish and offend you."

"I am not in the least afraid of your offending me, sir. I could not look in your face and feel its inspirations, and believe you capable of offending me."

"Thank you for the generous confidence, thank you. I am going and shall remember this so long as I live, and when in my native land, will think of it as too sacred for the keeping of any but myself."

"Are you really going to leave us, and so soon? I — I — would — but —"

"Miss Alice, I have trespassed too long already upon your brother's hospitality; beside, Miss Alice, I begin to feel that his welcome is worn out. Your brother, for some days, has seemed less cordial than was his wont during the first weeks of my stay here."

"My brother, sir, is a strange being — a creature of whims and caprices. There is nothing fixed or settled in his opinions or conduct. His inviting you to spend the summer with us was a whim: one that has astonished several who have not hesitated to express it. It is as likely on his return from his river place, that he will devour you with kindness as that he will meet you with the coldness he has manifested for some days. Do not let your conduct be influenced by his whims."

"Miss Alice, I am suspicious, perhaps, by nature. I have thought that you have avoided me lately. I have been very lonesome at times."

Alice lifted her bonnet from her head, and was swinging it by the strings as she walked along for a few steps, when she stopped, and, turning to her companion, said with a firm though timid voice: "I cannot be deceitful. You have properly guessed: I have avoided you. It was on your account as well as my own. My self-respect is in conflict with my respect for you. I need not tell you why I avoided you; but I will — conscious that I am speaking to a gentleman who will appreciate my motives and preserve inviolate my communications. You saw my cousin hurry away from here. She came to remain some weeks. The cause of her going was my brother. From some strange, unaccountable cause he became offended with her, and charged her with giving bad advice to me. What she has said to me as advice since she came was in the privacy of my bedroom, and in such tones that had he or another been in the chamber they could not have overheard it. I know, sir, and in shame do I speak it, that I am under the surveillance of the servants, who report to my brother and my sister my every act and every word; and I know, too, my brother's imagination supplies in many instances these reports. Why I am thus watched I know not.

"My brother is my guardian, and nature and duty, it would seem, should prompt him to guard my happiness as well as my interest; but I know in the one instance he fails, and I fear in the other I am suffering. All my family fear him, and none of them love me. I am my parents' youngest child. Oh, sir! England is not the only country where it is a curse to be a younger child. My father died when I was an infant. My mother was affectionate and indulgent; my sisters were harsh and tyrannical, and in very early girlhood taught me to hate them. My mother was made miserable by their treatment of me; and my brother, too, quarrelled with her because she would not subject me to the servility of the discipline he prescribed. This quarrel ripened into hate, and he never came to the house or spoke to my mother for years.

"The day before she died, and when her recovery was thought to be impossible, he came with a prepared will and witnesses, which in their presence he almost forced her to sign: in this will I was greatly wronged, and this brother has tauntingly told me the cause of this was my being the means of prejudicing our mother against him.

"He married a coarse, vulgar Kentucky woman, and brought her into the house. She was insolent and disrespectful toward my mother, and I resented it. She left the house, and died a few months after. Since that day, though I was almost a child, my life has been one of constant persecution on the part of my brother and sisters. I am compelled to endure it, but do so under protest; if not in words, I do in manner, and this I am persuaded you have on more than one occasion observed. Please do not consider me impertinent, nor let it influence you in your opinion of me, when I tell you my brother has rudely said to me that I was too forward in my intercourse with you. It is humiliating to say this to you; but I must, for it explains my conduct, which save in this regard has been motiveless.

"A lady born to the inheritance of fortune is very unpleasantly situated, both toward her family and to the world. These seem solicitous to take greater interest in her pecuniary affairs than in her personal happiness, and are always careful to warn her that her money is more sought than herself—distracting her mind and feelings, and keeping her constantly miserable. Since my school-days I have been companionless. If I have gone into society, I have been under the guard of one or the other of my sisters. These are cold, austere, and repulsive, and especially toward those who would most likely seek my society, and with whom I would most naturally be pleased. I must be retired, cold, and never to seem pleased, but always remarkably silent and dignified. I must be a goddess to be worshipped, and not an equal to be approached and my society courted companionably. In fine, I was to be miserable, and make all who came to me participate in this misery. It was more agreeable to remain at home among my flowers and shrubs, my books, and my visits to Uncle Toney. Do you wonder, sir, that I seem eccentric? You know how the young love companionship—how they crave the amusements which lend zest to life. I enjoy none of this, and I am sometimes, I believe, nearly crazy. I fear you think me so, now. I want to love my brother, but he will not permit me to do so. I fear he has a nature so unlovable that such a feeling toward him animates no heart. My sisters and a drunken sot of a brother-in-law pretend to love him—but they measure their affection by the hope of gain. They reside in Louisiana, and I am glad they are not here during your stay—for you would certainly be insulted, especially if they saw the slightest evidence of esteem for you on brother's part, or kindness on mine."

"Oh! sir, how true is the Scripture, 'Out of the fulness of the heart the mouth speaketh.' Out of my heart's fulness have I spoken, and, I fear you will think, out of my heart's folly, too; and in my heart's sincerity I tell you I do not know why I have done so to you — for I have never said anything of these things to any one but cousin Ann, before. Perhaps it is because I know you are going away and you will not come to rebuke me with your presence any more; for indeed, sir, I do not know how I could meet you and not blush at the memory of this evening's walk."

"Miss Alice, I have a memory, or it may be a fancy, that in the delirium of my fever, some weeks since, I saw you like a spirit of light flitting about my bed and ministering to my wants; and I am sure, when all supposed me *in extremis*, you came, and on my brow placed your soft hand, and pressed it gently above my burning brain. My every nerve thrilled beneath that touch; my dead extremities trembled and were alive again. The brain resumed her functions, and the nervous fluid flashed through my entire system, and departing life came back again. You saved my life. Were the records of time and events opened to my inspection and I could read it there, I could not more believe this than I now do. Then what is due from me to you? This new evidence of confidence adds nothing to the obligation — it was full without it. But it is an inspiration I had not before. We are here, Miss Alice, within a few steps of the threshold of the house in which you were born. I am far from the land of my nativity — our meeting was strange, and this second meeting not the less so."

"Ah! you have almost confessed that you are superstitious. You need not have acknowledged that you are romantic; your young life has proven this."

"Stay, Miss Alice: you asked me but now if there had never been the realization of previous predictions. You said you knew I would not offend you. I would not, but may. Now listen to me, here under the shade of this old oak. When I was a child, my nurse was an aged African woman; like all her race, she was full of superstition, and she would converse with me of mysteries, and spells, and wonderful revelations, until my mind was filled as her own with strange superstitions and presentiments. On one occasion, on the Sabbath day, I found her in the orchard, seated beneath a great pear-tree, and went to her — for though I was no longer her ward to nurse, I liked to be with her and hear her talk. It was a beautiful day, the fruit-trees were in bloom, and the spring-feeling in the sunshine was kindling life into activity through all nature. She asked me to let her see my hand and she would tell me my fortune. She pretended sagely to view every line, and here and there to press her index finger sharply down. At length she began to speak.

"'You will not stay with your people,' she said, 'but will be a great traveller; and when in some far-away country, you will be sick —mighty sick; and a beautiful woman will find you, and she will nurse you, and you will love that beautiful woman, and she will love you, and she will marry you, and you will not come to reside with your people any more.' Now, Miss Alice, I have wandered far away from my home, have been sick, very sick, and a beautiful woman has nursed me until I am well, and oh! from my heart I do love that beautiful woman. So far all of this wild prediction has been verified; and it remains with you, my dear Alice, to say if the latter portion shall be. You are too candid to delay reply, and too sincere to speak equivocally."

She trembled as she looked up into his face and read it for a moment. "You are too much of a gentleman to speak as you have, unless it came from your heart. O my God! is this reality, or am I dreaming?" She drooped her head upon his shoulder, and said: "'Whither thou goest I will go; thy house shall be my house, and thy God my God.'"

The full moon was just above the horizon, and the long dark shadows veiled them from view. The judge rode in at the gate, and leaving his horse, went directly into the house. A moment after a carriage drove into the court, and from it dismounted the brother-in-law sot and her weird sister; for indeed she was a very Hecate in looks and mischief. Alice stole away to her chamber; and the happy stranger to wander among the shrubs, regardless of the damp and chill.

Here were two young hearts conscious of happiness; but was it a happiness derived from the respective merits and congenial natures of the two known to each other? They were comparatively strangers, knowing little of the antecedents of each other. Each was unhappily situated — the one from poverty, the other owing to her wealth; the one ardently desirous of bettering pecuniarily his position, the other to release herself from restraints that were tyrannical and to enjoy that independence which she felt was her natural right. Might not these considerations override the purer impulses of the heart arising from that regard for qualities which win upon the mind until ripened first into deep respect, then mellowed into tender affection by association protracted and intimate? They had been reared in societies radically different: their early impressions were equally antagonistic; but their aims were identical — to escape from present personal embarrassments.

They had met romantically. He had been removed for many months from the presence of civilized society, though naturally fond of female association, and craving deeply in his heart the communion again of that intercourse, which had (as he had learned from sad experience) been the chief cause of the happiness of his youth. He met her first as he entered anew the relations of civilized and social society. She was young and exquisitely beautiful. Their meeting was but for a moment; their intercourse was intensely delightful to him, and the interest her ardent nature manifested toward him was extremely captivating. He had gone from her, with her in all his heart.

She for the time was free. She felt not the restraint of her female relatives, and the ardor of her heart burned out in the delighted surprise she experienced in the gentle and genial bearing of one to all seeming rude and uncultivated as the savage he so much resembled in the contour of his apparel. She had trembled with a strange ecstasy as he strolled by her side, and felt a thrill pierce her soul as she looked into his face and saw what she had never seen, beaming in his eyes. She had never seen it before; yet she knew it, and felt she had found what her heart had so long and so ardently craved. She had parted from him with a consciousness that she was never to meet him again; and yet his image was with her by day and by night — her fancy kept him by day, and her dreams by night. She loved him for the mellow civilization of his heart and for the wild savageness of his garb. Oh, the heart of dear woman! it is her world. Would that the realizations of life were as her heart paints and craves them! He had again come as unexpectedly to her; but the figure was without its surroundings: the diamond was there, but the setting was gone, and she was not agreeably surprised: hence the indifference manifested by her when he discovered to her his identity.

Intercourse had revived the tenderness of the woman as it dispelled the romance of the girl. Her affection she deemed was not a fancy, but a feeling now. Her heart had wandered and fluttered like a wounded bird seeking some friendly limb for support — some secluded shade for rest. She had found all, and she was happy. He was her future; she thought of none other — of nothing else. Was he as happy? He had seen the rough side of the world, and thought more rationally. His night was sleepless. In a moment of feeling he had asked and received the heart of a lovely being whom he felt he could always love. He knew she was more than anxious for a home where she was mistress, and he must prepare it — but how, or where? He was without means. It was humiliating to depend on hers; and this was the first alloy which stained and impoverished the bliss of his anticipations.

They met in the early morning. Her brow was clouded. None were up save themselves. Their interview was brief and explicit. He saw her in a new phase; she had business tact as well as an independent spirit.

"You must leave this morning," she said, "and immediately after breakfast. My sister has put the servants through the gantlet of inquiry. They knew what she wanted to know, and if inclination had been wanting, the fear of the stocks and torture would have compelled them to tell it to her. She has heard all she wished, to her heart's content. She was in my chamber until midnight, and, as usual, we have quarrelled. They have told her that I was constantly with you, and that I was in love with you, and a thousand things less true than this. She has upbraided me for entering your chamber when you were sick. She menacingly shook her finger at me, and almost threatened corporal punishment if I did not desist from your association. I shall be surprised if she does not insult you upon sight. Nothing will prevent it but fear of offending brother. This she would not do for less than half of his estate — for that, and even more, she is now playing. She pretends devotion to him; and they profess a mutual attachment. If this is sincere, it is the only love either of them ever felt. You must express to brother, the moment you see him, your determination to leave at once, and let it be decided. I don't know your means, but fear you will be embarrassed, as you are comparatively a stranger, in preparing a home for us. Give this to its address, and you will have all you want. Do not stop to look at it. Put it in your pocket — there. I shall not be at the table this morning; there would be unpleasantness for you, I am sure. I shall not see you again until you come to carry me to our own home, which shall be very soon. Despite this *contretemps* I am very happy; and now farewell. I will write to you; for to-day I mean to tell brother I am to be your wife. I know how he will receive it; but he knows me, and will more than simply approve it. He will wish to give us a wedding; but I will not receive it. Our marriage must be private. Again farewell!" Without a kiss they parted.

What were the reflections of this young man in his long morning's drive he will never forget. 'T was fifty years ago; but they are green in memory yet, and will be until the grave yonder at the hill's foot, now opening to view, shall close over — close out this mortality, and all the memories which have imbittered life so long.

CHAPTER XXIII.

WHEN SUCCESSFUL, RIGHT; WHEN NOT, WRONG.

Territorial Mississippi — Wilkinson — Adams — Jefferson — Warren — Claiborne — Union of the Factions — Colonel Wood — Chew — David Hunt — Joseph Dunbar — Society of Western Mississippi — Pop Visits of a Week to Tea — The Horse "Tom" and his Rider — Our Grandfather's Days — An Emigrant's Outfit — My Share — George Poindexter — A Sudden Opening of a Court of Justice — The Caldwell and Gwinn Duel — Jackson's Opposition to the Governor of Mississippi.

THE Counties of Wilkinson, Adams, Jefferson, Claiborne, and Warren are the river counties carved from the territory first settled in the State of Mississippi. The settlements along the Mississippi came up from New Orleans and went gradually up the stream. The English or American immigration to that river antedated but a very short time the war of the Revolution. The commencement of this war accelerated the settlement, many seeking an asylum from the horrors of war within the peaceful borders of this new and far-away land. The five counties above named constituted the County of Bourbon when the jurisdiction of the United States was extended to the territory. Very soon after it was divided into three counties — Wilkinson, Adams, and Jefferson; and subsequently, as the population increased, Claiborne and Warren were organized and established. These counties were named after John Adams, Thomas Jefferson, General Wilkinson, General Warren, who fell at Bunker's Hill, and General Ferdinand Claiborne, a distinguished citizen of the Territory. As a Territory, Mississippi extended to and comprised all the territory east to the Alabama River or to the Georgia line. In fact, there was no distinct eastern boundary until the admission of the State into the Union.

The leading men of the communities first formed in the five counties on the Mississippi were men of intelligence and substance. The very first were those who, to avoid the consequences of the war of the Revolution, had sought security here. Some, who conscientiously scrupled as to their duty in that conflict — unwilling to violate an allegiance which they felt they owed to the British crown, and equally unwilling to take part against their kindred and neighbors — had left their homes and come here. There were not a few of desperate character, who had come to avoid the penalties of the criminal laws of the countries from which they had fled. The descendants of all these constitute a large element of the population of these counties at the present moment. Some of these sustain the character of their ancestors in an eminent degree; others again are everything but what their parents were.

One feature of the country is different from that of almost any other portion of the United States. The descendants of the first pioneers are all there. There has been no emigration from the country. The consequence is that intermarriages have made nearly all the descendants of the pioneers relatives. In very many instances these marriages have united families whose ancient feuds are traditions of the country.

The opprobrium attached to the name of Tory (which was freely given to all who had either avoided the war by emigration, or who had remained and taken part against the colonies, and then, to avoid the disgrace they had earned at home, and also to escape the penalties of the laws of confiscation, had brought here their property) induced most families to observe silence respecting their early history, or the causes which brought them to the country, and especially to their children. This was true even as late as forty years ago. There were then in these counties many families of wealth and polish, whose ancestors were obnoxious on account of this damaging imputation; and it was remembered as a tradition carefully handed down by those who at a later day came to the country from the neighborhoods left by these families, and in most instances for crimes of a much more heinous character than obedience to conscientious allegiance to the Government. But success had made allegiance treachery, and rebellion allegiance. Success too often sanctifies acts which failure would have made infamous.

> "Be it so! though right trampled be counted for wrong,
> And that pass for right which is evil victorious,
> Here, where virtue is feeble and villany strong,
> 'T is the cause, not the fate of a cause, that is glorious."

The inviting character of the soil and climate induced (as soon as a settled form of government promised protection) rapid emigration to the country. This came from every part of the United States. Those coming from the same State usually located as nearly as practicable in the same neighborhood, and to this day many of these are designated by the name of the country or State from which they came. There are in the County of Jefferson two neighborhoods known to-day as the Maryland settlement and the Scotch settlement, and the writer has many memories — very pleasant ones, too — of happy hours in the long past spent with some of nature's noblemen who were inhabitants of these communities.

Who that has ever sojourned for a time in this dear old county, does not remember the generous and elegant hospitality of Colonel Wood, Joseph Dunbar, and Mr. Chew; nor must I forget that truly noble-hearted man, David Hunt, the founder of Oakland College, whose charitable munificence was lordly in character, but only commensurate with his soul and great wealth. It seems invidious to individualize the hospitality of this community, where all were so distinguished; but I cannot forbear my tribute of respect — my heart's gratitude — to Wood and Dunbar. I came among these people young and a stranger, poor, and struggling to get up in the world. These two opened their hearts, their doors, and their purses to me; but it was not alone to me. Should all who have in like circumstances been the recipients of their generous and unselfish kindnesses record them as I am doing, the story of their munificent generosity and open, exalted hospitality would seem an Eastern romance.

They have been long gathered to their fathers; but so long as any live who knew them, their memories will be green and cherished. In this neighborhood was built the first Protestant Episcopal Church in the State, and here worshipped the Woods, Dunbars, MacGruders, Shields, Greens, and others composing the settlement. The descendants of these families still remain in that neighborhood, where anterior to the late war was accumulated great wealth. The topography of the country is beautifully picturesque with hills and dales, and all exceedingly fertile. These hills are a continuation of the formation commencing at Vicksburg, and extending to Bayou Sara. They are peculiar, and seem to have been thrown over the primitive formation by some extraordinary convulsion, and are of a sandy loam. No marine shells are found in them; but occasionally trees and leaves are exhumed at great depths. No water is found in this loam by digging or boring; but after passing through this secondary formation, the humus or soil of the primitive is reached — the leaves and limbs of trees superincumbent on this indicating its character — then the sand and gravel, and very soon water, as in other primitive formations. These hills extend back from the river in an irregular line from ten to fifteen miles, and are distinguished by a peculiar growth of timber and smaller shrubs.

The magnolias and poplars, with linn, red oak, and black walnut, are the principal trees. There is no pine, but occasionally an enormous sassafras, such as are found in no other section on this continent. There is no stone, and no running water except streams having their rise in the interior, passing through these hills to their debouchment into the river. The entire formation is a rich compost, and in great part soluble in water; this causes them to wash, and when not cultivated with care, they cut into immense gullies and ravines. They are in some places almost mountainous in height and exceedingly precipitous. They are designated at different localities by peculiar names — as the Walnut Hills, Grand Hills, Petit Gulf Hills, Natchez Hills, and St. Catherine Hills. In primitive forest they presented a most imposing appearance.

Large and lofty timber covered from base to summit these hills, increasing their grandeur by lifting to their height the immense vines found in great abundance all over them. The dense wild cane, clothing as a garment the surface of every acre, went to the very tops of the highest hills, adding a strange feature to hill scenery. The river only approaches these hills in a few places and always at right angles, and is by them deflected, leaving them always on the outer curve of the semicircle or bend in the stream. From these points and from the summit of these cliffs the view is very fine, stretching often in many places far up and down the river and away over the plain west of the river, which seems to repose upon its lap as far as the eye can view. The scene is sombre, but grand, especially when lighted by the evening's declining sun. The plain is unbroken by any elevation: the immense trees rise to a great height, and all apparently to the same level — the green foliage in summer strangely commingling with the long gray moss which festoons from the upper to the lower limbs, waving as a garland in the fitful wind; and the dead gray of the entire scene in winter is sad and melancholy as a vast cemetery. There is a gloomy grandeur in this, which is only rivalled by that of the sea, when viewed from a towering height, lazily lolling in the quiet of a summer evening's calm.

To encounter the perils of a pioneer to such a country required men of iron nerve. Such, with women who dared to follow them, to meet and to share every danger and fearlessly to overcome every obstacle to their enterprise, coming from every section of the United States, formed communities and introduced the arts and industry of civilization, to subdue these forests and compel the soil to yield its riches for the use of man. From these had grown a population, fifty years ago, combining the daring and noble traits of human character which lie at the base of a grand and chivalrous civilization. Such men were the leaders and controllers of the society at that time, assuming a uniform and homogeneous character throughout the western portion of the State. The invasion of New Orleans had endangered this section, and to a man they rallied to meet the foe. More than half the male population of that portion of the State were at New Orleans and in the trenches on the memorable 8th of January, 1815. Their conduct upon that occasion was distinguished, and won from General Jackson high commendation. The charge of the Mississippi cavalry, commanded by General Thomas Hinds, the General, in his report of the battle, said, excited the admiration of one army and the astonishment of the other.

This campaign brought together the younger portion of the male population of the State, and under such circumstances as to make them thoroughly to know each other. These men were the prominent personages of the State forty years ago, and they formed the character of the population and inspired the gallantry and chivalry of spirit which so distinguished the troops of Mississippi in the late unfortunate civil war — in all, but in none so conspicuously, in this spirit and nobleness of soul and sentiment, as in the characters of Jefferson Davis and John A. Quitman — foremost to take up arms in the war with Mexico, resigning high positions for the duties of the soldier, to follow the flag, and avenge the insults of a presumptuous foe.

The society of Western Mississippi, forty years ago, was distinguished above any other in the Union, for a bold, generous, and frank character, which lent a peculiar charm. It was polished, yet it was free and unreserved, full of the courtesies of life, with the rough familiarity of a coarser people. The sports of the turf were pursued with enthusiastic ardor. The chase for the fox and the red deer pervaded almost universally the higher walks of life. The topography of the country was such as to make these, in the fearless rides they compelled, extremely hazardous, familiarizing their votaries with danger and inspiring fearlessness and daring. Almost every gentleman had his hunting steed and kennel of hounds; and at the convivial dinner which always followed the hunt, he could talk horse and hound with the zest of a groom or whipper-in, and at the evening *soirée* emulate D'Orsay or Chesterfield in the polish of his manners and the elegance of his conversation. This peculiarity was not alone confined to the gentlemen. The ladies were familiar with every household duty, and attended to them: they caught from their husbands and brothers the open frankness of their bearing and conversation, a confident, yet not a bold or offensive bearing in their homes and in society, with a polished refinement and an elevation of sentiment in all they said or did, which made them to me the most charming and lovely of their sex — and which made Mississippi forty years ago the most desirable place of rural residence in the Union.

The conduct of these people was universally lofty and honorable. A fawning sycophancy or little meannesses were unknown; social intercourse was unrestrained because all were honorable, and that reserve which so plainly speaks suspicion of your company was never seen. There was no habit of canvassing the demerits of a neighbor or his affairs. The little backbitings and petty slanders which so frequently mar the harmony of communities, was never indulged or tolerated. Homogeneous in its character, the population was harmonious. United in the same pursuits, the emulation was kind and honorable. The tone and purity was superior to low and debasing vices, and these and their concomitants were unknown. There were few dram-shops or places of low resort, and these only for the lower and more debased of the community. Fortunately, fifty years ago, there were but few such characters, no meetings for gaming or debauchery, and the social communion of the people was chaste and cordial at their hospitable and elegant homes.

A peculiar feature of the society of the river counties was the perfect freedom of manners, and yet the high polish, the absence of neighborhood discord, and the strict regard for personal and pecuniary rights: a sort of universal confidence pervaded every community, and in every transaction personal honor supplied the place of litigation. Strangers of respectable appearance were not met with apparent suspicion, but with hospitable kindness; and especially was this the case toward young men who professedly came in search of a new home and new fields for the exercise of their abilities professionally, or for the more profitable employment of any means they might to have brought to the country. Now, at seventy years of age, and after the experience of half a century of men and society in almost every portion of the Union, I can truthfully say, nowhere have I ever met so truthful, so generous, and so hospitable a people as the planters and gentlemen of the river counties of Mississippi, fifty years ago — nowhere women more refined, yet affable; so modest, yet frank and open in their social intercourse; so dignified, without austerity; so chaste and pure in sentiment and action, without prudery or affectation, as the mothers, wives, and daughters of those planters.

The Bench and the Bar were distinguished for ability and purity; many of these have left national reputations — all of them honorable names to their families and profession. Nor were the physicians less distinguished. The names of Provan, McPheters, Cartwright, Ogden, Parker, Cox, and Dennie will be remembered when all who were their compeers shall have passed away, as ornaments to their profession. There is one other, still living at a very advanced age, who was perhaps the superior of any I have mentioned—James Metcalf, who not only was and is an ornament to his profession, but to human nature. He is one of the few surviving monuments of the men of fifty years ago. His life has been eminently useful and eminently pure. He has lived to see his children emulating his example as virtuous and useful citizens, above reproach, and an honor to their parents.

There was not, perhaps, in the Union, a stronger Bar in any four counties than here — Childs, Gibbs, Worley, George Adams, (the father of Generals Daniel and Wirt Adams,) Robert H. Adams, (who died a Senator in the United States Congress when it was an honor to fill the position,) Lyman Harding, W. B. Griffith, John A. Quitman, Joseph E. Davis, (the elder brother of Jefferson Davis,) Thomas B. Reid, Robert J. and Duncan Walker. Time has swept on, and but one of all these remains in life — Robert J. Walker. Edward Tuner, then the presiding judge of the District Court, was a Kentuckian. Four brothers immigrated to the country about the same time. Two remained at Natchez, one at Bayou Sara, in Louisiana, and the fourth went to New Orleans. All became distinguished: three as lawyers, who honored the Bench in their respective localities, and the fourth as a merchant and planter accumulated an immense fortune.

The planters almost universally resided upon their plantations, and their habits were rural and temperate. Their residences were unostentatious, but capacious and comfortable, with every attachment which could secure comfort or contribute to their pleasure. The plantation houses for the slaves were arranged conveniently together, constituting with the barns, stabling, and gin-houses a neat village.

The grounds about the residences were covered with forest-trees carefully preserved; shrubs and flowers were cultivated with exquisite taste among these and over the garden grounds around and beyond them. Social intercourse was of the most cordial and unrestrained character. It was entirely free from that embarrassing ceremony which in urban communities makes it formal, stiff, and a mere ceremony. It was characterized by high-breeding, which made it not only unrestrained but polished, cultivating the heart and the manners to feeling and refinement; making society what it should be — a source of enjoyment and heart-happiness, free from jealousies, rivalries, and regrets.

The distances from plantation to plantation were such as to preclude visiting as a simple call; consequently calls were for spending a day to dine, or an evening to tea, to a rural ride, or some amusement occupying at least half a day, and not unfrequently half a week. Every planter built his house, if not with a view to architectural symmetry and beauty, at least with ample room to entertain his friends, come they in ever such numbers, and his hospitality was commensurate with his house — as capacious and as unpretending. It was the universal habit for both ladies and gentlemen to ride on horseback. The beauty of the forest, through which ran the roads and by-ways — its fragrant blooms — its dark, dense foliage, invited to such exercise; and social reunions were frequently accomplished in the cool shades of these grand old forests by parties ruralizing on horseback when the sun was low, and the shade was sweet, which led them to unite and visit, as unexpectedly as they were welcome, some neighbor, where without ceremony the evening was spent in rural and innocent amusement — a dance, a game of whist or euchre — until weary with these; and on the arrival of the hour for rest they left, and galloped home in the soft moonlight, respectively flushed with health-giving exercise, and only sufficiently fatigued to be able to sleep well.

Nowhere does a splendid woman appear to more advantage than on horseback. Trained from early girlhood to horseback exercise, she learns to sit fearlessly and control absolutely the most fiery steed, to accommodate herself to his every motion, and in his movements to display the ease and grace of this control and confidence. Nowhere on earth were to be found more splendid women or more intrepid riders than the daughters of the planters of Mississippi fifty years ago. Each was provided for her especial use with an animal of high blood, finished form, and well-trained gait. Daily intercourse familiarized rider and horse, and an attachment grew up between them that was always manifested by both upon meeting. It was said by Napoleon that his parade-horse knew and recognized him, and bore himself with more pride and spirit when he was in the saddle than when mounted by any other. Whoever has accustomed himself to treat kindly his saddle-horse, and to suffer no one but himself to ride him, can well understand this. I remember a horse and his rider among my early acquaintances on the banks of the Mississippi, whose mutual attachment was so remarkable as to excite the wonder of strangers. That rider was a true woman — kind, gentle, and yet full of spirit. Affectionate as she was fearless, she had importuned her brother for the gift of a fine young blood-horse, which he gave her upon the condition that she would ride him. She was an experienced rider, and promised.

After a few days of close intimacy, she ventured to mount him. To the astonishment of every one he was perfectly docile, and moved away gently, but with an air of pride, as if conscious of the precious burden he bore. From that time forward no one was permitted to ride him but the lady, who visited him every day in his stall, and always carried him a loaf of bread or a cup of sugar, and never mounted him without going to his front and holding a conversation with pretty Tom, stroking his head with her gentle hand, and giving him a lump of sugar or a biscuit. He was allowed the liberty of the yard, to graze on the young sweet grass of the front lawn, and luxuriate in the shade of the princely trees which grew over it. One or many ladies might go out upon the gallery and remain unnoticed by Tom. The moment, however, that his mistress came, and he saw her or heard her voice, he would neigh in recognition of her presence, and bound immediately forward to the house, manifesting in his eye and manner great pleasure. This was kindly returned by the lady always descending the steps and gently stroking his head, which he would affectionately rest against her person. He would follow her over the yard like a pet spaniel; but he would do this for no one else. He knew her voice, and would obey it, and bound to her call with the alacrity of a child. His pleasure at her coming to mount him, when saddled for a ride, was so marked as to excite astonishment. He would carefully place himself for her convenience, and stand quiet after she was in the saddle until her riding-skirt was adjusted and her foot well in the stirrup, and then she would only say, "Now, Tom!" when he would arch his neck and move off with a playful bound, and curvet about the grounds until she would lay her hand upon his mane, and, gently patting his neck, say, "There, Tom!" Then the play was over, and he went gallantly forward, obediently and kindly as a reasoning being.

The young reader will excuse this garrulity of age: it is its privilege; and I am writing my recollections of bygone years, and none are more pleasant than those which recall to me this great woman—the delightful hours spent in her society at the hospitable home of her family. She still lives, an aged woman, respected by all, and honored in the great merits of her children. Like Tom, they were affectionately trained; and like Tom, they were dutiful in their conduct, and live to perpetuate her intelligence and the noble attributes of her glorious heart. Should these lines ever meet her eye, she will remember the writer, and recall the delightful rides and happy hours spent together a long time ago. We are both in the winter of life, time's uses are almost ended, and all that is blissful now are the memories of the past. Dear Fannie, close the book and your eyes, turn back to fifty years ago, and to the memories common to us both, give the heart one brief moment to these, and, as now I do, drop a tear to them.

The population in the four river counties, at the time of which I write, was much more dense than of any other portion of the State: still there were numerous settlements in different parts of the State quite populous. That upon Pearl River, of these, perhaps, was most populous; but those eastern settlements were constituted of a different people: most of them were from the poorer districts of Georgia and the Carolinas. True to the instincts of the people from whom they were descended, they sought as nearly as possible just such a country as that from which they came, and were really refugees from a growing civilization consequent upon a denser population and its necessities. They were not agriculturists in a proper sense of the term; true, they cultivated in some degree the soil, but it was not the prime pursuit of these people, nor was the location sought for this purpose. They desired an open, poor, pine country, which forbade a numerous population.

Here they reared immense herds of cattle, which subsisted exclusively upon the coarse grass and reeds which grew abundantly among the tall, long-leafed pine, and along the small creeks and branches numerous in this section. Through these almost interminable pine-forests the deer were abundant, and the canebrakes full of bears. They combined the pursuits of hunting and stock-minding, and derived support and revenue almost exclusively from these. They were illiterate and careless of the comforts of a better reared, better educated, and more intelligent people. They were unable to employ for each family a teacher, and the population was too sparse to collect the children in a neighborhood school. These ran wild, half naked, unwashed and uncombed, hatless and bonnetless through the woods and grass, followed by packs of lean and hungry curs, hallooing and yelling in pursuit of rabbits and opossums, and were as wild as the Indians they had supplanted, and whose pine-bark camps were yet here and there to be seen, where temporarily stayed a few strolling, degraded families of Choctaws.

Some of these pioneers had been in the country many years, were surrounded with descendants, men and women, the growth of the country, rude, illiterate, and independent. Along the margins of the streams they found small strips of land of better quality than the pine-forests afforded. Here they grew sufficient corn for bread and a few of the coarser vegetables, and in blissful ignorance enjoyed life after the manner they loved. The country gave character to the people: both were wild and poor; both were *sui generis* in appearance and production, and both seeming to fall away from the richer soil and better people of the western portion of the State.

Between them and the inhabitants of the river counties there was little communication and less sympathy; and I fancy no country on earth of the same extent presented a wider difference in soil and population, especially one speaking the same language and professing the same religion. Time, and the pushing a railroad through this eastern portion of the State, have effected vast changes for the better, and among these quaintly called piney-woods people now are families of wealth and cultivation. But in the main they are yet rude and illiterate.

Not ten years since, I spent some time in Eastern Mississippi. I met at his home a gentleman I had made the acquaintance of in New Orleans. He is a man of great worth and fine intelligence: his grandfather had emigrated to the country in 1785 from Emanuel County, Georgia. His grandson says: "He carried with him a small one-horse cart pulled by an old gray mare, one feather bed, an oven, a frying-pan, two pewter dishes, six pewter plates, as many spoons, a rifle gun, and three deer-hounds. He worried through the Creek Nation, extending then from the Oconee River to the Tombigbee.

"After four months of arduous travel he found his way to Leaf River, and there built his cabin; and with my grandmother, and my father, who was born on the trip in the heart of the Creek Nation, commenced to make a fortune. He found on a small creek of beautiful water a little bay land, and made his little field for corn and pumpkins upon that spot: all around was poor, barren pine woods, but he said it was a good range for stock; but he had not an ox or cow on the face of the earth. The truth is, it looked like Emanuel County.

The turpentine smell, the moan of the winds through the pine-trees, and nobody within fifty miles of him, was too captivating a concatenation to be resisted, and he rested here.

"About five years after he came, a man from Pearl River was driving some cattle by to Mobile, and gave my grandfather two cows to help him drive his cattle. It was over one hundred miles, and you would have supposed it a dear bargain; but it turned out well, for the old man in about six weeks got back with six other head of cattle. How or where, or from whom he got them is not one of the traditions of the family. From these he commenced to rear a stock which in time became large.

"My father and his brothers and sisters were getting large enough to help a little; but my grandfather has told me that my father was nine years old before he ever tasted a piece of bacon or pork. When my father was eighteen years of age he went with a drove of beef cattle to New Orleans. He first went to Baton Rouge, thence down the river. He soon sold out advantageously; for he came home with a young negro man and his wife, some money, and my mother, whom he had met and married on the route. Well, from those negroes, and eight head of cattle, all the family have come to have something.

"I was born nine months after that trip, and grew up, as father had done before me, on the banks of that little creek. I doubt if there ever was a book in my grandfather's house. I certainly never remember to have seen one there, and I was sixteen years old when he died. I think I was very nearly that old before I ever saw any woman but those of the family, and I know I was older than that before ever I wore shoes or pants. Nearly every year father went to Mobile, or Natchez, or New Orleans. The first time I ever knew my mother had a brother, I was driving up the cows, and a tall, good-looking man overtook me in the road and asked where my father lived. I remember I told him, 'At home.' He thought it was impudence, but it was ignorance. However, he was quite communicative and friendly.

"That night, after the family had gone to bed, I heard him tell mother her father was dead, and that he had disinherited her for running off and marrying father. I did not know what this meant; but the next day father came and told mother that her brother wanted to be kind to her, and had proposed to give him a thousand dollars out of the estate of her father, if he and she would take it and sign off. That was the word. I shall not forget, so long as I live, my mother's looks as she walked up to father and said: 'Don't you do it, John. John, I say, don't you do it.' Uncle had gone down to grandfather's, and when he came back, mother had his horse saddled at the fence. She met him at the door, and said: 'You don't come in here. There 's your beast; mount him, and go. I am not such a fool as my John. I was raised in Louisiana, and I remember hearing my father say that all he hated in the laws was that a man could not do with his property, when he died, what he pleased. I haven't forgot that. I have not seen nor heard from any of you for fifteen years, and never should, if you had n't come here to try to cheat me.'

"I was scared, and father was scared; for we knew there was danger when mother's nap was up. Uncle did not reply to mother, but said: 'John, you can sign off.'

"'No, John can't; and I tell you John shan't! so now do you just mount that horse and leave.'

"As she said this she lifted the old rifle out of the rack over the door and rubbed her hand over the barrel to get the sight clear. 'I am not going to tell you to go any more.'

"It was not necessary—uncle went; but he kept looking back until he was at least a quarter of a mile from the house. Mother turned to father and said: 'Now, John, you go after my share of father's truck, and go quick.' He did as she bid him: everybody about the house did that. Well, he was gone three weeks, and came home with six thousand dollars, which he had taken for mother's share; but she said she knew he had been cheated.

"Every dollar of that money remained in the house until I got married and came off here. I got two thousand of it, one negro, and two hundred head of cattle. I had promised my wife's people that I would come and live with them. I am glad I did. I was twenty-one years old when I learned my letters. I have been lucky; have educated my children, and they have educated me, and are talking about running me for Congress. Well, my friend, I believe I could be elected; but that is a small part of the business. I should be of no service to the State, and only show my own ignorance. Come, Sue, can't you give the gentleman some music? Give me my fiddle, and I will help you."

Sue was a beautiful and interesting girl of nineteen, only a short time returned from a four-years residence at the famous Patapsco Institute. She had music in her soul, and the art to pour it out through her fingers' ends. It was an inheritance from her extraordinary father, as any judge of music would have said, who had heard the notes melting from that old black violin, on that rainy night in December. There are not many such instances of men springing from such humble origin in Eastern Mississippi; but this is not a solitary case.

There emigrated from different States, North and South, at a remote period in the brief history of this new country, several young men of talent and great energy, who not only distinguished themselves, but shed lustre upon the State. Among the first of these was George Poindexter, from Virginia; Rankin, from Georgia, (but born in Virginia;) Thomas B. Reid, from Kentucky; Stephen Duncan, and James Campbell Wilkins, from Pennsylvania. The most remarkable of these was George Poindexter. He was a lawyer by profession and a Jeffersonian Republican in politics. Very early in life he became the leader of that party in the State, and was sent to Congress as its sole representative. Very soon he obtained an enviable reputation in that body as a statesman and a powerful debater. His mind was logical and strong; his conception was quick and acute; his powers of combination and application were astonishing; his wit was pointed and caustic, and his sarcasm overwhelming. Unusually quick to perceive the weaker parts of an opponent's argument, his ingenuity would seize these and turn them upon him with a point and power not unfrequently confounding and destroying the effect of all he had urged. From Congress to the Gubernatorial chair of the State was the next step in his political career, and it was in this capacity that he rendered the most signal service to the State. As a lawyer, he was well aware of the wants of the State in statutory provisions for the protection of the people. These were wisely recommended, and, through his exertions, enacted into laws.

The several Governments which had claimed and held jurisdiction over the Territory of Mississippi had issued grants to companies and individuals for large tracts of country in different portions of the State. These grants had not been respected by the succeeding Governments, or else the records had been lost or carried from the country for a time; hence very many conflicting claims made insecure the titles of the proprietors now settled upon these tracts, and were fruitful of endless litigation. To remedy this evil, a statute was recommended by Governor Poindexter and enacted into a law, compelling suit to be commenced by all adverse claimants by a certain day. This effectually cured the evil, and a suit to establish titles is now very rare in Mississippi. As a judge he was able, prompt, impartial, unrivalled in talent, and, at the same time, unsurpassed by any lawyer in the State in legal learning. His administration of the laws was eminently successful. The country was new, with the exception of a few counties, and, as in all new and frontier countries, there were many bad and desperate men. To purge these from society it was necessary that the criminal laws should be strictly enforced. To do so required decision and sternness in the character and conduct of the judges. Very soon after Poindexter was placed on the Bench he manifested these attributes in an eminent degree.

The stern, impartial justice administered to these lawless men, soon created quite a sensation with the class to which they belonged, and threats were freely thrown out against his life; but these had no effect in intimidating him, or in changing his conduct. He went on fearlessly to administer the law, which at that time, instead of imprisonment, inflicted severe corporal punishments for many crimes most common in a new country. These were branding with a hot iron in the hand or on the cheek, whipping on the bare back, and public exposure in the pillory. Not a court went by without some one of these punishments being inflicted upon a male malefactor. Public opinion had begun to look upon these penalties as barbarous, and in very many cases great sympathy was manifested for the culprit.

This sentiment frequently operated with the jury, who were disposed to deal leniently with the accused. This was resisted by Poindexter, and effectually — for so clearly did he impress the minds of jurors with what was their duty, that few escaped where the proof was sufficient to convict; and once pronounced guilty, the extreme penalty of the law was surely awarded. The beneficial influence of this stern and inflexible administration of the laws was soon manifest, and the more orderly of the population unhesitatingly gave their approbation and support to the judge. He sustained in court the dignity of the Bench, restraining alike the license of the Bar and the turbulence of the populace. To do this, he was frequently compelled to exercise to the full the powers of his office.

An amusing anecdote is related of him in connection with the discharge of these duties. When holding court at one time in Natchez, he had sent to jail a turbulent and riotous individual, who could in no other way be restrained. This fellow, once incarcerated, professed great contrition, and humbly petitioned for release, but Poindexter had ordered the sheriff to keep him for a week, and could not be moved from his position. At the expiration of the week he was released, and though he was quiet and orderly, he remained lurking about town and the court-room until the adjournment of court. He watched his opportunity, and meeting the judge upon the street, commenced abusing him roundly; finally telling him he had waited purposely for the opportunity of whipping him, and that he intended then and there to do so. Poindexter, perceiving the sheriff on the opposite side of the street, called to him, and ordered him to open court then and there, which in all due form the sheriff proceeded to do. The bully was startled, and the judge, perceiving this, remarked to him authoritatively, "Now, you scoundrel, be off with yourself, or I will put you in jail for one year!" — when the blackguard speedily decamped, to the infinite amusement of the crowd upon the street.

Governor Poindexter found at Natchez, and a few other localities, strong opposition from the Federal party, then constituted almost entirely of emigrants from Western Pennsylvania, with a sprinkling from the more Eastern States. The party was small, but made up for this deficiency in numbers with zeal and violence. As with all heated and hating partisans, their malevolence was principally directed toward the leaders of the opposing party.

Poindexter was the acknowledged leader of the Republican or Jeffersonian party, and concentrated on himself the hatred of one and the adoration of the other party. His triumphs were complete and overwhelming in every election. He was not scrupulous in the use of terms when speaking of his enemies. These anathemas, darting in the caustic wit and voluble sarcasm so peculiarly his, went to the mark, and kindled hatred into fury. It was determined to get rid of him. His denunciations of Abijah Hunt, a prominent merchant and leading Federalist, being more pointed and personal than toward any other, it seemed incumbent on him to challenge Poindexter to mortal combat — an arbitrament for the settlement of personal difficulties more frequently resorted to at that period than at the present time. They met, and Hunt was killed. But such was the violence of feeling with his party friends, that they were determined Poindexter should not escape unscathed, and he was denounced as having fired before the word agreed upon in the terms of the conflict were fully enunciated. This, however, effected but little, and he continued the idol of his party.

Unfortunately, that bane of genius, dissipation, was poisoning his habits and undermining his reputation. It seems that exalted genius feeds upon excitement, and in some shape must have it. The excitement of active business at the Bar or in the halls of legislation must of necessity be temporary, and the relaxation which follows this is terrible to the excitable temperament of ardent genius. It craves restlessly its natural food, and in the absence of all others, it seeks for this in the intoxicating bowl or the gaming-table. How many brilliant examples of this fatal fact does memory call up from the untimely grave? These, culled from my seniors when I was a youth, from my compeers in early manhood, from the youth I have seen grow up about me, make a host whose usefulness has been lost to the world. Well may the poet sing in melancholy verse that genius is a fatal gift. It dazzles as a meteor with its superhuman light, and as soon fades into darkness, lighting its path with a blaze of glory, astonishing and delighting the world, but consuming itself with its own fire.

Poindexter had won greatly upon the affections of the people of the Territory, in the active part he had taken, in connection with General Ferdinand Claiborne and General Hinds, in stimulating the people to prepare to meet the exigencies of the war of 1812 with Great Britain. Her eastern territory was exposed to the inroads of the Creek Indians, a large and warlike tribe, who were hostile to the United States, and were in league with the English, and being armed by them. The Choctaws and Chickasaws were on her northern frontier, and were threatening. An invasion by the way of New Orleans by English troops was hourly expected. It required great energy and activity to anticipate and guard against these threatening dangers. Poindexter employed his time and his influence to prepare the people to act efficiently and at a moment's warning. When the threatened invasion became a reality, and General Jackson was descending the river with troops as the American commander, and when the militia were on the ground, and nothing remained to be done in Mississippi, he promptly repaired to the scene of action and volunteered his services to Jackson, who, accepting them, placed him on his staff as a volunteer aide.

In this capacity he continued to serve until the end of the campaign and the termination of the war. It was to him the negro or soldier brought the celebrated countersign of "Beauty and booty," found on the battle-field, and which he carried to General Jackson. His enemies laid hold of this incident and perverted it slanderously to his injury, by asserting the note to be a forgery of his, done for the purpose of winning favor with the General, and to cast odium upon an enemy incapable of issuing such an infamous countersign.

Those who have read the history of the various strongholds of the French in Spain which were stormed during the Peninsular war, will remember these were the same troops and the same commanders, who were quite capable of the excesses in New Orleans that they committed in Spain. This slander was never traced; but there were those remaining who, when the breach occurred between General Jackson and Governor Poindexter, asserted that General Jackson believed it, and who circulated industriously the contemptible slander. Poindexter was an active supporter of General Jackson's first election. He believed him honest and capable, and deserving of the reward of the Presidency for his services to the country. He thought, too, that he would bring back the Government to its early simplicity and purity, and administer it upon strictly republican principles. He, with very many of the Jeffersonian school, felt it had diverged from the true track.

These people were opposed to protective tariffs, internal improvements by the United States Government within the limits of a State without the consent of the State, and a national bank, deeming all these measures unconstitutional. The constitutionality of the bank had been affirmed by the Supreme Court, and Poindexter had acquiesced in the decision. Nevertheless, as a senator from the State of Mississippi, he was in harmony with the Administration of Jackson, until Jackson began to send his personal friends and especial favorites from Tennessee to fill the national offices located in Mississippi. Poindexter felt this as an insult to his State, and in the case of Gwinn's appointment as register of the Land-Office at Clinton, Mississippi, he opposed the nomination when sent to the Senate. He was successful in having it rejected.

He urged that though the office was national, and every man in the nation was eligible to fill it, yet it was due to the State that the incumbent should be selected from her own people, provided she could furnish one in every way qualified, and that it was a reflection upon the people of his State to fill the offices within her borders with aliens to her soil and interests — strangers to her people, with no motive to be obliging and respectful to them in the discharge of the duties of the office; that the offices belonged to the people and not to the President, and it was respectful to the people of a State to tender to her people these offices, as had been heretofore the custom; that simply being the President's favorite was not a qualification for office, and this departure from the established usages of former Administrations was a dangerous precedent, and would seem to establish a property in the office, belonging to the President.

This opposition enraged Jackson, who denounced Poindexter and persisted in his determination to give the office to Gwinn. In this he finally succeeded; but most unfortunately for Gwinn, for it embroiled him in quarrels with the citizens of the State. A duel with Judge Caldwell was the consequence, in which both fell. Caldwell died immediately; Gwinn survived to suffer intensely for a few months, when death relieved him.

The people of Mississippi were intensely devoted to General Jackson, and in the mad fury of partisan zeal forgot everything but party, nor permitted themselves for a moment to inquire into the official conduct of any political partisan, especially that of the President. Poindexter had been unhappy in his domestic relations. He had separated from his wife. He charged her with infidelity; forgot his affection for his children, and threw them off, because he doubted their paternity. In the agony of mind consequent upon this he became desperate, and for years was reckless in his dissipations. His wife's friends were respectable and influential. They, with every personal and political enemy he had, united in ascribing to him all the blame in this matter.

The northern portion of the State had been acquired from the Indians, and a population unacquainted with Poindexter or with his services to the State was crowding into the new Territory in such numbers as threatened politically to rule the State. These came principally from the West and South, and were eminently Jacksonian in their politics. Many young aspirants for fame had sprung up in different sections of the State, and these were in no way averse to seeing an old and talented politician shelved; and they joined in the huzza for Jackson and down with his opponents.

Seeing and feeling the tide setting in so strongly as to sweep everything before it except what comported with the views and wishes of General Jackson, and feeling also that he, with the minority in the Senate, could be of no possible use to the country, and beginning to experience the pressure of age, at the conclusion of his senatorial term he made no effort to be re-elected. He retired, disgusted with politics forever, and temporarily from the State. Subsequently an accident fractured both his legs below the knee, and for some years he was unable to walk. Prior to this event he had married a Boston lady — following the example of his divorced wife, who had married a Boston gentleman. With this lady he lived affectionately and happily. He located in Lexington, Kentucky, where he remained only a few years.

It was here I saw him, at his own house, for the last time — spending an evening in company with Daniel Webster, Henry Clay, John J. Crittenden, and the celebrated actress, Mrs. Drake. I enjoyed the hospitality, the wit, and a game of whist with him. He soon became weary of Lexington. His heart was in Mississippi, and thither he returned, old and worn. He took up his residence at Jackson, where in a short time he died, and is buried in the beautiful cemetery at that place. While paying a pilgrimage to the grave of a dear boy who died in defence of Jackson in 1866, I saw and paused at the modest stone which marks the grave of Governor Poindexter. Memory was busy with the past. My heart was sad. I had just looked upon the sod which covered my boy, and, thinking of the hours passed, long years ago, with him who was sleeping at my feet, I could not repress the tear due and dear to memory.

Few men have served more faithfully and more efficiently a people than did George Poindexter the people of Mississippi. His talents were indisputably of the first order, and, whatever may have been his short comings morally, none can say his political life was stained with selfishness or corruption. Every trust reposed in him was faithfully and ably discharged, and to him, more than to any of her public servants, is she indebted for the proud position she occupied before the tyrants' heel was upon her neck.

Few men can rise superior to the crushing effects of domestic infelicity: man's hopes, man's happiness, all centred in her whom he has chosen as the companion of his life. His love selects, and his love centres in her. The struggle for fortune, for happiness, for fame, is for her; she shares every success, every misfortune; and when she is kind and affectionate, there he meets with the true manliness of an honest and devoted heart. She smooths the brow of disappointment and sorrow, rejoices in his success, and, in the fulness of her confidence and affection, aids and encourages his exertions and enterprises. This reconciles him to life, and life's cares, troubles, and joys. His spirit is buoyant, come what may; for there is an angel at home, and there is happiness with her: she is the mother of his children; she unites with him in love and exertions for the benefit of these. They are one in these, and with every birth there is a new link to bind and gladden two hearts. Without the virtuous love of woman, man is a miserable being, worthless to himself and useless to his kind. But when the heart's wealth is given to one who has no sympathy with it, and gives only in return coldness and hate; who betrays every confidence and disappoints every hope; who is only happy when he is miserable, and refuses the generous aid a wife owes to his exertions; who rejoices in his failures, and intrigues to produce them, and weeps over his successes with the bitterness of disappointment; who hates her offspring, because they resemble their father; who spurns his caresses, and turns away from his love — then life's hopes are blighted, and all is black before. His energies die out with his hopes; the goading thought is eternally present; he shrinks away from society, and in solitude and obscurity hides him from the world — which too often condemns him as the architect of all his misery.

"Oh, a true woman is a treasure beyond price, but a false one the basest of counterfeits."

CHAPTER XXIV.

THE SILVER-TONGUED ORATOR.

JOHN A. QUITMAN — ROBERT J. WALKER — ROBERT H. ADAMS — FROM A COOPER-SHOP TO THE UNITED STATES SENATE — BANK MONOPOLY — NATCHEZ FENCIBLES — SCOTT IN MEXICO — THOMAS HALL — SARGENT S. PRENTISS — VICKSBURG — SINGLE-SPEECH HAMILTON — GOD-INSPIRED ORATORY — DRUNK BY ABSORPTION — KILLING A TAILOR — DEFENCE OF WILKINSON.

JOHN A. QUITMAN came to Mississippi in early life. He was a native of the State of New York; had, at first, selected a location in Ohio, but, not being pleased, he determined on coming South, and selected Natchez for his future home. His father was a Prussian; a minister of the German Lutheran Church, and a very learned man. He had preached in seven kingdoms, and in every one in the language of the country. He came to the State of New York when young, and was the bearer of the recognition of the independence of the United States by Frederick the Great, of Prussia. He settled in one of the interior counties of New York, where was born and reared his distinguished son.

When young Quitman came to Natchez, he found the Bar a strong one; but determined to follow the profession of law, and after a short time spent in the office of William B. Griffith, he was admitted to the Bar, and opened an office. Regardless of the overwhelming competition, his open, frank manners soon made him friends, and the stern honesty of his character won the confidence of every one. In a short time, he married the only daughter of Henry Turner, a wealthy planter, and was received into copartnership by William B. Griffith, a lawyer of great ability and eminence, then in full practice at Natchez, and who had married the daughter of Judge Edward Turner, and the cousin of Quitman's wife. Quitman's rise to eminence was rapid in his profession, but more so in the public estimation as a man of great worth. His affability, kindness, and courtesy were so genial and so unaffected as to fasten upon every one, and soon he was the most popular man in the county.

Soon after Quitman, came Duncan and Robert J. Walker — the

latter subsequently so distinguished as a senator in Congress from Mississippi, and still more distinguished as the Secretary of the Treasury during the Administration of Mr. Polk. A close intimacy grew up between Quitman and R. J. Walker. This intimacy influenced greatly the future of Quitman. Walker was from Pennsylvania, and had married Miss Bache, the niece of George M. Dallas, sister to the great Professor Bache, and great-granddaughter of Benjamin Franklin. Mrs. Walker was a lady of great beauty, of rare accomplishments, and distinguished for her modesty and womanly bearing. Mr. Bache, the father of Mrs. Walker, emigrated to Texas, was in the Senate of her Congress at the time she was received into the United States, and was the only man who voted against the union. He represented Galveston, and, after his death, that young city, in honor of his services, erected a monument to his memory.

Walker was of ardent temperament, great abilities, strong will, intense application, and was soon, at the Bar, among the first lawyers in the State. He wanted the softness and genial qualities of Quitman, but was superior to him mentally; and in prompt, decisive action his was the stronger character, and controlled. Quitman, being intimately associated with the leading men of the party supporting Mr. Adams, had adopted their opinions and politics; Walker was an ardent supporter of Jackson, and claimed to be the first man who brought forward his name for the Presidency, when he was a citizen of Pennsylvania. Soon after the election of General Jackson, Quitman, displeased with Mr. Clay, abandoned his Whig associates, and united himself with the Democratic party, and from that time until his death was a devoted Democratic partisan. These two men exercised, perhaps, more influence in the State than any others of their day.

Robert H. Adams and William B. Griffith, who were considered the ablest members of the Bar in the State, died young, and in the opening of their political career. Adams was a man of remarkable ability. He was a native of East Tennessee, and was a mechanic, with limited education, and without one single advantage save his talents. He came a stranger to Natchez, and in a few years was eminent in his profession, and intellectually one of the first men in the State—a man of fine appearance, with large head, and intellectual features. He was sent by the city of Natchez to the Legislature of the State, and such was the impression upon the members of his great abilities, that they, at the ensuing session, elected him to the United States Senate. He served but one session, but made, in that short period, a high reputation with the first minds of the nation. Returning home, he resumed his profession; and, after severe fatigue during the heated period of summer, he imprudently drank too freely of ice-water, and died from its effects.

There was, at this time, no man of more promise in all the country. He was but thirty-eight years of age, and, without patronage or patrimony, had risen from the cooper's shop to a distinguished position in the Senate of the United States.

Griffith preceded him to the grave one or two years, a victim of yellow fever.

Quitman and Walker came now prominently before the people. They resided in Natchez, and there was a strong prejudice in the east and the north of the State against the people of that city and the County of Adams. There were quite a number of families, in the city and county, of large fortunes. These were exclusive in their associations. With one or two exceptions they belonged to the Whig party, but none of them aspired to political preferment.

There was but one bank in the State — this was located in Natchez, and was under the control of these men of fortune. It had at the time of obtaining its charter paid an extravagant bonus to the State, upon condition no other bank should be chartered for the period granted to this. It was a monopoly, and was charged with great partiality in its management. Its accommodations were for the few, and these only granted for the purpose of enhancing the already bloated wealth of the stockholders, directors, and their special pets. This exclusive aristocracy was odious to the fierce democratic feelings of the masses. They counted their wealth by millions; their homes were palaces; their pleasure-grounds Edens; and all this was the fruit of an odious and oppressive monopoly. This fallacious and most ridiculous idea fastened itself upon the minds of the masses, and was fostered and encouraged by many who knew better, but who were willing to pander to the popular taste for popular preferment. R. J. Walker seized hold upon this popular whim, and leading the multitude, succeeded in procuring charters for several other banks, in defiance of the vested rights of the Bank of Mississippi.

Stephen Duncan was the president of the bank, and, under his advice, the directors surrendered the charter, and wound up the business of the bank. Duncan was one of the best business-men in the Union. From very small beginnings he had amassed an immense fortune —was a man of rare sagacity and wonderful energy. He was the cousin of Walker, but was always opposed to him in politics. This was the commencement of the era which culminated in the repudiation of the State's obligations and the general ruin of her people. It was about this period that Jefferson Davis first made his *début* as a public man in the State, with William M. Gwinn, and Henry S. Foote, McNutt, J. F. H. Claiborne, and Albert Gallatin Brown. Quitman was made chancellor of the State, and disappointed sadly his friends. His administration of this branch of the judiciary was weak and wild; a vast number of his decisions, or awards in chancery, were overruled, and, in disgust, or from a consciousness that a chancery judgeship was not his speciality, resigned. His mind was greatly overrated: it was neither strong, logical, nor brilliant. His classical attainments were of the first order, and I doubt if the Union furnished two better or more finished linguists than John A. Quitman and H. S. Foote.

Walker and Davis were the leading minds of the period. They were both men of education, extended reading; both men of fine oratorical powers; both men of strong will, ripe judgment, and exceedingly tenacious of purpose. Walker was many years the senior of Davis, and was in advance of him some years as a successful politician. Foote, as an orator, was greatly the superior of all of these; but there was in him want of judgment, want of fixed principles and fixity of purpose. When first appearing before the people of the State, he carried the multitude with him as a tempest drives a feather. In a contest for Governor he came out in opposition to Quitman, drove him from the canvass, and triumphed over Davis, who was placed by his party in nomination to fill the place of Quitman. This triumph was evanescent: he left the position, perhaps, the most unpopular man in the State.

Quitman's abilities were almost exclusively military. This proclivity of mind manifested itself in very early life. He organized a volunteer company, the Natchez Fencibles, soon after he came to the Bar, and took great pride in its drill and soldierly bearing and appearance. He seized with avidity the opportunity the Mexican war presented, and there greatly distinguished himself. After the termination of this war, he was engaged (very little to the honor of his sagacity) in endeavoring to organize a filibustering expedition against the Island of Cuba. In this he signally failed. He was elected to Congress, where he was principally distinguished by his extreme Southern views, but gained little or no reputation as a politician or statesman.

In the qualities of heart, Quitman was surpassed by no man; his moral character was unstained. In sincerity and devotion to his friends, no man was his superior. He had acquired large wealth by his marriage — this he had increased by judicious management, and none more freely used it for the benefit of his friends or the public interest. He was especially generous toward poor, enterprising young men; such instances of assistance rendered are innumerable. His friends never deserted him. To his command, during the Mexican war, he was exceedingly profuse with his means in aiding their necessities and supplying their wants. He was universally commented upon as the most munificent officer of the army. He was ambitious and courageous; and this ambition knew no bounds.

Upon his return from Mexico, I met him in New Orleans, in company with that ill-starred man, General Shields, of Illinois, and who, Irishman as he was, fell fighting to fasten upon the South the fetters she now wears. We had not conversed ten minutes before, taking my arm, he walked apart from his visitors and Shields, and commenced to converse upon the consequences of the war. Turning to me, he remarked: "General Scott is greatly wanting in ambition, he has no daring aspirations; he has thrown away the finest opportunity ever presented to man for aggrandizement. Had I commanded the army, and accomplished this great success, I would have established an empire, and made of Mexico a great nation. He had only to say so, and the Mexicans were ready to crown him emperor. He could have made dukes, marquises, lords, and barons of his officers, and endowed them with principalities; the soldiers would have remained with him; and in six months, enough from the United States and Europe would have joined his standard, to have held in check the lawless brigands who make anarchy for the country. The spoils of the Church would have rewarded the soldiers; immigration would have poured into the country, and his name and fame have been commensurate with time. Everything invited him to the act; he could not or would not see it — he had but one idea, 'This will make me President!' and a lifetime of glory and power was sacrificed for the empty hope of four years filling the Presidential chair."

It was a grand conception, but he seemed to take no account of the difficulties which would have interposed. He assumed that the United States would have been content with the great outrage, and have sanctioned the act; and that European nations would have immediately recognized the new empire. I knew him well enough to know that he would have attempted the enterprise and braved the consequences; but doubt whether he or Scott had the talent for the accomplishment of such an undertaking. General Quitman was one of the unfortunates who received a portion of the poison prepared for some victim or victims at Washington upon the inauguration of Mr. Buchanan. It was not immediately fatal, but he never fully recovered from it, and in a few months after sank into the grave.

No man ever died more regretted by his personal friends than John A. Quitman. He was in every relation of life a true man, chivalrously brave, nobly generous, and sternly faithful to all that ennobles human nature. Had his brain been equal to his soul, he had been the world's wonder. It was said of him by one who knew and loved him:

> "His spirit has gone to the Spirit that made him,
> The rest of the virtuous, chivalric, and brave;
> He sleeps where the friends of his early youth laid him,
> And green grows the laurel that springs by his grave."

Duncan Walker practised law with his brother until elevated to the Bench of the criminal court for the city of Natchez and County of Adams. He served with distinguished capacity for only one or two years, when he was prostrated by a severe attack of yellow fever. From this he never entirely recovered. Retiring from the Bench, he directed his attention to planting in Lower Louisiana; but his health continuing to decline, he was induced to try for the winter the climate of Cuba. It was but a few weeks after reaching there that he died at St. Jago de Cuba. Judge Walker was distinguished for great purity of character as well as superior legal attainments. His modesty was almost feminine; yet he was a man of remarkable firmness and decision. By many he was thought superior intellectually to his more distinguished and prominent brother. Few men may be truthfully termed superior to R. J. Walker.

In 1826, there came to Natchez, from Maine, a youth who was a cripple. He was without acquaintances or recommendations, and also without means. He was in search of a school, and expressed his intention of making the South his future home. His appearance was boyish in the extreme, for one who professed to be twenty years of age. At that time most of the planters in the region of Natchez employed private teachers in their families, who resided with the family as one of the household. A lady near Natchez, the widow of Judge Shields, was desirous of employing a teacher, and tendered the situation to the young Yankee. Mrs. Shields had grown-up sons, young men of fine attainments, and who subsequently distinguished themselves as men of sterling worth. They were soon delighted with the young stranger, who was busily employed in his new vocation with their younger brothers. I remember to have heard Mr. Thomas Shields say the young man teaching at his mother's was a most remarkable man, and narrate some instances of his great powers of memory, accompanied with facts which came within his own knowledge. These were so very extraordinary, that notwithstanding the high character for integrity borne by Shields, there were many who doubted them.

There lived at no great distance from Mrs. Shields, a planter, Mr. Thomas Hall. This man was a coarse and illiterate overseer for some years in the county, but having carefully husbanded his earnings, was enabled, in company with James C. Wilkins, to commence planting upon an extensive scale. At the time this young man was teaching at Mrs. Shields', Hall had accumulated quite a fortune, and was a man of comparative leisure. His mind was good, and now that he had an abundance of the world's goods, and was becoming a man of consideration in the community, he felt, in his intercourse with his educated neighbors, the want of that cultivation which would make him their equal. This had made him morbidly sensitive, and whenever an opportunity presented, he improved it in acquiring all the information possible.

On Saturdays the young schoolmaster would frequently ride over and converse with Hall. The strong mind and coarse but cordial manners of Hall pleased him. He was a specimen of the Southerner possessing salient points, and was a study for the Down-Easter. Never before had he met such a specimen, and it was his delight to draw him out, little deeming he was filling the same office for his friend. They were mutually agreeable the one to the other, and their association grew into intimacy. Each to their friends would speak of the other as a remarkable man. Assuredly they were; for neither had ever met such specimens as they presented to each other. They sometimes joined in a squirrel-hunt about the plantation of Hall. The schoolmaster's lameness compelled him to ride, while Hall preferred to walk. After a fatiguing tramp upon one occasion, they sat down upon the banks of Cole's Creek, where Hall listened with great delight to the conversation of his companion. Suddenly Hall started up, and exclaimed, with more than his usual warmth:

"You have taught me more than I ever knew before meeting with you; but I ought not to say what I am going to say. You, sir, were never made for a schoolmaster. By the eternal God!"—Hall was a Jackson man—"you know more than any man in the county, and you have got more sense than any of them, though you are nothing but a boy. Now, sir, go to town and study law with Bob Walker; he 's the smartest of any of them. In two years you will be ahead of him. If you have n't got the money to pay your way, I have, and you shall have it."

The term for which he had engaged was now expiring, and, as Hall had requested, he went into the office of Robert J. and Duncan Walker, and commenced the study of law.

This Yankee youth was Sargent S. Prentiss. Prentiss remained in the office of Walker for one year, and was a close student. When admitted to the Bar, he went to Vicksburg and opened an office. At that time Vicksburg was a new place, and presented peculiar inducements to young professional men. The country upon the Yazoo River—and indeed the entire northern portion of the State—had but recently been quit of its Indian population, and was rapidly filling up with an active and enterprising people. The soil was fertile, and the production of cotton, to which it is so eminently suited, was daily growing in importance. Vicksburg was the market-point. Trade was increasing daily, and rapidly filling up the town with mercantile men. The young and enterprising were hurrying thither, and in a few years there was met here more talent and more enterprise than at any other point in the State. The Bar had Prentiss, John Guion, McNutt, Sharkey, the three Yergers, Anderson, Lake, Brook,

Burwell, and many others of distinction, including the erratic H. S. Foote.

The entire population was a live one, and every branch of business was pushed with a *vim* commensurate with the abilities and enterprise of the population. The planters of the immediately adjacent country were men of intelligence and character, and were animated with the spirit of the people of the town, forming on the whole a community of almost reckless enterprise. It was at such a time and in the midst of such a people that young Prentiss had made his selection of a home, and a field for the future exercise of his professional abilities.

Young, ardent, and ambitious, he sought to rival his seniors at the Bar. Unwilling to wait on time, he aspired to leap at once to this equality. It was the daring of genius, and of a genius which counted as only a stimulant the obstacles intervening. To grapple with giants, such as he found in Guion, Yerger, Sharkey, McNutt, and Lake, would have intimidated a less bold and daring mind; but Prentiss courted the conflict *con amore*, and applying all his herculean powers with the vigor of youth and the ardency of enterprise, he soon found himself quite equal to any competitor.

When an infant, a fever settled in his leg, causing it to wither from the knee to the foot, and doomed him through life to lameness. Like Byron, he was sensitive upon the subject of this physical defect. It was a serious obstacle to his locomotion, and in speaking compelled a sameness of position injurious to the effect of his oratory. Scarcely had two years elapsed from the time of his admission to the Bar before his fame as a lawyer and advocate was filling the State. His business had increased to such an extent as to require his undivided attention, as he was employed in almost every important suit in that section of the State. His qualities of heart were as conspicuous as those of his brain, which had endeared him to the people of Vicksburg perhaps more than any other citizen. This social and professional popularity caused him to be elected to the Legislature of the State. He belonged to the Whig party, which was largely in the minority in the Legislature, but was powerful in talent.

Before this time, Colonel Adam L. Bingaman, of Adams County, had been the acknowledged leader of this party. He was a man of rare qualifications for a popular leader — highly gifted by nature in mind and personal appearance, which was most splendid and commanding, with a polished education and fascinating manners, and by nature an orator. Added to these advantages, he was a native of the State, the representative of great wealth, and with extensive family influence. These two met as friends personally and politically in the Legislature.

Prentiss — though known as a great lawyer and a powerful advocate at the Bar — had until now taken but little part in politics. None knew of his proficiency as a politician or as a popular political orator, and, long accustomed to the eloquence and the debating abilities of Bingaman, the lead was accorded to him as usual. Party excitement was fierce, and involved every one. The Democracy, armed with numbers and men of great abilities, felt secure in their position. They had no fears that any powers possessed by any man or set of men could operate a change in public opinion dangerous to their supremacy in the State.

Socially, Prentiss knew no party distinction. With all who were gentlemen he mingled, not as a partisan, but as a man. The kindness of his nature won upon all equally, and it was soon discovered that a personal favor to Prentiss would sometimes override party allegiance. His personal friends were all gentlemen, and once within the magic influence of his social circle was enough to bind him to the heart of every one. The session had made but little progress before his powers as an orator were beginning to be felt.

During an exciting debate, in which Bingaman had, as usual, taken the lead, when all the ablest of the Democracy had, as they supposed, exhausted the argument and demolished the position of their adversaries, and the House seemed impatient for the question, Prentiss rose, and claimed the attention of the chair. His clear and succinct statement of the pending question put a new phase upon it, and the House seemed surprised.

He proceeded then to debate the question; and very soon he was in *medias res*, and his bold and lucid argument won the attention of every one. The position of the Democracy was dissected to the separation of every fibre; its character and future effects denounced and exposed in a strain of invective eloquence which thrilled to every heart. Turning from this to the national policy of the Democracy, then in power, and which the measure under consideration was intended to aid and sustain, his powers seemed to expand with the magnitude of the subject, as he went on to analyze the policy and the measures of the Government, and to demonstrate the disastrous consequences which must follow these remotely, if not immediately, corrupting, undermining, and ultimately destroying the Constitution, and, of consequence, the Government. He spoke for three hours; his peroration was so grandly eloquent as to bring down the House and galleries in a round of applause.

From that day forward, Prentiss was the great man of the House and of the State. A fire in a prairie never spread or ran faster than his fame; it was on every tongue, in every newspaper. Such fame from one speech had never been won by any man in America, save Patrick Henry. Single - speech Hamilton, of the British Parliament, astonished England; but he was never afterward heard of, and is known to this day as "single-speech Hamilton." As with Henry, this was but the beginning of a fame which was to grow and expand into giant proportions. Prentiss was now a national man. Soon after this, he visited Boston and New York during an exciting political campaign. Throughout the North, wherever he appeared and spoke, he bore the palm from every rival.

The speech of Prentiss in Faneuil Hall will long be remembered as perhaps the finest specimen of oratory ever listened to in that venerable hall. It was at the time said by the men of the North to surpass the best efforts of Fisher Ames. Subsequently he spoke in New York, and for three hours held spell-bound an immense audience.

The writer was informed by a venerable judge, of New Jersey, that he had never believed any man possessed such powers of oratory as to interest him and chain his attention for that length of time. Hearing this young man from the wilds of Mississippi could do so, he embraced the first opportunity of hearing him. When he reached the place, he found the assemblage very great, and with difficulty he succeeded in reaching a point where he might hear well. He was unable to procure a seat, and was compelled to stand, thoroughly jammed by the crowd. He took out his watch to time him, as he commenced, and noting the minute, he essayed to replace his watch: something said arrested his attention and his hands from their work of putting the watch in its fob.

"There was something, sir, in his eye," said he, "which startled me, and then the words came bubbling up spontaneously as spring water, so full of power, so intensely brilliant, and his figures so bold, original, and illustrating, and the one following the other in such quick succession; the flights of imagination, so new, so eloquent, and so heart-searching — that I found it impossible to take my eyes from his face, or my ears from drinking in every word. At one time, so intense were my feelings under the effect of his words and the powerful impression they were making on my mind, that I thought I should faint. I forgot the presence of the crowd, and, though seventy years of age, felt no fatigue from my standing position. In truth, sir, I was unconscious of the time — equally so of the presence of any one but the speaker. I perceived that his physical man was failing under his effort, and so intense was my sympathy that I found myself breathing rapidly and painfully; and yet, when he exclaimed, 'My powers fail!' and sank into his seat completely exhausted, I regretted the necessity which compelled him to stop. It was not until then that I found my hand still holding my watch at the opening of its pocket, where, in my excitement, I had forgotten to deposit it. I looked, and I had been standing unmoved in the same position and intently listening for three hours and fifteen minutes. Near me stood one old as myself — a friend, a neighbor, and a minister of the gospel; he was livid with excitement, and his lips trembled as he said to me: 'Will you ever doubt again that God inspires man?' "

Notwithstanding the immense Democratic majority in the State, the Whigs determined to run Prentiss for Congress: the election, at that time, was by general ticket, and there were two members to be elected: the Whig nomination was Prentiss and Wood; the Democratic, Claiborne and Gholson.

Claiborne was a native of the State, and the son of General Ferdinand Claiborne, a young man of very superior abilities, and at the time a member of Congress. McNutt was the Democratic candidate for Governor. The campaign was a most animated one, and Prentiss addressed the people in very nearly every county in the State; the people, *en masse*, flocked to hear him, and his name was in every mouth. The Democratic nominees did not attempt to meet him on the stump. His march through the State was over the heads of the people, hundreds following him from county to county in his ovation. McNutt alone attempted to meet him and speak with him, and he only once. McNutt was a Virginian, and was a man of stupendous abilities; he was a lawyer by profession, and was Governor of the State. Next to Poindexter, he was the ablest man who ever filled the chair. Unfortunately, like most of the young and talented of that day in the West, he was too much addicted to the intoxicating bowl. Upon the only meeting of these, Prentiss and McNutt, the latter, in his speech, urged as a reason for the rejection or defeat of the former his dissipated habits, admitted his great abilities, his masterly genius, pronounced him the first man of the age intellectually, but deplored his habits, which were rendering him useless, with all his genius, learning, and eloquence.

Prentiss, in reply, said: "My fellow-citizens, you have heard the charge against my morals, sagely, and, I had almost said, soberly made by the gentleman, the Democratic nominee for the chief executive office of this State: had I said this, it would have been what the lawyers term a misnomer. It would be impossible for him to do or say anything soberly, for he has been drunk ten years; not yesterday, or last week, in a frolic, or, socially, with the good fellows, his friends, at the genial and generous board — but at home, and by himself and demijohn; not upon the rich wines of the Rhine or the Rhone, the Saone or the Guadalquivir; not with high-spirited or high-witted men, whose souls, when mellowed with glorious wine, leap from their lips sublimated in words swollen with wit, or thought brilliant and dazzling as the blood of the grape inspiring them — no; but by himself: selfish and apart from witty men, or ennobling spirits, in the secret seclusion of a dirty little back-room, and on corn-whiskey! — these only, communing in affectionate brotherhood, the son of Virginia and the spirits of old Kentucky! Why, fellow-citizens, as the Governor of the State, he refused to sign the gallon-law until he had tested, by experiment, that a gallon would do him all day!

"Now I will admit, fellow-citizens, that sometimes, when in the enjoyment of social communion with gentlemen, I am made merry with these, and the rich wines of glorious France. It is then I enjoy the romance of life. Imagination, stimulated with the juice of the grape, gave to the world the Song of Solomon, and the Psalms of that old poet of the Lord — glorious old David.

"The immortal verse of wandering old Homer, the blind son of Scio's isle, was the inspiration of Samian wine; and good old Noah, too, would have sung some good and merry song, from the inspiration of the juice of the vine he planted, but having to wait so long, his thirst, like the Democratic nominee's here, became so great, that he was tempted to drink too deeply, and got too drunk to sing; and this, I fancy, is the true reason why this distinguished gentleman never sings.

"Perhaps there is no music in his soul. The glug-glug-glug of his jug, as he tilts and pours from its reluctant mouth the corn-juice so loved of his soul, is all the music dear to his ear, unless it be the same glug-glug-glug as it disappears down his capacious throat. Now, fellow-citizens, during this ardent campaign, which has been so fatiguing, I have only been drunk once. Over in Simpson County I was compelled to sleep in the same bed with this distinguished nominee — this delight of the Democracy — this wonderful exponent of the principles and practices of the unwashed Democracy — and in the morning I found myself drunk on corn-whiskey. I had lain too close to this soaked mass of Democracy, and was drunk from absorption."

This was more than the Governor could stand, and, amidst the shouts and laughter of the assembled multitude, he left the stand, and declined to meet again, before the people, the young Ajax Telemon of the Whig party.

The memory of that campaign will probably never be forgotten in Mississippi. Mothers, in stories of Prentiss, tell it now to their children, and it and he have become a tradition of the early days of Mississippi. The election terminated in the choice of Prentiss and Wood, by a small majority; but the certificate was given, through the basest fraud, to Claiborne and Gholson.

This was contested before the House of Representatives in Congress assembled, and the contestants permitted to be heard on the floor of the House. It was here, in the presence of the assembled wisdom of the nation, Prentiss was to sustain the reputation which had preceded him, and gloriously did he do it. When he rose to commence his speech, all was silent, and every face expressed deep and excited expectation. The unfortunate deformity of his leg was forgotten, in viewing the noble contour of his head and face. Young, and for the first time in such a presence — standing there the impersonation of the State of Mississippi, demanding justice for her at the hands of the nation — he seemed conscious of the responsibility, and confident of his power to sustain this. There was little preliminary in his remarks opening the matter. He went at once, and as a strong man conscious of the right, to the core. He demonstrated, beyond a doubt, his election, and proceeded in a strain of burning invective to expose the fraud of the returning officer, who had shamefully disregarded the popular voice, and shamelessly violated the law he was sworn to obey, in giving the certificate to his defeated competitors. Never did the corruption of party receive so severe an exposition, or a more withering rebuke, than in this speech.

Very soon after he commenced, the Senate chamber was deserted, and the Vice-President and Secretary were left alone. Webster, Benton, Calhoun, Clay, Wright, and Evans came in and ranged themselves near him. Every space large enough, in the chamber, lobby, and galleries, was filled with a listener, and all were still and unmoving, however painful their position, until the enunciation of the last word of that wonderful oration. The speech occupied two hours and forty minutes, and the peroration was thrilling. When exhausted, and closing, he lifted his eyes to the national flag, floating above the Speaker's chair, and said, in an almost exhausted voice, "If, Mr. Speaker, in obedience to the necessities and corrupt behest of party, you are determined to wrest from Mississippi her rights as a sister, and coequal in this union of States, and turn from their seats her representatives constitutionally chosen, and place in their stead the repudiated of her people, strike from the flag which waves above you the star which represents her there; but leave the stripes, apt emblem of your iniquity and her degradation."

An adjournment was immediately moved; the painful excitement was relieved, the spell was broken, and from every side, and from every party, came men to congratulate him. Webster was the first to stretch forth his hand, and with more animation than was his wont, said, in his deep, sonorous tones, "New England claims her own, and is proud of her son."

The House, notwithstanding the demonstrative proof, and its enforcement by the powerful and unanswerable argument of Prentiss, sent the election back to the State, to be determined by a new election. In this, Prentiss and Wood were triumphantly elected. He was not again a candidate, retiring for the time from politics, and giving his undivided attention to his profession.

It was always a matter of astonishment, to all who could never make of a political enemy a personal friend, why it was that Prentiss, so bitter in his political denunciations of political partisans, and so bitter a partisan, should yet, among the opposition, have so many warm admirers and most devoted friends. His nature was sensitive, generous, and confiding. There was no malice festering in his heart, and in his opposition, he was only so to the politics, not the personal qualities of the man. By these he judged of the man, and the character of these regulated his conduct toward him. He did not pass through life without enemies. The man to whom this is possible is one of no positive points in his character, no strength of will, no fixity of purpose, and of but little intellect. Such men never occupy the public attention—are altogether negative, as well in action as in mind. The enemies of Prentiss were such from envy, or political hatred. His great abilities, when brought in contact with those suing for popular favor, so shrivelled and dwarfed them as to inspire only fear and hatred. But men of this character were scarce in that day in Mississippi. Such was the tone of society, and such the education of her sons, that traits so dishonorable rendered odious the man manifesting them, and those of talent and education emigrating to the country soon caught this spirit as by inoculation. If there were any who were influenced by such base and degrading motives, and who felt these a part of their nature, they most generally could command policy enough to conceal them.

No community is long in discovering the genuine from the counterfeit character. It did not require months to learn all the heart, all the nature of Prentiss. Too frequently are great abilities coupled with a mean spirit, and transcendent genius underlaid with a low, grovelling nature; but these may be known by the peculiar form or development of the cranium. The high coronal developments discover the intense moral organization: the lofty and expansive forehead, the steady, unblenching eye, and the easy self-possession of manner are all indications of high moral organization, and the possession of a soul superior to envy, malice, and vindictive hatred, and one to which little meannesses are impossible. Such a head and such a soul had S. S. Prentiss. His whole character was in his face, and so legible that the most illiterate could read it. This won to him like natures, and all such who knew him were instinctively his friends.

Judge Wilkinson was such a man, and though as ardently Democratic as Prentiss was Whig, and as uncompromising in his principles, yet these two were friends in the loftiest sense of the term. Judge

Wilkinson had a difficulty with a tailor in Louisville, Kentucky, who attempted an imposition upon him to which he would not submit. A quarrel ensued, and the knight of the needle and shears determined on revenge. Collecting about him his ready associates, they went to the hotel where Wilkinson lodged, and waylaid him at the door between the dining-parlor and the reception-room, and attacked him on his coming in from supper. In the rencontre three of the assailants were killed, and the remainder of the gang fled. Immediately surrendering himself, he was incarcerated and held for trial: although assaulted with murderous intent, and acting clearly in self-defence, he was denied bail. He was a stranger, and the prejudices of the court and the people of Louisville were so manifest that he demanded and obtained a change of venire.

The trial came off at Harrodsburg. Prentiss, learning the facts and the situation of his friend, volunteered immediately to defend him in court, and to befriend him in any manner possible to him. The celebrated Ben Hardin was employed to assist in the prosecution. The eyes of all Mississippi and Kentucky were turned to Harrodsburg when this trial commenced. Others volunteered — and among these was John Rowan — to assist in the defence. But the case for Wilkinson was conducted exclusively by Prentiss. It continued for some days. John Rowan — so celebrated in the State for his talents and great legal learning, as well as for his transcendent abilities as an advocate — sat by, and trusted all to Prentiss.

There were many sparrings in the course of the trial between Hardin and Prentiss upon points in the law of evidence, and as to the admissibility or rejection of testimony, as also upon many points of the criminal law of England, whether changed or not by statutory provisions of the State.

In one of these, Rowan handed an open authority to Prentiss, and was taunted by Hardin for the act, by saying: "Give your friend all the aid you can: he needs it."

"I only preserved the book open at the page where Mr. Prentiss had marked the law," said Rowan: "he requires no aid from me, brother Hardin. With all your learning and experience, he is more than a match for you."

This Hardin was not long in discovering, and especially did he feel it when Prentiss came to reply to his address to the jury. So long accustomed to defy competition as a criminal lawyer, Hardin was not only surprised at the tact and masterly talent displayed by his adversary, but he was annoyed, and felt that to maintain his prestige as the great criminal lawyer of Kentucky, he must put forth all his powers. He had done so; and in his summing up before the jury he seemed more than himself. When he had concluded there were many who deemed conviction sure.

Prentiss followed, and in his grandest manner tore to tatters every argument and every position advanced and assumed by Hardin. Towering in the majesty of his genius in one of those transcendent flights of imagination so peculiar to him, when his illustrations in figures followed each other in such quick and constant succession as to seem inexhaustible, he turned suddenly upon Hardin, and, stooping his face until it almost touched that of the stern old Kentuckian, he hissed forth: "Dare you, sir, ask a verdict of such a jury as is here sitting upon this testimony? — you, sir, who under the verdict of nature must soon appear before the awful bar to which you now strive prematurely to consign this noble, this gallant young man! Should you succeed, you must meet him there. Could you, in the presence of Almighty God — He who knows the inmost thoughts — justify your work of to-day? His mandate is not to the gibbet. Eternal Justice dictates there, whose decrees are eternal. Do you think of this? Do you defy it? If not — if you invoke it, do it through your acts toward your fellow-man. Have you to-day done unto this man as you would he should do unto you? I pause for a reply — none. Then shudder and repent, for the record even now is making up against you in that high court from which there is no appeal. You, gentlemen of the jury, are no hired advocates: you are not laboring for blood-money. Though your responsibility to your God is equal to his, you will not go to the bar of your Creator with blood — guiltless blood — upon your consciences. You will not, as he will, in that awful presence, on that eventful day, look around you for the accusing spirit of him whom you consigned to the gibbet with a consciousness of his innocence of murder. How will it be with you? (turning again to Hardin.) Ah! how will it be with you? Still silent. Despite the hardness of his features, mercy like a halo sweeps over them, and speaks to you, gentlemen, eloquently: 'Acquit the accused!' Look over yonder, gentlemen: within these walls is one awaiting your verdict in tearless agony — she who but for this untoward event would now have been happy as his bride: she who has cheered him in his prison-cell daily with her presence and lovely soul! Hers, not his fate, is in your hands. To him death is nothing: the brave defy death — the good fear it not; then why should he fear? But she! O God! it is a fearful thing to crush to death with agony the young, hopeful, and loving heart of virtuous woman. His death is only terrible in her future. Go with her, gentlemen, through life; contemplate the wan features of slow decay: see in these the one eternal, harrowing thought; list to the sigh which rives the heart; watch the tear which falls in secret; see her sink into the grave; then turn away, look up into heaven, and from your heart say: 'O God! I did it.' You will not; you cannot; you dare not."

Hardin's conclusion was tame, and without effect; the demonstrations on the part of the jury dispirited him, and his concluding speech had none of the power of his opening. The jury returned a verdict of not guilty, without hesitation. Wilkinson was immediately discharged, and in company with his friends was repairing to the hotel, when, in the warmth of his emotion, he said, laying his hand on the shoulder of Prentiss: "How shall I pay you, my friend, for this great service you have done me?"

"By never mentioning pay again," was the prompt and decisive reply.

CHAPTER XXV.

A FINANCIAL CRASH.

A Wonderful Memory — A Nation without Debt — Crushing the National Bank — Rise of State Banks — Inflated Currency — Grand Flare-up — Take Care of Yourself — Commencing Anew — Failing to Reach an Obtuse Heart — King Alcohol does his Work — Prentiss and Foote — Love Me, Love my Dog — A Noble Spirit Overcome — Charity Covereth a Multitude of Sins.

THE rare combination of the elements of the mind in Mr. Prentiss is only occasionally met with in time. Judgment, imagination, and memory were all transcendent and equal in their respective powers. With such a mind, everything possible to man may be accomplished. The invention is rapid; the combining and

31

applying responds as rapidly; the fitting and the proper wait on these in the judgment, and the emanation of the whole is perfect. The imagination conceives, the memory retains, and the judgment applies. The consummate perfection of all of these elements in one mind, assures greatness. Charles James Fox, one of England's ablest statesmen, said this combination, organized in the brain of Napoleon, was more complete than had existed with any man since the days of Julius Cæsar, and would have made him transcendently great in anything to which he might have addressed his powers. As a poet, he would have equalled Homer; as a lawyer, the author of the Pandects; as an architect, Michael Angelo; as an astronomer, Newton or Galileo; as an actor, Garrick, or his beloved Talma—as he had equalled Cæsar and Hannibal, and greatly surpassed Marlborough, Frederick the Great, and Charles XII.; as an orator, Demosthenes; and as a statesman, the greatest the earth ever knew.

This combination in the mind of Prentiss, with the great development of the organ of language, made him the unrivalled orator of his age. His powers of memory were so great as to astonish even those eminently gifted in the same manner. In reading, he involuntarily committed to memory, whether of prose or poetry. He seemed to have memorized the Bible, Shakspeare, Dryden, Ben Jonson, Byron, and many others of the modern poets. The whole range of literature was at his command: to read once, was always to remember. This capacity to acquire was so great that he would in a month master as much as most men could in twelve.

It appeared immaterial to what he applied himself, the consequence was the same. Scientific research, or light literature; the ordinary occurrences of the day, recorded in the newspapers, or detailed by an occasional visitor—all were remembered, and with truthful exactness. Dates, days, names, and events fastened upon his memory tenaciously, and remained there without an effort. Hence, the fund of information possessed by him astonished the best informed, who were gray with years and reading. The exuberance of his imagination continually supplied new and beautiful imagery to his conversation; and in private intercourse, such was the rich purity of his language, and his ideas so bold and original, that all were willing listeners: no one desired to talk if Prentiss was present and would talk.

The disasters which followed the commercial crisis of 1837

crushed almost every interest in Mississippi: especially was this true of the planting, the great interest of the State. On the healthy condition of him who tills the soil depends that of every other interest. The rapid rise in cotton, commencing in 1832, from the increased demand all over the world for cotton fabrics, caused a heavy immigration to the fertile cotton-lands of the West, and particularly to the extensive and newly acquired lands of Mississippi. The world was at peace, and great prosperity was universal; money was cheap, or rather its representative, bank paper. The system of finance, so wisely conceived and put in practical operation subsequently to the war of 1812, had been disturbed by being made an element in the political struggles of party. It had paid the war debt, and all the expenses of the Government — furnished a uniform currency, equal to, and at the holder's will convertible into coin. Its face was the nation's faith, and its credit equal in New York, London, and Calcutta. A surplus fund was accumulating in the United States Treasury, and the unexampled instance of a nation out of debt, and with an accumulating surplus of money in her treasury, was presented to the world by the United States.

The political economist, from this fact, would naturally infer that the people were heavily taxed: not so; there was not on earth a people who contributed, in proportion to their means, so little to the support of their Government. The tax-gatherer of the nation was never seen or known in the house of any citizen; he knew not that he contributed one dollar to the public treasury. So admirably was the source of revenue contrived, that no man knew or felt he paid a national tax. The Bank of the United States received and disbursed the moneys arising from customs, or tariffs upon imports, without one cent of expense to the Government; affording at the same time every healthy facility to the commerce of the country — holding in check and confining the local State banks to a legitimate business — and was the most complete and perfect fiscal agent ever organized. In the struggle for party ascendency, the idea was conceived of using the bank in aid of one of the factions which divided the country. The machinators of this scheme failed to accomplish it, and, being in power at the time, determined to destroy it, upon the plea of its unconstitutionality, and of having been used to overturn the Government — that is, the party in power. It was declared dangerous to the liberties of the country.

At the expiration of its charter, then approaching, it was refused a renewal. So intimately was it connected with every interest in the country, that its passing out of existence threatened universal bankruptcy. Its branches located at every important commercial point, its credit was universally employed. It furnished exchange at almost a nominal rate upon every commercial city of the world, and permeated every transaction, giving health and vigor as the circulating fluid does the animal system.

Suddenly to arrest and destroy this, was universal ruin. But to serve the behest of party in a double form, it was crushed. But a substitute was proposed by the party interested, and upon whom the responsibility rested — the creation of State banks without limit, which were recommended to discount liberally to the people, and supply the wants created by the withdrawal of the capital and accommodations of the national bank. This recommendation was literally and instantly obeyed. In every State where the dominant party held control — and they did so throughout the South and West — the legislatures made haste to create, without limit, State banks, with power to flood the country with irresponsible bank paper. Each assumed that it must supply not only its portion, but the entire amount of the banking capital withdrawn, and double or treble the circulation. The natural consequence was immense inflation of the currency, or circulating medium, and the rapid appreciation of every species of property in price. Everybody and every interest flourished most prosperously — gaunt poverty had fled the land, and bloated abundance laughed in every home. Suddenly men sprang into importance who a little while before were humble artizans or employed in the meanest capacities. A new El Dorado had been discovered; fortunes were made in a day, without enterprise or work; and unexampled prosperity seemed to cover the land as with a golden canopy — forests were swept away in a week; labor came in crowds to the South to produce cotton; and where yesterday the wilderness darkened over the land with her wild forests, to-day the cotton plantation whitened the earth — production was quadrupled — labor doubled in value, land rose to fearful prices, the wildest extravagance obtained; costly furniture, expensive equipages, ostentatious display — all were contributing to hasten the catastrophe. The wise saw what was impending, and the foolish thought it impossible. All of this was based on credit. The banks were irresponsible, for they were without capital: they had created a credit and loaned it in the shape of bank paper to every one. Finally, the hour came when all was to be paid for. The banks failed—like the fame of woman, a whisper destroys it; so a whisper blew away the banks. They could not redeem their promises to pay. These were no longer available for currency: they had driven from the country the coin, and there was no money. The merchants failed, the planters failed, money appreciated to the gold standard, and property correspondingly depreciated; and ruin—financial ruin—swept over the country as a consuming fire.

Nowhere was this destruction so complete as in Mississippi. The people of the State had been collected from all the States of the West and South. There was no common bond but interest; a healthy public sentiment, which must result from a homogeneous population, was unknown; there was no restraining influence upon the conduct of men, save only the law, and, for the want of efficient administration, this was almost powerless. Every one was making haste to be rich; speculation was wild, and every day was witnessing transactions of doubtful morality. Society was a chaos, and *sauve qui peut*, or, take care of yourself, the rule. Every one who owed money, however inconsiderable the sum, was ruined. Under such circumstances, Prentiss determined on removing from Mississippi, and selected New Orleans for his future home. The civil law, or Roman Code, was the law in Louisiana, and materially differed from the common or English law, which was the law of authority in Mississippi. Very few lawyers coming from the common-law States, have ever been able to succeed in Louisiana, especially after having practised in other States for any length of time. They have not only to learn the civil law, but to unlearn the common. Some, who did not know the extraordinary powers of Prentiss's mind, feared he, like many others who had made the attempt, would fail; but, almost from the moment of his advent at the New Orleans bar, his success was complete. To realize the expectations of the public, required abilities and attainments of the highest order. Fame had heralded his name and powers to every one: all had and did expect from him more than from any other man, and none were disappointed. From this time forward he eschewed politics, and devoted himself to his profession.

Some years before leaving Mississippi, Prentiss had married Miss

Williams, of Adams County. This lady was the daughter of James C. Williams, a large planter; her mother was a Percy, descended from the proud Percys of Northumberland, and was a most accomplished and intellectual woman. Her position was the first among the first, and her birth, blood, and attainments entitled her to the distinction. Her daughter, grown up under her eye and training, was the mother's equal, and fit companion for the man of her choice.

Prentiss had lost everything in the general crash, and was commencing anew, with a growing family to provide for. His business rapidly increased, and his displays at the Bar were frequent and wonderful. Some of these, recited here, might, if such a necessity existed, serve to illustrate his wonderful powers; but there are parties living whose feelings might suffer, and hence I forbear. It is my earnest wish, in recording these recollections, to offend no one; nor will I "set down aught in malice."

The ardent and excitable temperament of Prentiss, combined with his social qualities, required constant excitement. When employed with the duties of his profession, or engaged in any matter of business pertaining to politics, or his relations in any capacity with the world, requiring attention, he was sufficiently excited to afford escape for the restlessness of his mind; nor did this man seem fatigued in such occupations sufficiently to require repose and rest. On the contrary, it seemed to whet his desire for fiercer and more consuming excitement. Whenever he went abroad, the crowd followed him, and the presence of the increasing mass stimulated his feelings to mild, social delight, and this led him too frequently to indulge beyond a proper temperance in the exhilaration of wine. This, superadded to the fire of his genius, was wearing fearfully his vigorous physique.

For the first time, in the case of fraud against James Irwin, in which he made one of the most powerful efforts of his life, he manifested mental as well as physical fatigue. It was my good fortune to listen to that speech made to a New Orleans jury. I had listened many times to his speeches, and had thought some of these could never be surpassed by any man, not even by himself, and especially that delivered in Faneuil Hall, Boston, and the one delivered from the steps of the court-house at Vicksburg, after returning from his political campaign when a candidate for Congress. But this one was even grander and more powerful than any I had ever heard from him. Returning from the court-house with him upon that occasion, I remarked a flagging in the brilliancy of his conversation. For a moment he sat silent in the carriage, and then remarked: "I was never so much fatigued; I am afraid I am getting old. I have not an idea in my brain."

"Certainly, you have poured out enough to-day to empty any brain," was my reply; "and you should be content not to have another for a month. But I am sorry your invective was so severe."

"Ah! my old friend," he continued, "he deserved it all! From my heart I feel he deserved it all! The magnitude of his iniquities inspired the rebuke, and I exhausted my quiver in the attempt to pierce his shame; but I failed. The integuments of his sensibility are armor against the shafts from my bow; and I feel the failure, but I don't regret the attempt: the intention was as sincere as the failure has been signal."

"Why, what do you mean?" I asked; "for, assuredly, you have to-day made the most powerful and telling speech of your life."

"Yes, telling upon the audience, perhaps, but not upon the victim — he escapes unscathed. I care nothing for the crack of the rifle, if the bullet flies wide of the mark. I wanted to reach his heart, and crush it to remorse; but I have learned his moral obtusity is superior to shame. I have failed in my attempt."

This speech was followed by a challenge to Prentiss from the son of Irwin. This was promptly accepted, and a meeting was only prevented by the interference of parties from Kentucky, Mississippi, and Louisiana. The settlement was honorable to both parties. Soon after, young Irwin died by his own hand. He was a youth of brilliant parts, and promised a future of usefulness and distinction.

The habits of Prentiss were daily growing worse — the excitement he craved he found in the intoxicating bowl. The influence of his lovely and loving wife greatly restrained him; but when she was away, he was too frequently surrounded by his friends and admirers, and in social conviviality forgot the prudence of restraint, and indulged to excess. The more this indulgence was tolerated, the more exacting it became. The great strength of his nervous system had successfully resisted the influence of these indulgences, and after potations deep and long, it was remarked that they had no inebriating effect upon him. This nervous strength by degrees yielded to the power of alcohol, and as he advanced in life it was apparent the poison was doing its work.

Now it was that he found it necessary, in order to stimulate his genius to its wonted activity and vigor, on occasions demanding all his powers, to resort to artificial stimulants. His friends urged upon him temperance, to forbear altogether, to visit his mother and friends in Maine, recreate amidst the scenes of his childhood, and to do so in company with his wife and his lovely children, for they were all a parent could wish them to be. He promised to do so. Sad memory brings up our last meeting, and when the subject of his intemperance was the theme of our parting conversation. We stood together upon the portico of the St. Charles Hotel; he was preparing to leave for Maine; I was leaving for my home in the country.

"You still keep the old cane," he said, taking from my hand his gift many years before.

"I shall do so, Prentiss, while I live."

He continued to view the head, upon which our names were engraved, and a melancholy shade gathered upon his features. "Oh, were I," said he, "to-day, what I was the day I gave you this!" and he paused many minutes; still the shade darkened, and his voice trembled as he proceeded: "We were both young then, and how light our hearts were! We have gathered about us household gods, and we worship them; how sad to think we shall have to leave them! You married long before I did. Your children will grow up while yet you live; I shall never see mine other than children."

"Say not so, Prentiss. You are yet young. You have but one thing to do, and you will live to see those boys men; and what may you not expect of them, with such a mother to aid you in rearing them!"

"I know what you mean, and I know what I will; but, like Laocoon in the folds of the snake, the serpent of habit coils around me, and I fear its strength is too powerful for mine. Perhaps, had my angel of to-day been my angel when first a man, I had never wooed the scorpion which is stinging me to death; but all I can do I will. This is all I can promise. Keep this stick to remember me: it will support you when tottering with the weight of years, and with strength will endure. When age has done her work, and you are in the grave, give it to your son to remember us both. Farewell." With a clasp of the hand we parted, never to meet again. Not long after, he died at Natchez, and, in the family cemetery of the Sargents, sleeps near the city.

But few of the speeches of Prentiss were ever reported, and though they are like and have the ring of the true metal, yet not one of them is correctly reported. The fragment given in a former chapter is the report of one who heard it, and who wrote it the very hour of its delivery, to myself, that the information of the acquittal might be communicated to the friends of the lady Judge Wilkinson was about to be married to, who resided in my immediate neighborhood. There is not a word of it in the reporter's speech, which was some time after written out from notes. These speeches, with the traditions of his fame, will serve to perpetuate his memory as perhaps the most gifted man, as an orator, that adorned his generation.

In stature he was below the ordinary standard, and his lameness seemed to dwarf even this. His head was large, round, and high; his forehead expansive, high, and rising almost perpendicularly above his eyes, which were gray, deep set, and brilliant; his nose was straight and beautifully chiselled, thin, and the nostrils large, and swelling and expanding when excited. In speaking, his eyes blazed with a most peculiar expression. His chin was broad, square, and strong. His mouth was the most striking feature of his face — large and flexible, with a constant twitching about the corners. The entire contour of the face indicated humor, combined with firmness. This latter trait was also indicated in the large, strong under jaw — no trait was more prominent in his character than this. Yet he was slow to anger, and always conciliatory in language and manners. He was charitable in the extreme toward others for any laches in principle; always ready to find an excuse for the short-comings of others. Yet no man adhered more closely and more steadily to his principles and opinions. He never gave an insult, unless greatly provoked, but never failed to resent one; always loath to quarrel, but, once in, bore himself like a man, and a brave one. The high oval crown of his head confessed high moral qualities; here the moral organs were in wonderful development. Too generous to be malicious, he was ever ready to forgive, and too noble to permit his worst enemy to be slandered in his presence.

There was once a quarrel between Prentiss and that erratic man of wonderful genius, H. S. Foote. This culminated in a hostile meeting, in which Foote was wounded. In their impulsiveness these two were very like, as also in the generosity of their natures. Neither bore the other malice beyond the conflict, and neither ever permitted an insult to be offered to the name of the other in his absence. A short time after this affair, Prentiss was with some friends in Cincinnati. There is always to be found men who swell their importance by toadying men of character and eminence. Such are as frequently found in Cincinnati as elsewhere.

One of these had sought out Prentiss, and was attempting to make himself agreeable to him by abusing Foote: this abuse wound up by denouncing the distinguished Mississippian as a dog. Prentiss turned sharply upon him with the exclamation: "If he is a dog, sir, he is our dog, and you shall not abuse him in my presence!" The discomfiture of the toady may be easily imagined; he slunk away, nor did he again obtrude his unwanted presence upon Prentiss during his stay.

Few men have ever so fastened themselves upon the affections of their friends as did Prentiss: his qualities of heart and head were fascinating, almost beyond humanity; none ever met him for a day and went away unattached; strangers, who knew him not, listening to him, not only admired, but loved him. He never lost a friend; and all his enemies were political, or from envy. In the society of ladies he was extremely diffident and unobtrusive, and always apprehensive lest he should be unable to entertain them agreeably.

On one occasion, not long before our final parting, he said he had committed two great errors in his life: leaving his native home to find one in the South, and not marrying when he first commenced the practice of law. "My constitution was strong and suited to a northern climate, and there home-influences would have restrained propensities that have grown with indulgence, and are threatening in their consequences. I feel this: I am not the strong man I was; mind and body are failing, and the beautiful lines of our friend Wild are constantly recurring to my mind:

"'My life is like the autumn leaf,
Which trembles in the moon's pale ray:
Its hold is frail, its date is brief,
Restless, and soon to pass away.'

"Why did not Wild give his life to literature, instead of the musty maxims of the law. Little as he has written, it is enough to preserve his fame as a true poet; and though he has been a member of Congress, and a distinguished one, a lawyer, and a distinguished one, his fame and name will only be perpetuated by his verse, so tender, so touching, and so true to the feelings of the heart. It is the heart that he lives in. Ah! it is the heart only which forms and fashions the romance of life; and without this romance, life is scarcely worth the keeping.

"'T is midnight — on the mountains brown
The cold round moon shines deeply down;
Blue roll the waters, blue the sky
Spreads like an ocean hung on high,
Bespangled with those isles of light,
So wildly, spiritually bright;
Who ever gazed upon them shining,
And turned to earth without repining,
Nor wished for wings to flee away,
And mix with their eternal ray?"

We feel as Byron did when he imagined these lines. I see him with upturned eyes gazing on the blue expanse above, watching the stars; thinking of heaven; feeling earth, and hating it, and his soul flying away from it, to meet and mingle in the firmament above him with the spiritually bright and heavenly pure brilliants sparkling on her diadem. How mean — how miserably mean this earth, and all it gives! One diamond in a world of dirt. The soul that loves and contemplates the eternal — shall it shake off at once the miserable clod, and in a moment glisten among the millions, pure, bright, and lovely as these? There is but one idea of hell — eternal torture! But every man has his own idea of heaven: yet, with all, its chiefest attribute is eternal happiness. The wretch craves it for rest; he who never knew care or suffering, desires it for enjoyment; and the wildest imagination sublimates its bliss to love and beauty. And God only knows what it is, or in what it consists. But we shall know, and I, in a little time. On Him who gave me being I confidently rely for all which is destined in my future."

His spirit was eminently worshipful. The wisdom and goodness of God he saw in every creature; he contemplated these as a part of the grand whole, and saw a union and use in all for the harmony of the whole; he saw all created nature linked, each filling and subserving a part, in duties and uses, as designed, and, his mind filled with the contemplation, his soul expanded in love and worship of the great Architect who conceived and created all.

With all this might of mind and beauty of soul, there lurked a demon to mar and destroy. It worked its end: let us draw a veil over the frailties of poor human nature, and, in the admiration of the genius and the soul, forget the foibles and frailties of the body.

CHAPTER XXVI.

ACADIAN FRENCH SETTLERS.

Sugar *vs.* Cotton — Acadia — A Specimen of Mississippi French Life — Bayou La Fourche — The Great Flood — Theological Arbitration — A Rustic Ball — Old-fashioned Weddings — Creoles and Quadroons The Planter — Negro Servants — Gauls and Anglo-Normans — Antagonism of Races.

FORTY years ago, there was quite an excitement among the cotton-planters, in the neighborhood of Natchez, upon the subject of sugar-planting in the southern portion of Louisiana. At that time it was thought the duty (two and a half cents per pound) on imported sugars would be continued as a revenue tax, and that it would afford sufficient protection to make the business of sugar-planting much more profitable than that of cotton. The section of country attracting the largest share of attention for this purpose was the Teche, or Attakapas country, the Bayous La Fourche, Terre Bonne, and Black. The Teche and La Fourche had long been settled by a population, known in Louisiana as the Acadian French. These people, thus named, had once resided in Nova Scotia and Lower Canada, or Canada East as now known. When peopled by the French, Nova Scotia was called Acadia. Upon the conquest by the English, these people were expelled the country, and in a most inhuman and unchristian manner. They were permitted to choose the countries to which they would go, and were there sent by the British Government. Many went to Canada, some to Vincennes in Indiana, some to St. Louis, Cape Girardeau, Viedepouche, and Kaskaskia in Mississippi, and many returned to France.

Upon the cession, or rather donation to Spain of Louisiana by France, these, with many others of a population similar to these, from the different arrondissements of France, were sent to Louisiana, and were located in Opelousas, Attakapas, La Fourche, and in the parishes of St. John the Baptist, St. Charles, and St. James (parishes constituting the Acadian coast on the Mississippi). On the La Fourche they constituted, forty years ago, almost the entire population. They were illiterate and poor. Possessing the richest lands on earth, which they had reclaimed from the annual inundations of the Mississippi River by levees constructed along the margins of the stream — with a climate congenial and healthful, and with every facility afforded by the navigation of the bayou and the Mississippi for reaching the best market for all they could produce — yet, with all these natural advantages, promising to labor and enterprise the most ample rewards, they could not be stimulated to industry or made to understand them.

They had established their homes on the margin of the stream, and cleared a few acres of the land donated by the Government, upon which to grow a little corn and a few vegetables. With a limited amount of stock, which found subsistence upon the cane and grass of the woods, and with the assistance of a shot-gun, they managed to subsist — as Peake's mother served the Lord — after a fashion.

Their houses were unique: a slender frame, often of poles cut from the forest, and rudely squared, served the purpose. Into the studding were placed pins, extending from one to the other, horizontally, and about ten inches apart. The long gray moss of the country was then gathered and thrown by layers into a pit dug for the purpose, with the soil, until the pit was full, when water was added in sufficient quantities to wet the mass through; this done, all who are assisting in the construction of the house — men, women, boys, and girls — jump in upon it, and continue to tramp until mud and moss are completely intermingled and made of proper consistence, when it is gathered up and made into rolls about two feet long. These rolls are laid over the pins, commencing at the bottom or sill of the building, when each roll is bent down at the ends, covering the intervals between the pins, pressed hardly together, and smoothed with the hands, inside and out, forming a wall some five inches in thickness, with a perfectly smooth surface. The roof is first put on, and the floors laid. When this mud dries thoroughly it is white-washed; the house is then complete, and presents quite a neat appearance. It will continue to do so if the white-washing is annually continued. If, however, this is neglected, the lime falls off in spots, and the primitive mud comes out to view: then the appearance is anything but pleasant. No pains are taken to ornament their yards, or gather about them comforts. There is a pig or two in a pen in the corner of the yard, a hen-roost immediately at the house, a calf or two at large, and numerous half-starved, mangy dogs—and innumerable ragged, half-naked children, with little, black, piercing eyes, and dishevelled, uncombed hair falling about sallow, gaunt faces, are commingling in the yard with chickens, dogs, and calves. A sallow-faced, slatternly woman, bareheaded, with uncared-for hair, long, tangled, and black, with her dress tucked up to her knees, bare-footed and bare-legged, is wading through the mud from the bayou, with a dirty pail full of muddy Mississippi water.

A diminutive specimen of a man, clad in blue cottonade pants and hickory shirt, barefooted, with a palm-leaf hat upon his head, and an old rusty shot-gun in his hands, stands upon the levee, casting an inquiring look, first up and then down the bayou, deeply desiring and most ardently expecting a wandering duck or crane, as they fly along the course of the bayou. If unfortunately they come within reach of his fusee, he almost invariably brings them down. Then there is a shout from the children, a yelp from the dogs, and all run to secure the game; for too often, "No duck, no dinner." Such a home and such inhabitants were to be seen on Bayou La Fourche forty years ago, and even now specimens of the genuine breed may there be found, as primitive as were their ancestors who first ventured a home in the Mississippi swamps.

The stream known as Bayou La Fourche, or The Fork, is a large stream, some one hundred yards wide, leaving the Mississippi at the town of Donaldsonville, eighty miles above the city of New Orleans, running south-southeast, emptying into the Gulf, through Timbalier Bay, and may properly be termed one of the mouths of the Mississippi. Its current movement does not in high water exceed three miles an hour, and when the Mississippi is at low water, it is almost imperceptible. Large steamers, brigs, and schooners come into it when the river is at flood, and carry out three or four hundred tons of freight each at a time.

The lands upon the banks of this stream are remarkably fertile, entirely alluvial, and decline from the bank to the swamp, generally some one or two miles distant. This Acadian population was sent here during the Spanish domination, and with a view to opening up to cultivation this important tract of country. It was supposed they would become — under the favorable auspices of their emigration to the country, and with such facilities for accumulating money — a wealthy and intelligent population. This calculation was sadly disappointed. The mildness of the climate and the fruitfulness of the soil combined to enervate, instead of stimulating them to active industry, without which there can be no prosperity for any country. A few acres, though half cultivated, were found sufficient to yield an ample support, and the mildness of the climate required but little provision for clothing. Here, in this Eden upon earth, these people continued to live in a simplicity of primitive ignorance and indolence scarcely to be believed by any but an actual observer. Their implements of agriculture were those of two centuries before. More than half the population wore wooden shoes, when they wore any at all. Their wants were few, and were all supplied at home. Save a little flour, powder, and shot, they purchased nothing. These were paid for by the sale of the produce of the poultry-yard — the prudent savings from the labor of the women — to the market-boats from the city.

There were, at the period of which I write, but half a dozen Americans upon the bayou. These had found the country illy adapted to the growth of cotton, and some of them had commenced the planting of sugar-cane. The results from this were very satisfactory, and consequently stimulating to the enterprise of men of means, who felt they could be more profitably employed in this new culture than in cotton, even in the very best cotton regions.

There was one man of high intelligence and long experience who denied this — Stephen Duncan, of Natchez — and the subsequent experience of many brought bitter regret that they had not yielded to the counsels of Dr. Duncan.

The great flood of 1828 had not touched the La Fourche or Teche, while the entire alluvial plain above had been covered many feet, and for many months. This was the most terrible inundation, perhaps, ever experienced in that region; and every one appeared to be now satisfied that to continue to cultivate lands already reduced to man's dominion, or to open and prepare any more, subject to this scourge, was madness. Hence the emigration from this chosen section to the new El Dorado. Lands rose rapidly in South Louisiana as an effect of this, while above, in the flooded district, they were to be bought for almost a nominal price. Those who ventured to purchase these and reduce them to cultivation realized fortunes rapidly; for there was not a sufficient flood to reach them again for ten years. The levees by this time had become so extended as to afford almost entire immunity against the floods of annual occurrence. The culture of sugar received a new impetus and began rapidly to increase, and capital came flowing in. Population of an industrious and hardy character was filling up the West, and the demand from that quarter alone was equal to the production, and both were increasing so rapidly as to induce the belief that it would be as much as all the sugar lands in the State could accomplish to supply this demand. Steam power for crushing the cane was introduced — an economy of labor which enhanced the profits of the production — and a new and national interest was developed, rendering more and more independent of foreign supply, at least that portion of the Union most difficult of access to foreign commerce — the great and growing West.

The Americans, or those Americans speaking English alone, immigrating into these sections of Louisiana, so far as the language, manners, and customs of the people were concerned, were going into a foreign land. The language of the entire population was French, or a patois, as the European French term it — a provincialism which a Parisian finds it difficult to understand. The ignorance and squalid poverty of these people put their society entirely out of the question, even if their language had been comprehensible. They were amiable, kind, law-abiding, virtuous, and honest, beyond any population of similar character to be found in any country. Out of some fifty thousand people, extending over five or six parishes, such a thing as a suit for slander, or an indictment for malicious mischief, or a case of bastardy was not known or heard of once in ten years. This will seem strange when we reflect that at this time schools were unknown, and not one out of fifty of the people could read or write, and when it was common for the judge of the District Court to ask, when a grand jury was impanelled, if there was a man upon it who could write, that he might make him foreman. And not unfrequently was he compelled to call from the court-room one who could, and trump him on the jury for a foreman, as the action was termed. There was not upon the La Fourche, which comprised three large parishes, but one pleasure carriage, and not half a dozen ladies' bonnets. The females wore a colored handkerchief tastily tied about their heads, when visiting or at church; and when not, not anything but blowzed, uncombed hair.

The enterprise of the new-comers did not stimulate to emulation the action of these people. They were content and unenvious, and when kindly received and respectfully treated, were social and generous in their intercourse with their American neighbors. They were confiding and trustful; but once deceived, they were not to be won back, but only manifested their resentment by withdrawing from communicating with the deceiver, and ever after distrusting, and refusing him their confidence. They were universally Catholic; consequently, sectarian disputes were unknown. They practised eminently the Christian virtues, and were constant in their attendance at mass. The priest was the universal arbiter in all disputes, and his decision most implicitly acquiesced in. They had a horror of debt, and lawsuits, and would sacrifice any property they might have, to meet punctually an obligation. Fond of amusements, their social meetings, though of most primitive character, were frequent and cordial. They observed strictly the exactions of the Church, especially Lent; but indulged the Carnival to its wildest extent. Out of Lent they met to dance and enjoy themselves, weekly, first at one, and then at another neighbor's house; and with the natural taste of their race, they would appear neatly and cleanly dressed in the attire fabricated by their own hands in the loom and with the needle.

The method of invitation to these reunions was simple and speedy. A youth on his pony would take a small wand, and tie to its top end a red or white flag, and ride up and down the bayou, from the house where the ball was intended, for two or three miles; returning, tie the wand and flag to flaunt above the gate, informing all—"*This is the place.*" All were welcome who came, and everything was conducted with strict regard to decent propriety. Nothing boisterous was ever known—no disputing or angry wrangling, for there was no cause given; harmony and happiness pervaded all, and at proper time and in a proper manner all returned to their homes.

Marriages, almost universally, were celebrated at the church, as in all Catholic countries. The parsonage is at the church, and the priest always on hand, at the altar or the grave; and almost daily, in this dense population, a marriage or funeral was seen at the church. It was the custom for the bride and groom, with a party of friends, all on horseback, to repair without ceremony to the church, where they were united in matrimony by the good priest, who kissed the bride, a privilege he never failed to put into execution, when he blessed the couple, received his fee, and sent them away rejoicing. This ceremony was short, and without ostentation; and then the happy and expectant pair, often on the same horse, would return with the party as they had come, with two or three musicians playing the violin in merry tunes on horseback, as they joyfully galloped home, where a ball awaited them at night, and all went merry with the married belle.

These people are Iberian in race, are small in stature, of dark complexion, with black eyes, and lank black hair; their hands and feet are small, and beautifully formed, and their features regular and handsome; many of their females are extremely beautiful. These attain maturity very early, and are frequently married at thirteen years of age. In more than one instance, I have known a grandmother at thirty. As in all warm countries, this precocious maturity is followed with rapid decay. Here, persons at forty wear the appearance of those in colder climates of sixty years. Notwithstanding this apparent early loss of vigor, the instances of great longevity are perhaps more frequent in Louisiana than in any other State of the Union. This, however, can hardly be said of her native population: emigrants from high latitudes, who come after maturity, once acclimated, seem to endure the effects of climate here with more impunity than those native to the soil.

The Bayou Plaquemine formerly discharged an immense amount of water into the lakes intervening between the La Fourche and the Teche. These lakes have but a narrow strip of cultivable land. Along the right margin of the La Fourche, and the left of the Teche, they serve as a receptacle for the waters thrown from the plantations and those discharged by the Atchafalayah and the Plaquemine, which ultimately find their way to the Gulf through Berwick's Bay. They are interspersed with small islands: these have narrow strips of tillable land, but are generally too low for cultivation; and when the Mississippi is at flood, they are all under water, and most of them many feet. The La Fourche goes immediately to the Gulf, between Lake Barataria and these lakes, affording land high enough, when protected as they now are, for settlement, and cultivation to a very great extent. Its length is some one hundred miles, and the settlements extend along it for eighty miles. These are continuous, and nowhere does the forest intervene.

At irregular distances between these Acadian settlements, large sugar plantations are found. These have been extending for years, and increasing, absorbing the habitats of these primitive and innocent people, who retire to some little ridge of land deeper in the swamp, a few inches higher than the plane of the swamp, where they surround their little mud-houses with an acre or so of open land, from the products of which, and the trophies of the gun and fishing-line and hook, and an occasional frog, and the abundance of crawfish, they contrive to eke out a miserable livelihood, and afford the fullest illustration of the adage, " Where ignorance is bliss, it is folly to be wise."

The contrast between these princely estates, and the palatial mansions which adorn them, and make a home of luxuriant beauty, and the little log huts, their immediate neighbors, tells at once that the population is either very rich or very poor, and that under such circumstances the communication must be extremely limited; for the ignorance of the poor unfits them for social and intelligent intercourse with their more wealthy and more cultivated neighbors. This is true whether the planter is French or American. The remarkable salubrity of the climate, combined with the comforts and luxuries of home, causes the planter to spend most of his time there, where he can give his attention to his business and mingle with his brother planters in a style and manner peculiar to Louisiana and the tastes of her people. Intercommunication is facilitated by steamboat travel, and as every plantation is located upon a navigable stream, the planter and family can at any time suiting his business go with little trouble to visit his friends, though they may be hundreds of miles apart. Similarity of pursuit and interest draw these together. There is no rivalry, and consequently no jealousy between them. All their relations are harmonious, and their intercourse during the summer is continuous, for at that season the business of the plantation may be safely trusted to a manager, one of whom is found on every plantation.

This social intercourse is highly promotive of a general amity, as it cultivates an intimacy which at once familiarizes every one with the feelings, situation, and intentions of the other. Sometimes the contiguity of plantations enables the families of planters to exchange formal morning and evening calls, but most generally the distance to be overgone is too great for this. Then the visiting is done by families, and extends to days, and sometimes weeks. Provisions are so abundant that the extra consumption is never missed, and the residences are always of such dimensions that the visitors seem scarcely to increase the family — never to be in the way; and the suits of apartments occupied by them were built and furnished for the purpose to which they are then devoted. The visitor is at home. The character of the hospitality he is enjoying permits him to breakfast from seven till ten, alone, or in company with the family if he chooses. Horses, dogs, and guns for the gentlemen — billiards, the carriage, music, or promenading, with cards, chess, backgammon, or dominos for the ladies, to pass away the day until dinner. At this meal the household and guests unite, and the rich viands, wines, and coffee make a feast for the body and sharpen the wit to a feast of the soul. This society is the freest and most refined to be found in the country.

Upon the coast of the Mississippi, from Baton Rouge to many miles below the city, the proximity of the large plantations presents an opportunity of close and constant intercourse. A very large majority of these are the property and habitations of the cultivated and intelligent Creoles of the State. And here let me explain the term Creole, which has led to so many ludicrous, and sometimes to painful mistakes. It is an arbitrary term, and imported from the West Indies into Louisiana. Its original meaning was a native born of foreign parents; but universal use has made it to mean, in Louisiana, nothing more than simply "native;" and it is applied indiscriminately to everything native to the State — as creole cane, creole horse, creole negro, or creole cow. Many confound its meaning with that of quadroon, and suppose it implies one of mixed blood, or one with whose blood mingles that of the African — than which no meaning is more foreign to the word.

The Creole planters, or what are termed French Creoles, are descended from a very different race from the Acadian Creole, or Ibérian. The first colonists who came to Louisiana were men of the first blood and rank in France. The Ibervilles, the Bienvilles, St. Denises, and many others, were of noble descent; and the proud prestige of their names and glorious deeds still clings around their descendants now peopling the lands they conquered from the desert, the savage, and the flood. These daring men brought with them the chivalrous spirit which descended to their sons — the open, gallant bearing; the generous hospitality; the noble humanity; the honor which prefers death to a stain, and the soul which never stoops to a lie, a fraud, or a meanness degrading to a gentleman. They have been born upon the banks of the great river of the world; they have seen all the developments of talent, time, and enterprise which have made their country great as the river through which it flows. Accustomed from infancy to look upon this scene and these developments, their souls with their ideas have been sublimated, and they are a population unsurpassed in the higher attributes of humanity, and the nobler sympathies of man, by any on the face of the earth — surrounded by wealth, tangible and substantial, descending from generation to generation, affording to each all the blessings wealth can give.

The spirit of hospitality and independence has ennobled the sons, as hereditary wealth and privilege had the sires who planted this colony. These sires laid the foundation of this wealth, in securing for their posterity the broad acres of this fat land where now they are to be found. None have emigrated: conscious of possessing the noblest heritage upon earth, they have remained to eliminate from this soil the wealth which in such abundance they possess. As they were reared, they have reared their sons; the lessons of truth, virtue, honor have borne good fruit. None can say they ever knew a French Creole a confirmed drunkard or a professional gambler. None ever knew an aberration of virtue in a daughter of one.

The high-bred Creole lady is a model of refinement — modest, yet free in her manners; chaste in her thoughts and deportment; generous in her opinions, and full of charity; highly cultivated intellectually and by association; familiar from travel with the society of Europe; mistress of two, and frequently of half a dozen languages, versed in the literature of all. Accustomed from infancy to deport themselves as ladies, with a model before them in their mothers, they grow up with an elevation of sentiment and a propriety of deportment which distinguishes them as the most refined and polished ladies in the whole country. There is with these a softness of deportment and delicacy of expression, an abstinence from all violent and boisterous expressions of their feelings and sentiments, and above all, the entire freedom from petty scandal, which makes them lovely, and to be loved by every honorable and high-bred gentleman who may chance to know them and cultivate their association. Indeed, this is a characteristic of the gentlemen as well as the ladies.

These people may have a feud, and sometimes they do; but this rarely remains long unsettled. No one will ever hear it publicly alluded to, and assuredly they will never hear it uttered in slanderous vituperation of the absent party. I may be permitted here to narrate an incident illustrative of this peculiarity.

A gentleman, knowing of a dissension between two parties, was dining with one of them, in company with several others. This guest spoke to the hostess disparagingly of the enemy of her husband, who, hearing the remark, rebuked his officious guest by remarking to him: "Doctor, my lady and myself would prefer to find out the foibles and sins of our neighbors ourselves." The rebuke was effectual, and informed the doctor, who was new in the country, of an honorable feeling in the refined population of the land of his adoption alien to that of his birth, and which he felt made these people the superior of all he had ever known.

No one has ever travelled upon one of those palatial steamers abounding on the Mississippi, in the spring season of the year, when the waters swell to the tops of the levees, lifting the steamer above the level of the great fields of sugar-cane stretching away for miles to the forest on either bank of that mighty river, who has not been delighted with the lovely homes, surrounded with grounds highly cultivated and most beautifully ornamented with trees, shrubs, and flowers, which come upon the view in constant and quick succession, as he is borne onward rapidly along the accumulated waters of the great river. This scene extends one hundred and fifty miles up the river, and is one not equalled in the world. The plain is continuous and unbroken; nor hill nor stream intersects it but at two points, where the Plaquemine and La Fourche leave it to find a nearer way to the sea; and these are so diminutive, in comparison with all around, that they are passed almost always without being seen.

The fringe of green foliage which is presented by the trees and shrubs adorning each homestead, follows in such rapid succession as to give it a continuous line, in appearance, to the passers-by on the steamer. These, denuded of timber to the last tree, the immense fields, only separated by a ditch, or fence, which spread along the river — all greened with the luxuriant sugar-cane, and other crops, growing so vigorously as at once to satisfy the mind that the richness of the soil is supreme — and this scene extending for one hundred and fifty miles, makes it unapproachable by any other cultivated region on the face of the globe. Along the Ganges and the Nile, the plain is extensive. The desolate appearance it presents — the miserable homes of the population, devoid of every ornament, without comfort or plenty in their appearance — the stinted and sparse crops, the intervening deserts of sand, the waste of desolation, spreading away far as the eye can reach — the streams contemptible in comparison, and the squalid, degraded, thriftless people along their banks, make it painful to the beholder, who is borne on his way in some dirty little craft, contrasting so strangely with the Mississippi steamer. Yet, in admirable keeping with everything else, all these present a grand contrast to the valley of the Mississippi, and only prove the latter has no equal in all that pertains to grandeur, beauty, and abundance, on the globe. To appreciate all these, you must know and mingle with the population who have thus ornamented, with labor and taste, the margin of this stream of streams.

As this great expanse of beauty is a fairy-land to the eye, so is the hospitality of its homes a delight to the soul. In this population, if nowhere else in America, is seen a contented and happy people — a people whose pursuit is happiness, and not the almighty dollar. Unambitious of that distinction which only wealth bestows, they are content with an abundance for all their comforts, and for the comfort of those who, as friends or neighbors, come to share it with them. Unambitious of political distinction, despising the noisy tumult of the excited populace, they love their homes, and cultivate the ease of quiet in these delicious retreats, enjoying life as it passes, in social and elegant intercourse with each other, nor envying those who rush into the busy world and hunt gain or distinction from the masses, through the shrewdness of a wit cultivated and debased by trade, or a fawning, insincere sycophancy toward the dirty multitude they despise. By such, these people are considered anomalous, devoid of energy or enterprise, contented with what they have, nor ambitious for more — which, to an American, with whom, if the earth is obtained, the moon must be striven for, is stranger than all else — living indolently at their ease, regardless of ephemeral worldly distinctions, but happy in the comforts of home, and striving only to make this a place for the enjoyment of themselves and those about them.

To the stranger they are open and kind, universally hospitable, never scrutinizing his whole man to learn from his manner or dress whether he comes as a gentleman or a sharper, or whether he promises from appearance to be of value to them pecuniarily in a trade. There is nothing of the huckster in their natures. They despise trade, because it degrades; they have only their crops for sale, and this they trust to their factors; they never scheme to build up chartered companies for gain, by preying upon the public; never seek to overreach a neighbor or a stranger, that they may increase their means by decreasing his; would scorn the libation of generous wine, if they felt the tear of the widow or the orphan mingled with it, and a thousand times would prefer to be cheated than to cheat; despising the vicious, and cultivating only the nobler attributes of the soul.

Such is the character of the educated French Creole planters of Louisiana — a people freer from the vices of the age, and fuller of the virtues which ennoble man, than any it has fallen to my lot to find in the peregrinations of threescore years and ten. The Creoles, and especially the Creole planters, have had little communication with any save their own people. The chivalry of character, in them so distinguising a trait, they have preserved as a heritage from their ancestors, whose history reads more like a romance than the lives and adventures of men, whose nobility of soul and mind was theirs from a long line of ancestors, and brought with them to be planted on the Mississippi in the character of their posterity.

Is it the blood, the rearing, or the religion of these people which makes them what they are? They are full of passion; yet they are gentle and forbearing toward every one whom they suppose does not desire to wrong or offend them; they are generous and unexacting, abounding in the charity of the heart, philanthropic, and seemingly from instinct practising toward all the world all the Christian virtues. They are brave, and quick to resent insult or wrong, and prefer death to dishonor; scrupulously just in all transactions with their fellow-men, forbearing toward the foibles of others, without envy, and without malice. In their family intercourse they are respectful and kind, and particularly to their children: they are cautious never to oppress or mortify a child — directing the parental authority first to the teaching of the heart, then to the mind—instilling what are duties with a tenderness and gentleness which win the affections of the child to perform these through love only. Propriety of deportment toward their seniors and toward each other is instilled from infancy and observed through life. All these lessons are stamped upon the heart, not only by the precepts of parents and all about them, but by their example.

The negro servants constitute a part of every household, and are identified with the family as part of it. To these they are very kind and forbearing, as also to their children, to whom they uniformly speak and act gently. A reproof is never given in anger to either, nor in public, for the purpose of mortifying, but always in private, and gently—in sorrow rather than in anger; and where punishment must be resorted to, it is done where only the parent or master, and the child or servant, can see or know it. This is the example of the Church. The confessional opens up to the priest the errors of the penitent, and they are rebuked and forgiven in secret, or punished by the imposition of penalties known only to the priest and his repentant parishioner. Is it this which makes such models of children and Christians in the educated Creole population of Louisiana? or is it the instinct of race, the consequence of a purer and more sublimated nature from the blue blood of the exalted upon earth? The symmetry of form, the delicacy of feature in the males, their manliness of bearing, and the high chivalrous spirit, as well as the exquisite beauty and grace of their women, with the chaste purity of their natures, would seem to indicate this as the true reason.

All who have ever entered a French Creole family have observed the gentle and respectful bearing of the children, their strict yet unconstrained observance of all the proprieties of their position, and also the affectionate intercourse between these and their parents, and toward each other—never an improper word; never an improper action; never riotous; never disobedient. They approach you with confidence, yet with modesty, and are respectful even in the mirth of childish play. Around the mansions of these people universally are pleasure-grounds, permeated with delightful promenades through parterres of flowers and lawns of grass, covered with the delicious shade thrown from the extended limbs and dense foliage of the great trees. These children, when wandering here, never trespass upon a parterre or pluck unbidden a flower, being restrained only by a sense of propriety and decency inculcated from the cradle, and which grows with their growth, and at maturity is part of their nature. Could children of Anglo-Norman blood be so restrained? Would the wild energies of these bow to such control, or yield such obedience from restraint or love? Certainly in their deportment they are very different, and seem only to yield to authority from fear of punishment, and dash away into every kind of mischief the moment this is removed. Nor is this fear and certainty of infliction of punishment in most cases found to be of sufficient force to restrain these inherent proclivities.

Too frequently with such as these the heart-training in childhood is neglected or forgotten, and they learn to do nothing from love as a duty to God and their fellow-beings. The good priest comes not as a minister of peace and love into the family; but is too frequently held up by the thoughtless parent as a terror, not as a good and loving man, to be loved, honored, and revered, and these are too frequently the raw-head and bloody-bones painted to the childish imagination by those parents who regard the rod as the only reformer of childish errors — who forget the humanities in inspiring the brutalities of parental discipline, as well as the pastoral duties of their vocation. They persuade not into fruit the blossoms of the heart, but crush out the delicate sensibilities from the child's soul by coarse reproofs and brutal bearing toward them. The causes of difference I cannot divine, but I know that the facts exist, and I know the difference extends to the adults of the two races.

The Anglo-American is said to be more enterprising, more energetic and progressive — seeks dangers to overcome them, and subdues the world to his will. The Gallic or French-American is less enterprising, yet sufficiently so for the necessary uses of life. He is more honest and less speculative; more honorable and less litigious; more sincere with less pretension; superior to trickery or low intrigue; more open and less designing; of nobler motives and less hypocrisy; more refined and less presumptuous, and altogether a man of more chivalrous spirit and purer aspirations. The Anglo-American commences to succeed, and will not scruple at the means: he uses any and all within his power, secures success, and this is called enterprise combined with energy. Moral considerations are a slight obstacle. They may cause him to hesitate, but never restrain his action. The maxim is ever present to his mind: it is honorable and respectable to succeed — dishonorable and disreputable to fail; it is only folly to yield a bold enterprise to nice considerations of moral right. If he can avoid the penalties of the civil law, success obviates those of the moral law. Success is the balm for every wrong — the passport to every honor.

> "His race may be a line of thieves,
> His acts may strike the soul with horror;
> Yet infamy no soiling leaves —
> The rogue to-day's the prince to-morrow."

This demoralizes: the expedient for the just — that which will do, not that which should do, if success requires, must be resorted to. This idea, like the pestilence which rides the breeze, reaches every heart, and man's actions are governed only by the law — not by a high moral sense of right. Providence, it is supposed, prepares for all exigencies in the operations of nature. If this be true, it may be that the peculiarities of blood, and the consequence to human character, may, in the Anglo-American, be specially designed for his mission on this continent; for assuredly he is the eminently successful man in all enterprises which are essential in subduing the earth, and aiding in the spreading of his race over this continent. Every opposition to his progress fails, and the enemies of this progress fall before him, and success is the result of his every effort. That the French Creoles retain the chivalry and noble principles of their ancestry is certainly true; but that they have failed to preserve the persevering enterprise of their ancestors is equally true.

Emigration from France, to any considerable extent, was stayed after the cessation of Louisiana to the United States, and the French settlements ceased to expand. The country along and north of Red River, on the Upper Mississippi and the Washita, was rapidly filled up with a bold, hardy American population, between whom and the French sparsely peopling the country about Natchitoches on the Red, and Monroe on the Washita River, there was little or no sympathy; and the consequence was that many of those domiciled already in these sections left, and returned to the Lower Mississippi, or went back to France.

There had been, anterior to this cession, two large grants of land made to the Baron de Bastrop and the Baron de Maison Rouge, upon the Washita and Bartholomew, including almost the entire extent of what is now two parishes. These grants were made by the European Government upon condition of settlement within a certain period. The Revolution in France was expelling many of her noblest people, and the Marquis de Breard, with many followers, was one of these: he came, and was the pioneer to these lands. A nucleus formed, and accessions were being made, but the government being transferred and the country becoming Americanized, this tide of immigration was changed from French to American, and the requisite number of settlers to complete the grants was not reached within the stipulated period, and they were, after more than half a century, set aside, and the lands disposed of as public lands by the United States Government. Had the government continued in the hands of France, it is more than probable that the titles to these tracts would never have been contested, even though the requisite number of settlers had not been upon the lands to complete the grants at the specified period; and it is also probable there would have been, in proper time, the required number. But this transfer of dominion was exceedingly distasteful to the French population.

The antagonism of races itself is a great difficulty in the way of amalgamation, even though both may belong to the same great division of the human family; but added to this the difference of language, laws, habits, and religion, it would almost seem impossible. In the instance of Louisiana it has, so far, proved impossible. Although the French have been American subjects for more than sixty years, and there now remain in life very few who witnessed the change, and notwithstanding this population has, so far as the government is concerned, become thoroughly Americanized, still they remain to a very great extent a distinct people. Even in New Orleans they have the French part and the American part of the city, and do not, to any very great degree, extend their union by living among each other. Kind feelings exist between the populations, and the prejudices which have so effectually kept them apart for so long a time are giving way rapidly now, since most of the younger portion of the Creole-French population are educated in the United States, and away from New Orleans; consequently they speak the English language and form American associations, imbibe American ideas, and essay to rival American enterprise. Still there is a distinct difference in appearance. Perhaps the difference in bearing, and in other characteristics, may be attributable to early education, but the first and most radical is surely that of blood.

The settlements upon the Red and Washita Rivers did not augment the French population in the country; it has declined, but more signally upon the latter than the former river. There remain but few families there of the ancient population, and these are now so completely Americanized as scarcely to be distinguishable. The descendants of the Marquis de Breard, in one or two families, are there, but all who located on the Bayou Des Arc (and here was the principal settlement), with perhaps one family only, are gone, and the stranger is in their homes.

The French character seems to want that fixity of purpose, that self-denial, and steady perseverance, which is so necessary to those who would colonize and subdue a new and inhospitable country. The elevated civilization of the French has long accustomed them to the refinements and luxuries of life; it has entered into and become a part of their natures, and they cannot do violence to this in a sufficient degree to encounter the wilderness and all its privations, or to create from this wilderness those luxuries, and be content in their enjoyment for all the hardships endured in procuring them: they shrink away from these, and prefer the inconveniences and privations of a crowded community with its enjoyments, even in poverty, to the rough and trying troubles which surround and distress the pioneer, who pierces the forest and makes him a home, which, at least, promises all the comforts of wealth and independence to his posterity. He rather prefers to take care that he enjoys as he desires the present, and leaves posterity to do as they prefer. Yet there are many instances of great daring and high enterprise in the French Creole: these are the exceptions, not the rule.

CHAPTER XXVII.

ABOLITION OF LICENSED GAMBLING.

Baton Rouge — Florida Parishes — Dissatisfaction — Where there's a Will, there's a Way — Storming a Fort on Horseback — Annexation at the Point of the Poker — Raphignac and Larry Moore — Fighting the "Tiger" — Carrying a Practical Joke too far — A Silver Tea-Set.

THAT portion of Louisiana known as the Florida parishes, and consisting of the parishes east of the Mississippi, was part of West Florida, and was almost entirely settled by Americans when a Spanish province. Baton Rouge, which takes its name from the flag-staff which stood in the Spanish fort, and which was painted red, (*baton* meaning stick, and *rouge*, red, to Anglicize the name would make it red stick,) was the seat of power for that part or portion of the province. Here was a small Spanish garrison: on the opposite bank was Louisiana; New Orleans was the natural market and outlet for the productions of these Florida settlements.

When the cession of Louisiana to the United States occurred, these American settlers, desirous of returning to American rule, were restless, and united in their dissatisfaction with Spanish control. They could devise no plan by which this could be effected. Their people reached back from the river, along the thirty-first degree of north latitude, far into the interior, and extended thence to the lake border. On three sides they were encompassed by an American population and an American government. They had carried with them into this country all their American habits, and all their love for American laws and American freedom; to the east they were separated by an immense stretch of barren pine-woods from any other settlements upon Spanish soil. Pensacola was the seat of governmental authority, and this was too far away to extend the feeble arm of Spanish rule over these people. They were pretty much without legal government, save such laws and rule as had been by common consent established. These were all American in character, and, to all intents, this was an American settlement, almost in the midst of an American government, and yet without the protection of that or any other government. It was evident that at no distant day the Floridas must fall into the hands of the American Government. But there was to these people an immediate necessity for their doing so at once. They could not wait. But, what could they do? Among these people were many adventurous and determined men: they had mostly emigrated from the West—Tennessee, Kentucky, Western Pennsylvania, and Virginia; and some were the descendants of those who had gone to the country from the South, in 1777 and '8, to avoid the consequences of the Revolutionary War. This class of men met in council, and secretly determined to revolutionize the country, take possession of the Spanish fort, and ask American protection.

They desired to be attached to Louisiana as a part of that State. This, however, they could not effect without the consent of the State; and to ask this consent was deemed useless, until they were first recognized as part of the United States. In this dilemma, a veteran of the Revolution, and an early pioneer to Kentucky, and thence to West Florida, said: "'Wherever there is a will, there is a way:' we must first get rid of the Spanish authority, and look out for what may follow."

They secretly assembled a small force, and, upon a concerted day, met in secret, and under the cover of night approached the vicinity of the fort. Here they lay *perdu*, and entirely unsuspected by the Spanish Governor Gayoso. As day was approaching, they moved forward on horseback, and entered the open gate of the fort, and demanded its immediate surrender. The only opposition made to the assault was by young Gayoso, the governor's son, who was instantly slain, when the fort surrendered unconditionally. Perhaps this is the only instance in the history of wars that a fort was ever stormed on horseback. Thomas, Morgan, Moore, Johnson, and Kemper were the leaders in this enterprise. They were completely successful, and the Spanish authorities were without the means to subdue them to their duty as Spanish subjects.

The next step in their action was now to be decided. If the Government of the United States attempted their protection, it would be cause for war with Spain; and it was deemed best to organize under the laws of Louisiana, and ask annexation to that State. This was done. Members of the Legislature were elected in obedience to the laws of this State, and appeared at the meeting of that body, and asked to be admitted as members representing the late Florida parishes, then, as they assumed, a part and portion of the State.

When asked by what authority they claimed to be a part of the State, they answered, succinctly: "We have thrown off the Spanish yoke, and, as free and independent Americans, have annexed ourselves and the parishes we represent to this State, and claim as our right representation in this Legislature: we have joined ourselves to you, because it is our interest to do so, and yours, too; and we mean to be accepted." At the head of this representation was Thomas, who was the commander of the party capturing the fort; associated with him was Larry Moore. Thomas came from the river parishes; Moore from those contiguous to the lakes; both were Kentuckians, both illiterate, and both determined men. They did not speak as suppliants for favors, but as men demanding a right. They knew nothing of national law, and, indeed, very little of any other law; but were men of strong common sense, and clearly understood what was the interest of their people and their own, and, if determination could accomplish it, they meant to have it.

There were in the Legislature, at the time, two men of strong minds, well cultivated — Blanc and Raphignac; they represented the city, were Frenchmen — not French Creoles, but natives of *la belle* France. They led the opposition to the admission of the Florida parishes as part of the State, and their representatives as members of the Legislature. They were acquainted with national law, and appreciated the comity of nations, and were indisposed to such rash and informal measures as were proposed by Thomas and Moore. The portion of the State bordering upon this Spanish territory, and especially that part on the Mississippi, were anxious for the admission and union; they were unwilling that Spain should participate in the control and navigation of any part of the river; and, being peaceable and law-abiding, they wanted such close neighbors subject to the same government and laws. The influence of Blanc and Raphignac was likely to carry the majority and reject the application of the Floridans.

The pertinacious opposition of these men inflamed to anger Moore and Thomas. The matter, to them, was life or death. By some means they must get under the American flag, and they saw the only preventive in these two men. Moore (for it was a cold day when the decision was to be made) was seen to place the iron poker in the fire, and leave it there. Thomas was replying to Blanc in a most inflammatory and eloquent address; for, though rude and unlettered, he was full of native eloquence, and was very fluent: if he could not clothe his strong thoughts in pure English, he could in words well understood and keenly felt. They stimulated Moore almost to frenzy.

At that critical moment Raphignac walked to the fireplace, where Moore had remained sitting and listening to Thomas. Warm words were passing between Thomas and Blanc, when suddenly Moore grasped the heated poker — the end in the fire being at white heat — and calling to Thomas with a stentorian voice, "General Thomas! you take that white-headed French scoundrel, and I'll take blue-nose," and, brandishing his hot poker over his head, he charged, as with the bayonet, pointing the poker at the stomach of Raphignac. "*Tonnerre!*" exclaimed the frightened Frenchman, and, lifting both hands, he fell back against the wall. Moore still held the poker close to his stomach, as he called aloud, "Take the question, General Thomas! We come here to be admitted, and d— me if we won't be, or this goes through your bread-basket, I tell you, Mr. Raphy Blue-nose!" Raphignac was a tall, thin man, with a terribly large bottled nose. At the end it was purple as the grape which had caused it. The question was put, and the proposition was carried, amid shouts of laughter. "Oh!" said Raphignac, as the poker was withdrawn, and Moore with it, "vat a d— ole savage is dat Larry Moore!" Thus a part of West Florida became a part of Louisiana.

From that day forward, many of these men became most prominent citizens of the State. The son of Johnson — one of the leaders — became its Governor. Thomas was frequently a member of the Legislature, and once a member of Congress, from the Baton Rouge district, where he resided, and where he now sleeps in an honored grave. Morgan and Moore were frequently members of the Legislature. But of all the participants in this affair, Thomas was most conspicuous and most remarkable. He was almost entirely without education; but was gifted with great good sense, a bold and honest soul, and a remarkable natural eloquence. His manner was always natural and genial — never, under any circumstances, embarrassed or affected; and in whatever company he was thrown, or however much a stranger to the company, somehow he became the conspicuous man in a short time. The character in his face, the flash of his eye, the remarkable self-possession, the natural dignity of deportment, and his great good sense, attracted, and won upon every one. In all his transactions, he was the same plain, honest man — never, under any circumstances, deviating from truth — plain, unvarnished truth; rigidly stern in morals, but eminently charitable to the shortcomings of others. He was, from childhood, reared in a new country, amid rude, uncultivated people, and was a noble specimen of a frontier man; without the amenities of cultivated life, or the polish of education, yet with all the virtues of the Christian heart, and these, perhaps, the more prominently, because of the absence of the others. It was frequently remarked by him that he did not think education would have been of any advantage to him. It enabled men, with pretty words, to hide their thoughts, and deceive their fellow-men with a grace and an ease he despised; and it might have acted so with him, but it would have made him a worse and a more unhappy man. He now never did or said anything that he was ashamed to think of. He did not want to conceal his feelings and opinions, because he did not know how to do it; and he was sure if he attempted it he should make a fool of himself; for lies required so much dressing up in pretty words to make them look like truth, that he should fail for want of words; and truth was always prettiest when naked. In the main, the General was correct; but there are some who lie with a *naiveté* so perfect that even he would have deemed it truth naked and unadorned.

Larry Moore was a different man, but quite as illiterate and bold as Thomas, without his abilities; yet he was by no means devoid of mind. He resided upon the lake border, in the flat pine country, where the land is poor, and the people are ignorant and bigoted. Larry was far from being bigoted, save in his politics. He had been a Jeffersonian Democrat, he knew; but he did not know why. He lived off the road, and did not take the papers. He knew Jefferson had bought Louisiana and her people, and, as he understood, at seventy-five cents a head. He did not complain of the bargain, though he thought, if old Tom had seen them before the bargain was clinched, he would have hesitated to pay so much. But, anyhow, he had given the country a free government and a legislature of her own, and he was a Jefferson man, or Democrat, or whatever you call his party. He had been sent to the Legislature, and volunteered to meet the British under General Jackson.

From Jefferson to Jackson he transferred all his devotion; because the one bought, and the other fought for, the country. Some part of the glory of the successful defence of New Orleans was his, for he had fought for it, side by side with Old Hickory; and he loved him because he had imprisoned Louallier and Hall. The one was a Frenchman, the other an Englishman, and both were enemies of Jackson and the country.

Now he adored General Jackson, and was a Jackson Democrat. He did not know the meaning of the word, but he understood that it was the slogan of the dominant party, and that General Jackson was the head of that party. He knew he was a Jackson man, and felt whatever Jackson did was right, and he would swear to it. He was courageous and independent; feared no one nor anything; was always ready to serve a friend, or fight an enemy—*a fist-fight;* was kind to his neighbors, and always for the under dog in the fight. It would, after this, be supererogatory to say he was popular with such a people as his neighbors and constituents. Whenever he chose he was sent to the Senate by three parishes, or to the House by one; and in the Legislature he was always conspicuous. He knew the people he represented, and could say or do what he pleased; and for any offence he might give, was ready to settle with words, or a *fist-fight.* Physically powerful, he knew there were but few who, in a rough-and-tumble, could compete with him; and when his adversary yielded, he would give him his hand to aid him from the ground, or to settle it amicably in words. "Any way to have peace," was his motto.

There was, however, a different way of doing things in New Orleans, where the Legislature met. Gentlemen were not willing to wear a black eye, or bruised face, from the hands or cudgels of ruffians. They had a short way of terminating difficulties with them. A stiletto or Derringer returned the blow, and the Charity Hospital or potter's field had a new patient or victim. These were places for which Larry had no special *penchant,* and in the city he was careful to avoid rows or personal conflicts. He knew he was protected by the Constitution from arrest, or responsibility for words uttered in debate, and this was all he knew of the Constitution; yet he was afraid that for such words as might be offensive he would be likely to meet some one who would seek revenge in the night, and secretly. These responsibilities he chose to shun, by guarding his tongue by day, and keeping his chamber at night. Sometimes, however, in company with those whom he could trust, he would visit, at night, Prado's or Hicks's saloon, and play a little, just for amusement, with the "tiger."

Now, in the heyday of Larry's political usefulness, gaming was a licensed institution in the city of New Orleans. The magnificent charity of the State, the Hospital for the Indigent, was sustained by means derived from this tax.

It was the enlightened policy of French legislation to tax a vice which could not be suppressed by criminal laws. The experience of civilization has, or ought to have taught every people, that the vice of gaming is one which no law can reach so completely as to suppress *in toto*. Then, if it will exist, disarm it as much as possible of the power to harm—let it be taxed, and give the exclusive privilege to game to those who pay the tax and keep houses for the purpose of gaming. These will effectually suppress it. Everywhere else they are entitled to the game, and will keep close watch that it runs into no other net. Let this tax be appropriated to the support of an institution where, in disease and indigence, its victims may find support and relief. Make it public, that all may see and know its *habitués*, and who may feel the reforming influence of public opinion. For, at last, this is the only power by which the morals of a community are preserved. Let laws punish crimes—public opinion reform vices.

Larry was a lawmaker, and though he loved a little fun at times, even at the expense of the law, he was very solicitous as to the health of the public morals. In several visits at Prado's, he was successful in plucking some of the hair from the tiger. It was exceedingly pleasant to have a little pocket-change to evince his liberality socially with his friends, when it did not trench upon the crop, which was always a lean one on the sand-plains of St. Helena; for, like the great Corsican, Larry had a desolate home in St. Helena.

On one occasion, however, he went too close to the varmint, and returned to his little dirty apartments on the Rue Rampart minus all his gains, with a heavy instalment from the crop. His wonted spirits were gone. He moped to the State House, and he sat melancholy in his seat; he heeded not even the call of the yeas and nays upon important legislation. Larry was sick at heart, sick in his pocket, and was only seen to pluck up spirit enough to go to the warrant-clerk, and humbly insist upon a warrant on the treasurer for a week's pay to meet a week's board. On Monday, however, he came into the Senate with more buoyancy of spirit than had been his wont for some days; for Larry was a senator now, and had under his special charge and guardianship the people and their morals of three extensive parishes.

The Senate was scarcely organized and the minutes read, when it was plain Larry meant mischief. The hour for motions had arrived, and Larry was on his feet: he cleared his throat, and, throwing back his head, said: "Mr. President, I have a motion in my hand, which I will read to the Senate:

"'*Resolved*, That a joint committee, of one from the Senate, and two from the House, be appointed to report a bill abolishing licensed gaming in the city of New Orleans.'"

Larry had declared war, for he added, as he sent his resolution to the clerk's desk: "At the proper time I mean to say something about these damnable hells." Throughout the city there was a buzz; for at that time New Orleans had not the fourth of her present population. Any move of this sort was soon known to its very extremes. The trustees of the hospital, the stockholders in these licensed faro-banks — for they were, like all robbing-machines, joint-stock companies — and many who honestly believed this the best system to prevent gaming as far as possible, were seen hanging about the lobbies of the Legislature. Each had his argument in favor of continuing the license, but all were based upon the same motive — interest. The public morals would be greatly injured, instead of being improved; where there were only four gaming establishments, there would be fifty; instead of being open and public, they would be hid away in private, dark places, to which the young and the innocent would be decoyed and fleeced; merchants could not supervise the conduct of their clerks — these would be robbed by their employes. As the thing stood now, cheating operated a forfeiture of charter or license: this penalty removed, cheating would be universal. "What would become of the hospital?" the tax-payer asked. "God knows, our taxes are onerous enough now, and to add to these the eighty thousand dollars now paid by the gamblers — why, the people would not stand it, and this great and glorious charity would be destroyed."

To all of these arguments Larry was deaf; his constituents expected it of him; the Christian Church demanded it. They were responsible to Heaven for this great sin. The pious prayers of the good sisters of the holy Methodist Church, as well as those of the Baptist, had at last reached the ears of the Almighty, and he, Larry, felt himself the instrument in His hands to put down the *d——d infernal sons of b——*, who were robbing the innocent and unsuspecting. There was no use of urging arguments of this sort to him: if the Charity Hospital fell, *let* her fall, and if the indigent afflicted could not find relief elsewhere, why, they must die — they had to die anyhow at some time, and he did n't see much use in their living, anyhow; and as for the taxes, he was not much concerned about that: he had but little to be taxed, and his constituents had less. "I, or they, as you see, are not very responsible on that score. By the God of Moses, this licensed gambling was a sin and a curse, if it did support seven or eight thousand people in the Charity Hospital every year: that was the reason so many died there, the curse of God was on the place; for the Scripture says, the 'wages of sin is death,' and I see this Scripture fulfilled right here in that hospital, and the moral and religious portion of my constituents so feel it, and I am bound to represent them. And the d——d gamblers were no friends of mine or of the Church."

There was one, a little dark-moustached Spaniard, who was listening and peering at him, with eyes black and pointed as a chincapin, and, murmuring softly in Spanish, turned and went away. "What did that d——d black-muzzled whelp say?" Larry asked. "I don't understand their d——d lingo." An unobtrusive individual in the background translated it for him. He said: "He who strikes with the tongue, should always be ready to guard with the hands!" "What in the h— does he mean by that?" asked Larry. "*Je ne sais pas!*" said one whom Larry remembered to have seen in the tiger's den, and apparently familiar there, for he had been on the wrong side of the table.

"I suppose they mean to shoot me." The Frenchman shrugged his shoulders most knowingly. Larry grew pale, and walked from the lobby to his seat. Here he knew he was safe. He laid his head in his palm, and rested it there for many minutes. At last, he said sharply: "Let them shoot, and be d——d."

The committee was announced. Larry, who was the chairman, and two from the House, constituted this important committee. One of these loved fun, and never lost an opportunity to have it. The meeting of the committee soon took place, and the chairman insisted that the first named on the part of the House should draft the bill. This was the wag. He saw Larry was frightened, and peremptorily refused, declaring it was the chairman's duty. "I do not wish to have anything to do with this matter any way. It was a very useless thing, and foolish too, to be throwing a cat into a bee-gum; for this was nothing else. This bill will start every devil of those little moustached foreigners into fury: they are all interested in these faro-banks. It is their only way of making a living, and they are as vindictive as the devil. Any of them can throw a Spanish knife through a window, across the street, and into a man's heart, seated at his table, or fireside; and to-day I heard one of them say, in French, which he supposed I did not understand, that this bill was nothing but revenge for money lost; and if revenge was so sweet, why, he could taste it too. Now, I have lost no money there — have never been in any of their dens, and he could not mean me."

"Gentlemen, we will adjourn this meeting until to-morrow," said Larry, "when I will try and have a bill for your inspection." The morrow came, and the bill came with it, and was reported and referred to the committee of the whole House. On the ensuing morning, Larry found upon his desk, in the Senate chamber, the following epistle:

"MR. LARRY MOORE: You have no shame, or I would expose you in the public prints. You know your only reason for offering a bill to repeal the law licensing gaming in this city is to be revenged on the house which won honorably from you a few hundred dollars, most of which you had, at several sittings, won from the same house. Now, you have been talked to; still you persist. There is a way to reach you, and it shall be resorted to, if you do not desist from the further prosecution of this bill."

The hand in which this epistle was written was cramped and evidently disguised, to create the impression of earnestness and secrecy. It was a long time before Larry could spell through it. When he had made it out, he rose to a question of order and privilege, and sent the missive to the secretary's desk, to be read to the Senate. During the reading there was quite a disposition to laugh, on the part of many senators, who saw in it nothing but a joke.

"What in the h— do you see in that thar document to laugh at, Mr. Senators? D— it, don't you see it is a threat, sirs! — a threat to 'sassinate me? I want to know, by the eternal gods, if a senator in this house — this here body — is to be threatened in this here way? You see, Mr. President, that these here gamblers (d— 'em !) want to rule the State. Was that what General Jackson fit the battle of New Orleans for, down yonder in old Chemut's field? I was thar, sir; I risked my life in that great battle, and I want to tell these d——d scoundrels that they can't scare me — no, by the Eternal!"

"I must call the senator to order. It is not parliamentary to swear in debate," said the President of the Senate.

"I beg pardon of the chair; but I did n't know this Senate was a parliament before; but I beg pardon. I did n't know I swore before; but, Mr. President, I'll be d——d if this ain't a figure beyant me: for a parcel of scoundrels — d——d blacklegs, sir! — to threaten a senator in this Legislature with 'sassination, for doin' the will of his constituents."

"The chair would remind the senator that there is no question or motion before the Senate."

"Thar ain't? Well, that 's another wrinkle. Ain't that thar hell-fired letter to me, sir — a senator, sir, representing three parishes, sir — before this House? (or maybe you 'll want me to call it a parliament, sir?) It is, sir; and I move its adoption."

This excited a general laugh, and, at the same time, the ire of Moore.

"By G—, sir; I don't know if it would n't benefit the State if these hell-fired gamblers were to 'sassinate the whole of this House or parliament."

The laugh continued, and Moore left the Senate in a rage.

The next morning found a second epistle, apparently from a different source, on Moore's table. It was written in a fine, bold hand, and said:

"LARRY: You splurged largely over a letter found on your desk yesterday. I see you have carried it to the newspapers. I want you to understand distinctly and without equivocation, if the bill you reported to the Senate becomes a law, *you die.* *Verbum sapientis.*"

Larry had not returned to his seat during the day; but the next morning he came in, flanked by several senators, who had come with him from his quarters. There lay the threatening document, sealed, and directed to the "Honorable Larry Moore." In a moment the seal was broken. This he could read without much trouble. After casting his eyes over it, he read it aloud.

"Now, sir, Mr. President, here is another of these d——d letters, and this time I am told if this bill passes, I am to die. Maybe you'll say this ain't before the Senate."

"The chair would remind the senator that the simple reading of a private letter to the Senate raises no question. There must be a motion in relation to what disposition shall be made of the paper."

"I know that, sir. Mr. President, I'm not a greeny in legislater matters. I have been here before, sir; and did n't I move its adoption yesterday, sir? and was n't I laughed out of the house, sir? and I expect if I was to make the same motion, I should be laughed out of the house again, sir. Some men are such d——d fools that they will laugh at anything."

"The chair must admonish the senator that oaths are not in order."

"Well, by G—, sir, is my motion in order to-day? I want to know; I want you to tell me that."

"Order, Mr. Senator!"

"Yes, sir, 'order!' Mr. President, that's the word. Order, sir; is my motion in order, sir?"

"The chair calls the senator to order."

"Ah! that is it, is it? Well, sir, what order shall I take? I ask a question, and the chair calls me to order. Well, sir, I'm in only tolerable order, but I want my question answered — I want to know if I'm to be threatened with 'sassination by the hell-fired gamblers, and then laughed at by senators for bringing it before the Senate, and insulted by you, sir, by calling me to order for demanding my rights, and the rights of my constituents, here, from this Senate? This, sir, is a d——d pretty situation of affairs. If General Jackson was in your place, I'd have my rights, and these d——d gamblers would get theirs, sir: he would hang them under the second section, and no mistake."

The laugh was renewed, and the President asked Larry if he had any motion to make.

"Yes, sir," said Larry, now thoroughly aroused. "I move this Senate adjourn and go home, and thar stay until they larn to behave like gentlemen, by G—!" and away he went in angry fury.

For four consecutive days, this scene was enacted in the Senate. Each succeeding day saw Moore more and more excited, and the

Senate began to entertain the opinion that there was an intention to intimidate the Legislature, and thus prevent the passage of the bill. These daily missives grew more and more threatening, and terror began to usurp the place of rage with Moore. He would not leave the Senate chamber or his quarters without being accompanied by friends. In the mean time the bill came up, and Moore had made a characteristic speech, and the morning following there were half a dozen letters placed upon his table from the post-office. Their threats and warnings increased his alarm. Some of these purported to come from friends, detailing conversations of diabolical character which had been overheard — others told him only an opportunity was wanting to execute the threats previously made.

The city became excited — a public meeting was called, strong indignation resolutions were passed, and highly approbatory ones of the course and conduct of the intrepid senator, pledging him countenance and support. A subscription was taken up, and a splendid silver tea-set was presented him, and in this blaze of excitement the bill became a law — and the city one extended gambling-shop. The silver set was publicly exhibited, with the name of the senator engraved upon it, and the cause for presenting it, and by whom presented.

Moore was contemplating this beautiful gift with a group of friends: among them were the three individuals who had been the authors of all this mischief, when one of them asked Moore, "Where will you put this rich gift? It will show badly in your pine-pole cabin."

"I intend having the cabin, every log of it, painted red as lightning," said Moore. "The silver shan't be disgraced."

Originally it had been intended by those getting up the joke, when it had sufficiently frightened Moore, to laugh at him; but it took too serious a turn, and Moore died a hero, not knowing that every letter was written by the same hand, and that the whole matter was a practical joke. All, save only one, who participated in it, are in the grave, and only a few remain who will remember it.

Larry Moore was a Kentuckian by birth, and had many Kentucky characteristics. He was boisterous but kind-hearted, boastful and good at a fist-fight, decently honest in most matters, but would cheat in a horse-trade. Early education is sometimes greatly at fault in its inculcations, and this was, in Moore's case, peculiarly so. Had he not been born in Kentucky, these jockey tricks perhaps would not have been a part of his accomplishments. For there, it is said, no boy is permitted to leave home on a horse enterprise until he has cheated his father in a horse-trade. Moore left the State so young that it was by some doubted whether this trait was innate or acquired; but it always distinguished him, as a Kentuckian by birth at least.

He was remarkable for the tenacity of his friendships. He would not desert any one. It was immaterial what was the character of the man, if he served Moore, Moore was his friend, and he would cling quite as close to one in the penitentiary as in the halls of Congress. It made no difference whether he wore cloth or cottonade, lived in a palace or pine-pole cabin, whether honest or a thief, the touchstone to his heart was, "He is my friend, and I am at his service." Not only in this, but in everything else, he strove to imitate his great friend and prototype, General Jackson. He lived to be an old man, and among his constituents he was great, and made his mark in his day in the State. There was some fun in Larry, but he was the cause of much more in others. Larry, rest in peace, and light be the sand that lies on your coffin!

CHAPTER XXVIII.

THREE GREAT JUDGES.

A Speech in two Languages—Long Sessions—Matthews, Martin, and Porter—A Singular Will—A Scion of '98—Five Hundred Dollars for a Little Fun with the Dogs—Cancelling a Note.

THE Legislature of Louisiana, forty years ago, sat in New Orleans, and was constituted of men of varied nationalities. It was common to see in close union, Frenchmen, Germans, Italians, Englishmen, and Americans, with here and there a Scotchman, with his boat-shaped head and hard common sense. The Creole-French and the Americans, however, constituted the great majority of the body.

When the cession to the United States took place, and the colony soon after was made a State of the Union, the Constitution required all judicial and legislative proceedings to be conducted in English, which was the legal language. But as very few of the ancient population could speak or read English, it was obligatory on the authorities to have everything translated into French. All legislative and judicial proceedings, consequently, were in two languages. This imposed the necessity of having a clerk or translator, who could not only translate from the records, but who could retain a two-hours' speech in either language, and, immediately upon the speaker's concluding, repeat it in the opposite language.

This complicated method of procedure consumed much time, and consequently the sessions of the Legislature were protracted usually for three months, and sometimes four.

This fact caused many planters, whose business called them frequently to the city during the winter, to become members of the Legislature. At this time, too, representation was based on taxation, and the suffragist was he who paid a tax to the State. The revenues of the State were from taxation, and these taxes were levied alone upon property. There were no poll taxes, and very few articles except land, negroes, and merchandise were taxed. The consequence was, the government was in the hands of the property-holders only.

The constituency was of a better order than is usually furnished by universal suffrage, and the representation was of a much more elevated character than generally represents such a constituency.

Party spirit, at that time, had made little progress in dividing the people of the State, and the gentlemen representatives met cordially, and constituted an undivided society. There was no division of interest between different sections of the State, and the general good was consulted by all. The Legislature was then composed of substantial men. The seat of government being in the city, and the sessions held during the winter and spring months, men of business, and especially professional men, might represent the city constituency, and yet give a good portion of their time to their usual avocations.

Good laws were the consequence; and the Bench being filled by executive appointment, with the consent of the Senate, and their tenure of office being for life or good behavior, insured the selection of proper men for judges. The Supreme Court was composed at that time of three judges, Matthews, Martin, and Porter. Matthews was a Georgian by birth, Martin was a native of France, and Porter an Irishman: all of these were remarkable men, and each in his own history illustrative of what energy and application will effect for men, when properly applied in youth.

Chief-Justice George Matthews was the son of that very remarkable man, Governor George Matthews, of the State of Georgia. He was born in Oglethorpe County, Georgia, and received only such education as at that time could be obtained in the common country schools of the State. He read law in early life, and was admitted to the Bar of his native State. His father was Governor of the State at the time of the passage of the celebrated Yazoo Act, alienating more than half of the territory of the State.

This act was secured from the Legislature by corruption of the boldest and most infamous character. Governor Matthews was only suspected of complicity in this transaction from the fact that he signed the bill as governor. His general character was too pure to allow of suspicion attaching to him of corruption in the discharge of the duties of his office of governor.

At the period of passing this act, the United States Government was new. The States, under their constitutions, were hardly working smoothly; the entire system was experimental. The universal opinion that the people were sovereign, and that it was the duty of every public officer to yield obedience to the will of the majority, clearly expressed, operated strongly upon the Executives of the States, and very few, then, attempted to impose a veto upon any act of the Legislatures of the different States. Tradition represents Governor Matthews as opposed individually to the act, but he did not feel himself justified in interposing a veto simply upon his individual opinion of the policy or propriety of the measure, especially when he was assured in his own mind that the Legislature had not transcended their constitutional powers; and this opinion was sustained as correct by the Supreme Court of the United States in the case of Fletcher *vs.* Peck.

The great unpopularity of the transaction involved the Governor and his family. Men excited almost to frenzy, never stay to reflect, but madly go forward, and, in attempts to right great wrongs, commit others, perhaps quite as great as those they are seeking to remedy. Governor Matthews, despite his Revolutionary services and his high character for honesty and moral worth, never recovered from the effects of this frenzy which seized upon the people of the State, and is the only one of the early Governors of the State who has remained unhonored by the refusal of the Legislature, up to this day, to call or name a county for him. This unpopularity was keenly felt by the children of Matthews, who were men of great worth.

William H. Crawford was at this time filling a large space in the public confidence of the people of Georgia, and gave to Governor Matthews his confidence and friendship. It was he who persuaded George Matthews, the son, to emigrate to Louisiana. He frankly told him this unpopularity of his father would weigh heavily upon him through life, if he remained in Georgia. "You have talents, George," said he, "and, what is quite as important to success in life, common sense, with great energy: these may pull you through here, but you will be old before you will reap anything from their exercise in your native State. These prejudices against your father may die out, but not before most of those who have participated in them shall have passed away: truth will ultimately triumph, but it will be when your father is in the grave, and you gray with years. To bear and brave this may be heroic, but very unprofitable. I think I have influence enough with the President to secure an appointment in Louisiana—probably the judgeship of the Territory, or one of them."

Matthews feared his qualifications for such an appointment, and so expressed himself to Crawford. The civil law was the law of Louisiana, and he was entirely unacquainted with this. Crawford's reply was eminently characteristic. The great principles of all laws are the same. Their object is to enfore the right, and maintain impartial justice between man and man. In hearing a case, a judge of good common sense will generally find out the justice of the matter. Let him decide right, and do substantial justice, and he will, ninety-nine times out of one hundred, decide according to law, whether he knows anything about the law or not. And such a judge is always best for a new country, or, in truth, for any country. The appointment was secured, and George Matthews left his native State forever.

Soon after reaching Louisiana, he married Miss Flower, of West Feliciana—a lady in every way suited to him. She was of fine family, with strong mind, domestic habits, and full of energy. They were very much attached to each other, and were happy and prosperous through all the life of the great judge. Mrs. Matthews still lives, and in the immediate neighborhood of her birthplace, and is now active, useful, and beloved by all who know her, though extremely old.

When the Territory was organized into a State under the Constitution, Matthews was appointed chief justice of the Supreme Court by Governor Claiborne — an office he held through life, and the duties of which he discharged with distinguished ability, and to the honor of the State and the entire satisfaction of the Bar and the people.

The mind of Judge Matthews was strong and methodical. His general character largely partook of the character of his mind. He steadily pursued a fixed purpose, and was prudent, cautious, and considerate in all he did. There was no speculation in his mind. He jumped to no conclusions; but examined well and profoundly every question — weighed well every argument; but he never forgot the advice of Mr. Crawford, and sometimes would strain a point in order to effect strict and substantial justice. As a judge, he was peculiarly cautious. However intricate was any case, he bent to it his whole mind, and the great effort was always to learn the right — to sift from it all the verbiage and ambiguity which surrounded and obscured it, and then to sustain it in his decision. Upright and sincere in his pursuits, methodical, with fixity of purpose, he was never in a hurry about anything, and was always content, in his business, with moderate profits as the reward of his labor. As a companion, he was gentle, kind, and eminently social; but he gave little time to social entertainments or light amusements. In his decisions as a judge, he established upon a firm basis the laws, and the enlightened exposition of these, in their true spirit. A foundation was given to the jurisprudence of the State by this court, which entitles it justly to the appellation of the Supreme Court, and to the gratitude of the people of the State.

The life of Judge George Matthews was one of peculiar usefulness. Learned and pure as a judge, moral and upright as a citizen, affectionate and gentle as a husband and father, and humane and indulgent as a master, his example as a man was one to be recommended to every young man. Its influence upon society was prominently beneficial, and was an exemplification of moral honesty, perseverance, and success. He won a proud name as a man and as a jurist, and accumulated a large fortune, without ever trenching upon the rights of another. He secured the confidence and affection of every member of his wife's family — a very extensive one — and was the benefactor of most of them. He was beloved and honored by all his neighbors, through a long life. In his public duties and his private relations he never had an imputation cast upon his conduct, and he died without an enemy.

François Xavier Martin was a native of France. In early life he emigrated to the United States, and fixed his residence at Newbern, North Carolina. He was poor, and without a trade or profession by which to sustain himself, or to push his fortunes in a strange land. He labored under another exceedingly great obstacle to success: though pretty well educated, he could not speak the English language. But he had a proud spirit and an indomitable will. He sought employment as a printer, choosing this as a means of learning the English language. Though he had never fingered a type in his life, he had that confidence in himself which inspired the conviction that he could overcome any difficulty presenting itself between his will and success.

He found the editor of the newspaper kind, and apparently indifferent; for he asked no questions relative to his qualifications as a printer, but, requiring help, gave him immediate employment. He went to work — was very slow, but very assiduous and constant, never leaving his stand until he had completed his work. There was a compositor near him, and he watched and learned without asking questions. Owing to the little English he knew, no questions were asked; but it was observed in the office that he was rapidly improving in this, and in the facility of doing his work. The paper was a weekly one, consequently he had ample time for his work, and he improved every moment. The many mistakes he made in the beginning were attributed to his ignorance of the language, and it was not until he became the most expert compositor in the office that it was known that he had never, until he entered this office, been in a printing-office. He was so abstemious in his habits that those about the office wondered how he lived. He rarely left the composing-room, and, in his moments of rest from his work, was employed in studying the language, or reading some English author. A bit of cheese, a loaf of bread, some dried fish, and a cup of coffee constituted his bill of fare for every day, and these were economically used. He never spoke of home, of previous pursuits, or future intentions. He held communion with no one — his own thoughts being his only companions — but steadily persevered in his business. No amusements attracted him. He was never at any place of public resort. He was the talk of the town, though none had seen him unless they visited the little, dirty, inky office in which he was employed. He never seemed to know he was an object of curiosity, and when — as sometimes was the case — half a dozen persons would come expressly to see him, he never turned his head from his work, or seemed to be conscious of their presence.

In this office his progress was very rapid, and it was not very long before he became the foreman in the composing-room. He continued in that capacity until he became the owner of the entire establishment.

Not content with the life of a printer, he disposed of his printing establishment and paper, and came to New Orleans. Before leaving France he had read some law, and now he applied himself closely to its study. In a short time he rose to distinction, and was in a lucrative practice. It was a maxim with Judge Martin never to be idle, and never to expend time or money uselessly. He found time from his professional duties to write a history of Louisiana, which is, perhaps, more correct in its facts than any history ever written.

Early deprivations, and the necessity of a most rigid economy to meet the exigencies of this straitened condition, created habits of abstinence and saving which he never gave up. On the contrary, like all habits long indulged, they became stronger and more obdurate as life advanced. Before his elevation to the supreme Bench, he had accumulated a fortune of at least one hundred thousand dollars, which he had judiciously invested in the city of New Orleans. The tenure of his office was for life, and his ambition never aspired to anything beyond; but he devoted himself to the duties of this with the assiduity of one determined, not only to know, but faithfully to discharge them. Judge Martin was conscientious in all that he did as a man, and remarkably scrupulous as a judge. He was unwilling to hasten his judgments, and sometimes was accused of tardiness in rendering them. This resulted from the great care exercised in examining the merits of the case, and to make himself sure of the law applicable to it.

The peculiar organization of the Supreme Court of Louisiana imposes immense labor upon the judges; they are not only charged with the duty of correcting errors of law, but the examination of all the facts and all the testimony introduced in the trials in the District Court. In truth, the case comes up *de novo*, and is reviewed as from the beginning, and a judgment made up without regard to the proceedings below further than to determine from the record of facts and law sent up, holding in all cases jurisdiction as well of facts as law — and in truth it is nothing more than a high court of chancery.

Judge Martin was fond of labor, but did not like to do the same labor twice; hence his particularity in examining well both facts and law, in every case submitted for his adjudication. He wished the law permanently established applicable to every case, and disliked nothing so much as being compelled to overrule any previous decision of the Supreme Court. His mind was eminently judicial; its clear perceptions and analytical powers peculiarly fitted him for the position of supreme judge. But there was another trait of character, quite as necessary to the incumbent of the Bench, for which he was altogether as much distinguished. He was without prejudice, and only knew men before his court as parties litigant. It was said of him, by John R. Grymes, a distinguished lawyer of New Orleans, that he was better fitted by nature for a judge than any man who ever graced the Bench. "He was all head, and no heart."

This was severely said, and to some extent it was true, for Judge Martin appeared without sympathy for the world, or any of the world. He had no social habits; he lived in seclusion with his servant Ben, a venerable negro, who served him for all purposes. These two had been so long and so intimately associated, that in habits and want of feeling they seemed identical. Ben served him because he was his master and could compel it. He tolerated Ben because he could not well do without him. He kept an interest account with Ben. He had paid for him six hundred dollars, when first purchased. Ten per cent. upon this amount was sixty dollars. His insurance upon a life policy, which risk he took himself, was one hundred dollars. His services were regularly valued by what such a man would hire for. Ben accompanied him on the circuit, and died at Alexandria. When this was told him, he immediately referred to this account, and declared he had saved money by buying Ben, but should be loser if he paid his funeral expenses, which he declined to do. Judge Martin was very near-sighted, and it was amusing to see him with his little basket doing his marketing, examining scrupulously every article, cheapening everything, and finally taking the refuse of meats and vegetables, rarely expending more than thirty cents for the .lay's provisions. His penurious habits seemed natural: they had characterized him from the moment he came to the United States, and were then so complete as not to be intensified by age and experience. For many years, he had no relative in this country, and he created no relations, outside of his business, with the community in which he lived. His antisocial nature and his miserable manner of living kept every one from him. Secluded, and studious in his habits, he never seemed solitary, for his books and papers occupied his entire time. His thirst for knowledge was coequal with his thirst for money — and why, no one could tell. He never made a display of the one, or any use of the other but to beget money. There seemed an innate love for both, and an equal disposition to husband both. He seemed to have no ulterior view in hoarding — he endowed no charity, nor sought the world's praise in the grave, by building a church or endowing a hospital. With mankind, his only relations were professional. He never married, and had no taste for female society — was never known to attend a ball or private party, to unite himself with any society, or be at a public meeting — never indulged in a joke or frivolous conversation, and had no use for words unless to expound law or conclude a contract; strictly punctual to every engagement, but exceedingly chary in making any.

As Judge Martin advanced in years, his habits became more and more secluded. He had written for a brother, who came to him from France. This brother was quite as peculiar as himself — they lived together, and he in a great degree substituted Ben, at least so far as society was concerned. Now he was rarely seen upon the street, or mingling with any, save an occasional visit to some member of the Bar, who, like himself, had grown old in the harness of the law. During the early period of the State Government he reported the decisions of the Supreme Court: these reports are models, and of high authority in the courts of Louisiana.

Judge Martin's mind was one of peculiar lucidity and extraordinary vigor; its capacity to acquire, analyze, and apply was quite equal to that of the great Marshall; its power of condensation was superior to either of his compeers, while its capacity for application was never surpassed. It had been trained to close and continuous thought, and so long had this habit been indulged that it had become nature with him. His phlegmatic temperament relieved him from anything like impulsiveness in thought or action; all work with him was considerately approached and assiduously performed. His habits were temperate to austerity, and his mode of life penuriously mean; but, as said of another judge, this may have been the result of habit growing from extreme necessity—though the same characteristics were conspicuous in his brother: like the Judge, he was unmarried, and, though but little younger, was always spoken to and spoken of as his boy-brother. Like his confrère, he remained upon the Bench until he died, which was in extreme old age.

It has been asserted by some that Judge Martin soiled his reputation in his will. It was a very simple and brief will, giving all he possessed to his brother, and was autographic—that is, written in his own hand, and signed, dated, and sealed up, and upon the back of the document written, "This is my autographic will," and this signed with his own proper hand. Such a will is almost impervious to attack under the laws of Louisiana.

The law of Louisiana levies a tax of ten per cent. upon all estates or legacies made to leave the State for foreign countries. The brother of Judge Martin, as soon as his will was administered and the proceeds of his estate were in hand, left the United States for France, carrying with him three hundred thousand dollars, the entire amount of which the Judge died possessed; and it was subsequently ascertained that he had left written instructions with his brother to dispose among his European relatives this sum in obedience to this secret letter of instructions. This was considered as his will proper; and it was contended that the transaction was a fraud, to deprive the State of the legal percentage upon the amount going out of the country. An attempt was made to recover this amount from his executor, but failed; and the attorney for the State was rebuked by the Supreme Court for attempting an imputation dishonorable to the character of the deceased Judge—a legacy bequeathed to the State, in the distinguished services rendered to her by him and through so many years of his life. The facts are as stated. It is true, the will was a clear bequest of all his estate to his brother, a resident of the State, and the memorandum a mere request, and this might have been destroyed or disobeyed with impunity. The will alone was the authoritative disposition of his estate; the brother claimed under this, and the property once in his possession, it was his to dispose of at pleasure.

The death of Judge Martin was regretted by every one as a serious loss to the State, though he had attained very nearly to the age of fourscore. He had failed, from the entire want of social and sympathetic attributes in the composition of his nature, to fasten himself upon the affections of any one, though he commanded the respect of all for the high qualities of his intellect, his public services, and the consistent honesty of his life. He was followed to the grave by the entire Bench and Bar, and most of the distinguished people of his adopted city. But I doubt if a tear was shed at his funeral. He was without the ties in life which, sundered by death, wring tears and grief from the living who loved and who have lost the endeared one. All that the head could give, he had — the heart denied him all: in life he had given it to no one, and his death had touched no heart; and no tear embalmed his bier, no flower planted by affection's hand blooms about his grave. Still he has left an imperishable monument to his fame in his judicial career.

Alexander Porter, the junior by many years of Matthews and Martin, his associates on the Bench, was an Irishman by birth, and came in very early life to the United States. He was the son of an Irish Presbyterian minister of remarkable abilities and great learning. As a chemist, he was only inferior to Sir Humphrey Davy, of his day. During the troubles of 1798, (since known as the rebellion of '98,) he was travelling and delivering lectures upon chemistry through Ireland. He fell under suspicion as being an emissary of the Society of United Irishmen, who was covering, under the character of a scientific lecturer, his real mission to stir up and unite the Irish people in aid of the views of those who were organizing the rebellion. To be suspected was to be arrested, and to be arrested was wellnigh equivalent to being executed — sometimes with the mockery of a trial, and, where evidence was wanting to fix suspicion, even by drum-head court-martial. This latter was the fate of the accomplished and learned Porter. The wrath of the Government visited his family. The brother of the sufferer collected his own and the children of his murdered brother, consisting of two sons and several daughters, and emigrated to America. A number of emigrants from their immediate neighborhood had selected Nashville, Tennessee, as a home in the New World, and thither he came.

The education of Alexander, the eldest of the sons, had progressed considerably in Ireland, and was continued for some years at Nashville. Being poor, he was compelled to employ some of his time in pursuits foreign to study, in order to supply him with the means of pursuing the latter. This education was irregular, but was the foundation of that which in maturer life was most complete. He studied law when quite young, intending at first to remain at Nashville. The competition at the Bar in that place was formidable, and he could not hope to succeed as his ambition prompted, without patient application for years. Louisiana had just been ceded to the United States, Mississippi was filling with population: both these Territories would soon be States. Already they were inviting fields for enterprise and talent, and soon to be more so. Pondering these facts in his ardent mind, and riding alone on one occasion to a justice's court in the country to attend to some trifling matter, he chanced to overtake General Jackson. He had been frequently importuned by Jackson to remove to Louisiana. Jackson was, to some extent, familiar with the country, had frequently visited it, and at that time was interested in a retail store at Bruensburg, a place situated at the mouth of the Bayou Pierre, immediately on the bank of the Mississippi River. Mentioning his wish to emigrate to some point or place where he might expect more speedy success in his profession, Jackson, with his accustomed ardor and emphasis, advised him to go to one of these new Territories, and in such colors did he paint their advantages and the certain and immediate success of any young man of abilities and industry, that Porter's imagination was fired, and he immediately determined to go at once to one of these El Dorados — there to fix his home and commence the strife with fortune, to coax or command her approving smiles. Returning to Nashville, he communicated his intentions to his uncle; they met his approval, and in a short time he was ready to leave in search of a new home.

He was about to leave every friend, to find his home in the midst of strangers, without even an acquaintance to welcome and encourage him. But he was young, vigorous, and hopeful; alive, too, to all he had to encounter, and determined to conquer it. Still, to one of his natural warmth of feeling, the parting from all he had ever known, and all on earth he loved, wrung his heart, and he lingered, dreading the parting that was to come. His kind and devoted uncle, his brothers he loved so tenderly, his sisters, and the friends he had made, all were to be left — and perhaps forever. There were then no steamers to navigate the waters of the West. He might float away, and rapidly, to his new home; but to return through the wilderness, filled with savages and beset with dangers, was a long and hazardous journey, and would require, not only time, but means, neither of which were at his command.

He met General Jackson again. "What!" said he, "Alick, not gone yet? This won't do. When you determine, act quickly; somebody may get in before you. And remember, Alick, you are going to a new country—and a country, too, where men fight. You will find a different people from those you have grown among, and you must study their natures, and accommodate yourself to them. If you go to Louisiana, you will find nearly all the people French; they are high-minded, and fight at the drop of a hat; and now let me tell you, it is always best to avoid a fight; but sometimes it can't be done, and then a man must stand up to it like a man. But let me tell you, Alick, there are not half the men who want to fight that pretend to; you can tell this by their blustering. Now, when you find one of these, and they are mighty common, just stand right up to him, and always appear to get madder than he does—look him right in the eye all the time; but remember to keep cool, for sometimes a blusterer will fight; so keep cool, and be ready for anything. But, Alick, the best way of all is to fight the first man that offers, and do it in such a way as to let everybody know you will fight, and you will not be much bothered after that. Now, Alick, you will hear a great deal of preaching against fighting—well, that is all right; but I tell you the best preacher among them all loves a man who will fight, a thousand times more than he does a coward who won't. All the world respects a brave man, because all the better qualities of human nature accompany courage. A brave man is an honest man; he is a good husband, a good neighbor, and a true friend. You never saw a true woman who did not love a brave man. And now do you be off at once, look for a good place, and when you stop, stop to stay; and let all you say and all you do look to your advantage in the future."

Long years after this parting scene, and when Porter had become a national man, he used to love to recount this conversation to his friends, and the impression it created upon his mind of the wonderful man who had so freely advised him.

When Porter came, he explored the entire country, and selected for his home Opelousas, the seat of justice for the parish of St.

Landry. To reach this point from New Orleans, at that time, required no ordinary exertion. He came first to Donaldsonville, where he hired a man to bring him in a small skiff to the court-house of the parish of Assumption. There he employed another to transport him through the Verret Canal to the lakes, and on through these to Marie José's landing, in Attakapas; then another was engaged to take him up the Teche to St. Martinsville, and from there he went by land to Opelousas. This route is nearly three hundred miles.

The banks of the Teche he found densely populated with a people altogether different in appearance, and speaking a language scarcely one word of which he understood, and in everything different from anything he had ever before seen: added to this, he found them distrustful, inhospitable, and hating the Americans, to whose dominion they had been so recently transferred.

He used to relate an anecdote of this trip, in his most humorous manner. "I had," he said, "been all day cramped up in the stern of a small skiff, in the broiling sun, with nothing to drink but the tepid water of the Teche. I was weary and half sick, when I came to the front of a residence, which wore more the appearance of comfort and respectability than any I had passed during the day. It was on Sunday, and there were a number of decently dressed people, young and old, upon the gallery or piazza, and there were great numbers of cattle grazing out on the prairie. Here, I thought, I may find some cool water, and perhaps something to mix with it. I landed, and went to the front gate, and called. This was quite near the house, and I thought some one said, 'Come in.' I opened the gate, and started for the house. At this juncture, a tall, dark man, wearing a very angry look, came from the interior of the house, and stopping at the gallery door, looked scowlingly down upon me as I approached the steps. '*Arrêtez!*' he said, waving his hand. This wave I understood, but not the word, and stopped. He spoke to me in French: I did not understand. I asked for water: this he did not understand, as it was pronounced with considerable of the brogue. Turning abruptly round, he called aloud, '*Pierre!*' and a negro man came out, who was directed to ask me what I wanted. I told him, water: this he translated for his master. He spoke again angrily to the negro, who told me there was water in the bayou. 'Then, can I get a little butter-milk?' I asked. As soon as this was translated to him, he flew into a violent rage, and commenced gesticulating passionately. 'You better run, sir,' said the negro, 'he call de dogs for bite you.' I heard the yelp in the back yard, and started for the gate with a will: it was time, for in a moment there were a dozen lean and vicious curs at my heels, squalling and snapping with angry determination. I fortunately reached the gate in time to close it behind me and shut off my pursuers, amid the laughter and gibes of those in the gallery. I took my boat, and a few miles above found a more hospitable man, who gave me my dinner, plenty of milk, and a most excellent glass of brandy. I inquired the name of the brute, and recorded it in my memory for future use. Ten years after that, he came into my office, and told me he wished to have my services as a lawyer. He had quarrelled with his wife, and they had separated. She was suing him for a separation, and property, dotal and paraphernal. If she recovered, and there were strong reasons for supposing she would, he was ruined.

"'Why do you come to me?' I asked.

"'Ah! Advocat Porter, my friend tell me you de best lawyer, and in my trouble I want de best.' He stated his case, and I told him I would undertake it for a thousand dollars.

"'*Mon dieu!*' he exclaimed, with a desponding shrug, 'it is not possible to me for pay so much.'

"'Then you must employ some one else.'

"'But dere is none else dat be so good like you. Monsieur Brent is for my wife — Got damn! — an' you is de best now, so my friend tell me.'

"'Very well, then, if you want my services, you must pay for them; and you had better come to terms at once, for here is a note which I have just received from Mr. Brent, telling me he wishes to see me, and I expect it is to engage me to assist him in this very case.'

"'*O mon dieu! mon dieu!*' he exclaimed, in agony. 'Vell, I shall give you one thousand dollar.'

"I immediately wrote a note for the amount, payable when the suit was determined; but it was with great difficulty I could induce him to sign it. At length he did, however, and I gained his case for him. He came punctually to pay his note. When I had the money in hand, I told him I had charged him five hundred dollars for attending to his case, and five hundred for setting his dogs on me.

"'I been tink dat all de time,' he said, as he left the office."

There were then several men of eminence at the Bar in the Opelousas and Attakapas country — Brent, Baker, Bowen, and Bronson. The superior abilities of Porter soon began to be acknowledged. His practice increased rapidly, and when a convention was called to form a constitution for the State of Louisiana, Porter was elected from Opelousas as a delegate. Still very young, and scarcely known in the city or along the coast parishes, he came unheralded by any extraordinary reputation for abilities. Very soon, however, he was taking the lead amid the best talent in the State.

In every feature of this Constitution the mind of Porter is apparent; and to-day, to one who has witnessed the forming and passing away of many constitutions, and their effect upon public morals and the general interests of the country, it appears the best that was ever given to a State in this Union. To those who were most active in the formation of this Constitution, and who had most at heart the protection of every interest in the State, the judicial system was most interesting. The preserving of the civil law as the law of the land, and which was guaranteed by the treaty of cession, and at the same time to engraft American ideas upon that system, was a delicate and difficult matter. The French and the French Creoles were desirous of retaining as much of French law and French ideas as possible. To these they had always been accustomed: they thought them best, and were very loath to permit innovations. A written constitution was to these people entirely a new thing. Accustomed to almost absolute power in the hands of their Governors, with his council — these being appointed by the Crown, to which they owed allegiance — they could hardly comprehend a constitutional representative form of government, and, naturally distrustful of the Americans, they feared every move on their part. Porter was an Irishman, and they distrusted him and Henry Johnson less than any others of the convention speaking the English language. Where a difference of opinion seemed irreconcilable between the two interests, Porter was generally the referee, and he was always successful in reconciling these disputes, and bringing both parties to the support of his own views, which were those generally between the two extremes. In this way he succeeded in having a constitution framed as he wished it, upon the organization of the State Government. Under this Constitution, with Matthews and Martin, he was placed upon the Bench of the Supreme Court. Here he remained for many years; but his ambition sought distinction in the councils of the nation, and he resigned his seat to become a candidate for the Senate of the United States.

He had, years before, married the sister of Isaac L. Baker, of the Attakapas country, by whom he had two daughters. One of them had died in early life; the other — a most lovely woman — was under the care of his maiden sister, who resided with him, and had charge of his household until her death. Subsequently to the death of this lady, this only child was married to Mr. Alston, of South Carolina, but survived her marriage only a short time, dying childless.

He was successful in his canvass for the Senate, and in that body he soon became prominent as an orator of great powers, and as a most active business man. It was here the long-existing acquaintance with Mr. Clay ripened into deep friendship. Porter had always been the supporter of the views of Mr. Clay, and during his six years' service in the Senate, he gave a hearty and efficient support to the measures representing the policy of that great statesman.

After the expiration of his senatorial term he retired with an exhausted constitution to his elegant home in the parish of St. Mary, where he devoted himself to his planting interest, now very large. After the death of his daughter, his health declined rapidly; yet, notwithstanding his debilitated condition, he was chosen by a Democratic Legislature, a second time, as senator to the United States Congress; but he never took his seat. Just before the meeting of Congress, he visited Philadelphia for the purpose of obtaining medical advice. Dr. Chapman made a thorough examination of his case, which he pronounced ossification of the arteries of the heart, and which was rapidly progressing. He advised the Judge to return immediately home, and not to think of taking his seat in the Senate, as he was liable to die at any moment, and certainly must die in a very short time. He left immediately for his home.

Some years before this, Mr. Clay found himself so embarrassed that it was necessary for him to apply to his friends for aid. Judge Porter came forward and loaned him a large sum, for which he held his note. Upon reaching Maysville, in descending the Ohio, on his return from Philadelphia, Porter debarked, and went, by stage, to Lexington, where he visited Mr. Clay, and spent one night with him. Finding his disease increasing, and fearing, unless he hurried, that he might never reach home, he declined a longer visit. When in the carriage, (so it was stated at the time, but I do not vouch for the fact,) he took the hand of Mr. Clay, and, pressing it tenderly, said, "Farewell until eternity!" and bade the boy drive on. Mr. Clay found his note left in his hand, marked across the face, "Paid."

On reaching home, his health seemed for a short time to rally; but he began again to sink. Finding it impossible to lie down to sleep, he anticipated speedy dissolution. As a politician, he had been greatly harassed by a dissolute press, and, as a lawyer and prominent man, he had made some enemies. Among these was Thomas H. Lewis, a distinguished lawyer of Opelousas, who, of all his enemies, he hated most, and he was an honest hater. A clergyman was spending some time with him, and apprehending that he might pass suddenly away, remained, in company with Mr. James Porter, his brother, almost constantly with him. Only a day or two anterior to his death, after some conversation upon the subject of the great change, leaning back in his reclining easy-chair, he seemed to forget the presence of these two, and, after remaining for more than an hour entirely silent, without moving or opening his eyes, he commenced to speak, as if communing with himself. "I have," he said, "retrospected all my life, and am satisfied. Many things I have done I should not; but they were never from a bad motive. I have accomplished more than my merits were entitled to. To the inconsiderate generosity of the people of Louisiana I owe much of the success of my life. I have filled the highest offices in their gift, the duties of which I have faithfully discharged to the best of my abilities, and, I believe, to the satisfaction of the people of the State. I have differed with many of my fellow-citizens, and some of them are my enemies; but from my heart I have forgiven them all, as I hope to be forgiven by them, and by my God, before whom I must in a few hours appear." He paused many minutes, and then emphatically added: "Yes, Lord, even Tom Lewis."

The opinions of Judge Porter in the reports of the decisions of the Supreme Court are magnificent specimens of learning, logic, and eloquence. Of every question he took a bold and comprehensive view, and the perspicuity of his style and the clearness of his ideas made all he wrote comprehensible to the commonest capacity. In his decisions he was merciless toward a suitor where he discovered fraud, or the more guilty crime of perjury. His wit was like the sword of Saladin: its brilliancy was eclipsed by the keenness of the edge. In debate he was brilliant and convincing; in argument, cogent and lucid; in declamation, fervid and impassioned, abounding in metaphor, and often elucidating a position with an apposite anecdote, both pointed and amusing. His memory was wonderful, and his reading extensive and diversified. He had so improved the defective education of his youth as to be not only classical, but learned. Impulsive and impetuous, he was sometimes severe and arrogant toward his inferiors who presumed too much upon his forbearance. In his feelings and social associations he was aristocratic and select. He could not tolerate presumptuous ignorance; but to the modest and unobtrusive he was respectful and tolerant. For the whining hypocrisy of pretended piety he had the loftiest contempt, while he gave not only his confidence, but his most sincere respect, to him whose conduct squared with his religious professions. He was a Protestant in religion, as his father had been; but was superior to bigotry or the intolerance of little minds and lesser souls. Like all men of exalted genius, he was erratic at times, and uncertain in his temper. He died without pain, bequeathing his large estate to his brother, with legacies to his sister in Ireland, and to some friends there. To Mr. Clay he left his great diamond ring. He had, at his death, attained only to the age of fifty-seven years. Like Judge Martin, his besetting sin was love of money; but he was not a miser. To his slaves he was remarkably kind and indulgent, never permitting them to be persecuted by any one, and always treating them with paternal kindness — attentive to their comfort, furnishing them with good houses, beds, and an abundance of food and clothing — indeed, with everything which could contribute to their comfort or happiness. His hospitality was not surpassed by any gentleman in all the land. All who have visited at Woodlawn, the beautiful and beautifully improved residence of Judge Porter, will remember the warm Irish welcome and luxurious hospitality of its accomplished and talented master.

Thus have I attempted a slight sketch of the characters, minds, peculiarities, and services of these eminent men and jurists, who reduced to order and form the jurisprudence of Louisiana. It was the eminent abilities and extensive legal learning for which they were so eminently distinguished, as well as the stern integrity of each one of them, which prompted the executive of the State to select them for this delicate and onerous position. At this time, there were not three other men in the State combining so fully all these traits. Their long continuance in office systematized the law and the proceedings in the courts, making order out of chaos, and building up a jurisprudence not inferior to that of any country. Under the peculiar circumstances, this was no very easy or enviable task. The country was now American, and it was important that the judicial system should approximate as nearly as possible to the American system, and, at the same time, preserve the civil law as the law of the land. This law is a most beautiful system of equity, and is disrobed of many of the difficulties which surround the common law, and which oblige in every common-law country a separate and distinct system of equity.

The criminal code was that of the common law. It was so radically different from that which had heretofore prevailed in the country, that it was absolutely necessary, in order to secure to the accused the trial by jury, that this change should be made.

Owing to the extended commerce of New Orleans, many cases arose of contracts made in the common-law States, and this must control these cases. To reconcile and blend the two systems became, in many of these, a necessity. To do this required a knowledge of both on the part of the judges, and this knowledge, in order that no error might misdirect, should be thorough. It was happily accomplished, and now the system is clear and fixed, and will remain a monument to the learning and genius of this court.

Of the three judges, Matthews alone left descendants, and he but two — a son, who soon followed him to the grave, and a daughter, who is still living, the accomplished lady of Major Chase, formerly of the engineer corps of the army of the United States.

CHAPTER XXIX.

AMERICANIZING LOUISIANA.

Powers of Louisiana Courts — Governor William C. C. Claiborne — Cruel O'Reilly — Lefrenier and Noyan Executed — A Dutch Justice — Edward Livingston — A Caricature of General Jackson — Stephen Mazereau — A Speech in Three Languages — John R. Grymes — Settling a Ca. Sa. — Batture Property — A Hundred Thousand Dollar Fee.

THE Supreme Court of the State of Louisiana differs in this from that of the other States: it has jurisdiction as well of the facts as of the law.

In the trial of all cases in the district or lower courts, the testimony is made a part of the record, and goes up to the Supreme Court for supervision, as well as for the enlightenment of the court, which passes upon the facts as well as the law; thus making the judges in the lower courts merely masters in chancery, with the exception, that where the decision of the judge is considered correct, it is approved and made the judgment of the Supreme Court.

This court, by reason of its very extraordinary powers, becomes of the highest importance to every citizen, and is really by far the most important, as it is the most responsible branch of the Government.

The executive can only execute the law; the legislative acts are revisable and amendable, so often as the Legislature holds its sessions; but the judicial decisions of the Supreme Court become the permanent law of the land. True, these decisions may be revised and overruled, but this is not likely to be done by those judges who have made them, and the tenure of office is such as practically to make them permanent.

Under the first Constitution of the State, these judges were nominated by the executive, and confirmed by the Senate. This Senate consisted of seventeen members, chosen by the people from senatorial districts containing a large area of territory and a numerous population. This concentration of responsibility insured the selection of men of the first abilities, attainments, and moral character. So long as this system obtained, the Supreme Bench was ably filled, and its duties faithfully and wisely discharged, with one exception only; but for the sake of those who, though not blamable, would be deeply wounded, I forbear further remark.

Governor William C. C. Claiborne, who was the Territorial Governor, was elected by acclamation the first Governor of the State. He was a Virginian and a man of fine attainments. His peculiar temperament was well-suited to the Creole population, and identifying himself with that population by intermarrying with one of the most respectable families of New Orleans, and studiously devoting himself to the discharge of the duties of his office, he assumed some state in his style of living, and when going abroad kept up something of the regality of his colonial predecessors. Thus suiting the taste and genius of the people, and in some degree comporting with what they had been accustomed to, at the same time assuming great affability of manner, both in private and in the discharge of his public duties, he rendered himself extremely popular with both populations.

Governor Claiborne studiously promoted harmony between the people of the different races constituting the population of the State, and especially that of New Orleans. The State had been under the dominion of three separate nations. The mass of the population, originally French, very reluctantly yielded to Spanish domination, and not without an attempt at resistance. For a time this had been successful in expelling a hated Governor; but the famous O'Reilly, succeeding to the governorship of the colony, came with such a force as was irresistible, suppressing the armed attempt to reclaim the colony from Spanish rule. He made prisoners of the chiefs of the malecontents, with Lefrenier at their head, and condemned them to be shot. One of these was Noyan, the son-in-law of Lefrenier. He was a young man, and but recently united to the beautiful and accomplished daughter of the gallant Lefrenier. His youth, his chivalry, and extraordinary intrepidity excited the admiration of the cold, cruel O'Reilly, and he was offered a pardon. He refused to accept it, un less mercy should be extended to his father-in-law: this having been denied, he was executed, holding in his own the hand of Lefrenier, defiantly facing his executioners and dying with Roman firmness.

This bloody tragedy was transacted upon the square in front of the Cathedral, where now stands the colossal statue of Andrew Jackson, in the midst of the most lovely and beautiful shrubs and flowers indigenous to the soil of Louisiana. The orange, with her pale green foliage, and sweet, modest white flowers, so delicate and so delicious; the oleander, the petisporum, and roses of every hue unite their foliage and blend their fragrance to enchant and delight the eye and sense, and to contrast too the scene of carnage once deforming and outraging this Eden spot.

Scarcely had the people become reconciled to Spanish domination, before the colony was retroceded to France, and again in no great while ceded to the United States.

The French were prejudiced against the Spaniards and despised them, and now the Americans were flowing into the country and city, with manners and customs intolerable to both French and Spaniards, hating both and being hated by both, creating a state of society painfully unpleasant, and apparently irreconcilable.

This state of affairs made the Governor's position anything but pleasant. But distressing as it was, he accomplished more in preserving harmony than one well acquainted with the facts would have deemed possible.

In doing this he was skilful enough to preserve his popularity, and secure his election to the Gubernatorial chair upon the formation of the State. Indeed, so great was his popularity, that it was said some aspirants to Gubernatorial honors incorporated the clause in the Constitution which makes the Governor ineligible to succeed himself, lest Claiborne should be perpetual Governor.

Few men ever lived who could so suit themselves to circumstances as Governor Claiborne. There was a strange fascination in his manners, and a real goodness of heart, which spell-bound every one who came within the range of his acquaintance. He granted a favor in a manner that the recipient forever felt the obligation, and when he refused one, it was with such apparent regret as to make a friend. He sincerely desired the best interest of every one, and promoted it whenever he could. It was said of him that he never refused, but always promised, and always fulfilled his promise whenever it was in his power.

When coming to take charge of the Territorial Government he stopped at Baton Rouge, and spent the night with an honest Dutchman who kept entertainment for travellers. In the morning, when his guest was leaving, learning his official character, he took him aside, and solicited the appointment of justice of the peace for Baton Rouge. "Certainly, sir," said the Governor, "certainly;" and the Dutchman, supposing the appointment made, hoisted his sign above his door, and continued to administer justice in his way until his death, without ever being questioned as to the nature of his appointment. The Governor never thought a second time of the promise.

The selection and appointment of Governor Claiborne for the very delicate duties devolving on an American governor, with such a population as then peopled Louisiana, showed great wisdom and prudence in Mr. Jefferson: he was to reconcile discordant materials within the Territory, and reconcile all to the dominion of the United States. He was to introduce, with great caution, the institutions of a representative republican form of government among a people who had never known any but a despotic government; whose language and religion were alien to the great mass of the people of the nation. An American Protestant population was hurrying to the country, and of all difficulties most difficult, to reconcile into harmonious action two antagonistic religions in the same community is certainly the one. Claiborne accomplished all this. His long continuance in office showed his popularity, and the prosperity of the people and Territory, his wisdom.

In all his appointments he exercised great discretion, and in almost every case his judgment and wisdom were manifested in the result; and to this day his name is revered and his memory cherished as a benefactor. He was twice married, and left two sons — one by each marriage; both live, highly respected, and very worthy citizens of the city of their birth. His name is borne by one of the finest parishes of the State and one of the most beautiful streets in the city of New Orleans, and no man ever deserved more this high and honorable commemoration from a grateful people than did William C. C. Claiborne.

Among those most conspicuous in Americanizing the State and city at the early commencement of the American domination, after the Governor and Supreme Court, were Henry Johnson, Edward Livingston, James Brown, John R. Grymes, Thomas Urquhart, Boling Robinson, and General Philemon Thomas.

Edward Livingston was a citizen at the time of the cession, having emigrated from New York in 1801, where he had already acquired fame as a lawyer. He was the brother of the celebrated Chancellor Livingston, and had, as an officer of the General Government, in the city of New York, defaulted in a large amount. To avoid the penalties of the law he came to New Orleans, then a colony of a foreign government, and there commenced the practice of his profession. After the cession he was not disturbed by the Government, and continued actively to pursue his profession.

He was the intimate friend of Daniel Clark, who was the first Territorial representative in Congress; and it has been supposed that, through the instrumentality of Clark, the Government declined pursuing the claim against him. He first emerged to public view in a contest with Mr. Jefferson relative to the batture property in the city of New Orleans. Livingston had purchased a property above Canal Street, and claimed all the batture between his property and the river as riparian proprietor. This was contested by Mr. Jefferson as President of the United States. He claimed this as public land belonging to the United States under the treaty of purchase. The question was very ably argued by both parties; but the title to this immensely valuable property remained unsettled for many years after the death of both Jefferson and Livingston, and finally was decreed by the Supreme Court of the United States to belong to the city of New Orleans.

When, during the invasion of New Orleans by the English forces in the war of 1812 and '15, General Jackson came to its defence, Livingston volunteered as one of his aids, and rendered distinguished services to Jackson and the country in that memorable affair, the battle of New Orleans. A friendship grew up between Jackson and Livingston, which continued during their lives. Soon after the war, Livingston was elected to represent the New Orleans or First Congressional District in Congress. He continued for some time to represent this district; but was finally, about 1829, beaten by Edward D. White. At the succeeding session of the Legislature, however, he was elected a senator to Congress in the place of Henry Johnson. From the Senate he was sent as Minister to France, and was afterward Secretary of State during the administration of General Jackson. It was in his case that Jackson exercised the extraordinary power of directing the Treasurer of the United States to receipt Mr. Livingston for the sum of his defalcation thirty-four years before. At the time this was done, Tobias Watkins was in prison in Washington for a defalcation of only a few hundreds to the Government. These two events gave rise to the ludicrous caricature, which caused much amusement at the time, of General Jackson's walking with his arm in Livingston's by the jail, when Watkins, looking from the window, points to Livingston, saying to the General: "You should turn me out, or put him in."

Immediately upon this receipt being recorded, Livingston presented an account for mileage and per diem for all the time he had served in Congress, and received it. So long as he was a defaulter to the Government, he could receive no pay for public services.

As a lawyer, Mr. Livingston had no superior. He was master of every system prevailing in the civilized world; he spoke fluently four languages, and read double that number. As a statesman he ranked with the first of his country, and was skilled as a diplomatist. In every situation where placed by fortune or accident, he displayed ample ability for the discharge of its duties. It is not known, but is generally believed that, as Secretary of State, he wrote the state papers of General Jackson. The same has been said of that veteran Amos Kendall. There was one for which Livingston obtained the credit, which he certainly did not write — the celebrated proclamation to the people of South Carolina upon the subject of nullification. This was written by Mr. Webster. Upon one occasion, Mr. Webster, per invitation, with many members of Congress, dined with the President. When the company was about retiring, General Jackson requested Mr. Webster to remain, as he desired some conversation with him. The subject of South Carolina nullification had been discussed cursorily by the guests at dinner, and Jackson had been impressed with some of Webster's remarks; and when alone together, he requested Webster's opinions on the subject at length.

Mr. Webster replied, that the time was wanting for a full discussion of the question; but if it would be agreeable to the President, he would put them in writing and send them to him. He did so. These opinions, expressing fully Mr. Webster's views, were handed to Mr. Livingston, who, approving them, made a few verbal alterations, and submitted the document, which was issued as the President's proclamation. The doctrines politically enunciated in this paper are identical with those entertained in the great speech of Mr. Webster, in the famous contest with Robert T. Hayne, on Foote's Resolutions, some years before; and are eminently Federal. They came like midnight at noon upon the States-Rights men of the South, and a Virginian, wherever found, groaned as he read them.

Mr. Livingston, though a Jeffersonian Democrat in his early life, and now a Jackson Democrat, held very strong Federal notions in regard to the relations between the States and the United States Government, and was disposed to have these sanctioned by the adoption of General Jackson.

Jackson, probably, never read this paper; and if he did, did not exactly comprehend its tenor; for General Jackson's political opinions were never very fixed or clear. What he willed, he executed, and though it cut across the Constitution, or the laws, his friends and followers threw up their caps and cheered him.

Mr. Livingston was charged with the delicate duty of discussing the claims of our Government, representing its citizens, for spoliations committed upon our commerce under the celebrated Milan and Berlin decrees of Napoleon, and, backed by the determination of Jackson, happily succeeded in finally settling this vexatious question. A sum was agreed upon, and paid into the United States Treasury; but if I am not mistaken, none, or very little of it, has ever reached the hands of the sufferers. Upon the proof of the justice of their claims, France was compelled to pay them to the Government; but now the Government wants additional proof of this same fact, before the money is paid over to them.

Mr. Livingston's learning was varied and extensive; he was a fine classical scholar, and equally as accomplished in belles-lettres. In the literature of France, Germany, and Spain he was quite as well versed as in that of his native tongue. His historical knowledge was more extensive and more accurate than that of any public man of the day, except, perhaps, Mr. Benton. At the Bar, he met those eminent jurists, Grymes, Lilly, Brown, and Mazereau, and successfully. This is great praise, for nowhere, in any city or country, were to be found their superiors in talent and legal lore.

Livingston never had the full confidence of his party, and perhaps with the exception of General Jackson, that of any individual. In moneyed matters, he was eminently unreliable; but all admitted his great abilities. In social qualities, he was entirely deficient. He had no powers of attraction to collect about him friends, or to attach even his political partisans. These were proud of his talents, and felt honored in his representation, and with the rest of the world honored and admired the statesman, while they despised the man. He was illiberal, without generosity, unsocial, and soulless, with every attribute of mind to be admired, without one quality of the heart to be loved. In person he was tall and slender, and without grace in his movements, or dignity in his manners. With a most intellectual face, his brow was extremely arched, his eye gray, and his prominent forehead narrow but high and receding; his mouth was large and well formed, and was as uncertain and restless as his eye. No one could mistake from his face the talent of the man; yet there lurked through its every feature an unpleasant something, which forced an unfavorable opinion of the individual. Mr. Livingston lived very many years in Louisiana, and rendered her great services in codifying her laws, and making them clear and easy of comprehension. He shed lustre upon her name, by his eminent abilities as a jurist and statesman, and thus has identified his name most prominently with her history. But without those shining qualities which clasp to the heart in devoted affection the great man, and which constitute one great essential of true greatness. And now that he is in the grave, he is remembered with cold respect alone.

Stephen Mazereau was a Frenchman, a Parisian, and a lawyer there of the first eminence. When about to emigrate to Madrid, in Spain, the Bar of his native city presented him with a splendid set of silver, in respect for his position as a lawyer and his virtues as a man. He remained ten years in Spain's capital, and was at the head of the Bar of that city; and when leaving it to come to New Orleans, received a similar testimonial from his brethren there to his worth and talents. Immediately upon coming to New Orleans, he commenced the practice of the law, and at once took rank with Livingston, Lilly, Brown, and Grymes, who, though then a very young man, had already gained eminence in his profession.

Mr. Mazereau, except giving his State, in the Legislature, the benefit of his abilities, avoided politics, confining himself exclusively to his profession. In the argument of great questions before the Supreme Court of the State between these eminent jurists, was to be seen the combat of giants. Mazereau was a short, stout man, with an enormous head, which made his appearance singularly unique. In his arguments he was considerate, cautious, and eminently learned. Sometimes he would address the people on great political questions, and then all the fervor of the Frenchman would burst forth in eloquent and impressive appeals. I remember hearing him, when he was old, address an immense gathering of the people. He looked over the crowd, when he rose, and said: "I see three nations before me. Americans, I shall speak to you first. Frenchmen, to you next — and to you, my Spanish friends, last. I shall probably occupy two hours with each of you. It will be the same speech; so you who do not understand the English language, need not remain. You who understand French, may return when I shall dismiss these Americans — and you, my Spanish friends, when I am through with these Frenchmen." This he fulfilled to the letter in a six-hours' speech, and I never knew a political speech effect so much.

For many years he was attorney-general of the State, and legal adviser and counsellor of the Governor. Although his practice was eminently profitable, he was so careless and extravagant in money matters, that he was always poor and necessitous, especially in his old age.

It really seems one of the attributes of genius to be indifferent to this world's goods, and when time and labor have done their work, and the imbecility of years obscures its brilliancy, to droop neglected, and, if not in want, in despised poverty. Such was the fate for a short time of this great man — but only for a short time. His powerful intellect retained its vigor, and his brilliant wit all its edges, to within a little while of his death. Sadly I turn back, in memory, to the day he communicated to me that his necessities would compel him to dispose of the beautiful and valuable testimonials of the Bar of two proud nations to his character and abilities. His great intellect was beginning to fade out; but, as the sun, declining to rest canopied with increasing clouds, will sometimes pierce through the interstices of the dark masses, and dart for a moment the intensity of his light upon the earth, the mind of Mazereau would flash in all its youthful grandeur and power from the dimness that was darkening it out.

He was a noble specimen of a French gentleman: a French scholar, and a Frenchman. His memory is embalmed in the hearts of his friends of every nation who knew him in New Orleans. Strictly moral in his habits, full of truth and honor, and overflowing with generosity, social in his habits, and kindly in his feelings, he made friends of all who came in contact with him; and yet he had his enemies. His intolerance of everything that was little or mean, and his scorn and hatred of men of such character, was never concealed, either in his conversation or conduct. Such men were his enemies, and some, too, were his foes from the intolerance of political antagonism; but the grave obliterated these animosities, and the generous political antagonist cherishes now only respect for this truly great man. With deep gratitude my heart turns to his memory: his generous kindness, his warm friendship was mine for long years, and to me his memory is an incense.

John R. Grymes was a Virginian and close connection of John Randolph, of Roanoke, whose name he bore; but of this he never boasted, nor did any one hear him claim alliance of blood with Pocahontas. Mr. Madison appointed him district attorney of the United States for the district of Louisiana, when a very young man. This appointment introduced him to the Bar and the practice immediately. He was one of those extraordinary creations, who leap into manhood without the probation of youth: at twenty-two he was eminent and in full practice, ranking with the leading members of the Bar. Truly, Grymes was born great, for no one can remember when he was not great! Never, in company, in social life, with a private friend, at the Bar, or anywhere, was he even apparently simple or like other men; in private, with his best friend, he spoke, he looked, and he was the great man. He was great in his frivolities, great in his burlesques, great in his humor, great in common conversation; the great lawyer, the great orator, the great blackguard, and the great companion, the great beau, and the great spendthrift: in nothing was he little.

His language was ornate, his style was terse and beautiful; in conversation he was voluble and transcendently entertaining; knew everybody and everything; never seemed to read, and yet was always prepared in his cases, and seemed to be a lawyer by intuition. He was rarely in his office, but always on the street, and always dressed in the extreme of the fashion; lived nowhere, boarded nowhere, slept nowhere, and ate everywhere. He dined at a restaurant, but scarcely ever at the same twice in succession; would search for hours to find a genial friend to dine with him, and then, if he was in the mood, there was a feast of the body and flow of the soul; went to every ball, danced with everybody, visited the ladies; was learned r frivolous, as suited the ladies' capacities or attainments; appeared fond of their society, and always spoke of them with ridicule or contempt; married, and separated from his wife, no one knew for what cause, yet still claimed and supported her. She was the widow of Governor Claiborne, and a magnificent woman; she was a Spaniard by blood, aristocratic in her feelings, eccentric, and, intellectually, a fit companion for Grymes. She was to Claiborne an admirable wife, but there was little congeniality between her and Grymes. Grymes knew that it was not possible for any woman to tolerate him as a husband, and was contented to live apart from his wife. They were never divorced, but lived—she in New York, or at her villa on Staten Island; Grymes in New Orleans. He never complained of her; always spoke kindly, and sometimes affectionately of her; denied the separation, and annually visited her. Their relations were perfectly amicable, but they could not live together. Grymes could have lived with no woman. In all things he was *sui generis;* with no one like him in any one thing, for he was never the same being two consecutive days. He had no fixed opinions that any one knew of; he was a blatant Democrat, and yet never agreed with them in anything; a great advocate of universal equality, and the veriest aristocrat on earth; he would urge to-day as a great moral or political truth certain principles, and ridicule them with contemptuous scorn to-morrow. He was the most devout of Christians to-day, the most abandoned infidel to-morrow; and always, and with everybody, striving to appear as base and as abandoned as profligate man could be: to believe all he said of himself, was to believe him the worst man on earth. He despised public opinion and mankind generally; still he was kind in his nature, and generous to profligacy; was deeply sympathetic, and never turned from the necessitous without dropping a tear or giving a dollar—the one he bestowed generously, the other he rarely had to give; but, if an acquaintance was at hand, he would borrow and give, and the charity of heart was as sincere as though the money had been his own.

On one occasion I was with him when charity was solicited of him by a wretched old woman. "Give me five dollars," he said to me; the money was handed the woman, and she was sent away, to be drunk and in a police-station within the hour. I remarked: "That old wretch has brought all this upon her by an abandoned profligacy." "Then I owe her sympathy as well as charity," was his reply; "I do not know the cause of her suffering, but I know she is suffering: it may be for food, it may be for drink; if either obliterates her misery, your money is well spent."

He had no idea of the value of money; was constantly in the receipt of large fees, with a most lucrative practice, but was always embarrassed, owed everybody, loaned to everybody, gave to everybody, and paid nobody.

During the existence of the law which imprisoned for debt, he was constantly in the sheriff's hands, but always settling, by the most ingenious devices, the claim at the jail-door. It is told of him, that the sheriff on one occasion notified him that there was a *ca. sa.* in his hands, and that he did not want to arrest him. The sum was large, some two thousand dollars — Grymes had not a dollar. He paused a moment, then said, "Come to me to-morrow. I have a case of Milliadon's for trial to-morrow; he is greatly interested in it. When it is called, I will give you the wink, then arrest me." In obedience to directions, the sheriff came, the case was called, and Grymes arrested. Milliadon was in court, his hopes were in Grymes, and when he was informed that Grymes was in custody of the sheriff, he groaned aloud.

"Oh! Mr. Grymes, vat am I to do?"

"Why, you must employ other counsel," said Grymes.

"*Mon dieu*! but I have pay you for attend this case, and I want you. You know about it, and it must be try now."

"Yes," continued the imperturbable Grymes, "you have paid me, I know, and I know it would be dangerous to trust it to other counsel, but it is your only hope. I have no money, and here is a *ca. sa.*, and I am on my way to jail."

"Oh! *mon dieu! mon dieu!* vat is de amount of de *ca. sa.?*"

"Two thousand dollars," said the sheriff.

"Two thousand dollars!" repeated Milliadon.

"Goodall *vs.* Milliadon," said the Judge, "Preston, for plaintiff — Grymes, for defendant. What do you do with this case, gentlemen?"

"We are ready," said Preston.

"And you, Mr. Grymes?" asked the court.

"Vill you take my check for de *ca. sa.*, Mr. Sheriff?"

"Certainly, sir," replied the officer.

"Say we is ready too, Mr. Grymes — all my witness be here."

"I believe we are ready, your honor," answered Grymes. Milliadon was writing his check. "Enter satisfaction on the *ca. sa.*," said Grymes. The sheriff did so, as Milliadon handed him the check. Grymes now turned his attention to the case as coolly as though nothing had occurred. That was the last Milliadon ever heard of his two thousand dollars.

Laurent Milliadon and the millionaire John McDonough were litigious in their characters; and their names occur in the report of the Supreme Court decisions more frequently than those of any ten other men in the State. Grymes was the attorney for both of them for many years. They were both men of great shrewdness, and both speculative in their characters, and both had accumulated large fortunes. Without any assignable cause, McDonough ceased to employ Grymes, and intrusted his business to other counsel, who did not value their services so extravagantly. Mentioning the fact upon one occasion to Grymes, "Ah! yes," said he, "I can explain to your satisfaction the cause. In a certain case of his, in which he had law and justice with him, he suddenly became very uneasy. 'I shall certainly lose it, Grymes,' he said excitedly to me. I told him it was impossible; he had never had so sure a thing since I had been his attorney. In his dogmatical manner, which you know, he still persisted in saying, he was no great lawyer as I was, but some things he knew better than any lawyer, and 'I shall lose that case." At the same time he significantly touched his pocket and then his palm, signifying that money had been paid by his adversary to the court, or some member of it. 'Ah!' said I, 'are you sure — very sure?' 'Very sure — I know it; and you will see I shall lose this suit.' He was not wont to speak so positively, without the best evidence of any fact. 'Well, Mac,' said I, jestingly, 'if that is the game, who can play it better than you can — you have a larger stake than any of them, and of course better ability?' Well, sir, he did lose one of the plainest cases I ever presented to a court. From that day forward I have not received a fee from him: and now the secret is before the world. He has been detected in bribing one of the judges of the Supreme Court."

As an orator, Grymes was among the first of the country. All he wanted, to have been exceedingly eloquent, was earnestness and feeling; of this he was devoid. His manner was always collected and cool; his style chaste and beautiful, with but little ornament; he spoke only from the brain — there was nothing from the heart. In argument he was exceedingly cogent and lucid, and when the subject seemed most complicated, the acuteness of his analytical mind seemed to unravel and lay bare the true features of the case, with an ease and power that required scarce an effort. His powers of ratiocination were very great, and this was the forte of his mind; his conclusions were clearly deduced from arguments always logical.

There were times when he would be serious—and then there was a grandeur about him very striking. At such times, bursts of passionate feeling would break from him that seemed like volcanic eruptions. They appeared to come from a deep and intense tenderness of heart. These were momentary—the lightning's flash illuminating the gloom and darkness of its parent cloud. I have thought this was the man's nature, born with a heart capable of intense feeling, which had been educated to believe this weakness. Coming very young away from his home and early associations, to live and mingle with strangers of a different race—leaving the rural scenes and home associations which were forming and developing nature's glorious gifts, to come to a profligate and heartless city—the whole current of his susceptible nature was changed, and the feeling and good perverted and overshadowed, yet not entirely rooted out. Hence the contradictions in his character. Sometimes nature was too strong for art, and would break out in beauty, as the flower, rich in fragrance and delicate loveliness, when touched by the genial sun, will burst from the black and uninviting bud.

Upon one occasion, when there was a United States senator to be elected, and when the Democratic party held a majority in the Legislature, rendering it impossible for the Whigs to elect any member of their own party, yet, with the assistance of three from the Democratic party, could choose from this party any man they would select and unite upon—they determined to propose Grymes, and had secured the requisite assistance from the Democracy. I was a member, and a Whig, and was delegated to communicate the facts to Grymes. I knew the Senate had been his ambition for years. I knew he felt his powers would give him a position with the greatest of that body, and an immediate national reputation, and had no doubt of his cheerful acquiescence. To my astonishment he assumed a grave and most serious manner. "I am grateful, most grateful to you," he said, "for I know this has been brought about by you, and that you sincerely desire to gratify me; but I cannot consent to be a candidate. Most frankly will I tell you my reasons. I admit it has been my desire for years. It has been, I may say to you, my life-long ambition; but I have always coupled the possession of the position with the power of sustaining it reputably. I was never ambitious of the silly vanity of simply being a senator and known as such; but of giving to it the character and dignity due it. Louisiana is a proud State, her people are a noble and a proud people, they have a right to be so — look at her! With a soil and a climate congenial to the production of the richest staples now ministering to the luxuries and necessities of man — with a river emptying into her commercial mart the productions of a world, her planters are princes, in feeling, fortune, and position. At their mansions is dispensed a noble hospitality, rich in the feasts of body and mind, generous and open as was Virginia's in her proudest days. At Washington I would represent these, and the merchant-princes of her metropolis. You have said, as eloquently as truly, 'There is but one Mississippi River; but one Louisiana; but one New Orleans on the face of the earth.' As she is, and as her people are, I would represent her as her senator.

"I am a beggar, and cannot consent, in this character, to be made more conspicuous, by being made a beggarly senator. I cannot take a house in Washington, furnish it, and live in it as a gentleman. I could not, in any other manner, entertain my people visiting Washington, consistently with my ideas of what a senator should do. I cannot go to Washington, and, as one of them, stand among the great men of the Senate, in that magnificent hall, and feel my soul swell to theirs and its proportions, and then dodge you, or any other gentleman from Louisiana, and sneak home to a garret. My means would allow me no better apartment. I could not live in the mean seclusion of a miserable penury, nor otherwise than in a style comporting, in my estimation, with the dignity and the duty of a senator from Louisiana, as some have done, who were able to live and entertain as gentlemen, for the purpose of the degraded saving of half my *per diem* to swell my coffers at home.

"Now, my friend, I feel how miserably foolish I have been all my life. I have thrown away fortune because I despised it. It was too grovelling a pursuit, too mean a vocation, to make and to hoard money. In my soul I despised it, and now you see it is revenged; for without it, I have learned, there is no gratification for ambition — no independence of a sneering, envious world. A bankrupt is a felon, though his mind, his virtues, and his attainments may be those of a god. He is a useless waif upon the world; for all he has, or all he may be, is, to himself and the world, unavailable without money. I have discarded all my ambitious aspirations long since, and tried to reconcile myself to the fact that my life has been and is a failure. And I am sorry you have come to me to remind me that the aim of my young life was within my reach, when I have no means to grasp it, and, now that I am miserable, to show me what I might have been. No, my friend, I must go on with the drudgery of the law, to earn my bread, and thus eke out a miserable future. I am grateful to you and my other friends, who have delegated you to this mission. Say so to them, if you please. I must go to court. The horse of the bark-mill must go to his daily circle. Good morning!"

Some years after the event above mentioned, Grymes, as the attorney of the city of New Orleans, succeeded, before the Supreme Court of the United States, in making good the title to the batture property in the city. What is termed batture in Louisiana is the land made by accretion or deposits of the Mississippi. One strange feature of this great river is, that it never gets any wider. It is continually wearing and caving on one side or the other, and making a corresponding deposit on the other bank. Opposite a portion of the city of New Orleans this deposit has been going on for many years, while the opposite bank has been wearing away. There are living citizens who saw in youth the river occupying what is now covered by many streets and many blocks of buildings, and is one of the most valuable portions of the city. In truth, what was a century ago entire river, is now one-fourth of the city, and this deposit goes on annually without any decrease in its ratio.

By agreement of all parties, this batture was surveyed into squares and lots, and sold at public auction, and the money deposited in the Bank of Louisiana, to the credit of the Supreme Court of the United States, to abide the decision of that tribunal as to the rightful ownership. The decision gave it to the city. Grymes, as attorney for the city, by order of the court, received a check for the money. The bank paid the check, and Grymes appropriated one hundred thousand dollars of it, as a fee for his services, and then deposited the balance to the credit of the mayor and council of the city. This was a large fee, but was not really what he was entitled to, under the custom of chancery for collecting money. He had agreed to pay Daniel Webster for assistance rendered; but Mr. Webster, some years after, informed me that he had never received a cent, and I am sure he never did, after that.

Grymes was well aware, if the city fathers got their hands upon the money, it would be years before he got this amount, if ever. With a portion of this money he liquidated all claims not antiquated and forgotten by him, and the balance was intrusted to the hands of a friend to invest for his benefit. This, together with his practice, which was now declining, furnished a handsome support for him. Age appeared to effect little change in his *personnel*. At sixty-seven, he was as erect in person and as elastic in step as at thirty. There was none of that *embonpoint* usually the consequence of years and luxurious living. He was neither slender nor fat; but what is most agreeable to the eye — between the two, with a most perfectly formed person. His features were manly, and strikingly beautiful; his blue eyes beaming with the *hauteur* of high breeding and ripe intelligence. These features were too often disfigured with the sneer of scorn, or the curled lip of expressive contempt. His early hopes, his manhood's ambition had been disappointed; and, soured and sore, he sneered at the world, and despised it. He had no confidence in man or woman, and had truly reached Hamlet's condition, when "Man delighted him not, nor woman either." He felt the world was his debtor, and was niggardly in its payments. He grew more and more morose as the things of time receded. Others, full of youth, talent, and vigor, were usurping the positions and enjoying the honors of life, which were slipping away from him unenjoyed. He turned upon these the bitterness engendered by disappointment. Cynicism lent edge to his wit, and bitterness to his sarcasm. He was at war with himself, and consequently with all the world. His mind felt none of the imbecility of age, and to the last retained its perspicuity and power. As he came into life a man, and never knew a boyhood, so he went from it a man, without the date of years. At sixty-eight years of age, he went quietly from life without suffering, and, to himself, without regret. He was a man — take him all in all — whose like we shall not look on soon again.

The virtues and the vices, the loves and the hates of life were strangely blended in the character of John Randolph Grymes; but if we judge from the fact that he had and left many warm and devoted friends, and few enemies, we must suppose the good in his nature greatly preponderated. But notwithstanding the great space he had filled in the eyes of the people of the city, his death startled only for a moment, and straightway he was forgotten; as the falling pebble dimples for a moment the lake's quiet surface — then all is smooth again.

CHAPTER XXX.

DIVISION OF NEW ORLEANS INTO MUNICIPALITIES.

American Hotel — Introduction of Steamboats — Faubourg St. Mary — Canal Street — St. Charles Hotel — Samuel J. Peters — James H. Caldwell — Fathers of the Municipality — Bernard Marigny — An Ass — A. B. Roman.

FORTY years ago there was not a public hotel in the city of New Orleans which received and entertained ladies. There was but one respectable American hotel in the city. This was kept by John Richardson, who still lives, and was on Conti Street, between Chartres and the levee. About that time Madame Heries opened the Planter's Hotel on Canal Street, which some years after fell and crushed to death some thirty persons. There were many boarding-houses, where ladies were entertained, and to these were all ladies visiting the city constrained to resort. Some of these were well kept and comfortable, but afforded none or very few of the advantages of public hotels. They were generally kept by decayed females who were constrained to this vocation by pecuniary misfortunes. The liberal accommodation afforded in hotels, especially built and furnished for the purpose, was not to be found in any of them.

At this period all the means of travel between Mobile and New Orleans, across the Lake, consisted of one or two schooners, as regular weekly packets, plying between the two cities. It was about this time that the tide of emigration which had peopled the West, and the rapid increase of production, was stimulating the commerce of New Orleans. It was obeying the impulse, and increasing in equal ratio its population. This commerce was chiefly conducted by Americans, and most of these were of recent establishment in the city. That portion of the city above Canal Street, and then known as the Faubourg St. Mary, was little better than a marsh in its greater portion. Along the river and Canal Street, there was something of a city appearance, in the improvements and business, where there were buildings. In every other part there were shanties, and these were filled with a most miserable population.

About this time, too, steamboats were accumulating upon the Western waters — a new necessity induced by the increase of travel and commerce—affording facilities to the growing population and increasing production of the vast regions developing under the energy of enterprise upon the Mississippi and her numerous great tributaries. It seemed that at this juncture the whole world was moved by a new impulse. The difficulties of navigating the Mississippi River had been overcome, and the consequences of this new triumph of science and man's ingenuity were beginning to assume a more vigorous growth.

The Ohio and its tributaries were peopling with a hardy and industrious race; the Missouri, Arkansas, and Red rivers, too, were filling with a population which was sweeping away the great wild forests, and fields of teeming production were smiling in their stead. New Orleans was the market-point for all that was, and all that was to be, the growth of these almost illimitable regions. It was, as it ever is, the exigencies of man answered by the inspirations of God. The necessities of this extending population along the great rivers demanded means of transportation. These means were to be devised, by whom? The genius of Fulton was inspired, and the steamboat sprang into existence. The necessity existed no longer, and the flood of population poured in and subdued the earth to man's will, to man's wants. Over the hills and valleys, far away it went, crowding back the savage, demanding and taking for civilized uses his domain of wilderness, and creating new necessities—and again the inspired genius of man gave to the world the railroad and locomotive.

The great increase in the production of cotton in the West, and which went for a market to New Orleans, necessitated greater accommodations for the trade in that city—presses for compressing, and houses for merchants, where the business could be conducted with greater facility and greater convenience. American merchants crowded to the city, and located their places of business above Canal Street, beyond which there was not a street paved. There was not a wharf upon which to discharge freights, consequently the cotton bales had to be rolled from the steamers to the levee, which in the almost continued rains of winter were muddy, and almost impassable at times for loaded vehicles. Below Canal Street the levee was made firm by being well shelled, and the depth of water enabled boats and shipping to come close alongside the bank, which the accumulating batture prevented above.

The French, or Creole population greatly preponderated, and this population was all below Canal Street. They elected the mayor, and two-thirds of the council, and these came into office with all the prejudices of that people against the Americans, whom a majority of them did not hesitate to denominate intruders. The consequence was the expenditure of all the revenue of the city upon improvements below Canal Street. Every effort was made to force trade to the lower portion of the city. This was unavailing. The Faubourg St. Mary continued to improve, and most rapidly. Business and cotton-presses sprang up like magic. Americans were purchasing sugar plantations and moving into the French parishes, drawing closer the relations of fellow-citizens, and becoming more and more acquainted with the feelings and opinions of each other, and establishing good neighborhoods and good feelings, and by degrees wearing out these national prejudices, by encouraging social intercourse and fraternity. They were introducing new methods of cultivation, and new modes of making sugar; pushing improvements, stimulating enterprise, and encouraging a community of feeling, as they held a common interest in the country. In the country parishes these prejudices of race had never been so strong as in the city, and were fast giving way; intermarriages and family relations were beginning to identify the people, and this to some extent was true in the city. But here there was a conflict of interest, and this seemed on the increase. The improvements made in the Faubourg were suggested by the necessities of commerce, and this naturally went to these. There was a superior enterprise in the American merchant, there was greater liberality in his dealings: he granted hazardous accommodations to trade, and made greater efforts to secure it. This had the effect of securing the rapidly increasing commerce of the city to the American merchants, and of course was promoting the settlement and improvement of the Faubourg St. Mary. It excited, too, more and more the antipathies of the ancient population. These, controlling the city government constantly in a most envious spirit, refused to extend the public improvements of the Faubourg.

There was not, forty years ago, or in 1828, a paving-stone above Canal Street, nor could any necessity induce the government of the city to pave a single street. Where now stands the great St. Charles Hotel, there was an unsightly and disgusting pond of fetid water, and the locations now occupied by the City Hotel and the St. James were cattle-pens. There was not a wharf in the entire length of the city, and the consequence was an enormous tax levied upon produce, in the shape of drayage and repairs of injuries to packages, from the want of these prime necessities.

The navigation of the Bayou St. John commanded for the lower portion of the city the commerce crossing the lake, and to monopolize the profits of travel, a railroad was proposed from the lake to the river, and speedily completed. The people of the Faubourg, to counteract as much as possible these advantages, constructed a canal from the city to the lake, which was to enter the city, or Faubourg St. Mary, at the foot of Julia Street, one of the broadest and best streets in that quarter of the city. This was of sufficient capacity for schooners and steamboats of two hundred tons burden. When this was completed, with great difficulty the authorities were prevailed upon to pave Julia Street; still the greatly increasing demands of commerce were neglected, and while by these refusals the population of the city proper was doing all it could to force down to the city this increasing trade, they neglected to do anything there for its accommodation. The streets were very narrow; the warehouses small and inconvenient; the merchants close and unenterprising, seemingly unconscious of the great revolution going on in their midst.

From the growing greatness of the surplus products of the immense Valley, this was quadrupling annually. The cotton crop of the United States, forty years ago, scarcely reached half a million of bales, and of this New Orleans did not receive one-third; but in five years after, her receipts were very nearly one-half of the entire crop. At the same period, the sugar crop did not amount to more than twenty thousand hogsheads; five years thereafter, it had quadrupled, and the commerce from the upper rivers had increased a hundred-fold, and was going on in all the products of the soil to increase in like ratio. At this time the antipathy was at its acme between the two races or populations.

Then the Legislature held its sessions in New Orleans, and the

American residents, merchants, and property-holders determined to apply to the Legislature for an amendment of the city charter. A bill was introduced accordingly, proposing to divide the city into three municipalities, making Canal and Esplanade streets the lines of division; giving the city proper and each faubourg a separate government: in truth, making three cities where there had been but one. The excitement in the city became intense, and sectional animosities increased in bitterness. To the American population it was a matter of prime necessity; to the property-holders and merchants of the city proper it was a matter of life and death. To these it was apparent that the moment this bill became a law, and the Faubourg St. Mary controlled her own finances, her streets would be paved and warehouses spring up to meet every demand — wharves would be constructed, the quay or levee would be sheltered, capital would flow to the Faubourg, and, in a moment as it were, she would usurp the entire domestic trade of the country: in other words, the Faubourg St. Mary would become the City of New Orleans.

After carefully canvassing the Legislature, it was found very doubtful whether the bill would pass or not; the attempt had heretofore proved eminently unsuccessful, but now it was apparent that it had gained many friends, and it was not certain it could be defeated. Under these circumstances, overtures were made by the city government, to expend all the revenue in improvements above Canal Street, which should be collected from the inhabitants of that quarter. This proposition was declined, and the bill after a most exciting struggle became a law. Under its provisions a new council and recorder were chosen, and a new impetus was given the Faubourg St. Mary, which was now, under this law, the second municipality. Extensive wharves were erected along the front of the municipality; streets were paved, and the whole trading community felt the improvements were assuming gigantic proportions, and trade relieved of onerous and vexatious impositions. Property rose in value rapidly; Canal Street grew speedily into importance. The dry-goods trade, hitherto confined almost exclusively to Chartres Street, came out upon this magnificent street as rapidly as it could be accommodated. From an almost deserted suburb, it became the centre of business and the great boulevard of the city. A company built the great

St. Charles Hotel, and here were first opened hotel accommodations for ladies in New Orleans, thirty-one years ago.

The commercial crisis of 1837 retarded temporarily the improvements, but only for a day as it were, and in a few years there was a great American city, fashioned by American energy and American capital from the unsightly and miserable mire of the Faubourg St. Mary.

To the enterprise and perseverance of two men was mostly due this rapid improvement of the city and its new and extended accommodations to commerce — Samuel J. Peters and James H. Caldwell. Mr. Peters was a native of Canada, and came when quite a youth to New Orleans. He married a Creole lady, a native of the city; and, after serving as a clerk for some time in the business house of James H. Leverick & Co., commenced business as a wholesale grocer. In this business he was successful, and continued in it until his death. He was a man of splendid abilities and great business tact, great energy and application, and full of public spirit. New Orleans he viewed as his home; he identified himself and family with the people, and his fame with her prosperity. To this end he devoted his time and energies; around him congregated others who lent willingly and energetically their aid to accomplish his conceptions, and to fashion into realities the projections of his mind. I remember our many walks about the second municipality — when, where now is the City Hall, and Camp and Charles streets, and when these magnificent streets, now stretching for miles away, ornamented with splendid buildings and other improvements, were but muddy roads through open lots, with side-walks of flat-boat gunwales, with only here and there a miserable shanty, with a more miserable tenant — to contemplate and talk of the future we both lived to see of this municipality. Stopping on one occasion in front of what is Lafayette Square, at the time the bill was pending for the division of the city into municipalities, he said: "Here must be the City of New Orleans. You can pass the bill, now before the Legislature; and if you will, I promise you I will make the Faubourg St. Mary the City of New Orleans." Only a few months before his death, we stood again upon the same spot, surrounded by magnificent buildings — Odd-Fellows' Hall, the First Presbyterian Church, the great City Hall, and grand and beautiful buildings of every character. "Do you remember my promise made here?" he said. "Have I fulfilled it? Many days of arduous labor and nights of anxious

38

thought that promise cost me. You did your part well, and when I thought it impossible. Have I done mine?" I could but answer: "Well, and worthily!" I never saw him after—but I shall never cease to remember him as a great, true man.

James H. Caldwell was an Englishman, and by profession a comedian. It was he who first brought a theatrical company to the West. He had built the first theatres in Cincinnati, St. Louis, and New Orleans, and first created a taste for theatricals in the great West. Possessing fine natural abilities, and wonderful enterprise, he pushed his fortunes, as a theatrical manager, successfully for a number of years. He built the Camp Street Theatre, and made it exceedingly profitable. Away back, forty-five years ago, I remember my first meeting with him at Vicksburg, then a little hamlet, with but few houses and many hills, abrupt, and ugly. He and his company were descending to Natchez, and thence, after a short season, to New Orleans. Edwin Forrest, then a youth, was one of his company, which also included Russell and wife, Sol. Smith and brother, with their wives, Mrs. Rose Crampton, and, as a star, Junius Brutus Booth. How wild was the scene around us! The river was low and sluggish; the boat small and dirty; the captain ignorant and surly; the company full of life, wit, and humor. Slowly we labored on. The dense forest came frowning to the river's brink, with only here and there, at long intervals, an opening, where some adventurous pioneer had cut and burned the cane, and built his shanty. The time was whiled away with song, recitation, anecdotes, and laughter, until midnight brought us to Natchez. It was a terrible night—dark, and beginning to rain. Under the hill at Natchez, forty-five years ago, was a terrible place. The road up the bluff was precipitous and muddy. There were no accommodations for decent people under the hill. The dance-houses were in full blast. Boisterous and obscene mirth rang from them; men and women were drunk; some were singing obscene songs; some were shouting profanity in every disgusting term; some, overcome with debauchery, were insensible to shame, and men and women, rushing from house to house, gathered a crowd to meet us as we landed. One tremendous slattern shouted, as she saw us come on shore: "There are the show-folks; now we'll have fun!" If Mrs. Farren—the daughter of Russell—still lives, I will say to her that this was her advent to Natchez. Up that hill, through mire and rain, I bore her in my arms, on that terrible night. Caldwell alone was cheerful; Sol. Smith joked, and Russell swore.

> "How many, many memories
> Sweep o'er my spirit now!"

It was a peculiarity of James H. Caldwell to do whatever he did with all his might. No obstacle seemed to deter or impede the execution of any public or individual enterprise of his. Beside being a splendid performer, he was an accomplished gentleman, and a fine, classic scholar. His reading was select and extensive. At a very early day, he was impressed with the future importance of New Orleans as a commercial city, and commenced to identify himself with the American population, and to make this his future home. His ideas on this subject were in advance of those of many whose business had always been commerce, and they were generally deemed Utopian and extravagant; but his self-reliance was too great to heed any ridicule thrown upon any thought or enterprise of his. He invested his limited means in property in the second municipality, and lent himself, heart and soul, in connection with Peters, to its development into the proportions his imagination conceived it was ultimately capable of attaining, should the extent of its commerce reach the magnitude he supposed it would. Immediately upon the amendment of the city charter, creating the municipalities, and making independent the second, Caldwell conceived the idea of lighting the city with gas, and, at the same time, of building a city hall, and the establishment of a system of public schools.

Edward York, a merchant of the city, gave this idea his special attention, and co-operated with Peters and Caldwell in every project for the advancement of the interests of the municipality. Caldwell set to work in the face of difficulties, which really seemed insurmountable, to effect his scheme of lighting the city with gas. I was at that time a member of the Legislature. Caldwell's scheme was to obtain a charter for a bank, and with this carry into execution rapidly his scheme. He came to me, and opened up his views. He wanted my aid so far as assisting him in drafting the charter, and undertaking its passage through the Legislature. There was no delay, and in a short time the gas-light and banking company was chartered, the stock taken, and the bank in successful operation. Caldwell, though entirely unacquainted with the practical necessities of constructing the proper works to complete his plan, went energetically to work to acquire this, and did so, and in a few months everything was systematically and economically moving forward to completion. He alone conceived, planned, and superintended the whole work. Nor did he abate in energy and perseverance one moment until all was completed. All this while he was a member of the council, and giving his attention to many other matters of prime importance to the municipality.

Peters, Caldwell, and York may justly be said to have been the fathers of the municipality. To Edward York is justly due the system of public schools, which is so prominent a feature in the institutions of New Orleans. These three have passed away, and with them all who co-operated with them in this enterprise, which has effected so much for the city of New Orleans. They were unselfish public benefactors, and deserve this commemoration.

Among the remarkable men of New Orleans, at this period, was Bernard Marigny, a scion of the noble stock of the Marigny de Mandevilles, of France. His ancestor was one of the early settlers of Louisiana, and was a man of great enterprise, and accumulated an immense fortune, which descended to Bernard Marigny. This fortune, at the time it came into the hands of Marigny, was estimated at four millions. His education was sadly neglected in youth; so was his moral training. He was a youth of genius, and proper cultivation would, or might, have made him a man of distinguished fame and great usefulness. Coming into possession of his immense estate immediately upon his majority, with no experience in business matters, flushed with youth and fortune, courted by every one, possessing a brilliant wit, fond to excess of amusements, delighting in play, and flattered by every one, he gave up his time almost entirely to pleasure. A prominent member of the Legislature for many years, he had identified himself with the history of the State, as had his ancestor before him. He was the youngest member of the convention which formed the first Constitution of the State, and was the last survivor of that memorable body. Soon after succeeding to his fortune, and when he was by far the wealthiest man in the State, Louis Philippe, the fugitive son of Louis Égalité, Duke of Orleans, came to New Orleans, an exile from his native land, after his father had perished by the guillotine. Marigny received him, and entertained him as a prince. He gave him splendid apartments in his house, with a suite of servants to attend him, and, opening his purse to him, bade him take *ad libitum.* For some years he remained his guest, indeed until he deemed it necessary to leave, and when he went, was furnished with ample means. Long years after, when fortune had abandoned the fortunate, and was smiling upon the unfortunate — when the exile was a monarch, and his friend and benefactor was needy and poor — when Louis Philippe was king of France and the wealthiest man in Europe, they met again. Their circumstances were reversed. Marigny was old and destitute. The monarch waited to be importuned, though apprised of his benefactor's necessities and dependence, and answered his appeal with a snuff-box, and the poor old man learned that there was truth in the maxim, "Put not your trust in princes."

Wasteful habits, and the want of economy in every branch of his business, wrought for him what it must for every one — "ruin." During the discussion in the Legislature upon the bill dividing the city into municipalities, Marigny, then a member, exerted himself against the bill. He viewed it as the destruction of the property of the ancient population in value, and their consequent impoverishment, and threw much of his wit and satire at those who were its prominent supporters. Among them was Thomas Green Davidson, a distinguished member of Congress, (still living, and long may he live!) Robert Hale, and myself. Ridicule was Marigny's *forte.* Upon the meeting of the House, and before its organization for business, one morning, the writer, at his desk, was approached by Alexander Barrow, a member — and who afterward died a member of the United States Senate — who read to me a squib which Marigny was reading, at the same moment, to a group about him. It read thus:

"Sparks, and Thomas Green Davidson,
Rascals by nature and profession:
Dey can bos go to hell
Wid Colonel Bob Hailles."

I saw that the group would, with Marigny, soon approach me, and made haste to reply. It was only a day or two before we were to adjourn. When they came, and the squib was read, I read the following reply:

"Dear Marigny, we're soon to part,
So let that parting be in peace:

We 've not been angered much in heart,
But e'en that little soon shall cease.

"When you are sleeping with the dead,
The spars we've had I'll not forget:
A warmer heart, or weaker head,
On earth, I'll own, I never met.

"And on your tomb inscribed shall be,
In letters of your favorite brass,
Here lies, O Lord! we grieve to see,
A man in form, in head an ass."

He arched his brow, and, without speaking, retired. An hour after, he came to me, and said: "Suppose you write no more poetry. I shall stop. You can call me a villain, a knave, a great rascal: every gentleman have dat said about him. Mr. Clay, Mr. Webster, General Jackson, all have been call so. You can say dat; but I tell you, sir, I not like to be call ass."

He was the aggressor, and, though offended, was too chivalrous to quarrel. He had fought nineteen duels, and I did not want to quarrel either.

For many of his latter years he was destitute and miserable. He had seen all his compeers pass away, and he felt that he was in the way of a generation who knew nothing of him, or his history, and who cared nothing for either. At nearly ninety years of age he died in extreme poverty. Nature had done much for Bernard Marigny. His mind was of no ordinary stamp. He was a natural orator, abounding in humor and wit, and was the life of society. His person was symmetry itself, about five feet ten inches, and admirably proportioned; and, to the day of his death, he was truly a handsome man, so symmetrical and well-preserved were his features, and the sparkling light in his eyes. He long enjoyed the luxuries of life, and lived to lament its follies in indigence and imbecility.

Of all the Creole population, A. B. Roman was, at this time, the most prominent, and the most talented. In very early life he was elected Governor of the State, and discharged the duties of the office with great ability, and, after Claiborne, with more satisfaction to the people than any man who ever filled the office. The Constitution did not admit of his being elected a second time as his own successor, but he might be again chosen to fill the chair after the four years' service of another. He was elected to a second term, and when it expired, he was chosen president of the draining company, in which office he rendered most important services to the city, in planning and effecting a system of drainage which relieved the city of the immense swamp immediately in its rear.

In all the relations of life, A. B. Roman was a model — gentle and affable in his manners, punctiliously honorable, faithful in all his transactions, affectionate and indulgent as a husband and father, kind and obliging as a neighbor, faithful to all the duties of a citizen; and ambitious to promote the best interests of his native State, he gave his time and talents for this purpose, wherever and whenever they could be of service. The war, in his old age, left him destitute and heart-broken. I had the opportunity of several conversations with him, and found him despondent in the extreme. Our last interview was the week before his death.

"In my old age," he said, "I am compelled, for a decent support, to accept a petty office — recorder of mortgages — and I feel humiliated. I see no future for me or my people. My days are wellnigh over, and I can't say I regret it."

Only five days after, he fell dead in the street, near his own door. A wise and good man went to his God when A. B. Roman died. He was one of a large and respectable family, long resident in the State, and surely was one of her noblest sons.

CHAPTER XXXI.

BLOWING UP THE LIONESS.

Doctor Clapp — Views and Opinions — Universal Destiny — Alexander Barrow — E. D. White — Cross-Breed, Irish Renegade and Acadian — A Heroic Woman — The Ginseng Trade — I-I-I'll D-d-die F-f-first.

DR. CLAPP, so conspicuous in the annals of New Orleans, was from New England, and was located in New Orleans as a Presbyterian minister, as early as 1824, and about the same period that the great and lamented Larned died.

His mind was bold and original, analytical and independent. Soon after his location and the commencement of his ministry, he gave offence to some of his church, and especially to some of his brother pastors, by the enunciation of opinions not deemed orthodox.

There was at this time preaching at Natchez, one Potts, who was a Presbyterian, a Puritan, and extremely straight-laced in doctrine, and eminently puritan in practice, intolerant, bigoted, and presumptuous. Potts had accomplished one great aim of his mission: he had married a lady of fortune, and assumed more purity than any one else, and was a sort of self-constituted exponent of the only true doctrines of his church. Arrogant and conceited, he, though a very young man, thrust himself forward as a censor, and very soon was in controversy with Dr. Clapp. Without a tithe of his talent, or a grain of his piety, he assumed to arraign him on the ground of unfaithfulness to the tenets of the church. This controversy was bitter and continued. The result was, that Dr. Clapp dissolved connection with the Presbyterian Church, and, at the call of the most numerous and talented as well as wealthy congregation ever preached to, up to that time, in New Orleans, established himself as an independent, and continued to preach for many years — indeed, until age and infirmity compelled him to retire.

His peculiar religious opinions were more Unitarian than Presbyterian. They consisted of an enlightened philosophy derived from *natural revelation,* which elevated Deity above the passions, prejudices, loves, and hates of mortality. *His* GOD *was* INFINITE, ALL-PERVADING, *and* PERFECT.

The purity of his character, and his wonderful intellect, combined, brought around him the most intelligent and moral of the population, and his opinions won many converts. He preached and practised a rational religion, defined a rigid morality as the basis and main requisite to true piety, and the doing good toward his fellow-man, the duty of man toward God.

The faith he exacted was predicated upon works. . . . That he who had faith in the existence of the soul, and who believed its future dependent upon him, should be taught this faith was best exemplified by a faithful discharge of all the duties imposed by society and law. That he who was pious, was a good husband, father, and friend, a good neighbor, an honest, and sincere man, faithful in the discharge of all his duties as a citizen and member of society: resting here the hope of future reward, and not looking to the merits of any other for that salvation, which the mind hopes, and the heart craves for all eternity; fixing a responsibility individually and indivisibly upon each and every one, to earn salvation by discharging temporal duties which secure the harmony, well-being, and general love of mankind. Any other doctrine, he contended, destroyed man's free agency, and discouraged the idea that virtue and goodness were essential to true piety. God had created him for an especial mission. His existence in time was his chrysalis condition; to make this as nearly perfect as was possible to his nature, he was gifted with mind, passion, and propensities — the former to conceive and control the discharge of the duties imposed upon him in this state: this done, he perished as to time, and awoke prepared for eternity. These ideas were impressed with a logic irresistible to the enlightened mind — not clouded with the bigotry of fanaticism — and an eloquence so persuasive and sweet as to charm the heart and kindle it into love.

He never burned brimstone under the noses of his auditory, nor frenzied their imaginations with impassioned appeals to supernatural agencies. He expounded the Scriptures as the teachings of men. His learning was most profound, especially in the languages. He understood thoroughly the Hebrew and Greek. He read from the originals the Scriptures, and interpreted them to his hearers, as to their meaning in their originals, and disrobed them of the supernatural character which an ignorant fanaticism has thrown over them, and which time and folly has indurated beyond the possibility of learning and science to crack or crush.

A great original thinker, untrammelled by the schools, and independent of precedents, he saw nature before him, and studied closely all her developments. Eminently schooled in the philosophy of life, deeply read in the human mind and the heart, he searched for all the influences operating its conclusions, and the motives of human action: the relations of man to external nature, the connection of mind with matter, the origin of things, their design as developed in their creation, their connection and dependence, one upon the other, and the relation of all to the Creator, and in those the duty of man. It was his idea, that, commencing from the humblest, and ascending to man, through created nature, the design was manifest that these were all, in the animal and the vegetable kingdom, assigned by the Creator for man's uses. To him alone, in all these creations, are given the faculties necessary to a comprehension of the nature of all of these, as well as their uses.

From this fact, so powerfully prominent in all natural developments, he viewed man as the most intimate relation of the Creator on this globe, and discovering in him no designs beyond the cultivation of the great faculty of thought for time, the inference was natural that his future was not for time, or time's uses. That all was only fitting the soul, which his instincts tell him exists within, when, refined by time, and the probation of life, for the independence, and the fruition of the sublime designs of God in eternal life, he should ascend to his destined sphere, etherialized, and know his Creator and the future of his being; when speculation should cease, and reality and unambiguous truth be made manifest. Of this great truth his mind was so fully impressed that all his life was by it governed. His convictions were palpable in his conduct, for it was in strict conformity with these opinions. The aberrations from virtue and the laws of morals, as established by man for the better regulation of his conduct toward his fellow-men, he deemed the result of improper education, and especially the education of the heart, and the want of the training this gives to the natural desires of his organization. That these desires, passions, and instincts, are given as essential to his mission in time, and those properly educated, trained, and directed, are necessary to his fulfilment of life's duties, in the perfection of the Creator's design, and, when so educated and directed, secure to the individual, and to society, the consummation of this design; but when perverted, become a punishment to both society and the individual, for the neglect of a prime duty; and belong alone to time. Similar results he saw from similar causes, in the operations of inanimate life. The design of the tree was to grow upward, but an unnatural obstacle, in the falling of another, bends it away, and its growth is perverted from the original design, yet it grows on and completes the cycle of its destiny.

The stream flows onward, naturally obeying a natural law; but an obstacle interposes and interrupts the design; still it will go on to complete its cycle, obedient to its destiny, though turned from its natural channel: and these are the same in the end with those undisturbed in the fulfilment of their designs. All crime or vice is of time, and made such by the laws of man. The aggregation of men into societies or communities necessitate laws to establish moral, legal, and political duties, and to provide punishments for the infraction of these. The right to acquire and possess the fruits of labor — the right of free thought — the right to enjoy the natural relations of life, and the privileges conferred by society — the right to live undisturbed, all are the objects of legal protection; because the attributes of man's nature, unrestrained in the discharge of his duties to his fellow-man, will invade these rights, and hence the necessity of a universal rule of action. All these attributes are susceptible of education as to what is right, and what is wrong; and it is the duty of religion to impress upon the mind the importance of the one to the security of society, and the evil of the other in its effect upon the design of the Creator. This design is harmony and love universal, and pervades all nature, where a free will is not vouched; but with this free will is given a capacity to cultivate it into that love and harmony, and thus to consummate the great design of the Creator.

He taught, *religion was the sublimation of moral thought and moral action;* because it was in harmony with nature, and subserved the purposes of the Creator — because it brought man into harmony with every other creation, whose design was apparent to his capacity of understanding — that this design, made manifest to his mind, taught him his duty; and it was the province of the teacher to show to all this design, and illustrate this harmony. The teacher should know before he attempted to teach. He should disabuse his own mind of prejudices and superstitions at variance with nature, and study natural organization to learn the intention of the Creator; learn the nature of plants, the organization of the earth, its components how formed, and of what — all animal creation — the mechanism of the universe, its motions — the exact perfection of every creation for the design of that creation; see and know God's will, and God's wisdom, and God's power in all of them; descend to the minor and most infinitesimal creation; learn its organization, and see God here with a design, and a perfect organization, to work it out — learn truth, where only truth exists, from God in all created nature, and teach this, that all may learn and conserve to the same great end.

When comprehended, this planet, with all its creations, was designed for man, and to perfect him for the use of God's design. These are for consummation in eternity — all that relates to him in time, but subserves the great end. The relationship to him is apparent in all that surrounds him on earth. Step by step it comes up to him, and all is for his use. At this point, all stops except himself. What was his design as manifested in his nature? Surely, not solely to control and appropriate all created matter surrounding him — not simply to probate for a period, and pass away. It must be, that he is the link perfected in this probation for a higher creation, as a part of a more consummate perfection revealed through death. It cannot be, that the mind given to him, alone, was only given to learn in this combination of elements — earth, air, fire, and water — the startling and omnipotent wisdom of the all-wise Creator, and then to perish with knowing no more of that God, which this knowledge has created so consummate a desire to know.

The cycle of man's destiny is not in time, that of all else is; and that destiny centres in his use, and is complete. If for him there is not a future, why were the instincts of his nature given? Why the power to learn so much? To trace in the planetary system divine wisdom, and divine power; to see and know the same in the mite which floats in the sunbeam? If this is all he is ever to know, does this complete a destiny for use? if so, for what? Can it be, simply to propagate his species, and perish? and was all this grand creation of the earth, and all things therein, made to subserve him for so mean a purpose? It cannot be. Life is a probation, death the key which unlocks the portal through which we pass to the perfection of the design of God.

In these views and opinions Dr. Clapp lived and died. When worn out with labor and the ravages of time, he sought to renovate his exhausted energies, by removing to a higher latitude, and selected Louisville, Kentucky, for his future home. He had seen most of his early friends pass into eternity, in the fruition of time, and felt and knew it was only a day that his departure for eternity was delayed; yet how calmly and contentedly he awaited the mandate which should bid him home!

His belief in the universal destiny of man made him universally tolerant. His intimates were of every creed, and the harmony existing with these and himself made his life beautiful as exemplary. With the ministers of every creed he was affectionately social: he had no prejudices, cultivated no animosities, and was universally charitable. He inculcated his principles by example, encouraged social communion with all sects, teaching that he whose life is in the right cannot be in the wrong. To a very great extent he infused his spirit into the people of his adopted city. His most intimate associate was that very remarkable Israelite, Judah Luro. This man was a native of Newport, Rhode Island, and in early life came to New Orleans and commenced a small business, to which he gave his energetic attention. His means, though small at the beginning, were carefully husbanded, and ultimately grew into immense wealth. He was exceedingly liberal in his nature, philanthropic, and devoted to his friends. On the night of the 22d of December, 1814, he was engaged in the battle between the English and American forces, near New Orleans, and was severely wounded. In this condition he was found, when bleeding profusely from his wounds and threatened with speedy death, by a young merchant of the city, Resin D. Shepherd, who generously lifted him to his shoulder, after stanching his wounds, and bore him, through brambles and mire, in the darkness, to a place of security and comfort, some miles distant from the scene of the fight. He never lost sight of this friend. When he came to die, he made him executor to his will, and residuary legatee, after disposing of some half a million of money in other legacies. These were all immediately paid by Mr. Shepherd, who entered upon the possession of all the property the deceased died possessed of—consequently, the extent of his fortune was never publicly known.

This man built upon his own property, on Gravier Street, fronting St. Charles, and immediately across Gravier Street from the St. Charles Hotel, a church for Dr. Clapp, in which his congregation worshipped for many years. When the hotel was built, and business began crowding around this locality, it became necessary to remove his church. Again, Mr. Luro built for him a church, in a more private and eligible position, on the corner of Julia and St. Charles streets, and donated it to the pastor and congregation of the Gravier-Street Church. Here Mr. Clapp continued his ministry during the remaining time of his residence in New Orleans.

He found with the cultivated and intelligent of New Orleans an approval of his teachings and example. The consequence was, and is, the entire absence of sectarian dissensions, and a social intercourse between all, resulting in a united effort for the common good, and the maintenance of moral sentiments and moral conduct—the basis and source of true and triumphant religion.

"The deeds that men do, live after them." Of no man can this be more truly said than of Dr. Clapp. Through every phase of society his example and teachings continue to live; and every virtuous and intelligent man in the community of Dr. Clapp's ministry, in New Orleans, conspires to continue the effect of them.

In no community on earth is there a greater diversity of nationalities, than in that of New Orleans, where every sect of religionists is to be found. All pursue the worship of God after their own manner of belief, exciting no jealousies, heart-burnings, or hatreds. All agree that a common end is the aim of all, and that a common destiny awaits mankind.

In the pursuits of life, and the duties of time, nothing of religious intolerance enters. A man's opinions upon that subject are his own, and for these he is responsible to God only. His neighbor respects his prejudices and feelings, and appreciates him according to his conduct toward his fellow-man, and the discharge of his duties to society.

Good follows the honest discharge of the duties of his vocation, from every moral and religious teacher, if he is sincere and earnest, whether Jew or Christian. An intelligent and virtuous community appreciates this, and encourages such efforts as advance and sustain public morals and social harmony. How such a man is esteemed in New Orleans, a recent instance is ample illustration. A distinguished Jewish Rabbi, long a resident minister of his faith in that city, was called to minister in a synagogue in the city of New York. His walk and his work had been upright and useful. The good of all denominations were unwilling to give up so good and so useful a man. In the true spirit of pure religion, a large committee, appointed by a meeting of the citizens from among every sect, composed of the leading and most influential men of the city, waited upon him, and influenced him to remain among them, and continue his vocation and pious usefulness in the field where he had labored so long and so efficiently.

To the teachings of Dr. Clapp, much of this toleration is due. This tone of feeling is the offspring of enlightenment, the enemy of bigotry. His mission completed, he retired for health and quiet to a point from which he could contemplate the results of his labors.

He saw that they were good, and felt his whole duty had been done. In the fulness of years he awaited the coming of the hour when, released from his prison-house and freed from earth, he should go to his reward. It came, and ere the spirit was plumed for its final flight, he asked that its wornout casket should be carried and deposited by those he loved in life, in the city of his adoption and love; where, in death, the broken community of life should be restored. This was done, and now with them he sleeps well.

Memory turns sadly back to many, now no more, who were compeers of Dr. Clapp, and to New Orleans, as New Orleans was; but to none with more melancholy pleasure than to Alexander Barrow and E. D. White. These were both natives of the city of Nashville, Tennessee. Both came to New Orleans in early life: White, with his father when a child, and Barrow, when a young man. White was left an orphan when quite young, in Attakapas, where his father lived, and with very limited means. He struggled on in the midst of a people whose very language was alien to his own, and managed to acquire a limited education, with which he commenced the study of the law, the profession of his father. When admitted to practice, he located at Donaldsonville, in the Parish of Ascension, where he rose rapidly to distinction. Appointed subsequently to a judgeship in New Orleans, he removed there to reside. This appointment he did not continue to hold for any length of time, his popularity being such as to point him out as a fit person to contest with Mr. Livingston the seat in Congress then filled by the latter. In this contest he was successful, and continued to represent the district until he was chosen Governor. He filled this chair for the constitutional period of four years, and immediately upon the expiration of his term, he was again elected to Congress. He continued to represent the district until the treachery of a family, numerous and ignorant, yet influential with their ignorant, uneducated neighbors, caused him to be beaten. They succeeded subsequently in placing one of their family in his place, only to show the triumph of folly and stupidity over worth and intelligence. Yet this cross of an Irish renegade upon an Acadian woman was a fit representative of a large majority of his constituents.

The climate of Washington operated injuriously upon his constitution. Long accustomed to that of Louisiana, it failed to resist the terrible winter-climate of Washington, and he found his health broken. He returned to his plantation, on the Bayoú La Fourche, where he lingered for a year or more, and died, in the meridian of life, leaving a young and interesting family.

Governor White was a man of great eccentricity of character, but with a ripe intellect, and a heart overflowing with generous emotions and tenderness. He loved his kind, and his life was most unselfishly devoted to their service. Like all who have for any time made her their home, he loved Louisiana first of all things. He was too young when coming from his native land to remember it, and his first attachment was for the soil of his adoption. He was reared in the midst of the Creole population of the State; spoke French and Spanish as his mother-tongue, and possessed the confidence and affection of these people in a most remarkable degree.

Governor White was a passenger on board the ill-fated steamer Lioness, in company with many friends, among whom were Josiah S. Johnston, (the elder brother of A. Sidney Johnston, who fell at the battle of Shiloh,) and Judge Boyce, of the District Court. Josiah S. Johnston was, at the time, a Senator in Congress. Some miles above the mouth of Red River, and in that stream, the boat blew up, many of the passengers being killed, among whom was Judge Johnston. Governor White was terribly burned, and by many it was thought this led to his death. His disease was bronchitis, which supervened soon after this terrible disaster. The steamer had in her hold considerable powder. This, it was said at the time, was ignited by the mate of the boat, who had become enraged from some cause with the captain. The body of Judge Johnston was never found. The boat was blown to atoms, with the exception of the floor of the ladies' cabin. The upper works were all demolished. This floor was thrown, it seemed almost miraculously, intact upon the water. There were some six or eight ladies on board, who were saved on this floor. When the smoke had lifted sufficiently to permit a night view — for it was night — Governor White and Judge Boyce were seen swimming near this floor of the wreck. White was burned terribly in the face and on the hands, and was blinded by this burning. The ladies were in their night-clothes; but what will not woman do to aid the distressed, especially in the hour of peril? One of the most accomplished ladies of the State snatched from her person her *robe de chambre*, and, throwing one end to the struggling Governor, called to him to reach for it, and with it pulled him to the wreck, and kindly, with the aid of others, lifted him on. The same kind office was performed for Boyce, and they were saved. Though a stranger to the Governor, this great-hearted woman tore into strips her gown, and kindly did the work of the Good Samaritan, in binding up the wounds of one she did not know, had never before seen, and to whose rank and character she was equally a stranger; and when she was floating upon a few planks, at the mercy of the waters, and surrounded by interminable forests covering the low and mucky shores of Red River for many miles, where human foot had rarely trod, and human habitation may never rest — one garment her only covering, and all she could hope for, until some passing steamer should chance to rescue them, or until she should float to the river's mouth, and find a human habitation. She, too, is in the grave, but the memory of this act embalms her in the hearts of all who knew her. Blessed one! — for surely she who blessed all who came within her sphere, and only lived to do good, must in eternity and for eternity be blest, like thousands of others who have ministered in kindness for a day, and then went to the grave — in thy youth and loveliness thou wert exhaled from earth: like a storm-stricken flower in the morning of its bloom, wilted and dead, the fragrance of thy virtues is the incense of thy memory!

It was long before Governor White was fully restored to sight. No public man, and especially one so long in public life, ever enjoyed more fully the confidence of his constituents than Edward Douglass White. His private character was never impeached, even in the midst of the most excited political contests, nor did the breath of slander ever breathe upon his fair fame, from his childhood to the grave.

I am incompetent to write of Alexander Barrow as his merits deserve. In him all that was noble and all that was respectable was most happily combined. A noble and commanding person, a manly and intellectual face, an eye that bespoke his heart, a soul that soared in every relation of life above everything that was little or selfish, a ripe and accurate judgment, a purpose always honorable and always open, without concealment or deceit, and an integrity pure and unsullied as the ether he breathed, an affectionate father, a devoted husband, a firm and unflinching friend through every phase of fortune — in fine, every element which makes a man united in Alexander Barrow. Dear reader, if I seem extravagant in these words, pardon it to me. When seventy winters have passed over your head, and you turn back your memory upon all that has passed, recalling the incidents and the friends of life, and you remember those which have transpired with him you loved best and trusted most, and remember that he was always true, never capricious, always wise, never foolish, always sincere, never equivocal, and who never failed you in the darkest hours of adversity, but was always the same to you in kindness, forbearance, and devotion, remember such was ever to me Alexander Barrow, and forgive this wild outpouring of the heart to the virtues of the friend, tried so long, and loved so well. For more than twenty years he has been in his grave; but in all that time no day has ever passed that Alick has not stood before me as he was when we were young and life was full of hope. His blood with mine mingles in the veins of our grandchildren. O God! I would there were nothing to make this a painful memory.

Barrow served some years in the Legislature of the State, and was thence transferred to the United States Senate, where, after a service of six years, he died, in the prime of his manhood. Those who remember the speech of Hannegan, and the attempt of Crittenden, who, under the deep sorrow of his heart, sank voiceless and in tears to his chair — the feeling which filled and moved the Senate when paying the last tribute to his dead body, coffined and there before them in the Senate chamber — may know how those estimated the man who knew him best. Friend of my heart, farewell! We soon shall meet, with vernal youth restored, to endure forever.

There was another, Walter Brashear, our intimate friend for long years. He went to eternity after a pilgrimage of eighty-eight years in the sunshine and shadows of this miserable world. He was a native of the city of Philadelphia, but with his parents went to Kentucky, when a boy. These soon died, and Walter was left an orphan and poor, then but a boy. After attending a common neighborhood school in the County of Fayette, near Lexington, one year, he found it necessary to find support in some employment. Walking the streets of Lexington in search of this, the breeze blew to his feet a fragment of newspaper, which he picked up and read from curiosity. Here he found an advertisement inviting those who had ginseng for sale, to call. He knew there was plenty of this root to be found in portions of Kentucky, and determined immediately to embark in the speculation of searching for it and sending it to Philadelphia. He labored assiduously, and soon had acquired a considerable sum of money for those times, 1801. He employed several hands to assist him the ensuing season, and after forwarding the root collected, found there was no longer any market for it in Philadelphia. Suspecting the person to whom he had previously sold was deceiving him, in order to drive a profitable bargain with him, he determined to go himself with his venture to China. This he did, and, making so handsome a business of it, he returned and immediately went to work to procure a much larger amount for another venture. This he likewise accomplished, but was less fortunate than before, though he made some money. He was now twenty-one years of age, and had been twice to China; but had not contracted much love for commerce or voyaging upon the sea. He married soon after his return, read medicine, and commenced the practice of it in Kentucky. Forming an intimacy with Mr. Clay, they soon became close friends, being nearly of the same age, and very like in character. After some years' residence in Kentucky as a physician, he determined on emigrating to Louisiana, and embarking in the business of sugar-planting. Purchasing Belle Isle, an island off the coast of Attakapas, he removed his family there about 1824. He was successful in his new vocation; but not liking an island residence, where he was twenty miles from a neighbor, he purchased a residence upon Berwick's Bay, and a portion of Tiger Island, which was immediately opposite, and there made a new plantation, which is now the site of Brashear City. At this place he lies buried, by his children, all of whom, save one daughter, are there with him.

For many years he was a member of the Legislature of the State of his adoption, an honest and efficient one, of fine abilities, and great will. He usually triumphed in what he undertook. His fine social qualities attached to him many friends. His devotion to them was unflinching, and he rather preferred to fight for these than play with any others. His courage was truly chivalrous, and he is remembered by all who knew him, and yet live, as the man who never felt the sensation of fear.

An unfortunate difficulty with a neighbor, Dr. Tolls, brought on a personal rencontre. His antagonist was known to be brave and physically powerful; but in this affair, Brashear, after receiving a number of blows, wrested away his enemy's cane, and would soon have had the better of the fight, but persons interposing prevented it.

"Doctor," said Brashear, "this is not the way for gentlemen to settle their difficulties. As soon as I can bind up my head, which you have battered pretty severely, I shall be in the street armed. If you are as brave a man as your friends claim you to be, you will meet me there prepared to fight me as a gentleman."

"In forty minutes from this time, if you please," said his enemy.

At the appointed time and place they met, each with his friend, and each armed. When they had approached within ten paces, Brashear stopped and said, "Are you ready?" Being answered in the affirmative, "Then fire, sir; I scorn to take the first fire." Dr. Tolls did so, and, missing him, stood and received Brashear's ball through both thighs, and fell. There was no surgeon in town, and the wounds were bleeding profusely, when Brashear went to him, and proposed to dress the wounds. Tolls stuttered badly, and replied, "I-I-I'll d-d-die first." "I can do no more," said Brashear, and, bowing, left the ground.

This chivalry of character characterized him in everything. Fond of amusement, he indulged himself in hunting and innocent sports, when and where he was always the life of the party. Energetic and restless in his nature, he could not bear confinement, and, when a member of the Legislature, he was more frequently to be found walking rapidly to and fro in the lobby of the House than in his seat. To sit still and do nothing was impossible to him. A hundred anecdotes might be related of him, all illustrative of his lofty courage, and daring, and his utter contempt of danger. A noble and generous spirit was ever manifested by him, in every relation of life. His frankness and liberal hospitality, his kindness to his slaves, and his generosity to the poor, endeared him to his neighbors, who live to feel that his void can never be filled.

CHAPTER XXXII.

GRADUAL EXTINCTION OF THE RED MAN.

Line Creek Fifty Years Ago — Hopothlayohola — McIntosh — Undying Hatred — A Big Powwow — Massacre of the McIntoshes — Nehemathla — Onchees — The Last of the Race — A Brave Warrior — A White Man's Friendship — The Death-Song — Tuskega, or Jim's Boy.

I HAVE been to-day, the 23d of August, over the same spot I wandered over this day fifty years ago. What changes have supervened it is difficult to realize. This was then a dense, unsettled wilderness. The wild deer was on every hill, in every valley. Limpid streams purled rippling and gladly along pebbly beds, and fell babbling over great rocks. These alone disturbed the profound silence, where solitude brooded, and quiet was at home. These wild forests extended west to Line Creek, then the dividing line between the Indian possessions and the newly acquired territory now constituting the State of Alabama. Upon this territory of untamed wilderness there wandered then fifty thousand Indians, the remnant of the mighty nation of Muscogees, who one hundred and thirty years ago welcomed the white man at Yamacrow, now Savannah, and tendered him a home in the New World. Fifty years ago he had progressed to the banks of the Ocmulgee, driving before him the aboriginal inhabitant, and appropriating his domains. Here for a time his march was stayed. But the Indian had gone forward to meet the white man coming from the Mississippi to surround him, the more surely to effect his ultimate destruction and give his home and acres to the enterprise and capacity of the white man.

Wandering through these wilds fifty years ago, I did not deem this end would be so soon accomplished. Here now is the city and the village, the farm-house and extended fields, the railroads and highways, and hundreds of thousands of busy men who had not then a being. The appurtenances of civilization everywhere greet you: many of these are worn and mossed over with the lapse of time and appear tired of the weight of wasting years. The red men, away in the West, have dwindled to a mere handful, still flying before the white man, and shrinking away from his hated civilization.

Is this cruel and sinful — or the silent, mysterious operation of the laws of nature? One people succeeds another, as day comes after day, and years follow years. Upon this continent the Indian found the evidences in abundance of a preceding people, the monuments of whose existence he disregards, but which, in the earth-mounds rising up over all the land, arrest the white man's attention and wonder. He inquires of the Indian inhabitant he is expelling from the country, Who was the architect of these, and what their signification? and is answered: We have no tradition which tells; our people found them when they came, as you find them to-day. These traditions give the history of the nations now here, and we find in every Southern tribe that they tell of an immigration from the southwest.

The Muscogee, Natchez, Choctaw, and Chickasaw, all have the history of their flying from beyond the Mississippi, and from the persecutions of superior and more warlike nations, and resting here for security, where they found none to molest them, and only these dumb evidences of another people, who once filled the land, but had passed away.

When the white man came, he found but one race upon the two continents. Their type was the same and universal, and only these mounds to witness of a former race. Ethnology has discovered no other. All the remains of man indicate the same type, and there remains not a fossil to record the existence of those who reared these earth-books, which speak so eloquently of a race passed away.

How rapidly the work of demolition goes on! Will a century hence find one of the red race upon this continent? Certainly not, if it shall accomplish so much as the century past. There is not one for every ten, then; and the tenth remaining are now surrounded on all sides, and, being pushed to the centre, must perish.

They are by nature incapable of that civilization which would enable them to organize governments and teach the science of agriculture. They were formed for the woods, and physically organized to live on flesh. The animals furnishing this were placed with them here, and the only vegetable found with them was the maize, or Indian corn. The white man was organized to feed on vegetables, and they were placed with him in his centre of creation, and he brought them here, and with himself acclimated them, as a necessity to his existence in America.

No effort can save the red man from extermination that humanity or Christianity may suggest. When deprived of his natural food furnished by the forest, he knows not nor can he be taught the means of supplying the want. The capacities of his brain will not admit of the cultivation necessary to that end. And as he has done in the presence of civilization, he will know none of its arts; and receiving or commanding none of its results, he will wilt and die.

Here, on the very spot where I am writing, is evidence in abundance of the facts here stated. Every effort to civilize and make the nomadic Indian a cultivator of the earth — here has been tried, and within my memory. Missionary establishments were here, schools, churches, fields, implements, example and its blessings, all without effect. Nothing now remains to tell of these efforts but a few miserable ruins; nothing in any change of character or condition of the Indian. And here, where fifty years ago, with me, he hunted the red deer and wild turkey for the meat of his family and the clothing of himself and offspring — to-day he would be a curiosity, and one never seen by half the population which appropriates and cultivates the soil over which he wandered in the chase. His beautiful woods are gone; the green corn grows where the green trees grew, and the bruised and torn face of his mother earth muddies to disgust, with her clay-freighted tears, the limpid streams by which he sat down to rest, and from which he drank to quench his thirst from weariness earned in his hunt for wild game, which grew with him, and grew for him, as nature's provision. The deer and the Indian are gone. The church-steeple points to heaven where the wigwam stood, and the mart of commerce covers over all the space where the camp-fires burned. The quarrels of Hopothlayohola and McIntosh are history now, and the great tragedy of its conclusion in the death of McIntosh is now scarcely remembered.

True to his hatred of the Georgians, Hopothlayohola, in the recent war, away beyond the Mississippi, arrayed his warriors in hostility to the Confederacy, and, when numbering nearly one hundred winters, led them to battle in Arkansas, against the name of his hereditary foe, and hereditary hate — McIntosh; and by that officer, commanding the Confederate troops, was defeated, and his followers dispersed. Since that time, nothing has been known of the fate of the old warrior-chief.

It had been agreed between the United States and Georgia, and the famous Yazoo Company, in order to settle the difficulties between the two latter, that the United States should purchase, at a proper time, from the Indian proprietors, all the lands east of the Chattahoochee and a line running from the west bank of that stream, starting at a place known as West Point, and terminating at what is known as Nickey Jack, on the Tennessee River. The increase of population, and the constant difficulties growing out of the too close neighborhood of the Indians, induced the completion of this agreement. Commissioners on the part of the Government were appointed to meet commissioners or delegations from the Indians, to treat for the sale of their lands within the limits of the State of Georgia. McIntosh favored the sale, Hopothlayohola opposed it. As a chief, McIntosh was second to his great antagonist in authority, and, in truth, to several other chiefs. But he was a bold man, with strong will, fearless and aggressive, and he assumed the power to sell. In the war of 1812–15, he had sided with the Americans, Hopothlayohola with the English; and leading at least half the tribe, McIntosh felt himself able to sustain his authority. The commissioners met the Indian delegation at the Indian Springs, where negotiations were commenced by a proposition placed before the chiefs, and some days given for their consideration of it. Their talks or consultations among themselves were protracted and angry, and inconclusive. Every effort was made to induce Hopothlayohola to accede to the proposition of McIntosh. The whites united in their efforts to win his consent to sell: persuasions, threats, and finally large bribes were offered, but all availed nothing. Thus distracted and divided, they consumed the time for consultation, and met the white commissioners to renew the strife, in open council with these. Each chief was followed to this council by the members of his band, sub-chiefs, and warriors. McIntosh announced his readiness to sell, and sustained his position with reasons which demonstrated him a statesman, and wise beyond his people.

"Here in the neighborhood of the whites," he said, "we are subject to continual annoyance and wrong. These have continued long, and they have dwarfed our mighty nation to a tribe or two, and our home to one-tenth of its original dimensions. This must go on if we remain in this proximity, until we shall be lost, and there will be none to preserve our traditions. Let us sell our lands, and go to the proffered home beyond the Great River. Our young men have been there: they have seen it, and they say it is good. The game is abundant; the lands are broad, and there is no sickness there." Turning to Hopothlayohola, who stood, with dignified and proud defiance in his manner, listening, he proceeded: "Will you go and live with your people increasing and happy about you: or will you stay and die with them here, and leave no one to follow you, or come to your grave, and weep over their great chief? Beyond the Great River the sun is as bright, and the sky is as blue, and the waters are as clear and as sweet as they are here. Our people will go with us. We will be one, and where we are altogether, there is home. To love the ground is mean; to love our people is noble. We will cling to them — we will do for their good; and the ground where they are will be as dear to us as this, because they will be upon it, and with us.

"The white man is growing. He wants our lands. He will buy them now. By and by he will take them, and the little band of our people left will wander without homes, poor and despised, and be beaten like dogs. We must go to a new home, and learn like the white man to till the earth, grow cattle, and depend on these for food and life. Nohow else can many people live on the earth. This makes the white man like the leaves; the want of it makes the red men weak and few. Let us learn how to make books, how to make ploughs, and how to cultivate the ground, as the white man does, and we will grow again, and again become a great people. We will unite with the Cherokee, the Choctaw, and the Seminole, and be one people. The Great Spirit made us one people. Yes, we are all the children of one family: we are the red men of the Great Spirit, and should be one people for strength and protection. We shall have schools for our children. Each tribe shall have its council, and all shall unite in great council. They will be wise through learning as the white man is, and we shall become a great State, and send our chiefs to Congress as the white man does. We shall all read, and thus talk, as the white man does, with the mighty dead who live in books; and write and make books that our children's children shall read and talk with, and learn the counsels of their great fathers in the spirit-land. This it is which makes the white man increase and spread over the land. In our new home he promises to protect us — to send us schools and books, and teach our children to know them; and he will send us ploughs, and men to make them, and to teach our young men how to make them.

"The plough will make us corn for bread, for the strength of the body; the books will be food for the head, to make us wise and strong in council. Let us sell and go away, and if we suffer for a time, it will be better for our children. You see it so with the white man; shall we not learn from him, and be like him?"

When he had concluded his talk, it was greeted in their own peculiar manner by his followers as good. Hopothlayohola, the great red chief, turning from McIntosh as if disdaining him, addressed the commissioners of the Government:

"Our great father, your head chief at Washington, sent us a talk by you, which is pleasant to hear, because it promises the red man much — his friendship, his protection, and his help; but in return for this he asks of us much more than we are willing to give even for all his promises. The white man's promises, like him, are white, and bring hope to the red man; but they always end in darkness and death to him.

"The Great Spirit has not given to the red man, as He has to the white man, the power to look into the dark, and see what to-morrow has in its hand; but He has given him the sense to know what experience teaches him. Look around, and remember! Away when time was young, all this broad land was the red man's, and there was none to make him afraid. The woods were wide and wild, and the red deer, and the bear, and the wild turkey were everywhere, and all were his. He was great, and, with abundance, was happy. From the salt sea to the Great River the land was his: the Great Spirit had given it to him. He made the woods for the red man, the deer, the bear, and the turkey; and for these He made the red man. He made the white man for the fields, and taught him how to make ploughs, to have cattle and horses, and how to make books, because the white man needed these. He did not make these a necessity to the red man.

"Away beyond the mighty waters of the dreary sea, He gave the white man a home, with everything he wanted, and He gave him a mind which was for him, and only him. The red man is satisfied with the gifts to him of the Great Spirit; and he did not know there was a white man who had other gifts for his different nature, until he came in his winged canoes across the great water, and our fathers met him at Yamacrow. The Great Spirit gave him a country, and He gave the red man a country. Why did he leave his own and come to take the red man's? Did the Great Spirit tell him to do this? He gave him His word in a book: do you find it there? Then read it for us, that we may hear. If He did, then He is not just. We see Him in the sun, and moon, and stars. We hear Him in the thunder, and feel Him in the mighty winds; but He made no book for the red man to tell Him his will, but we see in all His works justice. The sun, and the moon, and the stars, and the ground keep their places, and never leave them to crowd upon one another. They stay where He placed them, and come not to trouble or to take from one another what He had given. Only the white man does this. A few — a little handful — came in their canoe to the land of the red man, as spirits come out of the water. The red man gave them his hand. He gave them meat, and corn, and a home, and welcomed them to come and live with him. And the flying canoes came again and again, and many came in them, and at last they brought their great chief, with his long knife by his side, and his red coat, and he asked for more land. Our chiefs and warriors met him, and sold him another portion of our lands; and his white squaws came with him, and they made houses and homes near our people. They made fields, and had horses and herds, and grew faster than our people, and drove away the deer and the turkeys deeper into the woods. And then they wanted more land, and our chiefs and warriors sold them more land, and now again another piece, until now we have but a little of our all. And you come again with the same story on your forked tongues, and wish to buy the last we have of all we had, and offer us a home away beyond the Great River, and money, and tell us we shall there have a home forever, free from the white man's claims, and in which we shall dwell in peace, with no one to make us afraid.

"Our traditions tell us that our fathers fled before the powerful red men who dwell beyond the Great River, and who robbed us of our homes and made them their own, as you, the white men, have done. Have you bought the home of our fathers from these red men? or have you taken it? that you bid us take it from you, and go back, and make a new home where the fathers of our fathers sleep in death? If you have not, will they not hunt us away again, as you have? How shall we know you will not come and make us sell to you, for the white man, the homes you promise shall always be ours and a home for our children's children?

"We love the land where we were born and where we have buried our fathers and our kindred. It is the Great Spirit which teaches us to love the land, the wigwam, the stream, the trees where we hunted and played from our childhood, where we have buried out of sight our ancestors for generations. Who says it is mean to love the land, to keep in our hearts these graves, as we keep the Great Spirit? It is noble to love the land, where the corn grows, and which was given to us by the Great Spirit. We will sell no more; we know we are passing away; the leaves fall from the trees, and we fall like these; some will stay to be the last. The snow melts from the hills, but there is some left for the last; we are left for the last, like the withered leaf and little spot of snow. Leave to us the little we have, let us die where our fathers have died, and let us sleep where our kindred sleep; and when the last is gone, then take our lands, and with your plough tear up the mould upon our graves, and plant your corn above us. There will be none to weep at the deed, none to tell the traditions of our people, or sing the death-song above their graves — none to listen to the wrongs and oppressions the red man bore from his white brother, who came from the home the Great Spirit gave him, to take from the red man the home the Great Spirit gave him. We are few and weak, you are many and strong, and you can kill us and take our homes; but the Great Spirit has given us courage to fight for our homes, if we may not live in them — and we will do it — and this is our talk, our last talk."

He folded back the blanket he had thrown from his shoulders, and, followed by his band, he stalked majestically away. They had broken up their camp and returned to their homes upon the Tallapoosa.

Unawed by the defection of the Tuscahatchees, the band attached to Hopothlayohola, McIntosh went on to complete the treaty. This chief, because he had been the friend of the United States in the then recent war, assumed to be the principal chief of the nation, as he held the commission of a brigadier-general from the United States; a commission, however, which only gave him command with his own people. This assumption was denied by Hopothlayohola, chief of the Tuscahatchees, Tuskega, and other chiefs of the nation, who insisted upon the ancient usages, and the power attaching through these to the recognized head-chief of the nation. Strong representations and protests against the treaty were sent to Washington, and serious complications were threatened, very nearly producing collision between the State of Georgia and the General Government. The hostility to McIntosh and his party culminated in a conspiracy for his assassination. Fifty warriors were selected, headed by a chief for the purpose. These received their orders, which were that on a day designated they should concentrate at a given spot, and at night proceed to the house of McIntosh, in secret, and surrounding it at or near daylight, call him up, and as he came forth, all were to fire upon him. His brother, his son, and son-in-law, Rolla and Chillie McIntosh, and Hawkins, were all doomed to die, and by the hands of this executory band. That there might be no mistake as to the day, each warrior was furnished with a bundle of sticks of wood, each of these represented a day—the whole, the number of days intervening between the time of receiving them, and the day of execution. Every night upon the going down of the sun one of these was to be thrown away—the last one, on the night of concentration and assassination. It was death to betray the trust reposed, or to be absent from the point of rendezvous at the time appointed.

The secret was faithfully kept—every one was present. The house of McIntosh stood immediately upon the bank of the Chattahoochee River, at the point or place now known as McIntosh's Reserve. It was approached and surrounded under the cover of night, and so stealthily as to give no warning even to the watch-dogs. McIntosh and his son Chillie were the only victims in the house, the two others were away. Hawkins was at his own home, Rolla McIntosh no one knew where. Hopothlayohola had accompanied this band, but not in the character of chief. The command was delegated to another. This chief knocked at the door, and commanded McIntosh to come out and meet his doom. The Reverend Francis Flornoy, a Baptist preacher, was spending the night with the chief, and was in a room with Chillie. The chief McIntosh knew his fate, and, repairing to the apartment of his guest and son, told them he was about to die, and directing his son to escape from the rear of the house, and across the river, said he would meet his fate as a warrior. Taking his rifle, he went to the front door, and throwing it open, fired upon the array of warriors as he gave the war-whoop, and, in an instant after, fell dead, pierced with twenty balls. Chillie, at this moment, sprang from the window, leaped into the river, and made his escape, though fired at repeatedly. A detachment was immediately sent to execute Hawkins at his home, which was successful in effecting it.

Soon after this tragic occurrence, the McIntosh party, consisting of fully one-half the nation, emigrated to the lands granted them west of the State of Arkansas, and made there a home. The remainder of the Creeks retired to the district of country between the Chattahoochee and Line Creek, only to learn that to remain upon this circum scribed territory was certain destruction.

The whites soon populated the acquired territory, and the Chattahoochee was no barrier to their aggressions upon the helpless Indian beyond. Feuds grew up: this led to killings, and in the winter of 1835-6 active hostilities commenced. This war was of short duration. Before the nation was divided, Hopothlayohola was opposed to war. In his communication with General Jessup, he told him: "My strength is gone; my warriors are few, and I am opposed to war. But had I the men, I would fight you. I am your enemy—I shall ever be; but to fight you would only be the destruction of my people. We are in your power, and you can do with us as you will." But the chiefs of the lower towns would not yield, and made the fight. In a short time this was concluded by the capture of their leading chief, Nehemathla. He was decoyed by treachery into the power of General Jessup, who detained him as a prisoner, and almost immediately his band surrendered.

Nehemathla was an Onchee chief. This was the remnant of a tribe absorbed into the nation of the Creeks or Muscogees, and was probably one of those inferior bands inhabiting the land when this nation came from the West and took possession of the country. Their language they preserved, and it is remarkable it was never acquired by white or red man, unless he was reared from infancy among the tribe. It was guttural entirely, and spoken with the mouth open, and no word or sound ever required it to be closed for its pronunciation. They had dwindled to a handful at the time of his capture, but more obstinately determined to remain and die upon their parental domain, than any other portion of the nation.

Nehemathla was more than eighty years of age at the time of his capture. When brought into the presence of General Jessup, he expected nothing short of death. The General told him of his crimes, upbraided him with bad faith to his great father, General Jackson, and drawing his sword, told him he deserved to die.

The chief, seeing the sword lifted, snatched the turban from his head, and fiercely and defiantly looking the General in the face, as the wind waved about his brow and head the long locks white as snow, said firmly and aloud: "Strike, and let me sleep here with my father and my children! Strike, I am the last of my race! The Great Spirit gave me seven sons — three of them died at Emucfaw, two at Talladega, and two at Aletosee. General Jackson killed them all, and you call him my great father! When did a father wash his hands in his children's blood? When did a father rob his children of their homes? When did a father drive his children in anger into the wilderness, where they will find an enemy who claim it as the gift of the Great Spirit, and who will fight to retain it? Strike, and let me die — no time, no place like this! The mother of my sons, their sisters, perished for food, when I with my sons was fighting for our homes. I am alone, and not afraid to die! Strike: eighty winters are on my head — they are heavier than your sword! They weigh me to the earth! Strike, and let me go to my squaw, my sons, and my daughters, and let me forget my wrongs! Strike, and let my grave be here, where all I have is in the ground! Strike: I would sleep where I was born — all around me are the graves of my people, let mine be among them; and when the Great Spirit shall come, let Him find us all together, here with our fathers of a thousand winters, who first built their wigwams here, and who first taught their children to be more cautious than the panther — more watchful than the turkey!"

"I will not strike you," said the General. "No, I will not strike my foe, a prisoner; but here is my hand in friendship."

"No," said the chief; "you have put your sword in its pocket, put your hand in its pocket; do not let it reach out to blind me, or to take my home. I am the white man's enemy; his friendship I fear more than his anger. It is more fatal to the red man. It takes away his home, and forces him living to go away and grieve for his country, and the graves of his fathers, and to starve in a strange land. In his anger he kills, and its mercy shuts his eyes and his heart away from the wrongs and the miseries of his people. I have lived and I will die the white man's enemy. I have done you all the harm in my power. If I could, I would do you more. My tongue is not forked like yours, my heart has no lies to make it speak to deceive. Strike, and let me go to the happy hunting-grounds where all my people are."

He sat down upon the ground, and, in a low, monotonous, melancholy tone, chanted the death-song.

"Who-ah-who-allee! wait for me, I am coming. Who-ah-who-allee! prepare the feast, the great warrior's feast. Who-ah-who-allee! let my boys and my braves come down to welcome me. Who-ah-who-allee! those who went before me, tell them the old warrior is coming. Who-ah-who-allee! the white man has come, he treads on their graves, and the graves of their fathers. Who-ah-who-allee! the last of the Onchee is coming, prepare—his bow is broken, his arrows are all gone. Who-ah-who allee!" Concluding his song with one shrill whoop, he dropped his head and lifted up his hands — then prone upon the earth he threw himself, kissed it, rose up, and seemed prepared for the fate he surely expected.

Nehemathla spoke English fluently, and all his conversation was in that language. He was informed that there was no intention of taking his life, but that he would be kept a close prisoner, until his people could be conquered and collected — when they would be sent to join their brethren, who had gone with the Cussetas and Cowetas and Broken Arrows, beyond the Great River of the West. Tamely and sullenly he submitted to his confinement, until the period approached, when all were collected and in detachments forwarded to their future homes.

It was my fortune to be in New Orleans when the old chief and his little band arrived at that place. It was winter, and the day of their debarkation was cold and rainy. The steamer chartered to take them to Fort Smith, upon the Arkansas, from some cause did not arrive at the levee at the time appointed for their leaving, and they, with their women and children, were exposed upon the levee to all the inclemencies of rain and cold, through a protracted winter night. Many propositions were made to give them shelter, which were rejected. One warm-hearted, noble spirit, James D. Fresett, the proprietor of an extensive cotton-press, went in person to the aged chief, and implored him to take his people to shelter there. He declined, and when the importunity was again pressed upon him, impatient of persuasion, he turned abruptly to his tormentor and sternly said:

"I am the enemy of the white man. I ask, and will accept, nothing at his hands. Me and my people are children of the woods. The Great Spirit gave them to us, and He gave us the power to endure the cold and the rain. The clouds above are His, and they are shelter and warmth enough for us. He will not deceive and rob us. The white man is faithless; with two tongues he speaks: like the snake, he shows these before he bites. Never again shall the white man's house open for me, or the white man's roof shelter me. I have lived his enemy, and his enemy I will die." The grunt of approval came from all the tribe, while many rough and stalwart men stood in mute admiration of the pride, the spirit, and the determination of this white-haired patriarch of a perishing people. The next day he went away to his new home, but only to die. About this time a delegation from both the Tuscahatchees or Hopothlayohola band and the McIntosh band met by private arrangement, in New Orleans, to reconcile all previous difficulties between these parties. Hopothlayohola and Tuskega, or Jim's Boy, and Chillie McIntosh and Hawkins, constituted the delegations. I was present at the City Hotel, and witnessed the meeting. It was in silence. McIntosh and Hopothlayohola advanced with the right hand extended and met. The clasping hands was the signal for the others: they met, clasping hands, and unity was restored, the nations reconciled and reunited, and Hopothlayohola and his people invited to come in peace to their new homes.

It was evidently a union of policy, as there could be no heart-union between McIntosh and Hopothlayohola; and though the latter placed his conduct upon the broad basis of national law and national justice, yet this was inflicted upon the parent of the other, who denied the law, or the power under the law, supposing it to exist, of the other to adjudge and to execute its sentence. In the meeting of these chiefs, and their apparent reconciliation, was to be seen a desire that the nation should reunite, and that there should be amity between the bands, or divided parties, for the national good, and for the good of all the parties or people. But there could never be between the two representative chiefs other than a political reconciliation. There was no attempt on the part of either to deceive the other. Both acted from the same high motives, while their features told the truth — personally they were enemies. The son held the hand of his father's executioner, red with the life-blood of him who gave him being — a father he revered, and whose memory he cherished. The filial and hereditary hatred was in his heart. The feeling was mutual. Both knew it, and the cold, passive eye, and relaxed, inexpressive features but bespoke the subdued, not the extinguished passion. Chillie McIntosh is only one-fourth Indian in blood. Hopothlayohola is a full-blooded Indian. His features are coarse and striking. His high forehead and prominent brow indicate intellect, and his large compressed mouth and massive underjaw, terminating in a square, prominent chin, show great fixity of purpose, and resolution of will. Unquestionably he was the great man of his tribe.

Tuskega, or Jim's Boy, was a man of herculean proportions. He was six feet eight inches in height, and in every way admirably proportioned. He was the putative son of a chief whose name he bore, and whose titles and power he inherited. But the old warrior-chief never acknowledged him as such. The old chief owned as a slave a very large mulatto man, named Jim, who was his confidant and chief adviser, and to him he ascribed the parentage of his successor, and always called him Jim's boy. His complexion, hair, and great size but too plainly indicated his parentage. He was not a man of much mark, except for his size, and would probably never have attained distinction but through hereditary right.

In their new home these people do not increase. The efforts at civilization seem only to reach the mixed bloods, and these only in proportion to the white blood in their veins. The Indian is incapable of the white man's civilization, as indeed all other inferior races are. He has fulfilled his destiny, and is passing away. No approximation to the pursuits or the condition of the white man operates otherwise than as a means of his destruction. It seems his contact is death to every inferior race, when not servile and subjected to his care and control.

CHAPTER XXXIII.

FUN, FACT, AND FANCY.

EUGENIUS NESBITT — WASHINGTON POE — YELVERTON P. KING — PREPARING TO RECEIVE THE COURT — WALTON TAVERN, IN LEXINGTON — BILLY SPRINGER, OF SPARTA — FREEMAN WALKER — AN AUGUSTA LAWYER — A GEORGIA MAJOR — MAJOR WALKER'S BED — UNCLE NED — DISCHARGING A HOG ON HIS OWN RECOGNIZANCE — MORNING ADMONITION AND EVENING COUNSEL — A MOTHER'S REQUEST — INVOCATION — CONCLUSION.

TO-DAY I parted from Eugenius Nesbitt and Washington Poe, two of only four or five of those who commenced life and the practice of law with me in the State of Georgia. We had just learned of the death of Y. P. King, of Greensboro, Georgia, who was only a few years our senior. The four of us were young together, and were friends, but I had been separated from them for more than forty years. Yet the ties of youthful attachment remained, and together we mourned the loss of our compeer and companion in youth.

I was a member of the Legislature when Judge Nesbitt, by act of the Legislature, was admitted to the Bar, he having not attained his majority, and by a rule could not be admitted in the ordinary manner. Nesbitt, though so young, was known through the up-country of Georgia as a young man of more than ordinary promise. The same was the case with Poe. They had so deported themselves as to win the confidence and affection of the wise and the good. There were some in the Legislature who were lawyers, and who conscientiously believed that no one so young as Nesbitt was could be sufficiently matured mentally to properly discharge the duties of the profession. These men themselves were naturally dull, and ignorantly supposed all minds, like their own, were weak in youth, and could only be strengthened and enlightened by time and cultivation. They honestly opposed the bill admitting the applicant. There was one though, who held no such ridiculous notions — himself an example to the contrary — but from some cause he strenuously opposed the bill. It was the celebrated Seaborne Jones, one of the very ablest lawyers the State ever produced. It seemed ever a delight to him to bear heavily upon young lawyers. It would be difficult to divine his motives. He was at the head of the Bar, unapproached by competition, especially by any young man.

I was young and ardent, and felt offended at this opposition, and gave all the aid I could to the passage of the bill. Fortunately for our cause, there were many young lawyers in the Legislature, and these were a unit, and we succeeded in carrying the measure. From that day Nesbitt seemed nearer to me than any other of the Bar in our circuit. We have been separated over forty years, he remaining in his native State, while I have wandered away to the West. Still that warmth of heart toward him has never died out. And now, when both are on the grave's brink, we meet, not to renew, but to find the old flame burning still. King, Nesbitt, and myself were born in the same county, and our ancestors worshipped at the same church — Old Bethany — and to-day we recalled the fact as we mourned the death of our early friend and compeer at the Bar.

Time has swept on. Our children are gray with years. One by one, all who were at the Bar with us are gone, save two or three, and to-morrow we shall be gone. But the oblivious past has not curtained from memory yet the incidents and the men of that past, and while I may I will bear testimony to these, and to the men who were their chief actors. Nesbitt justified in his subsequent life all that his friends and the public hoped from him. In every relation of life he has done his duty ably, honestly, and purely. As a member of the Legislature, of Congress, as a judge of the Supreme Court, as a worthy member of the Presbyterian Church, and, above all, as a father, husband, and citizen, he has been good, wise, and faithful. Is not his measure full? Who deserves it more? We were sad to-day. One said, "King is dead." "Yes," answered the other, and we were silent. Memory was busy. We could not talk. In his office, where yet he wears the harness of the law, surrounded by musty, well-thumbed books, and piles of papers with hard judicial faces, we sat and mused. Perhaps we thought of the past, when those to whom eternity is a reality were with us and joyous. At such times the mind turns quickly back to youth's joys, nor lingers along the vista of intervening time. All of that day will revive, but these memories sadden the heart, and we are fain to think, but not to talk. Perhaps we wondered what were the realizations of the dead. What are they? Who knows, except the dead? Do the dead know?

Unprofitable thought! Faith and hope only buoy the heart, and time brings the end. Well, time has whitened our heads, but not indurated our hearts, and time is now as busy as when in the joyousness of youth we heeded not his flight, and to-morrow may bring us to the grave. Ah! then we shall know the secret, and we will keep it, as all who have gone before. Oh, what a blessed hope is that which promises that we shall, forgetful of the cares and sorrows of time, meet those whom death has refined, and be happy as they in eternity! But the doubt, and then the fear! But why the fear? We come into time without our knowledge or consent, fulfil a destiny, and without our knowledge or consent die out of time. This is the economy of man's life, and was given him by his Creator. Then why should he fear? If it is wise for him to be born, to live, it is surely wise that he should die, since that is equally a part of his economy. Then why fear? Reason is satisfied, but instinct fears.

Yelverton P. King never removed from the county of his birth, nor abandoned his profession, remaining upon the soil of his nativity and among those with whom he had been reared, maintaining through life the character of an upright man. Many memories are connected with his name. When we were young at the Bar, there were as our associates very many who attained eminence as lawyers, and fame as politicians; but these distinctions are not connected with the endearing attributes which make them so cherished in memory — the incidents of social intercourse, the favors, the kindnesses of good neighborhood, the sympathies of young life, the unity of sentiment, the sameness of hopes, little regarded at the moment; but oh! how they were rooting in the heart, to bear, away in the coming time, these fruits of memory, in which is the most of happiness when age whitens the head, and the heart is mellowed with the sorrows of time.

Though all were affectionate and social in their intercourse with each other, yet each had his favorites, because of greater congeniality in nature, more intense sympathies, and more continual intercourse. Little incidents were of frequent occurrence which drew these continually closer, until friendships ripened into confidences — some more special favorites of some, and some more general favorites of all. This latter was Y. P. King; and yet this favoritism was never very demonstrative, but perhaps the stronger and more permanent for this. Such, too, was Nesbitt: the older members of the profession loved him, and those of his own age were unenvious and esteemed him.

Our circuit consisted of seven counties, and the ridings were spring and fall, occupying about two months each term. In each court-house town was a tavern or two. These houses of entertainment were not then dignified with the sonorous title of hotel. The proprietors were usually jolly good fellows, or some staid matronly lady, in black gown and blue cap, and they all looked forward with anxious delight to the coming of court week. Every preparation was made for the judge and lawyers. Beds were aired and the bugs hunted out. Saturday previous to the coming Monday was a busy day in setting all things to rights, and the scrubbing-broom was heard in consonance with calls to the servants to be busy and careful, as Sally and Nancy sprang to their work with a will. With garments tucked up to their knees, they splashed the water and suds over the floors, strangers to the cleansing element until then for months ago. A new supply of corn and fodder was arriving from the country; stables and stable lots were undergoing a scraping eminently required for the comfort of decent beasts, who gave their lives in labor to exacting man. The room usually appropriated to the Bench and Bar was a great vagabond-hall, denominated the ball-room, and for this purpose appropriated once or twice a year. Along the bare walls of this mighty dormitory were arranged beds, each usually occupied by a couple of the limbs of the law, and sometimes appropriated to three. If there was not a spare apartment, a bed was provided here for the judge. And if there were no lawyers from Augusta, this one was distinguished by the greatest mountain of feathers in the house. Here assembled at night the rollicking boys of the Georgia Bar, who here indulged, without restraint, the convivialities for which they were so celebrated. Humor and wit, in anecdotes and repartee, beguiled the hours; and the few old taverns time has spared, could they speak, might narrate more good things their walls have heard, than have ever found record in the *Noctes Ambrosianæ* of the wits of Scrogie.

There are but few now left who have enjoyed a night in one of these old tumble-down rooms, with A. S. Clayton, O. H. Prince, A. B. Longstreet, and John M. Dooly. Here and there one, old, tottering, and gray, lives to laugh at his memories of those chosen spirits of fun. Yes, that is the word — fun — for these *ancients* possessed a fund of mirth-exciting humor, combined with a biting wit, which, in the peregrinations of a long life, I have met nowhere else. Were I to select one of these inns, it would be the old Walton Tavern, in the mean little hamlet of Livingston in Oglethorpe County, or the old house, kept long and indifferently, by that mountain of mortal obesity, Billy Springer, in Sparta, Hancock County. It was here, and when Springer presided over the fried meat and eggs of this venerable home for the weary and hungry, after a night of it, that all were huddled to bed like pigs in a sty.

This bulky Boniface was polite to all, but especially to an Augusta lawyer. Freeman Walker, of that ilk, usually attended this court, and was the great man of the week. A man of splendid abilities and polished manners, dressed and deporting himself like a gentleman, as he was, he shone among the lesser lights which orbed about him, a star of the first magnitude. The choice seat, the choice bed, and choice bits at the table, were ever for Major Walker. Big Billy, with his four hundred and ten pounds of adipose flesh, was always behind Major Walker's chair. He was first served; the choicest pieces of the pig were pointed out, cuts from the back and side bones and breast were hunted from the dish of fried chicken, a famous Georgia dish, for Major Walker. It was a great thing in those days in Georgia, to live in a little town of three thousand inhabitants, and wear *store clothes.* It was this and these which made a Georgia major.

Judge Dooly, upon one occasion, when attempting to usurp the seat of honor, was unceremoniously informed by Big Billy that it was Major Walker's seat.

Custom since has familiarized the retention of special seats for special persons, and now such a remark from a host astonishes no one. But in those days of unadulterated democracy, to assume a right to an unoccupied seat, startled every one. Dooly, amid the astonished gaze of the assembled guests, unmurmuringly retired to an unoccupied seat of more humble pretensions near the foot of the extended table. The occurrence was canvassed at night with full house in the democratic dormitory. When the jests incidental were hushed, and one after another had retired to bed, Judge Dooly, then on the Bench, went slowly to the only unappropriated bed, and undressing, folded down the bed-clothes. Suddenly, as if he had forgotten something, he slipped to the landing of the stairway and called anxiously for the landlord. "Come up, if you please," he said to the answering host. Springer commenced the ascent with slow and heavy tread; at length, after a most exhausting effort, and breathing like a wounded bellows, he lifted his mighty burden of flesh into the room.

"What is your will, Judge Dooly?" he asked, with a painful effort at speech.

Dooly, standing in his shirt by the bedside and pointing to it, asked, with much apparent solicitude, if that "was Major Walker's bed."

Springer felt the sarcasm keenly, and, amid the boisterous outburst of laughter from every bed, turned and went down.

A thousand anecdotes might be related of the peculiar wit, sarcasm, and drollery of this remarkable man. One more must suffice. When Newton County was first organized, it was made the duty of Dooly to hold the first court. There then lived and kept the only tavern in the new town of Covington, a man of huge proportions, named Ned Williams, usually called Uncle Ned — he, as well as Dooly, have long slept with their fathers. The location of the village and court-house had been of recent selection, and Uncle Ned's tavern was one of those peculiar buildings improvised for temporary purposes — a log cabin, designated, in some parts of Georgia at that time, as a two-storied house, with both stories on the ground; in other words, a double-penned cabin with passage between. Uncle Ned had made ample provision for the Bench and Bar. One pen of his house was appropriated to their use. There was a bed in each corner, and there were nine lawyers, including the judge. The interstices between the cabin poles were open, but there was no window, and but one door, which had to be closed to avoid too close companionship with the dogs of the household. It was June, and Georgia June weather, sultry, warm, and still, especially at night. In the centre there stood a deal table of respectable dimensions, and this served the double purpose of dining-table and bed-place for one. Uncle Ned was polite and exceedingly solicitous to please. He had scoured the county for supplies; it was too new for poultry or eggs, but acorns abounded, and pigs were plenty. They had never experienced want, and consequently were well-grown and fat. Uncle Ned had found and secured one which weighed some two hundred pounds. This he divided into halves longitudinally, and had barbecued the half intended for the use of the Bar and Bench. At dinner, on Monday, it was introduced upon a large wooden tray as the centre substantial dish for the dinner of the day. It was swimming in lard. There were side-dishes of potatoes and cold meats, appellated in Georgia collards, with quantities of corn-bread, with two bowls of hash from the lungs and liver of the pig, all reeking with the fire and summer heat. A scanty meal was soon made, but the tray and contents remained untouched.

The court continued three days, and was adjourned at noon of the fourth day, until the next term. Each day the tray and contents were punctual in their attendance. The depressed centre of the tray was a lake of molten lard, beneath which hid a majority of the pig. After dinner of the last day, all were ready to leave. When the meal was concluded, Dooly asked if all were done. "Landlord," said the Judge, "will you give us your attention?" Uncle Ned entered. "Your will, Judge," he asked. "I wish you, sir, to discharge this hog on his own recognizance. We do not want any bail for his appearance at the next term." The dinner concluded in a roar of laughter, in which Uncle Ned heartily joined.

Only one of the nine who assisted to organize that county, now remains in life. There were four men there whose names are inscribed on the scroll of fame — whose names their fellow-citizens have honored and perpetuated by giving them to counties: Cobb, Dawson, Colquitt, and Dougherty. Warner and Pierman died young. I alone remain. The children of most of them are now gray with years, and have seen their grandchildren. The name of Dooly remains only a memory.

The affections arising from youthful associations are more enduring than those which come of the same cause in riper years. They are more disinterested and sincere. They come with the spring of life, root deep into the heart, and cling with irradicable tenacity through life. We find in mature life dear friends, friends who will share the all they have with you, who will for you hazard even life, and you love them — but not as you love the boys who were at school with you, who ran with you wild through the woods, when you hunted the squirrel and trapped the quail. When fortuitous time forces your separation, and long intervening years blot the features, in their change, from your recognition, and chance throws you again with a loved companion of life's young morn — the thrill which stirs the heart, when his name is announced, comes not for the friend found only when time has grown gray.

Go and stand by the grave of one loved when a boy, the little laughing girl you played with at hide-and-seek, through the garden shrubbery and the intricacies of the house and yard, one who was always gentle and kind, she for whom you carried the satchel and books when going to school, who came at noon and divided her blackberry-pie with you, and always gave you the best piece — and see how all these memories will come back; and if the green grass upon the roof-top of her home for eternity does not bear, when you have gone away, a tear-drop to sparkle and exhale, a tribute to endearing memory, your heart is not worth the name. It is not given to us to love all with whom we may be familiar in early life. But every one will sincerely love some few of the companions of his school-days and early manhood. This is really the sugar of life, and the garrulity of age loves to recount these, for in his narrative he lives over and revives the attachments of boyhood. Woman may confess only to her own heart these memories — she must love only in secret. When the heart is fresh and brimming with affection, she may love with all the devotion of woman's heart; but if her love meets no return its birthplace must be its grave. She may only tell, when she is old, of her successful and more fortunate love. Ah! how many recount to their grandchildren their love, in budding youth, for their grandfather, who hide in the secret alcoves of the heart a more sacred memory of one who found his way there before dear old grandfather came. What sorrows these memories have sown along the way of life! but they have winced not when the thorn has pricked; and how she has folded to her bosom dear John, while imagination made him the more dear Willie, her first and foremost love! These endure in secret, and are the more sacred for this; they die only with the dead heart. Oh! the grave, the secrets of the grave, are they hidden there for ages, or shall they survive as treasures for eternity?

I have been wandering among the graves of those loved best when the heart could love most, and dead memories sprouted anew, and with them a flash of the feelings which made them treasures of the heart. Yonder is the grave of Thomas W. Cobb; near me is that of him most loved — William C. Dawson; and here, in this green grave, is Yelverton P. King; and near him is the last resting-place of Adeline Harrison. Dear, sweet Adeline, you went, in truth, to heaven, ere yet the bud of life had opened into flower! This is the county of my birth, and all of these, save Cobb, were natives, too, of the dear old land.

To me, how near and dear were these! Turn back, O Time, thy volume for fifty years, and let me read over anew the records of dead days, and make memories once more realities, as they were real then — else hurry on to the end, that I may know with these, or with these forget forever! I would not linger in the twilight of life, with all of time dimming out, and nothing of eternity dawning upon my vision. Let me sleep in the forgetfulness of the one, to awake to the fruition of the other!

I have been to the graves of my father and my mother. For more than a third of a century they have been sleeping here. I sat down in the moonlight, and placed my hand upon the cold, heavy stone which rests above them: they do not feel its pressure, but sleep well. They are but earth now — and why am I here? The moon and the stars are the same, and as sweetly bright, looking down upon this sacred spot, as they were when, a little child, I sat upon the knee of her who is nothing here, and listened to her telling me the names of these, as she would point to them, and ask me if I did not see them winking at me. Yet they are there, and the same now as then. But where is that gentle, sweet, affectionate mother? Is she up among these gems of heaven? Is she yonder in the mighty Jupiter, looking down, and smiling at me? Is she permitted, in her new being, to come at will, and breathe to my mind holy thoughts and holy feelings? Disembodied, is she, as God, pervading all, and knowing all? Does she, with that devotion of heart which was so much hers in time, still love and protect me? Shall I, when purified by death, go to her? and shall this hope become a reality, and endure forever? Surely, this must be true; or, why are these thoughts and hopes in the mind — why this affection sublimated still in the heart — why this link between the living, and the dead, if its fruition shall be denied in eternity? Why this question, which implies a doubt of the goodness of God? Sweet is the belief, sweeter the hope, that I shall see that smile of benignity, feel that gentle, loving caress, and forever, in unalloyed bliss, participate heaven with her. My mother — my mother! see you into my heart, here by your gravestone, to-night? Hast thou gone with me through my long pilgrimage of time? If I have kept thy counsels, and walked by their wisdom, hast thou approved, my mother? My mother, all that is good and pure in me has come of thee! If the allurements of vice have tempted, and frail nature has threatened to yield, the morning's admonition, the evening's counsel in our long walks, would strengthen me to forbearance. These bright memories have lived and remained with me a guide and salvation; and now they are the morning's memory, the evening's thought. As I have remembered and loved thee, I have been guided and governed by these. Surely there can be no loss to the child like the loss of the mother! How those are to be pitied! They go through life without the holy influences for good coming from a mother; they stumble on, and learn here and there, as time progresses, the moral lessons only taught to childhood from a mother's lips: they stumble and fall for the want of these; and, by experience, too often bitter experience, learn in youth what in childhood should be taught, which should grow up with them as a part of their being, to be the guides and comforts of life. And oh, how many never learn this!

Go, and converse with the wise and good, and they will tell you of their mothers' teachings; go to the condemned criminal, whose crimes have cast him from society, and ask him why he is thus—and he will tell you he disregarded the teachings of his mother; or, 'I had a wicked and vicious mother, who taught me evil instead of good;' or, 'I had no mother, to plant in my childhood's heart the fear of God and the love of virtue.'

Here, to me, to-night, in grateful memory, comes the Sabbath morning in the garden at the home of my childhood, more than sixty years ago, when this dead mother here sleeping pointed to the drunken man passing on the highway, and, kindly looking up into my face, asked me to look at him, and, when he had passed out of sight, said: "My child, will you here, this beautiful morning of God's day, promise your mother that you will not drink one drop of ardent spirits until you are twenty-one years of age? You are so full of animal spirits, I fear, should you touch it at all, that you will come to drink to excess, and fill a drunkard's grave before you shall have passed half the days allotted to man's life." I see that pleading face, those soft brown eyes to-night, as they looked from where she was seated into my face; I see the soft smile of satisfaction, as it came up from her heart and illumined her features, when I lifted up my hand and made the promise! And, oh, shall I ever forget the thrill which gladdened my heart when she rose up and kissed me, and murmured so gently, so tenderly, so full of hope and confidence: "I know you will keep it, my child." That promise is a holy memory! It was kept with sacred fidelity.

Angel of love and light — my mother — look down upon thy child here to-night, and for the last time by thy grave, with whitened head and tottering step, and see if I have ever departed from the way you taught me to go! Soon I shall be with you.

MY WORK IS OVER, MY TASK IS DONE!

FINIS.

www.ingramcontent.com/pod-product-compliance
Lightning Source LLC
LaVergne TN
LVHW020921110826
845150LV00004B/735

* 9 7 8 1 4 2 5 5 5 4 8 5 9 *